Resolving Difficult
Clinical Syndromes

D1607368

Other Books in the Series

Overcoming Resistant Personality Disorders: A Personalized Psychotherapy Approach
Theodore Millon and Seth Grossman

Moderating Severe Personality Disorders: A Personalized Psychotherapy Approach
Theodore Millon and Seth Grossman

Resolving Difficult Clinical Syndromes

A Personalized Psychotherapy Approach

Theodore Millon **Seth Grossman**

BICENTENNIAL
1807
WILEY
2007
BICENTENNIAL

John Wiley & Sons, Inc.

Library of Congress Cataloging-in-Publication Data:

Millon, Theodore.
Resolving difficult clinical syndromes : a personalized psychotherapy approach /
    Theodore Millon, Seth Grossman.
      p. ; cm.
    Includes bibliographical references.
    ISBN 978-0-471-71770-6 (pbk. : alk. paper)
    1. Clinical neuropsychology.   2. Psychotherapy.   3. Neuropsychiatry.
  I. Grossman, Seth.   II. Title.
  [DNLM: 1. Psychotherapy-methods.   WM 420 P4675 2007]
  RC386.6.N46P474 2007
  616.89′14—dc22

                         2006029329

Printed in the United States of America.

10 9 8 7 6 5 4 3 2 1

To our patients of the past 50 years

CONTENTS

Preface   ix

Part One

CHAPTER 1   **The Wisdom of Personalized Therapy**   3

Part Two

CHAPTER 2   **Personalized Therapy of Mood-Related Syndromes:**
            Dysthymic, Major Depressive, and Bipolar Disorders   81

CHAPTER 3   **Personalized Therapy of Acute, Posttraumatic, and
            Generalized Anxiety Syndromes**   115

CHAPTER 4   **Personalized Therapy of Anxiety-Related
            Psychological Syndromes:** Phobic, Dissociative, and
            Obsessive-Compulsive Disorders   153

CHAPTER 5   **Personalized Therapy of Anxiety-Related Physical
            Syndromes:** Somatoform and Conversion Disorders   191

CHAPTER 6   **Personalized Therapy of Cognitive Dysfunction Syndromes:** Substance-Related and Schizophrenia Spectrum Disorders   **221**

References   **253**
Index   **265**

PREFACE

W ould it not be a great step forward in our field if diagnosis or psychological assessment, following a series of interviews, tests, or laboratory procedures, actually pointed clearly to what a clinician should do in therapy? Would it not be good if all evaluations could spell out which specific features of a patient's psychological makeup are fundamentally problematic—biological, cognitive, interpersonal—and therefore deserved primary therapeutic attention? Is it not time for clinicians to recognize that diagnosis can lead directly to the course of therapy?

This diagnosis-to-therapy goal can be achieved by employing treatment-oriented assessment tools (e.g., the Millon Clinical Multiaxial Inventory III Facet Scales, the Millon-Grossman Personality Disorder Checklist).

"Personalized psychotherapy" is not a vague concept or a platitudinous buzzword in our treatment approach, but an explicit commitment to focus first and foremost on the *unique composite* of a patient's psychological makeup. That focus should be followed by a precise formulation and specification of therapeutic rationales and techniques to remedy those personal attributes that are assessed as problematic.

Therapists should take cognizance of the *person* from the start, for the psychic parts and environmental contexts take on different meanings and call for different responses depending on the specific person to whom they are anchored. To focus on one social structure or one psychological realm of expression, without understanding its undergirding or reference base, is to engage in potentially misguided, if not random, therapeutic techniques.

Fledgling therapists should learn further that the *symptoms and disorders we diagnose represent but one or another segment of a complex of organically interwoven psychological elements.* The significance of each clinical feature can best be grasped by reviewing a patient's unique psychological experiences and his or her overall psychic pattern or configurational dynamics, of which any one component is but a single part.

Therapies that conceptualize clinical disorders from a single perspective, be it psychodynamic, cognitive, behavioral, or physiological, may be useful, and even necessary, but are not sufficient in themselves to undertake a therapy of the patient, disordered or not. The revolution we propose asserts that clinical disorders are not exclusively behavioral or cognitive or unconscious, that is, confined to a particular expressive form. The overall pattern of a person's traits and psychic expressions are systemic and multioperational. No part of the system exists in complete isolation from the others. Every part is directly or indirectly tied to every other, such that there is an emergent synergism that accounts for a disorder's clinical tenacity.

Personality is real; it is a composite of intertwined elements whose totality must be reckoned with in all therapeutic enterprises. The key to treating our patients, therefore, lies in *therapy that is designed to be as organismically complex as the person himself or herself;* this form of therapy should generate more than the sum of its parts. Difficult as this may appear, we hope to demonstrate its ease and utility.

If our wish takes root, this book will serve as a revolutionary call, a renaissance that brings therapy back to the natural reality of patients' lives.

It is our hope that the book will lead all of us back to reality by exploring both the unique intricacy and the wide diversity of the patients we treat. Despite frequent brilliance, most single-focus schools of therapy (e.g., behavioral, psychoanalytic) have become inbred. Of more concern, they persist in narrowing the clinicians' attention to just one or another facet of their patients' psychological makeup, thereby wandering ever farther from human reality. They cease to represent the full richness of their patients' lives, considering as significant only one of several psychic spheres: the unconscious, biochemical processes, cognitive schemas, or some other. In effect, what has been taught to most fledgling therapists is an artificial reality, one that may have been formulated in its early stages as an original perspective and insightful methodology, but has drifted increasingly from its moorings over time, no longer anchored to the complex clinical reality from which it was abstracted.

How does our therapeutic approach differ from others? In essence, we come to the treatment task not with a favored theory or technique, but with the patient's unique constellation of personality attributes given center stage. *Only after* a thorough evaluation of the nature and prominence of these personal attributes do we think through which combination and sequence of treatment orientations and methodologies we should employ.

It should be noted that a parallel personalized approach to physical treatment has currently achieved recognition in what is called *genomic medicine.* Here medical scientists have begun to tinker with a particular patient's DNA so as to decipher and remedy existing, missing, or broken genes, thereby enabling the physician to tailor treatment in a highly personalized manner, that is, specific to the underlying or core genetic defects of that particular patient. Anomalies that are etched into a patient's unique DNA are screened and assessed to determine their source, the vulnerabilities they portend, and the probability of the patient's succumbing to specific manifest diseases.

As detailed in the first chapter of this first book of this *Personalized Psychotherapy* series, *Resolving Difficult Clinical Syndromes,* we have formulated eight personality components or domains comprising what we might term a *psychic DNA,* a framework that conceptually parallels the four chemical elements composing biologic DNA. Deficiencies, excesses, defects, or dysfunctions in these psychic domains (e.g., mood/temperament, intrapsychic mechanisms) effectively result in a spectrum of 15 manifestly different variants of personality styles and pathology (e.g., avoidant style, borderline disorder). It is the unique constellation of vulnerabilities as expressed in and traceable to one or several of these eight potentially problematic psychic domains that become the object and focus of personalized psychotherapy (in the same manner as the vulnerabilities in biologic DNA result in a variety of different genomically based diseases).

In this first book of the personalized series, we attempt to show that *all the clinical syndromes that constitute Axis I can be understood more clearly and treated more effectively when conceived as an outgrowth of a patient's overall personality style.* To say that depression is experienced and expressed differently from one patient to the next is a truism; so general a statement, however, will not suffice for a book such as this. Our task requires much more.

This first book focuses on resolving difficult clinical syndromes of Axis I of the *Diagnostic and Statistical Manual of Mental Disorders;* it provides extensive information and illustrations on how patients with different personality vulnerabilities react to and cope with life's stressors. With this body of knowledge in hand, therapists should be guided to undertake more precise and effective treatment plans. For example, a dependent person will often respond to a divorce situation with feelings of helplessness and hopelessness, whereas a narcissist faced with similar circumstances may respond in a disdainful and cavalier way. Even when both a dependent and a narcissist exhibit depressive symptoms in common, the precipitant of these symptoms will likely have been quite different; furthermore, treatment—its goals and methods—should likewise differ. In effect, similar symptoms do not call for the same treatment *if* the pattern of patient vulnerabilities and coping styles differ. In the case of dependents, the emotional turmoil may arise from their feelings of lower self-esteem and their inability to function autonomously; in narcissists, depression may be the outcropping of failed cognitive denials as well as a consequent collapse of their habitual interpersonal arrogance.

Whether we work with a clinical syndrome's "part functions" as expressed in behavior (social isolation), or cognitions (a delusional belief), or affect (depression), or a biological defect (appetite loss) *or* we address contextual systems that focus on the larger environment, the family, or the group, or the socioeconomic and political conditions of life, the crossover point, the place that links the varieties of clinical expression to the individual's social context, is the person. The person is the intersecting medium that brings functions and systems together. Persons, however, are more than just crossover mediums. As we elaborate in this first book of the series on resolving difficult clinical syndromes, they are the only organically integrated system in the psychological domain, inherently created from birth as natural entities. Moreover, it is the person who lies at the heart of the therapeutic experience, the substantive being who gives meaning and coherence to symptoms and traits—be they behaviors, affects, or mechanisms—as well as that being, that singular entity, who gives life and expression to family interactions and social processes.

Looking at a patient's totality can present a bewildering if not chaotic array of therapeutic possibilities, potentially driving even the most motivated young clinician to back off into a more manageable and simpler worldview, be it cognitive or pharmacologic. But as we contend here, complexity need not be experienced as overwhelming; nor does it mean chaos, if we can create a logic and order to the treatment plan. We try to provide logic and order by illustrating that the systematic integration of an Axis I syndrome into its foundation in an Axis II disorder is not only feasible, but is one that is conducive to both briefer and more effective therapy. We should note, however, that a therapeutic method, no matter how logical and rational it may be, can never achieve the precision of the physical sciences. In our field we must be ever alert to the many subtle variations and sequences, as well as the constantly evolving forces, that compose the natural course of human life.

THEODORE MILLON
SETH D. GROSSMAN

Coral Gables, Florida

PART **ONE**

CHAPTER 1

The Wisdom of Personalized Therapy

Introduction

Are not all psychotherapies personalized? Do not all therapists concern themselves with the person who is the patient they are treating? What justifies our appropriating the name "personalized" to the treatment approach we espouse? Are we not usurping a universal, laying claim to a title that is commonplace, routinely shared, and employed by most (all?) therapists?

We think not. In fact, we believe most therapists only incidentally or secondarily attend to the *specific personal qualities* of their patients. The majority come to their treatment task with a distinct if implicit bias, a preferred theory or technique they favor, one usually encouraged, sanctioned, and promoted in their early training, be it cognitive, group, family, eclectic, pharmacologic, or what have you.

How does our therapeutic approach differ? In essence, we come to the treatment task not with a favored theory or technique, but giving center stage to the patient's unique constellation of personality attributes. *Only after* a thorough evaluation of the nature and prominence of these personal attributes do we think through which combination and sequence of treatment orientations and methodologies we should employ.

As noted in the preface, "personalized" is not a vague concept or a platitudinous buzzword in our approach, but an explicit commitment to focus first and foremost on the unique composite of a patient's psychological makeup, followed by a precise formulation and specification of therapeutic rationales and techniques suitable to remedying those personal attributes that are assessed as problematic.

We have drawn on two concepts from our earlier writings, namely, personality-guided therapy (Millon, 1999) and synergistic therapy (Millon, 2002), integrating them into what we have now labeled "personalized psychotherapy." Both prior concepts remain core facets of our current treatment formulations in that, first, they are *guided* by the patient's overall personality makeup and, second, they are methodologically *synergistic* in that they utilize a combinational approach that employs reciprocally interacting and mutually reinforcing treatment modalities that produce a greater total result than the sum of their individual effects.

The preface recorded a parallel "personalized" approach to physical treatment in what is called *genomic medicine.* Here medical scientists have begun to investigate a particular patient's DNA so as to decipher and remedy existing, missing, or broken genes, thereby enabling the physician to tailor treatment in a highly personalized manner, that is, specific to the underlying or core genetic defects of that particular patient. Anomalies that are etched into a patient's unique DNA are screened and assessed to determine their source, the vulnerabilities they portend, and the probability of the patient's succumbing to specific manifest diseases.

Personalized psychological *assessment* is *therapy-guiding;* it undergirds and orients personalized psychotherapy. Together, they should be conceived as corresponding to genomic medicine in that they seek to identify the unique constellation of *underlying vulnerabilities* that characterize a particular mental patient and the consequent likelihood of his or her succumbing to specific mental clinical syndromes. In personalized assessment (Millon, Bloom, & Grossman, in press) we seek to employ *customized instruments,* such as the Grossman Facet Scales of the Millon Clinical Multiaxial Inventory (MCMI-III), to identify the patient's vulnerable psychic domains (e.g., cognitive style, interpersonal conduct). These assessment data furnish a foundation and a guide for implementing the distinctive individualized goals we seek to achieve in personalized psychotherapy.

As will be detailed in later sections, we have formulated eight personality components or domains constituting what we term a *psychic DNA,* a framework that conceptually parallels the four chemical elements composing biologic DNA. Deficiencies, excesses, defects, or dysfunctions in these psychic domains (e.g., mood/temperament, intrapsychic mechanisms) effectively result in a spectrum of 15 manifestly different variants of personality pathology (e.g., Avoidant Disorder, Borderline Disorder). It is the unique constellation of vulnerabilities as expressed in and traceable to one or several of these eight potentially problematic psychic domains that becomes the object and focus of personalized psychotherapy (in the same manner as the vulnerabilities in biologic DNA result in a variety of different genomically based diseases).

The reader may wish to glance ahead to pages 28–30 in this chapter and review Figures 1.1, 1.2, and 1.3, as well as survey the assessment tables that detail the Millon-Grossman Personality Domain Checklist (pp. 50–68) to gain a more complete picture of the elements composing these vulnerable psychic domains and their associated 15 personality style/disorder spectra.

Reflections on Psychotherapeutic Practice Today

As we look back over the long course of scientific history we see patterns of progress and regress, brilliant leaps alternating with foolish pursuits and blind stumblings.

Significant discoveries often were made by capitalizing on accidental observation; at other times, progress required the clearing away of deeply entrenched but erroneous beliefs.

As the study of the sciences of psychopathology and psychotherapy progressed, different and occasionally insular traditions and terminology evolved to modify these beliefs. Separate disciplines with specialized educational and training procedures developed, until today we have divergent professional groups involved in the enactment of psychotherapy, for example, the medically oriented psychiatrist with his tradition in biology and physiology; the psychodynamic psychiatrist with her concern for unconscious intrapsychic processes; the clinical-personology psychologist with his interest in cognitive functions and the measurement of personality; and the academic psychologist with her experimental approaches to the basic processes and modification of behavior. Each has studied these complex questions with a different emphasis and focus. Yet the central issues remain the same.

Beset with troublesome "mental" difficulties, patients are given a bewildering "choice" of therapeutic alternatives that might prove emotionally upsetting in itself, even to the well-balanced individual. Thus, patients may not only be advised to purchase this tranquilizer rather than that one, or told to take vacations or leave their job or go to church more often, but if they explore the possibilities of formal psychological therapy, they must choose among myriad schools of treatment, each of which is claimed by its adherents to be the most efficacious, and by its detractors to be both unscientific and ineffective.

Should patients or their family evidence a rare degree of "scientific sophistication," they will inquire into the efficacy of alternative therapeutic approaches. What they will learn, assuming they chance upon an objective informant, is that the outcome of different treatment approaches is strikingly similar, and that there are few data available to indicate which method is "best" for the particular difficulty they face. Moreover, they will learn the troublesome fact that many patients improve *without benefit of psychotherapy*.

This state of affairs is most discouraging. However, the science, as opposed to the art, of psychotherapy is relatively new, perhaps no older than 3 or 4 decades. Discontent concerning the shoddy empirical foundations of therapeutic practices was registered in the literature as early as 1910 (Patrick & Bassoe, 1912), but systematic research did not begin in earnest until the early 1950s and has become a primary interest of able investigators only in the past 30 to 40 years (Bergen & Garfield, 1994; Drake, Merrens, & Lynde, 2005; Fisher & O'Donohue, 2006; Frank & Frank, 1991; A. P. Goldstein & Dean, 1966; Goodheart, Kazdin, & Sternberg, 2006; Gottschalk & Auerbach, 1966; Hoch & Zubin, 1964; Lazarus & Messer, 1991; Nathan & Gorman, 2002; Norcross & Goldfried, 1992; Rubinstein & Parloff, 1959; Shlien, 1968; Stollak, Guerney, & Rothberg, 1966; Strupp & Luborsky, 1962).

The varied settings, goals, processes, and orientation that differentiate psychological treatment methods may lead one to conclude that the field of psychotherapy comprises a motley assemblage of techniques. However, despite substantive differences in verbalized rationales and technical procedures, psychotherapies sound more dissimilar than they are in practice. Close inspection reveals that the aims of many are fundamentally alike and that their methods, although focusing on different facets or levels of psychological functioning, deal essentially with similar pathological processes.

It should be noted that psychotherapy is a constantly changing science of treatment. As new research, theory, and clinical experience enlarge our range of knowledge, many of the treatment techniques described in this and the associated books of this series may call for modification. These personalized psychotherapeutic texts are intended exclusively for graduate students and clinical professionals; moreover, the reader is not expected to utilize their suggestions without an extensive range of information about a specific patient to guide his or her treatment. Although every effort has been made to furnish guidelines that live up to medical and psychological standards, the authors cannot make any warranty as to the effectiveness of the methods contained herein. This caveat is especially addressed to nonprofessionals who may be seeking methods for self-treatment: nonprofessionals are urged to consult their psychologist and/or physician for advice and treatment.

As noted, psychotherapy has been dominated until recently by what might be termed domain- or modality-oriented therapy. That is, therapists identified themselves with a single-realm focus or a theoretical school (behavioral, intrapsychic) and attempted to practice within whatever prescriptions for therapy it made. Rapid changes in the therapeutic milieu, all interrelated through economic pressures, conceptual shifts, and diagnostic innovations, have taken place in the past few decades. For better or worse, these changes show no sign of decelerating and have become a context to which therapists, far from reversing, must now themselves adapt.

Ironically, changes wrought by the confluence of economics, the diagnostic revolution that began with the third edition of the *Diagnostic and Statistical Manual of Mental Disorders* (*DSM-III*), the increasing awareness of minority- and gender-related issues, and the managed care revolution in the 1980s perhaps represent an accidental example of the emergent synergism for which the authors believe therapists should strive in their everyday work. Alone, the reinvention of the form and substance of the official nosology that occurred with the *DSM-III* in 1980 probably would not have been enough to overturn domain- or school-oriented psychotherapy, though certainly the emancipation of the *DSM* from the psychodynamic paradigm, and in favor of an atheoretical posture, did in fact hold the philosophical seeds of the recent coup that followed. Nonetheless, it may be argued that the essential force that provided, and continues to provide, the latent agenda for therapeutic innovation came from without, in the form of reluctance on the part of almost all third-party payers to reimburse psychosocially grounded psychotherapy. The study of such economic influences—through which the substance of what a discipline postures as truth changes to conform with new requirements for its continued existence—is worthy of a treatise in itself. Here, however, we sketch only a few broad strokes.

Today it is economic forces, not theoretical developments or evidence-based empirical research, that increasingly drive the direction of developments in psychotherapy.

Although modern times continue to see an explosion in the total number of all therapies, it is the demands of managed care that require an accounting of the efficacy of more inclusive therapies. The message to psychotherapists today is "Do more with less," meaning, unfortunately, not only fewer sessions, but more patients, and therefore less time spent thinking about the dynamics of any one patient's problems. The emphasis on efficiency is today the primary impetus in the development of programmatic forms of therapy across the spectrum of disorders. Moreover, these forms have been adapted to variables at levels of analysis congruent with what is afforded by current economic constraints. So therapy becomes more behavioral and operational and less dynamic and inferential.

Trend toward Briefer and Evidence-Based Therapies

Whatever the economic constraints, psychopathology would seem to stand squarely and intrinsically in opposition, not just to managed therapies, but to most forms of brief and research-evaluated therapy. The more concentrated Axis I disorders do admit to more focal, and therefore briefer, more explicit interventions. The disorders of Axis II, however, essentially more long-standing and pervasive disorders constituting the entire matrix of the patient, may stand like stone monoliths unmoved in the face of these fiscal demands.

Is it reasonable to expect 10, or even fewer, hours with a therapist to "cure" such complex disorders? These disorders are not clay to be passively resculpted. Functioning in a manner similar to the immune system, the psychic system actively resists any external influence that would disrupt its homeostasis. To uproot a complex disorder, one must wrangle with the ballast of a lifetime, a developmental pathology that has grown to become the entire structure of the person, manifested and perpetuated across a lifetime. By any reasoning, the pervasiveness and entrenched tenacity of the psychic pathology is likely to soak up therapeutic resources without end, leading inevitably to pessimism and disaffection for both therapists and payers.

The general term "brief therapy" encompasses a wide range of approaches, techniques, and philosophical orientations, often obscuring important elements more than it may actually reveal. Similarly, despite its relative recency, segments signifying brief approaches to treatment can be traced back to the earliest of therapeutic efforts at the beginning of the twentieth century (Millon, 1999).

Trend toward Culturally Sensitive Therapies

Psychotherapists are faced with an increasing challenge of cultural diversity and gender issues in their work in Western societies. The profession has been remiss in taking cognizance of these factors in the past, displaying indifference, neglect, or inadequate preparation in our graduate training programs and in our daily practice. The part that these sociocultural issues play in our work has become more fully recognized in recent times. Numerous books and papers on socially relevant topics have been published this past decade; many compensate for the almost pernicious character of our multicultural insensitivities of the past. Fortunately, the special roles and perspectives required on the part of therapists dealing with increasingly diverse societal subgroups have become a significant trend in our professional work.

As in the past, the United States continues to be enriched by its *growing diversity of ethnic and racial minorities*. A transformation is rapidly taking place in our society. Close to 80% of those entering the United States and its labor force are composed of minorities, drawn from a vast arena of other countries and cultures. Further, owing to the fact that the fertility rate of the dominant American culture has been declining and that the newborn population of ethnic/racial minorities continues to grow, it is clear that minority groups will become the numerical majority by midcentury. This trend calls for an important reassessment of our traditional therapeutic attitudes and responsibilities. Psychotherapists are only now being prepared for diverse patient populations with appreciably different cultural values and social experiences than has typified our practice in earlier years.

The core unit in the dominant American society is the nuclear family; here, parents live alone with their children, while other significant relatives (aunts, uncles, grandparents) live separately in independent family units. Many racial/ethnic subgroups, however, live in extended family systems, with diverse relatives of all ages living together or in very close proximity. Family therapy in our dominant social system tends to include only members of the nuclear family; other relatives are rarely brought into treatment. For example, the central role that grandparents have may be overlooked in treating Asian American families.

As a consequence of the diversity of racial/ethnic value systems, the primary orientation of many established therapeutic schools of thought may not prove as relevant and suitable as one might hope. We must recognize that the ancestry of many of the therapeutic theories we utilize is to be found in Western societal thought and, hence, reflects an English or European cultural perspective, with their implicit goals, values, and attitudes. The suitability, for example, of psychodynamic therapy is questionable owing to its focus on the key role of the individual, the desire to aid the person "to know oneself," to recognize that the problem that faces the patient is one that inheres within himself, with the consequent task of working through intrapsychic or unconscious mental distortions. This contrasts sharply with minority patient values and experiences in which primary attention may best be placed on the key role of sociocultural factors, such as racism, poverty, and social marginality. Similarly, the orientation in cognitive approaches stresses thought distortions that undermine the patient's effective functioning; in fact, the troublesome cognitions of the patient may represent the awful but actual realities experienced in everyday life. Similarly, self-actualizing modalities orient patients toward achieving psychic growth and self-esteem, but such an emphasis may cause considerable conflict or guilt for patients who come from cultural groups that are grounded in the importance of the collective, the family, or a traditional community.

Although the United States has benefited greatly these past 3 decades by the emergence of the feminist movement, especially as manifested in an *increase in women's rights and opportunities,* this valued progress has been a mixed blessing for some. For both men and women, there is a deep struggle between the wish for mastery and self-determination, on the one hand, and the wish for protection and security, on the other. The feminist movement has sought to facilitate the development of women's autonomy, self-assertion, and psychic independence. This same ideal, however, is often experienced as a threat when it opposes the female tradition of deserving protection from the uncertainties of a complex and competitive world. Success and achievement, therefore, can be sources of discomfort, if not anxiety, because they may threaten to disrupt the fulfillment of conflicting life-nurturing needs. Despite the worthy values of the feminist movement, many women have been socialized not to master competitive tasks, but to develop social rather than professional skills. Behaviors that run contrary to traditional feminine roles are a special problem for women who often see their efforts at autonomy and achievement as a sign of rebelliousness, if not deviance in contemporary society.

Therapists have observed that women, in efforts to compete with men, often anticipate troublesome social consequences for their effort. Whereas men assume that success will lead to further opportunities and cultural rewards, women are often in conflict about achievement, such as feeling guilty about surpassing their mother, the fear of losing a less adequate male partner, and consequent anxieties about aloneness in a less-than-accepting world. Historically, female identity has been shaped to be pleasing to men and to downgrade women's own abilities and confidence. It has been difficult, therefore, to integrate a sense of work achievement as a source of one's self-identity.

No therapist would wish to return to the days when women were encouraged to be quiet and sedate, to be seen and not heard, to be obedient and passive. But on the other hand, good therapists must recognize that ours is a time of cultural transition, when countervailing voices are to be heard, hence creating internalized conflicts for many women who will come to seek their guidance and support. There is little doubt that part of the conflict that women face stems from a social system sharply divided in its attitudes. However, in a society in which women are denied equal access to opportunities and resources, it should be a priority of therapists to help resolve the conflicts in those able women who struggle with their role-breaking efforts to find a more egalitarian life that will enable them to synthesize their deeper emotional needs with the authenticity of autonomy and independence.

There is a growing receptiveness and open-mindedness in the United States today regarding the *diverse forms of gender proclivity and sexual preference.* Although this trend has numerous benefits for many, problematic residuals remain for some that may call for therapeutic action. Although gay men and lesbians are some 10 to 15% of the overall population in the United States, their status, until the past decade or so, has been that of an invisible minority. Pervasive negative attitudes in society and insufficient professional training have prevented the delivery of thoughtful and sensitive therapeutic services to this subculture group. The trend toward greater knowledge and more egalitarian attitudes has only recently led to increased knowledge and skills necessary to work effectively with these patients.

Gay people, both male and female, experience a unique position among the socially rejected groups in that they are reared largely in nongay families, families who fail to provide adequate models of self-respect and self-esteem and rarely provide an attitude of acceptance and affirmation for their progeny's socially problematic identity. Homophobia is commonplace and characterizes how most families and others react to gay people. Moreover, gay men and lesbians often grow up learning the same rejecting and hostile attitudes toward same-sex intimacies as do nongays. This internalization of homophobia is distressing for many gays, one that further complicates their already troubled self-identity.

The problems presented by gay persons are not unexpected. Typical is a young person who might come to a therapist because he has been degraded, if not beaten, by his family, has been thrown out of his home, and is now homeless. The most frequent presenting problem among young gays is that of isolation. Youngsters report having no one to talk to and feeling alone in most social situations, especially within the family, at school, or in their religious community. Such isolation is usually associated with their fear of discovery and the constant need to hide. Even where a network of gay social companions is available, there is often a sense that others are interested only in exploiting them. Not to be overlooked is a sense of deep emotional isolation, the belief that one cannot trust bonding or attaching to others owing to the assumption that the gay lifestyle tends to be transient and incidental rather than genuine and enduring. Lacking a consistent and appropriate role model, many young gays often demonstrate an appalling ignorance regarding what it is to be homosexual, frequently holding to the worst stereotypes about homosexuals—and therefore about themselves.

There is no reason to believe that the homosexually oriented, as a group, are less well-adjusted than their heterosexual counterparts, but there are specific factors that typify the problems that gays do experience when difficulties have arisen; isolation, family rejection, abuse, and intrapsychic identity conflicts represent the problems for which they seek guidance. The task of therapists is not invariably a complex one. Many gays simply need access to accurate information; others need opportunities for socialization with a wider network of peers than can be achieved in same-sex settings. Of course, it is extremely difficult for gays to "actualize" themselves in a social context of public rejection. Moreover, gays and lesbians need support before they can fully express themselves and their individuality. Therapists must also learn to feel comfortable with their own sexuality and seek to rid themselves of homophobic feelings if they are to work openly and honestly with gay and lesbian patients. Most important, they must aid their patients to be free of their own homophobic stereotypes and conflicts, enabling them to develop a healthier attitude toward their own genuine feelings and authentic identities.

As with all issues discussed in this section on minority, feminist, and gay/lesbian perspectives, most of the "standard" therapeutic approaches discussed in this chapter can be carefully examined so as to reorient underlying biases and assumptions. Most may thereby not only prove useful, but may be applied with an informed sensitivity to the patient's special life conditions.

Trend toward Integrative Therapies

The simplest way to practice psychotherapy is to approach all patients as possessing essentially the same disorder, and then utilize one standard modality of therapy for their treatment. Many therapists still employ these simplistic models. Yet everything we have learned in the past 2 or 3 decades tells us that this approach is only minimally effective and deprives patients of other, more sensitive and effective approaches to treatment. In the past 2 decades, we have come to recognize that patients differ substantially in the clinical syndromes and personality disorders they present. It is clear that not all treatment modalities are equally effective for all patients, be it pharmacologic, cognitive, intrapsychic, or another mode. The task set before us is to maximize our effectiveness, beginning with efforts to abbreviate treatment, to recognize significant cultural considerations, to combine treatment, and to outline an integrative model for selective therapeutics. When the selection is based on each patient's personal trait configuration, integration becomes what we have termed *personalized psychotherapy*, to be discussed in the next section.

Present knowledge about combinational and integrative therapeutics has only begun to be developed. In this section we hope to help overcome the resistance that many psychotherapists possess to the idea of utilizing treatment combinations of modalities that they have not been trained to exercise. Most therapists have worked long and hard to become experts in a particular technique or two. Though they are committed to what they know and do best, they are likely to approach their patients' problems with techniques consonant with their prior training. Unfortunately, most modern therapists have become expert in only a few of the increasingly diverse approaches to treatment and are not open to exploring interactive combinations that may be suitable for the complex configuration of symptoms most patients bring to treatment.

In line with this theme, Frances, Clarkin, and Perry (1984, p. 195) have written:

> The proponents of the various developing schools of psychotherapy tended to maintain the pristine and competitive purity of their technical innovations, rather than attempt to determine how these could best be combined with one another. There have always been a few synthesizers and bridge builders (often derided from all sides as "eclectic") but, for the most part, clinicians who were trained in one form of therapy tended to regard other types with disdain and suspicion.

The inclination of proponents of one or another modality of therapy to remain separate was only in part an expression of treatment rivalries. During the early phases of a treatment's development, innovators, quite appropriately, sought to establish a measure of effectiveness without having their investigations confounded by the intrusion of other modalities. No less important was that each treatment domain was but a single dimension in the complex of elements that patients bring to us. As we move away from a simple medical model to one that recognizes the psychological complexity of patients' symptoms and causes, it appears wise to mirror the patients' complexities by developing therapies that are comparably complex.

As will be elaborated throughout the text, certain combinational approaches have an additive effect; others may prove to possess a synergistic effect (Klerman, 1984). The term additive describes a situation in which the combined benefits of two or more treatments are at least equal to the sum of their individual benefits. The term synergistic describes a situation in which the combined benefits of several treatment modalities exceed the sum of their individual components; that is, their effects are potentiated. This entire book series is intended to show that several modalities— pharmacotherapy, cognitive therapy, family therapy, intrapsychic therapy—may be combined and integrated to achieve additive, if not synergistic effects.

It is our view that psychopathology itself contains structural implications that legislate the form of any therapy one would propose to remedy its constituents. Thus, the philosophy we present derives from several implications and proposes a new integrative model for therapeutic action, an approach that we have called *personalized psychotherapy.* This model, which is guided by the psychic makeup of a patient's personality—and not a preferred theory or modality or technique—gives promise, we believe, of a new level of efficacy and may, in fact, contribute to making therapy briefer. Far from being merely a theoretical rationale or a justification for adhering to one or another treatment modality, it should optimize psychotherapy by tailoring treatment interventions to fit the patient's specific form of pathology. It is not a ploy to be adopted or dismissed as congruent or incongruent with established therapeutic preferences or modality styles. Despite its name, we believe that what we have termed a personalized approach will be effective not only with Axis II personality disorders, but also with Axis I clinical syndromes, as illustrated in this first volume of the three-part series on the topic.

What exactly do we mean when we say that therapy must be integrated and should be grounded in the inherent characteristics of the patient (Arkowitz, 1992; Millon, 1988)? Unfortunately, much of what travels under the "eclectic" or "integrative" banner sounds like the talk of someone desiring to be nice to all sides and to say that everybody is right. These labels have become platitudinous buzzwords, philosophies with which open-minded people certainly would wish to ally themselves. But "integrative theory and psychotherapy" must signify more than that.

First, the approach to therapy that we propose is not eclecticism. Perhaps it might be considered posteclecticism, if we may borrow a notion used to characterize modern art just a century ago. Eclecticism is not a matter of choice. We all must be eclectics, engaging in differential (Frances et al., 1984) and multimodal (Lazarus, 1981) therapeutics, selecting the techniques that are empirically the most efficacious for the problems at hand (Beutler & Clarkin, 1990).

Integration should be more than the coexistence of two or three previously discordant orientations or techniques. We cannot simply piece together the odds and ends of several theoretical schemas, each internally consistent and oriented to different data domains. Such a hodgepodge will lead only to illusory syntheses that cannot long hold together (Messer, 1986, 1992). Efforts such as these, meritorious as they may be in some regards, represent the work of peacemakers, not innovators and not integrationists. Integration is eclectic, of course, but more.

As we will argue further, it is our belief that integration should be a synthesized system to mirror the problematic configuration of traits (personality) and symptoms (clinical syndromes) of a specific patient-at-hand. In the next section, we discuss integration from this view. Many in the past have sought to coalesce differing theoretical orientations and treatment modalities with interconnecting bridges. By contrast, those of us in the *personalized* therapeutic persuasion bypass the synthesis of theory. Rather, primary attention should be given to the *natural synthesis or inherent integration that may be found within patients* themselves.

As Arkowitz (1997) has noted, efforts to create a theoretical synthesis are usually not fully integrative in that most theorists do not draw on component approaches equally. Most are oriented to one particular theory or modality, and then seek to assimilate other strategies and notions to that core approach. Moreover, assimilated theories and techniques are invariably changed by the core model into which it has been imported. In other words, the assimilated orientation or methodology is frequently transformed from its original intent. As Messer (1992, p. 151) wrote, "When incorporating elements of other therapies into one's own, a procedure takes its meaning not only from its point of origin, but even more so from the structure of the therapy into which it is imported." Messer illustrates this point by describing a two-chair gestalt procedure that is brought into a primary social-learning model; in this assimilation, the two-chair procedure will likely be utilized differently and achieve different goals than would occur in the hands of a gestalt therapist using the same technique.

Furthermore, by seeking to impose a theoretical synthesis, therapists may lose the context and thematic logic that each of the standard theoretical approaches has built up over its history. In essence, intrinsically coherent theories are usually disassembled in the effort to interweave their diverse bits and pieces. Such an integrative model composed of alternative models (behavioral, psychoanalytic) may be pluralistic, but it reflects separate modalities with varying conceptual networks and their unconnected studies and findings. As such, integrative models *do not* reflect that which is inherent in nature, but *invent* a schema for interweaving that which is, in fact, essentially discrete.

As will be discussed in the following section, it is argued that intrinsic unity cannot be invented, but can be discovered in nature by focusing on the intrinsic unity of the person, that is, the full scope of a patient's psychic being. It will be asserted that integration based on the natural order and unity of the person avoids the rather arbitrary efforts at synthesizing disparate and sometimes disjunctive theoretical schemas.

Efforts at synthesizing therapeutic models have been most successful in desegregating the field rather than truly integrating it. As Arkowitz (1997, pp. 256–257) explains:

> Integrative perspectives have been catalytic in the search for new ways of thinking about and doing psychotherapy that go beyond the confines of single-school approaches. Practitioners and researchers are examining what other theories and therapies have to offer. . . .
>
> Several promising starts have been made in clinical proposals for integrative therapies, but it is clear that much more work needs to be done.

As noted, it is the belief of the authors that integration cannot stem from an intellectual synthesis of different theories, but from the inherent integration that is discovered in each patient's personal style of functioning, a topic to which we now turn.

Emergence of Personalized Psychotherapy

Unlike eclecticism, integration insists on the primacy of an overarching gestalt that gives coherence, provides an interactive framework, and creates an organic order among otherwise discrete units or elements. Whereas the theoretical syntheses previously discussed attempt to provide an intellectual bridge across several theories or modalities, personalized integrationists assert that a natural synthesis already exists within the patient. As we better understand the configuration of traits that characterize each patient's psyche, we can better devise a treatment plan that will mirror these traits and, we believe, will provide an optimal therapeutic course and outcome.

As noted previously, integration is an important concept in considering not only the psychotherapy of the individual case but also the place of psychotherapy in clinical science. For the treatment of a particular patient to be integrated, the elements of a clinical science—theory, taxonomy, assessment, and therapy—should be integrated as well (Millon, 1996b). One of the arguments advanced earlier against empirically based eclecticism is that it further insulates psychotherapy from a broad-based clinical science. In contrast to eclecticism, where techniques are justified empirically, *personalized psychotherapeutic integration* should take its shape and character from an integrative theory of human nature. Such a grand theory should be inviting because it attempts to explain all of the natural variations of human behavior, normal or otherwise; moreover, personalized psychotherapy will grow naturally out of such a personalized theory. Theory of this nature will not be disengaged from therapeutic technique; rather, it will inform and guide it.

Murray (1983) has suggested that the field must develop a new, higher order theory to help us better understand the interconnections among cognitive, affective, self, and interpersonal psychic systems. It is the belief of personalized therapeutic theorists, such as ourselves, who claim that interlinked configurations of pathology deduced from such a theory can serve to guide psychotherapy.

Although differential treatment gives special weight to the specific problem areas of the patient, most theorists and therapists pay little attention to the particular domains composing different diagnostic categories. We argue for considering the configuration of personality traits that characterize each specific patient. Differential treatment recognizes that current diagnostic information, such as listed in *DSM-IV,* provides only a surface coverage of the complex elements that are associated with a patient's inner and outer worlds.

As noted previously, whether we work with "part functions" that focus on behaviors, cognitions, unconscious processes, or biological defects, or whether we address contextual systems that focus on the larger environment, the family, the group, or the socioeconomic and political conditions of life, the crossover point, the place that links parts to contexts, is the person. The individual is the intersecting medium that brings them together.

Persons, however, are more than crossover mediums. They are the only organically integrated system in the psychological domain, inherently created from birth as natural entities rather than experience-derived gestalts constructed via cognitive attribution. Moreover, it is persons who lie at the heart of the psychotherapeutic experience, the substantive beings that give meaning and coherence to symptoms and traits—be they behaviors, affects, or mechanisms—as well as those beings, those singular entities, that give life and expression to family interactions and social processes.

The cohesion (or lack thereof) of intrinsically interwoven psychic structures and functions is what distinguishes most complex disorders of psychopathology; likewise, the orchestration of diverse yet synthesized modalities of intervention is what differentiates synergistic from other variants of psychotherapy. These two parallel constructs, emerging from different traditions and conceived in different venues, reflect shared philosophical perspectives, one oriented toward the understanding of mental disorders, the other toward effecting their remediation.

It is not that one-modality or school-oriented psychotherapies are inapplicable to more focal or simple syndrome pathologies, but rather that synergistically planned therapies are required for the intricate relationships that interconnect personality and clinical syndromes (whereas depression may successfully be treated either cognitively or pharmacologically); it is the very interwoven nature of the components that compose such complex disorders that makes a multifaceted and synthesized approach a necessity.

In the following pages we present a few ideas in sequence. First, personalized therapies require a foundation in a coordinating theory of nature, that is, they must be more than a schema of eclectic techniques, a hodgepodge of diverse alternatives assembled de novo with each case. Second, although the diagnostic criteria that make up *DSM* syndromes are a decent first step, these criteria must become comprehensive and comparable, that is, be systematically revised so as to be genuinely useful for treatment planning. Third, a logical rationale can be formulated as to how one can and should integrate diverse modality-focused therapies when treating complex psychopathologies.

Broadening the Base of Personologic Science

Before turning to these themes, we would like to comment briefly on some philosophical issues. They bear on a rationale for developing a wide-ranging theory of nature to serve as a basis for treatment techniques, that is, universal principles that transcend the merely empirical (e.g., electroconvulsive therapy for depressives). It is our conviction that the theoretical foundations of our personologic science must be advanced further if we are to succeed in constructing a personalized approach to psychotherapy.

Obviously, a tremendous amount of knowledge, both about the nature of the patient's disorders and about diverse modes of intervention, is required to perform personalized therapy. To maximize synergism among numerous modalities requires that the therapist be a little like a jazz soloist. Not only should the professional be fully versed in the various musical keys, that is, in techniques of psychotherapy that span all trait domains, but he or she should also be prepared to respond to subtle fluctuations in the patient's thoughts, actions, and emotions, any of which could take the composition in a wide variety of directions, and integrate these with the overall plan of therapy as it evolves. After the instruments have been packed away and the band goes home, a retrospective account of the entire process should reveal a level of thematic continuity and logical order commensurate with that which would have existed had all relevant constraints been known in advance.

The integrative processes of personalized therapy should be dictated by the nature of personality itself. The actual logic and foundation of this therapy, however, must be grounded on some other basis. Psychopathology is by definition a patterning of intraindividual variables, but the nature of these variables must be supplied by a set of fundamental principles or on some basis beyond the personologic construct. In our view, for example, the structure and functions of personality and psychopathology are grounded in evolutionary theory, a discipline that informs but exists apart from our clinical subject. In and of itself, pathologic personality is a structural-functional concept that refers to the intraorganismic patterning of variables; it does not in itself say what these variables are or how they relate, nor can it.

As stated previously (Millon, 1990, 2004), we believe that several elements characterize all mature clinical sciences: (a) They embody *conceptual theories* based on universal principles of nature from which their propositional deductions can be derived; (b) these theories provide the basis for *coherent taxonomies* that specify and characterize the central features of their subject domain (in our case, that of personality and psychopathology, the substantive realm within which scientific psychotherapeutic techniques are applied); (c) these taxonomies are associated with a variety of *empirically oriented assessment instruments* that can identify and quantify the concepts that constitute their theories (in psychopathology, methods that uncover developmental history and furnish cross-sectional assessments); and (d) in addition to natural theory, clinical taxonomy, and empirically anchored assessment tools, mature clinical sciences possess *change-oriented intervention* techniques that are therapeutically optimal in modifying the pathological elements of their domain.

Most current therapeutic schools share a common failure to coordinate these four components of a mature science. What differentiates them has less to do with their scientific grounding than with the fact that they attend to different levels of data in the natural world. It is to the credit of those of an eclectic persuasion that they have recognized, albeit in a fuzzy way, the arbitrary if not illogical character of single-focus positions, as well as the need to bridge schisms among these approaches that have evolved less by philosophical considerations or pragmatic goals than by the accidents of history (Millon, 2004). There are numerous other knotty issues with which the nature of psychic pathology and personalized therapy must contend (e.g., differing worldviews concerning the essential nature of psychological experience). There is no problem, as we see it, in encouraging active dialectics among these contenders.

However, there are two important barriers that stand in the way of personalized psychotherapy as a treatment philosophy. The first is the *DSM*. The idea of diagnostic prototypes was a genuine innovation when the *DSM-III* was published in 1980. The development of diagnostic criteria work groups was intended to provide broad representation of various points of view, while preventing any single perspective from foreclosing on the others. Even some 25 years later, however, the *DSM* has yet to officially endorse an underlying set of principles that would interrelate and differentiate the categories in terms of their deeper principles. Instead, progress proceeds mainly by way of committee consensus, cloaked by the illusion of empirical research.

The second barrier is the human habit system. The admonition that different therapeutic approaches should be pursued with different patients and different problems has become almost self-evident. But given no logical basis from which to design effective therapeutic sequences and composites, even the most self-consciously antidogmatic clinician must implicitly lean toward one orientation or another.

What specifically are the procedures that distinguish personalized therapy from other models of an eclectic nature?

The integrative model labeled 2 decades ago by the senior author as "personologic psychotherapy" (Millon, 1988) insisted on the primacy of an overarching gestalt that gave coherence, provided an interactive framework, and created an organic order among otherwise discrete polarities and attributes. It was eclectic, but more. It was derived from a substantive theory whose overall utility and orientation derives from that old chestnut "The whole is greater than the sum of its parts." The problems our patients bring to us are often an inextricably linked nexus of interpersonal behaviors, cognitive styles, regulatory processes, and so on. They flow through a tangle of feedback loops and serially unfolding concatenations that emerge at different times in dynamic and changing configurations. Each component of these configurations has its role and significance altered by virtue of its place in these continually evolving constellations. *In parallel form, personalized therapy should be conceived as an integrated configuration of strategies and tactics in which each intervention technique is selected not only for its efficacy in resolving particular pathological attributes, but also for its contribution to the overall constellation of treatment procedures of which it is but one integral part.*

Although the admonition that we should *not* employ the same therapeutic approach with all patients is self-evident, it appears that therapeutic approaches accord more with where training occurred than with the nature of the patients' pathologies. To paraphrase Millon (1969/1985), there continues to be a disinclination among clinical practitioners to submit their cherished techniques to detailed study or to revise them in line with critical empirical findings. Despite the fact that most of our therapeutic research leaves much to be desired in the way of proper controls, sampling, and evaluative criteria, one overriding fact comes through repeatedly: Therapeutic techniques must be suited to the patient's problem. Simple and obvious though this statement is, it is repeatedly neglected by therapists who persist in utilizing and argue heatedly in favor of a particular approach to *all* variants of psychopathology. No school of therapy is exempt from this notorious attitude.

Why should we formulate a personalized therapeutic approach to psychopathology? The answer may be best grasped if we think of the psychic elements of a person as analogous to the sections of an orchestra, and the trait domains of a patient as a clustering of discordant instruments that exhibit imbalances, deficiencies, or conflicts within these sections. To extend this analogy, therapists may be seen as conductors whose task is to bring forth a harmonious balance among all the sections, as well as their specifically discordant instruments, muting some here, accentuating others there, all to the end of fulfilling the conductor's knowledge of how the composition can best be made consonant. The task is not that of altering one instrument, but of altering all, in concert. What is sought in music, then, is a balanced score, one composed of harmonic counterpoints, rhythmic patterns, and melodic combinations. What is needed in therapy is a likewise balanced program, a coordinated strategy of counterpoised techniques designed to optimize sequential and combinatorial treatment effects.

If clinical syndromes were anchored exclusively to one particular trait domain (as phobias are thought of being primarily behavioral in nature), modality-bound psychotherapy would always be appropriate and desirable. Psychopathology, however, is not exclusively behavioral, cognitive, biologic, or intrapsychic, that is, confined to a particular clinical data level. Instead, it is multioperational and systemic. No part of the system exists in complete isolation. Instead, every part is directly or indirectly tied to every other, such that a synergism lends the whole a tenacity that makes the full system of pathology "real"—a complex that needs to be fully reckoned with in a comprehensive therapeutic endeavor. Therapies should mirror the configuration of as many trait and clinical domains as the syndromes and disorders they seek to remedy. If the scope of the therapy is insufficient relative to the scope of the pathology, the treatment system will have considerable difficulty fulfilling its meliorative and adaptive goals. Both unstructured intrapsychic therapy and highly structured behavioral techniques, to note the extremes, share this deficiency.

Most psychotherapists have had the unsettling experience of developing a long-term treatment plan, only to have the patient make some startling revelation several sessions later, requiring a significant change of course. Although some therapists will always administer the same form of therapy regardless of the problem, a good theory should allow techniques across many modalities to be dynamically adapted or integrated as ongoing changes in the patient occur or as new information comes to light.

In contrast to this ideal, the state of the art in psychotherapy can be characterized as either linear, but dogmatic, or eclectic, but uncoordinated. Linear perspectives hail mainly from the historical schools that have dominated psychotherapy's classical past. Major viewpoints include the psychodynamic, interpersonal, neurobiological, behavioral, and cognitive, but more esoteric conceptions could also be included, such as the existential, phenomenological, cultural, and perhaps even religious. Theorists within each perspective usually maintain that their content area is core or fundamental and thus serves as the logical basis for the treatment of its disorders. In the earlier, dogmatic era of therapeutic systems, psychologists strongly wedded to a particular perspective would either assert that other points of view were peripheral to their own pet contents, or just stubbornly ignore the existence of other schools of thought. Behaviorists, for example, denied the existence of the mental constructs, including self and personality. In contrast, psychodynamic psychologists held that behavior is useful only as a means of inferring the properties and organization of various mental structures, namely, the id, ego, and superego, and their "drive derivatives." Theorists took this stance essentially for two reasons. First, history remembers only those that contribute significantly to the development of a particular point of view. Hence, there are no famous eclectics. Second, the fact that other content areas operate according to their own autonomous principles could impugn the completeness of one's own approach. As a result, various perspectives within psychology have tended to develop the dogmatic schools of psychotherapy to high states of internal consistency. It is not at all clear how one conceptual system might falsify another, or how two systems might be put against one another experimentally. Instead, the proponents of one perspective usually seek to assimilate the variables of other domains to their own perspective, which is then put forward as the best candidate for a truly personalized model for the treatment of its disorders.

In contrast to the modality- or school-oriented perspectives, which appeal to organizing principles that derive from a single system of psychotherapy, we might ask whether there is any theory that honors the nature of psychopathology as the pattern of variables across the entire matrix of the person. Psychopathology is neither exclusively behavioral, exclusively cognitive, nor exclusively interpersonal, but is instead a genuine integration of each of its subsidiary domains. Far from overturning established paradigms, such a broad perspective simply allows a given phenomenon to be treated from several angles, so to speak. Even agnostic therapists, with no strong allegiance to any one point of view, may avail themselves of a kaleidoscope of modalities. By turning the kaleidoscope, by shifting paradigmatic sets, the same phenomenon can be viewed from any of a variety of internally consistent perspectives. Eclecticism becomes a first step toward synthesizing modalities that correspond to the natural configuration of each patient's traits and disorders.

The open-minded therapist is left, however, with several different modality combinations, each with some currency for understanding the patient's pathology, but no real means of bringing these diverse conceptions together in a coherent model of what, exactly, to do. The therapist's plight is understandable, but not acceptable. For example, modality techniques considered fundamental in one perspective may not be so regarded in another. The interpersonal model of Lorna Benjamin and the neurobiological model of Robert Cloninger are both structurally strong approaches to understanding personality and psychopathology. Yet their fundamental constructs are different. Rather than inherit the modality tactics of a particular perspective, then, a theory of psychotherapy as a total system should seek some set of principles that can be addressed to the patient's whole psyche, thereby capitalizing on the naturally organic system of the person. The alternative is an uncomfortable eclecticism of unassimilated partial views. Perhaps believing that nothing more is possible, most psychotherapists have accepted this state of affairs as an inevitable reality.

Fortunately, modality-bound psychotherapies are increasingly becoming part of the past. In growing numbers, clinicians are identifying themselves, not as psychodynamic or behavioral, but as eclectic or integrative. As noted earlier, eclecticism is an insufficient guide to personalized therapy. As a movement, and not a construct, it cannot prescribe the particular form of those modalities that will remedy the pathologies of persons and their syndromes. Eclecticism is too open with regard to content and too imprecise to achieve focused goals. The intrinsically configurational nature of psychopathology, its multioperationalism, and the interwoven character of clinical domains simply are not as integrated in eclecticism as they need be in treating psychopathology.

Evolution as a Unifying Theoretical Orientation

Before proceeding to an abbreviated outline of assessment and treatment techniques that derive from our specific model, we would like to make a comment in favor of the utility of theory. Kurt Lewin (1936) wrote some 70 years ago that "there is nothing so practical as a good theory." Theory, when properly grounded, ultimately provides more simplicity and clarity than unintegrated and scattered information (Millon & Grossman, 2006a). Unrelated knowledge and techniques, especially those based on surface similarities, are a sign of a primitive science, as has been effectively argued by contemporary philosophers of science (Hempel, 1961; Quine, 1961).

We will present a précis of the general theoretical model we have employed in analyzing personality and psychopathology (Millon, 1969/1985, 1990; Millon, with Davis, 1996a). This is a digression in a way, but it is one that we believe is only proper for our readers to reflect on, especially those who may wish to know more about the underlying logic and grounding on which our diagnostic and therapeutic model adheres.

It is logically impossible for any single perspective on psychotherapy to develop constructs that embrace the person as a whole, that is, a scope and level of synthesis at which the psychopathologic phenomenon itself exists. Perspectives are necessarily analytic, whereas personality is inherently synthetic. An intrinsically synthetic treatment design is exactly what is required to transcend the hodgepodge of eclecticism. Only such a theory can allow for the construction of logically meaningful therapeutic composites and sequences.

Unfortunately, the field does not as yet have an accepted, unifying theory for human behavior. We have generated microtheories that encompass and give coherence to certain facets that compose our psychopathological subject domain. It is toward a larger end that the authors have sought to develop an integrative and unified theory of personality and psychopathology (Millon, 1969/1985, 1981, 1986a, 1990, 1991, 1996b; Millon with Davis, 1996a; Millon & Grossman, 2006a, 2006b) with exemplar integrative concepts for the larger domain of mental disorders. The reader is encouraged to read Millon with Davis (1996a) for a comprehensive review of the development and derivation of these disorders.

We have gone beyond current conceptual boundaries in our field to explore hypotheses that drew their principles, if not their substance, from other established, adjacent sciences. Not only have such steps generated new conceptual fruits, but they provided a foundation that could undergird and guide our own discipline's explorations. Much of psychopathology, no less psychology as a whole, has remained adrift these past decades, divorced from broader spheres of scientific knowledge, isolated from firmly grounded, if not universal principles, leading us to continue building the patchwork quilt of concepts and data domains that characterize the field. Preoccupied with but a small part of the larger puzzle, or fearing accusations of reductionism, many scientists of the mind have failed to draw on the rich possibilities to be found in other realms of scholarly pursuit. With few exceptions, cohering concepts that would connect psychotherapy and psychopathology to those of its sister sciences have not been developed.

Our effort has been to find theoretical principles for psychopathology that fall outside the field of psychology proper. Otherwise, we would only repeat the error of the past by asserting the importance of some new set of variables heretofore unemphasized, building yet another perspective inside the totality of the person but thereby missing a scientific understanding of our place in the whole of nature. As stated, we went beyond traditional conceptual boundaries in our field to explore hypotheses that drew their inspiration from more established, adjacent sciences.

The fundamental principles we uncovered (Millon, 1990) began with human evolution. Just as each person is composed of a total patterning of variables across all domains of human expression, it is the total organism that survives and reproduces, carrying forth both its adaptive and its maladaptive potentials into subsequent generations. Although lethal mutations sometimes occur, the evolutionary success of organisms with "average expectable genetic material" is dependent on the entire configuration of the organism's characteristics and potentials. Similarly, psychological fitness derives from the relation of the entire configuration of personal characteristics to the environments in which the person functions. Beyond these analogies, the principles of evolution also serve as principles that lie outside personality proper, and thus form a foundation for the integration of the various historical schools that escapes the part-whole fallacy of a dogmatic past. The creation of a taxonomy of personality and psychotherapy based on evolutionary principles is faced with one central question: How can these processes best be segmented so that their relevance to the individual person is placed and highlighted in the foreground?

The evolutionary theory comprises three imperatives (Millon, 1990; Millon & Grossman, 2004), each of which is a necessary aspect of the progression of evolution. First, each organism must survive. Second, it must adapt to its environment. And third, it must reproduce. To each of these imperatives is coupled a polarity that expresses the manifestation of that imperative in the life of the individual organism, thereby giving the theory content and putting metapsychology on a solid basis. To survive, an organism seeks to *maximize pleasure* and *minimize pain,* its **existential aims.** To adapt, an organism must either *passively conform* to resources and the constraints an environment offers, or *actively reform* the environment to meet its needs and make its opportunities, its **adaptation modes.** And finally, to reproduce, an organism must adopt a classically male and *self-oriented* strategy of producing many offspring with little further investment, or a classically female and *other-oriented* strategy of producing a few or a single offspring, while making a great investment of time and resources, its **replication strategies** (Millon, 1990). These are the fundamental evolutionary concerns of sustainable organisms on earth, and there are none more fundamental.

Polarities, that is, *contrasting* functional directions, representing these three evolutionary processes (pleasure-pain, passive-active, other-self) have been used to construct a theoretically generated classification system of personality styles and clinical disorders (Millon with Davis, 1996a). Such bipolar or dimensional schemes are almost universally present throughout the literatures of mankind, as well as in psychology at large (Millon, 1990). The earliest may be traced to ancient Eastern religions, most notably the Chinese *I Ching* text and the Hebrew Kabala.

In the life of the individual organism, each sequence of evolution is recapitulated and expressed *ontogenetically;* that is, each individual organism moves through developmental stages whose functional goals are related to their respective phases of evolution. Within each stage, every individual acquires character dispositions representing a balance of or predilection toward one of the two polarity inclinations; which inclination emerges as dominant over time results from the inextricable and reciprocal interplay of intraorganismic and extraorganismic factors. For example, during early infancy, the primary organismic function is to "continue to exist." Here, evolution has supplied mechanisms that orient the infant toward life-enhancing environments (pleasure) and away from life-threatening ones (pain).

The expression of traits or dispositions acquired in early stages of development may be transformed as later faculties or dispositions develop (Millon, 1969/1985). Temperament is a classic example. An individual with an active temperament may develop, contingent on contextual factors, into several personality styles, for example, an avoidant or an antisocial, the consequences being partly determined by whether the child has a fearful or a fearless temperament when dealt with a harsh environment. The transformation of earlier temperamental characteristics takes the form of what we have called "personological bifurcations" (Millon, 1990). Thus, if the individual is inclined toward a *passive* orientation and later learns to be self-focused, a narcissistic style ensues. But if the individual possesses an *active* orientation and later learns to be self-focused, an antisocial style may ensue. Thus, early developing dispositions may undergo vicissitudes, whereby their meaning in the context of the whole organism is subsequently re-formed into complex personality configurations.

The evolutionary model that has been presented, as well as its biosocial-learning forerunner (Millon, 1969/1985, 1981, 1986a), has generated several new diagnostic categories, several of which have found their way into the *DSM-III* and *DSM-IV* (Kernberg, 1984). Drawing on the three key components of the polarity framework—pain-pleasure, active-passive, self-other—a series of basic person prototypes and severe variants were deduced, of which a few have proved to be original derivations in the sense that they had never been formulated as categories in prior psychiatric nosologies (e.g., portraying and coining the avoidant personality designation; Millon, 1969/1985). Progressive research will determine if the network of concepts composing this theory provides an optimal structure for a comprehensive nosology of personality pathology. At the very least, it contributes to the view that formal theory can lead to the deduction of new categories worthy of clinical evaluation and consensual verification.

Before proceeding to elaborate the theory-derived nosology of psychopathology, that is, Axes I and II of the *DSM*, it should be emphasized that the theory provides a basis for deriving the so-called clinical syndromes as well as the personality disorders. To illustrate briefly, the most prevalent mental disorder according to recent epidemiologic studies is that of the anxiety disorders. Without explicating its several variants, a low pain threshold on the pleasure-pain polarity would dispose such individuals to be sensitive to punishments, which, depending on covariant polarity positions, might result in the acquisition of complex syndromal characteristics, such as ease of discouragement, low self-esteem, cautiousness, and social phobias. Similarly, a low pleasure threshold on the same polarity might make such individuals prone to experience joy and satisfaction with great ease; again, depending on covariant polarity positions, such persons might be inclined toward impulsiveness and hedonic pursuits, be intolerant of frustration and delay, and, at the clinical level, give evidence of a susceptibility to manic episodes.

To use musical metaphors again, *DSM-IV*'s Axis I clinical syndromes are composed essentially of a single theme or subject (e.g., anxiety, depression), a salient melodic line that may vary in its rhythm and harmony, changing little except in its timing, cadence, and progression. In contrast, the diversely expressed domains in Axis II seem constructed more in accord with the compositional structure known as the fugue, where there is a dovetailing of two or more melodic lines. Framed in the sonata style, the opening exposition in the fugue begins when an introductory theme is announced (or analogously in psychopathology, a series of clinical symptoms become evident), following which a second and perhaps third and essentially independent set of themes emerge in the form of answers to the first (akin to the unfolding expression of underlying personality traits). As the complexity of the fugue is revealed (we now have identified a full-blown personality disorder), variants of the introductory theme (i.e., the initial symptom picture) develop countersubjects (less observable, inferred traits), which are interwoven with the preceding in accord with well-known harmonic rules (comparably, mechanisms that regulate intrapsychic dynamics). This matrix of entwined melodic lines progresses over time in an episodic fashion, occasionally augmented, at other times diminished. It is sequenced to follow its evolving contrapuntal structure, unfolding a musical quilt, if you will, or better yet, an interlaced tapestry (the development and linkages of several psychological traits). To build this metaphorical elaboration further, not only may personality be viewed much like a fugue, but the melodic lines of its psychological counterpoints are composed of the three evolutionary themes presented earlier (the polarities, that is). Thus, some fugues are rhythmically vigorous and rousing (high "active"), others kindle a sweet sentimentality (high "other"), still others evoke a somber and anguished mood (high "pain"), and so on. When the counterpoint of the first three polarities is harmonically balanced, we observe a well-functioning or so-called normal person; when deficiencies, imbalances, or conflicts exist among them, we observe one or another variant of the personality disorders.

Personal styles we have termed *deficient* lack the capacity to experience or to enact certain aspects of the three polarities (e.g., the schizoid style has a faulty substrate for both pleasure and pain); those spoken of as *imbalanced* lean strongly toward one or another extreme of a polarity (e.g., the dependent style is oriented almost exclusively to receiving the support and nurturance of others); and those we judge in conflict struggle with ambivalences toward opposing ends of a bipolarity (e.g., the negativistic style vacillates between adhering to the expectancies of others and enacting what is wished for oneself).

Evolutionary theory is not undertaken for purposes of understanding alone. Its ultimate aim is to lead to intelligent remedial action.

Personality Styles and Disorders: Focusing on the Whole Person

As stated earlier, not all patients with the same diagnosis should be viewed as possessing the same problem. Platitudinous though this statement may be, care must be taken not to force patients into the procrustean beds of our theoretical models and nosological entities. Whether or not they are derived from mathematical analyses, clinical observations, or a systematic theory, all taxonomies are essentially composed of prototypal classes. Clinical categories must be conceived as flexible and dimensionally quantitative, permitting the full and distinctive configuration of characteristics of patients to be displayed (Millon & Grossman, 2006b). The multiaxial schema of *DSM-IV* is a step in the right direction in that it encourages multidimensional considerations as well as multidiagnoses that approximate the natural heterogeneity of patients. It is our view, however, that the atheoretical orientation of the *DSM-IV* does a disservice to assessment and psychotherapy because it bypasses highly informative interpretations that can be generated by a comprehensive theory, be it cognitive, psychoanalytic, or evolutionary.

Applying the Polarities of the Evolutionary Model

As will be elaborated later, the *DSM* personality prototypes simply list characteristics that have been found to accompany a particular disorder with some regularity and specificity. This approach is necessary, but insufficient. The *DSM* does put forward several domains in which personality is expressed, notably, cognition, affectivity, interpersonal functioning, and impulse control. However, these psychological domains are neither comprehensive nor are they applied comparably to all personality disorders.

Both the nature of the person as a synthetic construct and the laws of evolution require that the several domains of personality be organized in a logical fashion. The antagonism that exists among the competing domain approaches (cognitive, biological) in our discipline is largely an illusion wrought by human habits. No clinical trait domain should be seen as an autonomous entity. Rather, both the structure and the content of personality are mediated by the evolutionary imperatives of survival, adaptation, and reproductive success. It is always the entire organism as a whole that survives and evolves. The domains of the person are synthesized as a coherent unity. What we call the *functional* domains relate the organism to the external world; other domains serve as the *structural* substrates for such functioning. The distinction between function and structure parallels the distinction between the biological fields of physiology and anatomy. Anatomy investigates embedded and essentially permanent structures, which serve, for example, as substrates for mood and memory, whereas physiology examines functions that regulate internal dynamics and external transactions.

These functional and structural domains have parallels in numerous historical traditions as well as current major approaches to our field (Millon, 2004). This should not be surprising, given that progress in the softer sciences has proceeded slowly through the elucidation of previously neglected yet relevant variables. For example, the recent rise of the cognitive and the interpersonal perspectives were all but inevitable. The particulars of history influenced the timing at which these evolutions occurred but could not prevent their emergence. Thus, among the functional domains we have the Expressive Behavior domain representing the modern legacy of Thorndike, Skinner, and Hull, for example, while the Interpersonal Conduct domain represents the interpersonal tradition originating with Sullivan and expressed today by Kiesler (1986) and L. S. Benjamin (1993), among others. The Cognitive Style domain obviously represents the cognitive tradition, of which Beck (1976) is the most notable modern exponent, while the Regulatory Mechanisms and Object Representations domains parallel the ideas of defense mechanisms and object relations of the psychodynamic school (Millon, 2004). All of these are legitimate approaches to personality and through their very existence provide empirical support for the position advanced earlier: that person pathologies are best thought of as disorders of the entire matrix of the person. The alternative is a reduction of this complex matrix to one perspective, be it behavioral, cognitive, or psychodynamic—in other words, to substitute a part for the whole.

Three treatment themes may usefully be made to illustrate the combinatorial variations among the three polarities.

At the simplest level of analysis a number of personologic consequences of a single polar extreme are briefly noted. A high standing on the pain pole—a position typically associated with a disposition to experience anxiety—will be used for this purpose. The upshot of this singular sensitivity will take different forms depending on a variety of factors that lead to the learning of diverse styles of anxiety-neutralizing. For example, *avoidants* learn to deal with their pervasively experienced anxiety sensitivity by removing themselves across the board, that is, actively withdrawing from most relationships unless strong assurances of acceptance are given. The *compulsive,* often equally prone to experience anxiety, has learned that there are sanctioned but limited spheres of acceptable conduct; the compulsive reduces anxiety by restricting activities to those that are permitted by more powerful and potentially rejecting others, as well as to adhere carefully to rules so that unacceptable boundaries will not be transgressed. And the anxiety-prone *paranoid* has learned to neutralize pain by constructing a semidelusional pseudocommunity (Cameron, 1963), one in which environmental realities are transformed to make them more tolerable and less threatening, albeit not very successfully. In sum, a high standing at the pain pole leads not to one, but to diverse personality outcomes.

Another of the polar extremes illustrates the diversity of forms that personal styles may take as a function of covariant polarity positions, in this case, a shared position on the "passivity" pole. Six primary personality disorders demonstrate the passive style, but their passivity derives from and is expressed in appreciably different ways that reflect disparate polarity combinations. *Schizoids,* for example, are passive owing to their relative incapacity to experience pleasure and pain; without the rewards these emotional valences normally activate, they will be devoid of the drive to acquire rewards, leading them to become rather indifferent and passive observers. *Melancholic* personalities have given up on life and passively accept their misfortunes. Unwilling to make efforts to overcome their "fate," they exhibit little initiative to change their circumstances. *Dependents* typically are average on the pleasure and pain polarity, yet they are usually no less passive than schizoids or depressives. Strongly oriented to others, they are notably weak with regard to self. Passivity for them stems from deficits in self-confidence and self-competence, leading to deficits in initiative and autonomous skills as well as a tendency to wait passively while others assume leadership and guide them. Passivity among *compulsives* stems from their fear of acting independently owing to intrapsychic resolutions they have made to quell hidden thoughts and emotions generated by their intense self-other ambivalence. Dreading the possibility of making mistakes or engaging in disapproved behaviors, they become indecisive, immobilized, restrained, and passive. High on pain and low on both pleasure and self, *masochistic* personalities operate on the assumption that they dare not expect nor do they deserve to have life go their way; giving up any efforts to achieve a life that accords with their "true" desires, they passively submit to others' wishes, acquiescently accepting their fate. Finally, *narcissists,* especially high on self and low on others, benignly assume that good things will come their way with little or no effort on their part; this passive exploitation of others is a consequence of the unexplored confidence underlying their self-centered presumptions.

To turn to slightly more complex cases, there are individuals with appreciably different personality patterns who are often characterized by highly similar clinical features. To illustrate: To be correctly judged as "humorless and emotionally restricted" may be the result of diverse polarity combinations. *Schizoids,* as noted previously, are typically at the low end of both dimensions of the pleasure-pain bipolarity, experiencing little joy, sadness, or anger; they are quite humorless and though not restricted emotionally, do lack emotional expressiveness and spontaneity. By contrast, *avoidants* are notably high at the pain polar extreme; whatever their other traits may be, they are disposed to choose neither interpersonal humor nor emotional openness in their social interactions. Finally, the self-other–conflicted *compulsive* has learned to deny self-expression as a means of assuring the approval of others. Rarely will the compulsive let down his or her guard, lest any true oppositional feelings be betrayed; a compulsive rarely is relaxed sufficiently to engage in easy humor or willing to expose any contained emotions. All three personalities are humorless and emotionally restricted, but for different reasons and as a consequence of rather different polarity combinations.

The seeming theoretic fertility of the evolutionary polarities secures but a first step toward a systematic treatment framework. Convincing professionals of the validity of the schema requires detailed explications, on the one hand, and unequivocal evidence of utility, on the other. We must not only clarify what is meant by each term of the polarities—for example, identifying or illustrating their empirical referents—but also specify ways they may combine and manifest themselves clinically. It is toward those ends that the clinical chapters of this and other books of this personalized therapy series are addressed.

As may be inferred from the foregoing, it is both feasible and productive to employ the key dimensions of the bipolar evolutionary model to make the clinical features of the basic styles of personality functioning more explicit, from the actively pain-sensitive avoidant to the passively self-centered narcissist, and from the actively other-oriented histrionic to the self-other–conflicted negativistic (passive-aggressive; see Figure 1.1). The bias toward adaptive modes that is inherent in an evolutionary thesis does enable the identification of alternative mixtures in which these more pathological syndromes are expressed—hence, the clinical presence of frequent comorbidity, such as histrionic borderlines, sadistic paranoids, avoidant schizotypals, and passive-aggressive borderlines.

Responses to the preceding issues point to the inadequacy of any approach that links taxonomic criteria to intervention without theoretical guidance, as well as one that encompasses the functional-structural nature of the person (to be elaborated in the forthcoming sections on domain characteristics). The argument is merely that diagnosis should constrain and guide therapy in a manner consonant with accepted standards of the theoretically derived prototypal model. The scope of the interventions that might be considered appropriate and the form of their application has been left unattended. Any set of interventions or techniques might be applied singly or in combination, without regard to the diagnostic complexity of the treated disorder. In the actual practice of therapy, techniques within a particular pathological data level (i.e., psychodynamic techniques, behavioral techniques, and so on) are, in fact, often applied conjointly. Thus, systematic desensitization might be followed by in vivo exposure, or a patient might keep a diary of his or her thoughts while at the same time reframing those thoughts in accordance with the therapist's directions when they occur. In these

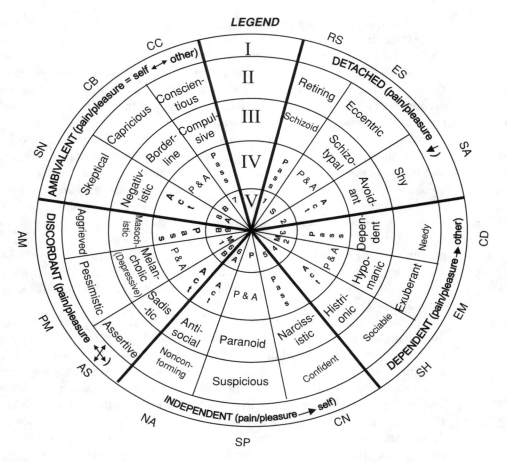

FIGURE 1.1 Personality spectra circulargram I: Normal and abnormal personality patterns. Evolutionary foundations of the normal and abnormal extremes of each personality prototype of the 15 spectra. I: Evolutionary Orientation; II: Normal Prototype; III: Abnormal Prototype; IV: Adaptation Style; V: MCMI-III-E Scale number/letter.

formulations, however, there is no strong a priori reason why any two therapies or techniques should be combined at all. As noted previously, when techniques from different modalities are applied together successfully, it is because the combination mirrors the composition of the individual case, not because it derives its logic on the basis of a theory or the syndrome.

Personality Spectra and Domains

The text, figures, and tables in this chapter will provide the reader with a brief synopsis of the personality-based evolutionary model; other sources should be pursued for a

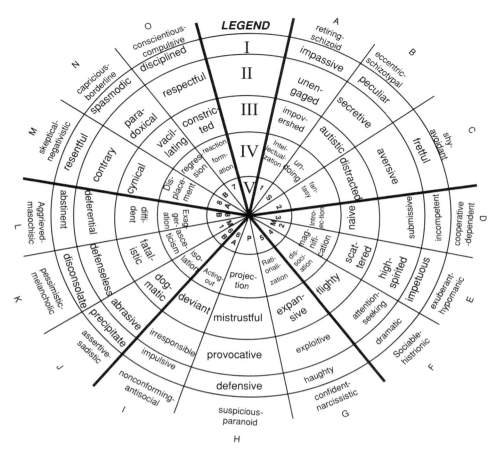

FIGURE 1.2 Personality circulargram IIA: Functional personologic domains.
I: Expressive Behavior; II: Interpersonal Conduct; III: Cognitive Style/Content;
IV: Intrapsychic Mechanisms; V: MCMI-III Scale.

more extensive elaboration of these ideas (Millon, Bloom, & Grossman, in press; Millon & Davis, 1996; Millon & Grossman, in press).

Three figures, 1.1, 1.2, and 1.3, present circumplex representations of the overall theoretically derived personality spectra of normal and abnormal patterns and their associated clinical domains. Figure 1.1, the Personality Spectra Circulargram, portrays the 15 prototypal variants derived from the theory. Legend I of Figure 1.1 relates to the prototype's primary evolutionary foundation (e.g., the retiring/schizoid reflects a detached pattern that stems from deficiencies in the pain-pleasure polarity). Figure 1.2 represents the four *functional* domains for each of the 15 personality prototype patterns. Legend II of Figure 1.2, for example, relates to the prototype's characteristic interpersonal conduct (e.g., the retiring/schizoid's conduct is noted as unengaged).

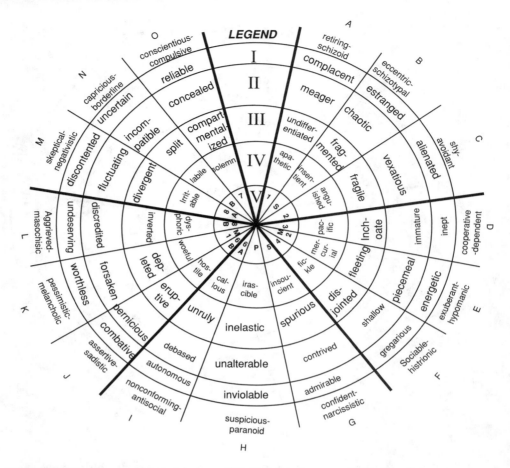

FIGURE 1.3 Personality circulargram IIB: Structural personologic domains.
I: Self-Image; II: Intrapsychic Content; III: Intrapsychic Structure; IV: Mood-Affect;
V: MCMI-III Scale.

Figure 1.3 portrays the four *structural* domains for all of the 15 personality prototypes. Legend IV of Figure 1.3, to illustrate, concerns the prototypal fundamental mood/affect (e.g., the retiring/schizoid's typical mood is recorded as apathetic).

Scores on these functional and structural domains, as calculated by MCMI-III analyses and/or obtained on the Millon-Grossman Personality Domain Checklist (MG-PDC), to be described shortly, serve as the basis for identifying, selecting, and coordinating the major foci and techniques of therapeutic action. Thus, high ratings on the pessimistic/melancholic interpersonal and mood/affect domains may identify the more problematic realms of a patient's psychological makeup. It also suggests the use of a combination of two therapeutic techniques: interpersonal methods (e.g., L. S.

Benjamin's approach, 2003) and pharmacologic medications (e.g., daily regimen of Prozac).

Complex Syndromes: Focusing on Symptom Clusters

A historic and still frequently voiced complaint about diagnosis, based or not on an official classification system, is its inutility for therapeutic purposes. Most therapists, whatever their orientation or mode of treatment, pay minimal attention to the possibility that diagnosis can inform the philosophy and technique they employ. It matters little what the syndrome or disorder may be, a family therapist is likely to select and employ a variant of family therapy, a cognitively oriented therapist will find that a cognitive approach will probably work best, and so on, including integrative therapists who are beginning to become a school and join this unfortunate trend of asserting the "truth" that their approach is the most efficacious.

A clinical study that attempted to unravel all of the elements of a patient's past and present would be an exhausting task indeed. To make the job less onerous, clinicians must narrow their attention to certain features of a patient's past history and behavior that may prove illuminating or significant. This reduction process requires that clinicians make a series of discriminations and decisions regarding the data they observe. They must find a constellation of core characteristics (e.g., cognitive style, interpersonal behavior) that capture the essential personal pattern of the patient and will serve as a framework to guide assessment and treatment.

Several assumptions are made by diagnosticians in narrowing their focus to this limited configuration of symptom domains. They assume that a patient possesses a core of interrelated behaviors, feelings, and attitudes that are central to his or her manifest pathology, that these characteristics are found in common among distinctive and identifiable groups of patients, and that prior knowledge regarding the features of these distinctive patient groups, hereby termed *complex clinical syndromes,* will facilitate therapists' clinical responsibilities and functions.

What support is there for these assumptions?

There are both theoretical and empirical justifications for the belief that people display a composite of linked characteristics, and that there is an intrinsic unity among these traits over time. Careful study of individuals with complex clinical syndromes will reveal a congruency among behaviors, cognitive reports, intrapsychic functioning, and biophysical disposition. This coherence or unity of psychic functioning is a valid phenomenon; that it is not merely imposed upon clinical data as a function of theoretical bias is evident by the fact that similar patterns of complex syndromes are observed by diagnosticians of differing theoretical persuasions. Moreover, these findings follow logically from the fact that people possess relatively enduring biophysical dispositions that give a consistent coloration to their experiences, and that the actual range of experiences to which they have been exposed throughout their lives is highly limited and repetitive. It should not be surprising, therefore, that individuals develop a complex pattern of distinguishing, prepotent and deeply ingrained behaviors, attitudes, and needs. Once several elements of these complex syndromes are identified, the clinician should have a fruitful basis for inferring the likely presence of other, unobserved, but frequently correlated features of the patient's life history and current functioning.

If we accept the assumption that people display covariant symptoms, we are led next to the question of whether certain patients evidence a commonality in the pattern of characteristics they display. The notion of complex clinical syndromes rests on the assumption that there are a limited number of symptom patterns that can be used profitably to distinguish certain groups of patients. The hope is that the diagnostic placement of a patient within one of these complex syndromal groups will clue the diagnostician to a wider pattern of the patient's difficulty, thereby simplifying the clinical task immeasurably. Thus, once diagnosticians identify clusters of clinical characteristics in a particular patient, they will be able to utilize the knowledge they have learned about other patients evidencing that syndrome and apply that knowledge to the present patient.

The fact that patients can profitably be categorized into complex clinical syndromes does not negate the fact that patients so categorized will display differences in the presence and constellation of their characteristics. The philosopher Grunbaum (1952, pp. 665–676) illustrates this thesis in the following:

> Every individual is unique by virtue of being a distinctive assemblage of characteristics not precisely duplicated in any other individual. Nevertheless, it is quite conceivable that the following... might hold: If a male child having specifiable characteristics is subjected to maternal hostility and has a strong paternal attachment at a certain stage of his development, he will develop paranoia during adult life. If this... holds, then children who are subjected to the stipulated conditions in fact become paranoiacs, however much they may have differed in other respects in childhood and whatever their other differences may be once they are already insane.

There should be little concern about the fact that certain "unique" characteristics of each patient will be lost when he or she is grouped in a complex syndrome; differences among members of the same syndrome will exist, of course. The question that must be raised is *not* whether the syndrome is entirely homogeneous, as no complex category meets this criterion, but whether placement in the category impedes or facilitates a variety of clinically relevant objectives. Thus, if this grouping of key characteristics simplifies the task of clinical analysis by alerting diagnosticians to features of the patient's past history and present functioning that they have not yet observed, or if it enables clinicians to communicate effectively about their patients or guides their selection of beneficial therapeutic plans or assists researchers in the design of experiments, then the existence of these syndromal categories has served many useful purposes. No single classification schema can serve all of the purposes for which clinical categories can be formed; all we can ask is that it facilitate certain relevant functions.

As noted previously, the diagnostic criteria of the *DSM-IV* have *not* been explicitly constructed to facilitate treatment, no less personalized psychotherapy. Criteria should do more than classify persons into categories, a rather minimalistic function. Instead, diagnostic criteria should encourage an integrative understanding of the patient across all those psychic domains in which the person's mental impairments are expressed. The *DSM-IV* criteria, disproportionately weighted in some symptom domains and nonexistent in others, cannot perform this function. At this point in time, personalized psychotherapy requires that the official diagnostic criteria be supplemented by clinical judgment. Obviously, effective synergistic therapy requires a detailed assessment of all those symptom domains that can exist as constraints on system functioning. Because the *DSM-IV* therapist simply would not be cognizant of such abnormalities, techniques appropriate to those domains would not be used either combinatorially or in series. Using *DSM-IV* criteria alone as a guide to the substantive characteristics of personality and syndromes would effectively leave some systems constraints completely unobserved, free to operate insidiously in the background to perpetuate the pathological tenacity of the system as a whole. Consequently, a *DSM-IV*-based therapy is not necessarily a personalized therapy.

We next review some of the distinctions between *complex* clinical syndromes and *simple* clinical reactions. In essence, the distinction is traceable to the interweaving of intrapsychic, cognitive, and interpersonal elements in the complex syndrome. The residuals of the past intrude on the individual's present perceptions and behaviors, often giving rise to seemingly irrational symptoms. Both complex clinical syndromes and simple reactions are classed among the *DSM-IV* Axis I disorders, an unfortunate decision that overlooks important distinctions. It is only in the complex syndromes that we see the compounding of pervasive interpersonal relations, unconscious emotions, cognitive assumptions, self-images, and so on.

Differentiating Simple Reactions from Complex Syndromes

Simple clinical reactions, complex clinical syndromes, and personality styles and disorders lie on a continuum such that the simple clinical reaction is essentially a straightforward singular symptom, unaffected by other clinical domains of which the-person-as-a-whole is composed (Millon, 1969/1985). At the other extreme are personality styles and disorders which comprise an interrelated mix of cognitive attitudes, interpersonal styles, and biological temperaments and intrapsychic processes. Complex clinical syndromes lie in between, manifestly akin to simple syndromes but interwoven and mediated by pervasive personality traits and embedded vulnerabilities.

Clinical signs in *personality disorders* reflect the operation of a pattern of deeply embedded and pervasive characteristics of functioning, that is, a system of traits that systematically "support" one another and color and manifest themselves automatically in all facets of the individual's everyday life. By contrast, *simple clinical reactions* are relatively direct responses that derive from specific neurochemical dysfunctions or are prompted by rather distinctive stimulus experiences. Simple reactions operate somewhat independently of the patient's overall personality pattern; their form and content are determined largely by the character of a biologic vulnerability or the specifics of an external precipitant; that is, they are not contaminated by the intrusion of other psychic domains or forces. Simple clinical reactions are best understood *not* as a function of the intricate convolutions among intrapsychic mechanisms, interpersonal behaviors, cognitive misperceptions, and the like, but as simple and straightforward responses to an endogenous liability or to adverse and circumscribed stimulus conditions. To paraphrase Eysenck (1959): There are no obscure "causes" that "underlie" simple clinical reactions, merely the reaction itself; modify the reaction, or the conditions that precipitate it, and you have eliminated all there is to the pathology.

The overt clinical features of the simple clinical reactions and the *complex clinical syndromes* are often indistinguishable; moreover, both are prompted *in part* by external precipitants.

How are they different?

Complex clinical syndromes are rooted in part to pervasive personality vulnerabilities and coping styles, whereas simple clinical reactions are not. Complex syndromes usually arise when the patient's established personality equilibrium has been upset or threatened. At that point, numerous domains of expression come into play in the patient's effort to reestablish a modicum of stability. Unfortunately, as often occurs in medical diseases, the reparative process itself becomes highly problematic, creating additional difficulties. Hence, therapy must attend not only to the primary clinical domain that has begun the process, but to many of the secondary domains of expression. Complex clinical syndromes often arise in response to what objectively is often an insignificant or innocuous event; despite the trivial and specific character of the precipitant, the patient exhibits a mix of complicated responses that have minimal relationship to how normal persons respond in these circumstances. Thus, complex clinical syndromes often do not "make sense" in terms of actual present realities; they signify an unusual vulnerability and an overreaction on the part of the patient, that is, a tendency for objectively neutral stimuli to touch off and activate cognitive misperceptions, unconscious memories, and pathological interpersonal responses. Complex syndromes usually signify the activation of several traits that make up the varied facets of a personality style or disorder. They are seen in individuals who are encumbered with the residues of deeply embedded past experiences or adverse life events that have led to the acquisition of problematic cognitive beliefs and behavioral habits.

As suggested, unconscious memories, self-attitudes, and interpersonal dispositions intervene in the expression of complex syndromes, complicating the connection between present stimuli and the patient's response to them. As we see it, intrusions of this nature do not occur in simple clinical reactions. In the latter, the patient's vulnerabilities are neither deep nor widespread, but restricted to a limited class of biological vulnerabilities or environmental conditions. These pathological responses do not pass through a chain of complicated and circuitous intrapsychic and cognitive transformations before they emerge in manifest form. Thus, in addition to the restricted number of precipitants that give rise to them, simple reactions are distinguished from complex syndromes in the more or less direct route through which they are channeled and expressed clinically.

In complex syndromes, a precipitating stimulus will stir up a wide array of intervening thoughts and emotions which then take over as the determinant of the response; reality stimuli serve merely as catalysts that set into motion a complex chain of intermediary processes that transform what might otherwise have been a fairly simple and straightforward response. Because of the contaminating intrusion of these transformations the complex response acquires an irrational and often symbolic quality. For example, in complex phobias the object that is feared often comes to represent something else; a phobia of elevators might come to symbolize a more generalized and unconscious anxiety about being closed in and trapped by others.

Because of the frequent pervasiveness of complex syndromal vulnerabilities, thoughts and behaviors become entangled in a wide variety of dissimilar stimulus situations, for example, the feeling of being trapped may give rise to a phobia not only of elevators but also of rooms in which the doors are shut, of riding in cars in which the windows are closed, of tight clothes. Moreover, these complicated processes vary in their form and degree of intrusion; for example, a phobic patient may feel well on certain days and agree to the closing of room doors; on other days, however, all doors and windows must be wide open. Thus, the responses of complex syndromes not only are elicited by a wide variety of stimulus conditions, but these diverse responses wax and wane in their relative salience.

All this fluidity and variability in complex clinical syndromes contrast with the relative directness and uniformity of responses found in simple clinical reactions. Uninfluenced by the intricate and circuitous transformations of other facets of the person's psyche, simple reactions tend to be consistent and predictable. They are manifested in essentially the same way each time the endogenous vulnerability or troublesome stimulus to which they have been attached occurs. Moreover, they are rarely exhibited at other times or in response to events that are dissimilar to the stimulus to which they were originally attached. In short, simple clinical reactions are ingrained, but they are *isolated responses* to specific inner or outer stimulus events. They tend not to vary or be influenced by the patient's general personal makeup. They are relatively compartmentalized stimulus-response reactions that are isolated in large measure from the patient's larger and characteristic pattern of functioning. They may be narrowly focused behaviors, displaying themselves only in response to specific types of stimulus events. To use an analogy, we might speak of complex syndromes emerging from several interwoven domains of personality structure and function; they are both body and basic design of a fabric, whereas the simple reaction may be seen as an embroidered decoration that has been sewn onto it. One may remove (extinguish) the embroidery with relative ease (as conditioning therapists have done in treating the simple clinical reactions) without involving or altering the body of the cloth (personality). Simple clinical reactions, then, do not permeate and intrude on the many facets of the individual's transactions with his or her world, as do the trait covariants of complex disorders; rather, they are stimulus-specific responses to either a circumscribed inner or outer class of stimuli.

Despite the preceding, there are many similarities between simple reactions and complex syndromes. For example, anxiety can be either simple or complex. Both are characterized by feelings of tension and by a rapid increase in sympathetic nervous system reactivity (perspiration, muscular contraction, and rapid heartbeat). They differ in that the origins of complex anxiety disorders are difficult to decode and are often unanchored and free-floating. In contrast, simple anxiety reactions usually are connected to a readily identifiable stimulus.

As another illustration, complex phobic syndromes and simple phobic reactions are alike in that both may be precipitated by a tangible external stimulus, leading taxonomists to question whether any difference exists between them. As we conceive it, the difference is a matter of the degree and complexity with which other clinical domains contribute to the pathological response. Complex phobias, as we define them, signify that intricate and highly convoluted cognitive and emotional processes have played a determinant role in "selecting" a provocative stimulus that subjectively represents, but is objectively different from, that which may actually be feared; for example, a phobia for open places may symbolize a more generalized fear of assuming independence of others. In contrast, what we have termed a simple phobic reaction is a direct, nonsymbolic response to the actual stimulus the patient has learned to fear, for example, a fear of Asian persons that is traceable to distressing encounters in childhood with a Chinese teacher. Of course, some measure of generalization occurs in simple reactions, but the individual tends to make the simple response only to objects or events that are essentially similar or closely allied with the original fear stimulus; for example, learning to fear a cat in early life may be generalized into a fear of dogs because these animals are barely discriminable in the eyes of the very young. At most, then, the simple phobic reaction may reflect an uncomplicated generalization. Although often appearing irrational to the unknowing outsider, they can be traced directly to these reality-based and well-circumscribed experiences.

Complex clinical syndromes tend to occur in persons whose histories are replete with innumerable instances of adverse experience. Given their repeated exposure to mismanagement and faulty learning experiences, these individuals have built up an obscure psychic labyrinth, a residue of complex, tangentially related, but highly interwoven cognitions, emotions, and interpersonal behaviors that are easily reactivated under the pressure of new stressors. Because these intervening processes are stirred up under new stressful conditions, no simple and direct line can be traced between the overt response and its associated precipitant. The final outcome, as in complex phobias, often appears to be symbolic rather than simply generalized because the associative route is highly circuitous, involving both the residuals of the past and numerous distortion mechanisms. Complex syndromes are formed by the crystallization of diffusely anchored and transformed past learnings acquired in response to a wide and diverse range of faulty experiences; this pervasively adverse background and the rather circuitous sequence of distortions are what are activated among pathological persons. Because "normals" are not likely to have had such pervasively adverse experiences, they have had little reason to develop a complex of behavioral styles and defensive maneuvers to avoid the reactivation of distressing memories and emotions; as a result, what we observe in them are relatively clean, that is, simple and direct.

It should be noted that the continuum we have drawn between simple and complex syndromes cannot be drawn with ease in describing characteristics of the first years of life. During this early period, learnings have not crystallized into ingrained, pervasive, stable, and consistent styles of life. In many respects, childhood personality is a loose cluster of scattered habits and beliefs learned in response to a wide variety of odds-and-ends experiences. Over time, however, as certain of the conditions that gave rise to these habits and beliefs are repeated and attached to an increasing variety of stimuli, and as the child's own self-perpetuating processes accentuate and spread the range of these events further, some of these simple reactions become more dominant than others, until they may take shape as pervasive and ingrained personality traits. Thus, early simple reactions may become the precursors of later complex syndromes and personality patterns; it is a continuous developmental process.

Let us briefly recapitulate and extend several points.

Coping refers to processes of instrumental activity that are learned as a function of experience. These processes enable individuals to maintain an optimum level of psychological integration by increasing the number of life-enhancing satisfactions they achieve (e.g., attention, comfort, pleasure, and status) and avoiding as many life-endangering experiences as they can (e.g., punishment, frustration, rejection, and anxiety).

Psychic pathologies utilize coping behaviors to achieve several goals, such as counteracting external precipitants that threaten to upset their equilibrium and tenuous controls; blocking reactivated anxieties and impulses from intruding into conscious awareness, thereby avoiding potentially upsetting social condemnation; discharging tensions engendered by external stressors and their intrapsychic residuals; and soliciting attention, sympathy, and nurture from others.

It is the synthesis of goals such as these that also distinguishes simple reactions from complex clinical syndromes. Diluting tensions while at the same time blocking awareness of their true source, avoiding social rebuke, and evoking social approval and support in their stead, is characteristic of the complex syndromes, a task of no mean proportions. It requires the masking and transformation of one's true thoughts and feelings by the intricate workings of several psychic mechanisms. The resulting complex syndrome symptom represents the interplay and final outcome of numerous psychic and interpersonal maneuvers. Not only have the patient's anxieties and impulses been disguised sufficiently to be kept from conscious awareness, but they also managed to solicit interpersonal acceptance as well as achieve a measure of cognitive resolution and tension discharge.

Alexander (1930) reports a classic case of phobia in which the patient's symptom achieved her goals through a complex psychic resolution:

> A young woman dreaded going into the street alone, the thought of which made her feel faint and extremely anxious. Upon clinical investigation it became clear that a forbidden and unconscious sexual impulse was associated with her phobia; each time she would go out her impulse would be stimulated by the thought that a man might "pick her up" and seduce her. The thought both excited her and caused her intense anxiety. To avoid the true character of her forbidden desire and the tension it provoked she displaced her tension to an associated and more generalized activity, that of going into the street; thus, her phobia. However, she was able to venture out quite undisturbed if accompanied by a relative. In this way she could engage in fleeting sexual fantasies as she passed attractive men, without the fear that she might be carried away and shamed by her forbidden impulse. Her symptom was extremely efficient; not only did it enable her to maintain psychological cohesion by controlling her impulse, blocking her awareness of its true source and keeping her behavior within acceptable social boundaries, but, at the same time, it solicited the assistance of others who enabled her to find some albeit skimpy means of gaining both tension and impulse release.

The case just described brings us to another aspect of complex clinical syndromes: the tendency for symptoms to achieve what are known as secondary gains. According to traditional theory, the primary function of clinical syndromes is the avoidance, control, and partial discharge of anxiety, or, as we would be inclined to call it, the elimination of a strong upsurge of negative feelings stemming from unconscious sources. But, in addition, the psychic maneuver may produce certain positive consequences; that is, as a result of his of her clinical syndrome, the patient may obtain secondary advantages or rewards. In the case just described, for example, the woman's phobic symptom achieved a positive result above and beyond the reduction of the negatively toned anxiety; in the role of a sick and disabled person, she solicited attention, sympathy, and help from others and was freed of the responsibility of carrying out many of the duties expected of a healthy adult. In this fashion her symptom not only controlled and partially vented her anxieties, but enabled her to gratify a more basic dependency need.

The distinction between primary gains (anxiety neutralization) and secondary gains (positive rewards) may be sharply drawn at the conceptual level but is difficult to make when analyzing actual cases because the two processes intermesh closely in reality. However, the conceptual distinction may be extremely important. As we view it, secondary gains play no part in the formation of simple clinical reactions. Here, patients are prompted to develop their symptom not as a means of gaining secondary or positive rewards, but as a means of avoiding, controlling, or discharging anxiety.

This sharp distinction between primary and secondary gains seems rather arbitrary and narrow. Although it is true that anxiety neutralization is centrally involved in complex syndromes, this, in itself, could not account for the variety of symptoms that patients display (e.g., somatoform, obsessive-compulsive). We may ask: Why are certain forms of interpersonal conduct and psychic mechanisms employed by some patients and different ones by others, and why do certain symptoms rather than others emerge? If the sole purpose of syndrome formation were anxiety abatement, then any set of mechanisms could fulfill that job, giving rise to any number and variety of different syndromes.

This, however, is not the case. It seems that most complex syndrome maneuvers both neutralize anxiety (primary gain) and, at the same time, achieve certain positive advantages (secondary gain). We believe that complex clinical syndromes reflect the joint operation of both primary and secondary gain strategies (neither of which, we should note, is consciously planned). Furthermore, we propose that complex clinical syndromes, albeit different overtly, have a common and covert secondary gain characteristic that distinguishes them from simple reactions; that is, their symptoms (phobias, conversions) serve to neutralize tensions, and do so without provoking social condemnation, eliciting, in its stead, support, sympathy, and nurture.

Personality Domain Traits Underlying Complex Syndromes

The prognostic course of simple reactions is relatively predictable and uncomplicated, assuming that the diagnosis is correct. It can safely be expected that the patient will regain normal composure and functioning shortly following the removal of the stressful inner or outer precipitant.

As noted earlier, complex clinical syndromes display themselves in such ways as both to avoid social derogation and to elicit support and sympathy from others. In Alexander's (1930) example, a phobic patient manipulated members of her family into accompanying her in street outings, where she gained the illicit pleasures of sexual titillation; through her unfortunate disablement, she fulfilled her dependency needs, exerted interpersonal control over the lives of others, and achieved partial impulse gratification without social condemnation. Let us look at two other examples. A depressed woman not only may be relieved of family responsibilities, but through her subtly angry symptom makes others feel guilty and limits their freedom while still gaining their concern, and yet does not provoke retribution. A hypochondriacal woman experiences diverse somatic ailments that preclude sexual activity; she not only gains her husband's compassion and understanding, but does so without his recognizing that her behavior is a subtle form of punishing him; she is so successful in her maneuver that her frustration of his sexual desires is viewed, not as an irritation or a sign of selfishness, but as an unfortunate consequence of her physical illness. Her plight evokes more sympathy for her than for her husband.

Why do the symptoms of complex clinical syndromes take this particular, devious route? Why are their anxieties or otherwise socially unacceptable impulses masked and transformed so as to appear not only socially palatable, but evocative of support and sympathy? To answer this question we must examine which of the various personality styles and disorders tend to exhibit these clinical syndromes. When we do, we discover that they are found primarily among avoidants, depressives, dependents, histrionics, compulsives, negativists, masochists, and borderlines. More will be said when we discuss these syndromes and personalities in later chapters and other books in this series.

What rationale can be provided for the covariation of certain personality patterns and complex clinical syndromes?

We previously stated that a clearer understanding of complex clinical syndromes is achieved by a study of the context of a patient's personality. Complex syndromes are largely an outgrowth of deeply rooted habits, vulnerabilities, and coping strategies. What events a person perceives as threatening or rewarding and what behaviors and mechanisms he or she employs in response to them depend on the history to which he or she was exposed. If we wish to uncover the reasons for the particular syndromes a patient "chooses," we must first understand the source and character of the goals he or she seeks to achieve. As elaborated in Millon and Davis (1996), the character of the symptoms a patient chooses has not been a last-minute decision, but reflects a long history of interwoven biogenic and psychogenic factors that have formed his or her basic personality pattern. As noted earlier, in analyzing the distinguishing goals of complex syndromal behaviors, we are led to the following observations: Susceptible patients appear especially desirous of avoiding the negative experiences (pain) of social disapproval and rejection; moreover, where possible, they wish to evoke the positive experiences (pleasure) of attention, sympathy, and nurture.

Although each personality pattern (or syndrome context) has had different prior experiences, they tend to share in common a hypersensitivity to social rebuff and condemnation, to which they hesitate reacting with counteraggression. In the *dependent* patterns, for example, there is a fear of losing the security and rewards that others provide; these patients must guard themselves against acting in such ways as to provoke disapproval and separation; rather, where feasible, they will maneuver themselves to act in ways that evoke favorable responses.

There are endless variations in the *specific* life experiences to which different members of the same personality style or disorder have been exposed. Let us compare, for example, two individuals who have been "trained" to become *compulsive* personalities. One may have been exposed to a mother who was chronically ill, a pattern of behavior that brought her considerable sympathy and freedom from many burdens. With this as a background factor, the person may be inclined to follow the model she observed in her mother when she is faced with undue anxiety and threat, thereby displaying hypochondriacal syndromes. A second compulsive personality may have learned to imitate a father who expressed endless fears about all types of events and situations. In his case, there is a greater likelihood that phobic syndromes would arise in response to stressful and anxiety-laden circumstances. In short, the specific "choice" of the complex syndrome is not a function solely of the patient's personality pattern, but may reflect more particular and entirely incidental events of prior experience and learning.

Although each complex syndrome crops up with greater frequency among certain personalities than others, they do arise in a number of different patterns. For example, *somatoform* syndromes occur most commonly among patients exhibiting a basic avoidant, dependent, histrionic, compulsive, or negativistic personality pattern; *conduct disorders* are found primarily in narcissistic, antisocial, and sadistic patterns. This observation points up the importance of specifying the basic personality style or disorder from which a complex syndrome arises. The dominant symptom a patient displays cannot, in itself, clue us well enough to the basic dispositions and vulnerabilities of the patient. In later chapters, we shall make it a practice to discuss complex clinical syndromes with reference to the specific pathological personality pattern from which they issue.

Three cases of the complex clinical syndrome labeled dysthymia are presented next to illustrate the fact that the appraisal of an Axis I syndrome should be approached in terms of the patient's larger context of personality dispositions and vulnerabilities. In the first of these cases, a dysthymic syndrome is described in a *dependent* personality. In the second, the dysthymia is interpreted as it is likely to occur in a *negativistic* (passive-aggressive) personality. In the third dysthymic description, the characterization of the patient derives its significance in the context of a *masochistic* personality:

Dysthymia in a dependent personality: This woman may be characteristically tense and sad; however, her apprehensiveness appears to have achieved dysphoric levels that are sufficient to classify her as experiencing a mixed anxiety and dysthymic disorder. Dependent and dejected, but also ambivalent about her relationships, she may struggle to restrain her sadness and resentment, but with only partial success. The strain of her vacillations may precipitate a variety of behavioral syndromes, such as restlessness and distractibility, as well as physical discomfort such as insomnia and fatigue. Holding back her dysphoric mood is stressful, but discharging it is equally problematic in that it may provoke those on whom she depends.

Dysthymia in a negativistic personality: A pattern of anxiety and dysthymia is likely to have emerged over time in this edgy and actively ambivalent man. Unsure of the fealty of those on whom he has learned to depend and conflicted about his neediness in this regard, he experiences strong emotions of a resentful and hostile nature. Because of his dread of rebuke and rejection, he tries to restrain these emotions but is only partially successful. Rather than chance total abandonment, he turns much of his anger inward, leading to self-generated feelings of unworthiness and guilt. His increasingly hopeless feeling springs from a wide and pervasive range of events that have caused him to see his life as being filled with inadequacies, resentments, fears, diminished pleasures, and self-doubts.

Dysthymia in a masochistic personality: The self-demeaning comments and feelings of inferiority expressed by this dysthymic woman are part of her overall and enduring characterological structure, a set of chronic self-defeating attitudes and depressive emotions that are intrinsic to her psychological makeup. Feelings of emptiness and loneliness are mixed with expressions of low self-esteem, preoccupations with ostensive failures and physical unattractiveness, and assertions of guilt and unworthiness. Although she complains about being aggrieved and mistreated, she is likely to assert that she deserves the anguish and abuse she receives. Such self-debasement is consonant with her self-image, as are her tolerance and perpetuation of relationships that foster and aggravate her misery.

Despite the short-term gains made by complex syndromal efforts, the symptoms they give rise to are frequently self-defeating in the end. By restricting their environment (e.g., phobias), limiting their physical competencies (e.g., conversions), preoccupying themselves with distracting activities (e.g., obsessions-compulsions), or deprecating their self-worth (e.g., dysthymia), patients avoid confronting and resolving their real difficulties and tend to become increasingly dependent on others. This psychic maneuver, then, is a double-edged sword. It relieves for the moment passing discomforts and strains, but in the long run fosters the perpetuation of faulty attitudes and coping strategies.

Complex syndromal patients exhibit a blend of several traits and symptoms that rise and subside over time in their clarity and prominence. This complex and changing picture is further complicated by the fact that it is set within the context of the patient's broader personality pattern of attitudes and behaviors. In planning a treatment approach, the therapist is faced with an inextricable mixture of focal and transitory symptoms that are embedded in a pattern of more diffuse and permanent traits.

Separating these clinical features for therapeutic attention is no simple task. To decide which features make up the "basic personality" and which represent the "clinical syndrome" cannot readily be accomplished as both are elements of the same system of vulnerabilities and coping strategies. Even when clear distinctions can be drawn, as when a symptom suddenly emerges in clear and sharp relief, a judgment must be made as to whether therapeutic attention should be directed to the focal symptom or to the "underlying" personality trait pattern from which it has sprung. In certain cases, it is both expeditious and fruitful to concentrate solely on the manifest clinical syndrome; in other cases, however, it may be advisable to rework the more pervasive and ingrained pattern of personality domains.

Before we proceed, let us again be reminded that the descriptive label given to each of the clinical syndromes may be misleading in that it suggests that a single symptom stands alone, uncontaminated by others. This is not the case, especially in what we have termed the complex clinical syndromes. Although a particular symptom may appear dominant at one time, it often coexists and covaries with several others, any one of which may come to assume dominance. As a further complication, there is not only covariation and fluidity in symptomatology, but each of these clinical syndromes arise in a number of different personality patterns.

Much of the confusion that has plagued diagnostic systems in the past can be attributed to this overlapping and changeability of symptom pictures. For reasons discussed in previous sections, it has been argued that greater clarity can be achieved in diagnosis if we focus on the basic personality of the patient rather than limit ourselves to the particular dominant symptom he or she manifests. Moreover, by focusing our attention on enduring personality traits and pervasive clinical domains of expression, we may be able to deduce the cluster of different symptoms the patient is likely to display and the sequence of symptoms he or she may exhibit over the course of the illness. For example, knowing the vulnerabilities and habitual coping strategies of *paranoid* personalities, we would predict that they will evidence either together or in sequence both delusions and hostile mania, should they become psychotically disordered. Similarly, *compulsive* personalities may be expected to manifest cyclical swings between catatonic rigidity, agitated depression, and manic excitement, should they decompensate into a psychotic state. Focusing on ingrained personality patterns rather than transient symptoms enables us to grasp both the patient's complex syndrome and the symptoms he or she is likely to exhibit, as well as the possible sequence in which they will wax and wane.

Simple Reactions: Focusing on Singular Symptoms

There is a close correspondence in simple clinical reactions between classical assessment *domains* (e.g., *DSM* diagnostic criteria) and modern *therapeutic* modalities. This concurrence greatly facilitates our understanding and selection of optimal techniques of treatment among these reactions. It addresses the long-held desire to connect diagnostic assessment with therapeutic methodology.

Unfortunately, the diagnostic criteria of the *DSM-IV* are both noncomprehensive (no real scheme through which to coordinate and anchor domain attributes has been developed) and noncomparable (the criteria run the gamut from very broad to very narrow). Further, these problems exist both within and between disorders, so that different disorders evince different content distortions. Consider, for example, the Obsessive-Compulsive Personality Disorder. Criterion 5 is relatively narrow and behavioral: "Is unable to discard worn-out or worthless objects even when they have no sentimental value." In contrast, criterion 8 requires more inference: "Shows rigidity and stubbornness." In fact, the inability to discard worthless objects could well be considered simply a behavioral manifestation of the trait of rigidity. Failure to coordinate criteria across domains may also lead to redundancies. Consider, for example, the Dependent Personality Disorder. Criterion 1 states, "Has difficulty making everyday decisions without an excessive amount of advice and reassurance from others." Criterion 2, however, says almost the same: "Needs others to assume responsibility for most major areas of his or her life." In fact, five of the eight dependent personality criteria seem oriented toward the interpersonal conduct domain, two seem oriented toward the self-image domain, and only one is concerned with cognitive style, leaving the domains of regulatory mechanisms, object representations, morphologic organization, mood/temperament, and expressive behavior completely unaddressed.

Failure to multioperationalize psychopathology via comprehensive and comparable symptom domains certainly means that the content validity of the criteria sets has been compromised, quite probably contributing to diagnostic invalidity and therapeutic inefficiency. Because the *DSM* is usually taken as the gold standard by which other measures of psychic pathology are judged, the degree of distortion is an open question at this point—there is no gold standard for the gold standard. The worst-case scenario reads as follows: Clinical wisdom states correctly that, in principle, multiple data sources and construct operationalizations should be sought as a means of obtaining convergent validity for one's assessment findings, where possible. Because the *DSM* criteria sets are noncomprehensive and noncomparable, there are substantive reasons, reasons that go beyond mere principle, for bringing extra-*DSM* notions and instruments to bear on an individual's assessment case. To the extent that *DSM* criteria are successfully operationalized, distortions that are latent in these criteria are built into an instrument, thereby providing users with information confirmatory of a *DSM* diagnosis, but in fact diagnosis is valid only through redundancy. Thus, the role of freewheeling clinical judgment has by no means been usurped by such instrumentalities and criteria sets (Westen & Weinberger, 2004).

Ideally, a diagnosis functions as a means of narrowing the universe of therapeutic techniques to some small set of choices, and within this small set, uniquely personal factors come into play between alternative techniques or the order in which these techniques might be applied.

Let us *briefly* examine how a few of the simple reaction symptoms correspond to various modes of therapy; more extensive discussions are provided in later chapters of this text.

Therapists who subscribe to the *behavioral* orientation emphasize simple reactions that can be directly observed. As a consequence, their interest centers on environmental stimuli and overt behavioral responses. Most clinical reactions are considered to be deficient or maladaptive learned behaviors. They avoid, where possible, reference to unobservable or subjective processes such as intrapsychic conflicts or cognitive attitudes. Because inner states are anathema to them, they are inclined to an action-suppressive rather than an insight-expressive process. Because the most clearly formulated schema of behavior change has been developed in the laboratories of learning theorists, they borrow their methods and procedures from that body of research. It follows logically, they contend, that simple reactions can best be altered by the same learning principles and procedures that were involved in their acquisition. Thus, behavior therapists design their treatment programs in terms of conditioning and imitative modeling techniques that provide selective rewards and punishments. In this way, simple syndromal behaviors that had been connected to provocative stimuli are systematically eliminated and more adaptive behavioral alternatives carefully formed.

Cognitive therapists believe that treatment for both simple reactions and complex syndromes should be conceived in terms of the patient's beliefs, assumptions, and expectancies. Because individuals react to their present world in accord with their current perception of it, cognitivists contend that the goal of treatment should not be to unravel the early causes of difficulties, but to assist people in developing a clearer understanding of how their distorted attitudes and beliefs generate and prolong their problems. As their perception of events and people is clarified, they will be able to approach life with fewer problematic assumptions and expectancies, enabling them to act in ways that will eliminate the syndrome in question.

As we know, *intrapsychic* therapists focus their efforts on the elusive and obscure data of the unconscious. To them, the crucial elements underlying most syndromes are repressed childhood anxieties and the unconscious adaptive processes that have evolved to protect against their resurgence. The task of therapy, then, is to unravel these hidden residues of the past and to bring them into consciousness, where they can be reevaluated and reworked in a constructive fashion. Shorn of insidious unconscious forces through the unfolding of self-insight and the uprooting of forbidden feelings, the patient may now be free to explore a more wholesome and productive way of life.

As we know it, the concept of a system must be brought to the forefront, even when discussing reactions and syndromes. Systems function as a whole, but are composed of parts. As noted, we have partitioned mental disorders into simple reactions, complex syndromes, and personality patterns, but we segregated these disorders with reference to the eight structural and functional domains described in the figures and tables in this chapter (Millon, 1984, 1986a, 1990; Millon & Davis, 1996). These domains encompass the greater part of a person's makeup. Simple reactions are essentially expressed in only one major symptom domain (e.g., behavior, relationships); complex syndromes usually engage three or four clinical domains, whereas personality patterns are likely to comprise almost all of the trait domains. They serve as a means of classifying the parts or constructs in accord with established therapeutic traditions. In every complex syndrome, elements from several domains constrain what can exist in other domains of the system. An individual born with a phlegmatic temperament, for example, is unlikely to mature into a histrionic adult. An individual whose primary defensive mechanism is intellectualization is more likely to mature into a schizoid than an antisocial. The nature and intensity of the constraints in each of these domains limit the potential number of states that the system can assume at any moment in time; this total configuration of operative domains results in each patient's distinctive pattern of individuality.

Millon-Grossman Personality Domain Checklist (MG-PDC)

Several words may usefully be said regarding the newly devised MG-PDC instrument (Millon & Grossman, in press). Clinicians and personologists employ numerous sources to obtain assessment data on both persons in general and their patients. These range from incidental to well-structured observations, casual to highly systematic interviews, and cursory to formal analyses of biographic history; also employed are a variety of laboratory tests, self-report inventories, and performance-based or projective techniques. All of these have proven to be useful grounds for diagnostic study.

How do we put these diverse data sources together to systematize and quantify the information we have gathered? It is toward the end of organizing and maximizing the clinical utility of our personality findings that the MG-PDC has been developed.

On their own, observations and projective techniques are viewed as excessively subjective. Laboratory procedures (e.g., brain imaging) are not yet sufficiently developed, and biographical data are often too unreliable to depend on. And despite their popularity with many a distinguished psychometrician, the utility of self-report inventories is far from universally accepted.

Whether assessment tools are based on empirical investigations, epidemiologic research, mathematical analyses, or theoretical deductions, they often fail to characterize persons in the language and concepts traditionally employed by clinical personologists. Although many instruments have proven of value in numerous research studies, such as demonstrating reasonable intercorrelations or a correspondence with established diagnostic systems (e.g., the *DSM*), many an astute clinician has questioned whether these tools yield anything beyond the reliability of surface impressions. Some (Westen & Weinberger, 2004) doubt whether self-report instruments, for example, successfully tap into or unravel the diverse, complex, and hidden relationships among difficult-to-fathom processes. Other critics have contended that patient-generated responses may contain *no* clinically relevant information beyond the judgments of nonscientists employing the vocabulary of a layperson's lexicon.

Data obtained from patient-based self-judgments may be contrasted with the sophisticated clinical appraisals of mental health professionals. We must ask whether clinical language, concepts, and instruments encoded in the evolving professional language of the past 100 years or so generate information incremental to the naive descriptions of an ordinary person's everyday lexicon. We know that clinical languages differ from laypersons' languages because they serve different and more sophisticated purposes (Livesley, Jackson, & Schroeder, 1989). Indeed, clinical concepts reflect the experienced contributions of numerous historical schools of thought (Millon, 2004). Each of these clinical schools (e.g., psychodynamic, cognitive, interpersonal) have identified a multitude of diverse and complex psychic processes that operate in our mental life. Surely the concepts of these historical professional lexicons are not reducible to the superficial factors drawn from the everyday vocabulary of nonscientists.

It is to represent and integrate the insights and concepts of the several major schools of thought that has led us to formulate a domain-based, clinician-rated assessment (Millon, 1969/1985, 1981, 1984, 1986a, 1990, 1996b; Tringone, 1990, 1997), and now to develop, following numerous empirical and theoretical refinements, the MG-PDC. In contrast with the five-factor method, popular among research-oriented psychologists, the Personality Domain Checklist (PDC) is based on the contributions of five of the major *clinical traditions:* the behavioral, the interpersonal, the self, the cognitive, and the biological. Three optional domains are listed additionally in the instrument to reflect the psychoanalytic tradition; the use of these intrapsychic domains has diminished in recent decades and they are therefore included as elective, that is, not required components of the instrument.

Several criteria were used to select and develop the clinical domains listed in the checklist: (a) that they be *broad-based and varied* in the features they embody, that is, not limited just to biological temperaments or cognitive processes, but instead encompass a full range of personality characteristics that are based on frequently used clinical terms and concepts; (b) that they correspond to the major *therapeutic modalities* employed by contemporary mental health professionals to treat their patients (e.g., *cognitive* techniques for altering dysfunctional beliefs, group procedures for modifying *interpersonal* conduct) and, hence, are readily employed by practicing therapeutic clinicians; (c) that they be *coordinated with* and reflect the official personality disorder prototypes established by the *International Classification of Diseases* (*ICD*) and *DSM* and, thereby, be understood by insurance and other management professionals; (d) that a *distinctive psychological trait* can be identified and operationalized in each of the clinical trait domains for each personality prototype, assuring thereby both scope and comparability among personological criteria; (e) that they lend themselves to the appraisal of domain characteristics for both *normal and abnormal* personalities and, hence, further promote advances in the field of normality, one of growing interest in the psychological literature; and (f) that they can serve as an *educational clinical tool* to sensitize mental heath workers in training (psychologists, psychiatrists, clinical social workers, etc.) to the many distinctions, subtleties, and domain interactions that are worth considering in appraising personality attributes.

The *integrative perspective* encouraged in the MG-PDC views personalities as a multidetermined and multireferential construct. One, albeit problematic, means by some clinical researchers of dealing with the conceptual alternatives that characterizes personality study today is to oversimplify the task. They choose to assess the patient in accord with a single conceptual orientation, eliminating thereby the integration of divergent perspectives by an act of regressive dogmatism. A truly effective assessment, however, one that is logically consonant with the modern integrative character of personality, both as a construct and as a reality, requires that the individual be assessed systematically across multiple characterological domains, thereby ensuring that the assessment is comprehensive, useful to a broad range of clinicians, and more likely valid. In assessing with the MG-PDC, clinicians should refrain, therefore, from regarding each domain as an independent entity and thereby falling into a naive, single-minded approach. Each of the domains is a legitimate but highly contextualized part of a unified or integrated whole, a necessary composite that ensures that the full integrity of the person is represented.

As noted previously, the domains of the instrument can be organized in a manner similar to distinctions drawn in the biological realm; that is, they may be divided and characterized as *structural* and *functional* attributes. The functional domains of the instrument represent dynamic processes that transpire between the individual and his or her psychosocial environment. These transactions take place through what we have termed the person's *modes of regulatory action,* that is, his or her demeanor, social relations, and thought processes, each of which serve to manage, adjust, transform, coordinate, and control the give-and-take of inner and outer life. Several functional domains relevant to each personality are included among the major components of the MG-PDC.

In contrast to the functional characteristics, structural domains represent templates of deeply embedded affect dispositions and imprinted memories, attitudes, needs, and conflicts that guide experience and orient ongoing life events. These domains may be conceived as *quasi-permanent substrates for identity and temperament.* These residues of the past and relatively enduring affects effectively constrain and even close off innovative learnings and limit new possibilities to already established habits and dispositions. Their persistent and preemptive character perpetuates the maladaptive behavior and vicious circles of a patient's extant personality pathology.

Of course, individuals differ with respect to the domains they enact most frequently. People vary not only in the degree to which they approximate each personality prototype but also in the extent to which each domain dominates their behavior. In conceptualizing personality as a system, we must recognize that different parts of the system will be dominant in different individuals, even when those individuals are patients who share the same prototypal diagnosis. It is the goal of the MG-PDC to *differentiate, operationalize,* and *measure quantitatively* those domain features that are primary in contributing to the person's functioning. Thus identified, the instrument should help orient the clinical therapist to modify the person's problematic features (e.g., interpersonal conduct, cognitive beliefs), and thereby enable the patient to acquire a greater variety of adaptive behaviors in his or her life circumstances.

The reader may wish to review the trait options that constitute the choices for each of the domains. While reading and thinking about the several domain descriptions, and to help guide your choices, feel comfortable in moving freely, back and forth, as you proceed. For example, while working on reviewing the trait options for the Expressive Behavior domain, do not hesitate to look at the trait descriptions for any of the other domains (e.g., Interpersonal Conduct) if by doing so you may be aided in understanding the characteristics of the Expressive Behavior group of choices.

For each of the following domain pages, beginning with Expressive Behavior, you will see 15 descriptive trait choices. Locate the descriptive choice that appears to you to *best fit* in characterizing a patient you may be thinking about. You would encircle that choice in the 1st best fit column.

Because most people can be characterized by more than one expressive behavior trait, locate a second-best-fit descriptive characteristic, one not as applicable to this person as the first best fit you selected, but notable nonetheless. Encircle the 2nd best fit choice.

Should there be other listed descriptive trait features that are applicable to this person, but less so than the one selected as second best, encircle the 3rd best fit choice.

You may encircle up to three choices in the 3rd best fit column. (Note that only one trait description may be marked in each of the 1st and 2nd best fit columns.)

Consider the following points as you proceed. The 15 descriptive traits for each domain were written to characterize patients. Further, each trait is illustrated with several clinical characteristics and examples. Note that the person you are rating need not display precisely the characteristics that are listed; they need only be the best fit of the listed group of features. It is important to note also that for rated persons of a nonclinical character, that is, normal personalities who display only minor or mild aspects of the trait characteristic, you should, nevertheless, fully mark the best-fit columns (even though the descriptor is characterized with a more serious clinical description than suits the person). In short, *do not* leave any of the best-fit columns blank. Fill them in, in rank best-fit order, even when the features of the trait are only marginally present.

After completing ratings for the Expressive Behavior domain, you would proceed to fill in your choices for the next seven domains, one at a time, using the same first, second, and third ratings you followed previously.

Because readers of this text are not actually completing the following MG-PDC judgment forms, it will be useful for them to know which personality prototype corresponds to the letters that precede each of the descriptors. For example, in the Expressive Behavior domain, note that the letter A precedes the first descriptor, "Impassive." The letter A signifies that this descriptor characterizes the Retiring/Schizoid Prototype. Each of the following letters on all eight domains corresponds to the following associated prototypes:

A. Retiring/Schizoid

B. Eccentric/Schizotypal

C. Shy/Avoidant

D. Needy/Dependent

E. Exuberant/Hypomanic

F. Sociable/Histrionic

G. Confident/Narcissistic

H. Suspicious/Paranoid

I. Nonconforming/Antisocial

J. Assertive/Sadistic

K. Pessimistic/Melancholic (Depressive)

L. Aggrieved/Masochistic

M. Skeptical/Negativistic

N. Capricious/Borderline

O. Conscientious/Compulsive

Table 1.1 *MG-PDC* I. Expressive Behavior DOMAIN

These attributes relate to observables at the *behavioral level* of emotion and are usually recorded by noting how the patient acts. Through inference, observations of overt behavior enable us to deduce what the patient unknowingly reveals about his or her emotions or, often conversely, what he or she wants others to think about him or her. The range and character of expressive actions are wide and diverse and they convey distinctive and worthwhile clinical information, from communicating a sense of personal incompetence to exhibiting emotional defensiveness to demonstrating disciplined self-control, and so on.

1st Best Fit	2nd Best Fit	3rd Best Fit	Characteristic Behavior
1	2	3	**A. Impassive:** Is colorless, sluggish, displaying deficits in activation and emotional expressiveness; appears to be in a persistent state of low energy and lack of vitality (e.g., phlegmatic and lacking in spontaneity).
1	2	3	**B. Peculiar:** Is perceived by others as eccentric, disposed to behave in an unobtrusively aloof, curious, or bizarre manner; exhibits socially gauche habits and aberrant mannerisms (e.g., manifestly odd or eccentric).
1	2	3	**C. Fretful:** Fearfully scans environment for social derogation; overreacts to innocuous events and judges them to signify personal derision and mockery (e.g., anxiously anticipates ridicule/humiliation).
1	2	3	**D. Incompetent:** Ill-equipped to assume mature and independent roles; is passive and lacking functional competencies, avoiding self-assertion and withdrawing from adult responsibilities (e.g., has difficulty doing things on his or her own).
1	2	3	**E. Impetuous:** Is forcefully energetic and driven, emotionally excitable and overzealous; often worked up, unrestrained, rash, and hotheaded (e.g., is restless and socially intrusive).
1	2	3	**F. Dramatic:** Is histrionically overreactive and stimulus-seeking, resulting in unreflected and theatrical responsiveness; describes penchant for sensational situations and short-sighted hedonism (e.g., overly emotional and artificially affected).
1	2	3	**G. Haughty:** Manifests an air of being above conventional rules of shared social living, viewing them as naive or inapplicable to self; reveals an egocentric indifference to the needs of others (e.g., acts arrogantly self-assured and confident).

Table 1.1   (*Continued*)

1st Best Fit	2nd Best Fit	3rd Best Fit	Characteristic Behavior
1	2	3	*H. Defensive:* Is vigilantly guarded, hyperalert to ward off anticipated deception and malice; is tenaciously resistant to sources of external influence (e.g., disposed to be wary, envious, and jealous).
1	2	3	*I. Impulsive:* Since adolescence, acts thoughtlessly and irresponsibly in social matters; is shortsighted, heedless, incautious, and imprudent, failing to plan ahead or consider legal consequences (e.g., Conduct Disorder evident before age 15).
1	2	3	*J. Precipitate:* Is stormy and unpredictably abrupt, reckless, thick-skinned, and unflinching, seemingly undeterred by pain; is attracted to challenge, as well as undaunted by punishment (e.g., attracted to risk, danger, and harm).
1	2	3	*K. Disconsolate:* Appearance and posture convey an irrelievably forlorn, heavy-hearted, if not grief-stricken quality; markedly dispirited and discouraged (e.g., somberly seeks others to be protective).
1	2	3	*L. Abstinent:* Presents self as nonindulgent, frugal, and chaste, refraining from exhibiting signs of pleasure or attractiveness; acts in an unpresuming and self-effacing manner, placing self in an inferior light (e.g., undermines own good fortune).
1	2	3	*M. Resentful:* Exhibits inefficiency, erratic, contrary, and irksome behaviors; reveals gratification in undermining the pleasures and expectations of others (e.g., uncooperative, contrary, and stubborn).
1	2	3	*N. Spasmodic:* Displays a desultory energy level with sudden, unexpected self-punitive outbursts; endogenous shifts in emotional state places behavioral equilibrium in constant jeopardy (e.g., does impulsive, self-damaging acts).
1	2	3	*O. Disciplined:* Maintains a regulated, emotionally restrained, and highly organized life; often insists that others adhere to personally established rules and methods (e.g., meticulous and perfectionistic).

Table 1.2 *MG-PDC* **II. Interpersonal Conduct DOMAIN**

A patient's style of relating to others may be captured in a number of ways, such as how his or her actions affect others, intended or otherwise; the attitudes that underlie, prompt, and give shape to these actions; the methods by which he or she engages others to meet his or her needs; and his or her way of coping with social tensions and conflicts. Extrapolating from these observations, the clinican may construct an image of how the patient functions in relation to others.

1st Best Fit	2nd Best Fit	3rd Best Fit	Characteristic Conduct
1	2	3	**A. Unengaged:** Is indifferent to the actions or feelings of others, possessing minimal "human" interests; ends up with few close relationships and a limited role in work and family settings (e.g., has few desires or interests).
1	2	3	**B. Secretive:** Strives for privacy, with limited personal attachments and obligations; drifts into increasingly remote and clandestine social activities (e.g., is enigmatic and withdrawn).
1	2	3	**C. Aversive:** Reports extensive history of social anxiety and isolation; seeks social acceptance, but maintains careful distance to avoid anticipated humiliation and derogation (e.g., is socially pan-anxious and fearfully guarded).
1	2	3	**D. Submissive:** Subordinates needs to a stronger and nurturing person, without whom will feel alone and anxiously helpless; is compliant, conciliatory, and self-sacrificing (e.g., generally docile, deferential, and placating).
1	2	3	**E. High-Spirited:** Is unremittingly full of life and socially buoyant; attempts to engage others in an animated, vivacious, and lively manner; often seen by others, however, as intrusive and needlessly insistent (e.g., is persistently overbearing).
1	2	3	**F. Attention-Seeking:** Is self-dramatizing, and actively solicits praise in a showy manner to gain desired attention and approval; manipulates others and is emotionally demanding (e.g., seductively flirtatious and exhibitionistic).
1	2	3	**G. Exploitive:** Acts entitled, self-centered, vain, and unempathic; expects special favors without assuming reciprocal responsibilities; shamelessly takes others for granted and uses them to enhance self and indulge desires (e.g., egocentric and socially inconsiderate).

Table 1.2   (*Continued*)

1st Best Fit	2nd Best Fit	3rd Best Fit	Characteristic Conduct
1	2	3	*H. Provocative:* Displays a quarrelsome, fractious, and distrustful attitude; bears serious grudges and precipitates exasperation by a testing of loyalties and a searching preoccupation with hidden motives (e.g., unjustly questions fidelity of spouse/friend).
1	2	3	*I. Irresponsible:* Is socially untrustworthy and unreliable, intentionally or carelessly failing to meet personal obligations of a marital, parental, employment, or financial nature; actively violates established civil codes through duplicitous or illegal behaviors (e.g., shows active disregard for rights of others).
1	2	3	*J. Abrasive:* Reveals satisfaction in competing with, dominating, and humiliating others; regularly expresses verbally abusive and derisive social commentary, as well as exhibiting harsh, if not physically brutal behavior (e.g., intimidates, coerces, and demeans others).
1	2	3	*K. Defenseless:* Feels and acts vulnerable and guilt-ridden; fears emotional abandonment and seeks public assurances of affection and devotion (e.g., needs supportive relationships to bolster hopeless outlook).
1	2	3	*L. Deferential:* Relates to others in a self-sacrificing, servile, and obsequious manner, allowing, if not encouraging others to exploit or take advantage; is self-abasing, accepting undeserved blame and unjust criticism (e.g., courts others to be exploitive and mistreating).
1	2	3	*M. Contrary:* Assumes conflicting roles in social relationships, shifting from dependent acquiescence to assertive independence; is obstructive toward others, behaving either negatively or erratically (e.g., sulky and argumentative in response to requests).
1	2	3	*N. Paradoxical:* Needing extreme attention and affection, but acts unpredictably and manipulatively and is volatile, frequently eliciting rejection rather than support; reacts to fears of separation and isolation in angry, mercurial, and often self-damaging ways (e.g., is emotionally needy, but interpersonally erratic).
1	2	3	*O. Respectful:* Exhibits unusual adherence to social conventions and proprieties; prefers polite, formal, and "correct" personal relationships (e.g., interpersonally proper and dutiful).

Table 1.3 *MG-PDC* **III. Cognitive Style/Content DOMAIN**

How the patient focuses and allocates attention, encodes and processes information, organizes thoughts, makes attributions, and communicates reactions and ideas to others represents key cognitive functions of clinical value. These characteristics are among the most useful indices of the patient's distinctive way of thinking. By synthesizing his or her beliefs and attitudes, it may be possible to identify indications of problematic cognitive functions and assumptions.

1st Best Fit	2nd Best Fit	3rd Best Fit	Characteristic Cognitive Style
1	2	3	**A. Impoverished:** Seems deficient in human spheres of knowledge and evidences vague thought processes about everyday matters that are below intellectual level; social communications are easily derailed or conveyed via a circuitous logic (e.g., lacks awareness of human relations).
1	2	3	**B. Autistic:** Intrudes social communications with personal irrelevancies; there is notable circumstantial speech, ideas of reference, and metaphorical asides; is ruminative, appears self-absorbed and lost in occasional magical thinking; there is a marked blurring of fantasy and reality (e.g., exhibits peculiar ideas and superstitious beliefs).
1	2	3	**C. Distracted:** Is bothered by disruptive and often distressing inner thoughts; the upsurge from within of irrelevant and digressive ideation upsets thought continuity and interferes with social communications (e.g., withdraws into reveries to fulfill needs).
1	2	3	**D. Naive:** Is easily persuaded, unsuspicious, and gullible; reveals a Pollyanna attitude toward interpersonal difficulties, watering down objective problems and smoothing over troubling events (e.g., childlike thinking and reasoning).
1	2	3	**E. Scattered:** Thoughts are momentary and scrambled in an untidy disarray with minimal focus to them, resulting in a chaotic hodgepodge of miscellaneous and haphazard beliefs expressed randomly with no logic or purpose (e.g., intense and transient emotions disorganize thoughts).
1	2	3	**F. Flighty:** Avoids introspective thought and is overly attentive to trivial and fleeting external events; integrates experiences poorly, resulting in shallow learning and thoughtless judgments (e.g., faddish and responsive to superficialities).
1	2	3	**G. Expansive:** Has an undisciplined imagination and exhibits a preoccupation with illusory fantasies of success, beauty, or love; is minimally constrained by objective reality; takes liberties with facts and seeks to redeem boastful beliefs (e.g., indulges fantasies of repute/power).

Table 1.3 *(Continued)*

1st Best Fit	2nd Best Fit	3rd Best Fit	Characteristic Cognitive Style
1	2	3	***H. Mistrustful:*** Is suspicious of the motives of others, construing innocuous events as signifying conspiratorial intent; magnifies tangential or minor social difficulties into proofs of duplicity, malice, and treachery (e.g., wary and distrustful).
1	2	3	***I. Deviant:*** Construes ordinary events and personal relationships in accord with socially unorthodox beliefs and morals; is disdainful of traditional ideals and conventional rules (e.g., shows contempt for social ethics and morals).
1	2	3	***J. Dogmatic:*** Is strongly opinionated, as well as unbending and obstinate in holding to his or her preconceptions; exhibits a broad social intolerance and prejudice (e.g., closed-minded and bigoted).
1	2	3	***K. Fatalistic:*** Sees things in their blackest form and invariably expects the worst; gives the gloomiest interpretation of current events, believing that things will never improve (e.g., conceives life events in persistent pessimistic terms).
1	2	3	***L. Diffident:*** Is hesitant to voice his or her views; often expresses attitudes contrary to inner beliefs; experiences contrasting and conflicting thoughts toward self and others (e.g., demeans own convictions and opinions).
1	2	3	***M. Cynical:*** Skeptical and untrusting, approaching current events with disbelief and future possibilities with trepidation; has a misanthropic view of life, expressing disdain and caustic comments toward those who experience good fortune (e.g., envious or disdainful of those more fortunate).
1	2	3	***N. Vacillating:*** Experiences rapidly changing, fluctuating, and antithetical perceptions or thoughts concerning passing events; contradictory reactions are evoked in others by virtue of his or her behaviors, creating, in turn, conflicting and confusing social feedback (e.g., erratic and contrite over own beliefs and attitudes).
1	2	3	***O. Constricted:*** Constructs world in terms of rules, regulations, time schedules, and social hierarchies; is unimaginative, indecisive, and notably upset by unfamiliar or novel ideas and customs (e.g., preoccupied with lists, details, rules, etc.).

Table 1.4 *MG-PDC* IV. Self-Image DOMAIN

As the inner world of symbols is mastered through development, one major configuration emerges to impose a measure of sameness on an otherwise fluid environment: the perception of self-as-object, a distinct, ever-present identity. Self-image is significant in that it serves as a guidepost and lends continuity to changing experience. Most patients have an implicit sense of who they are but differ greatly in the clarity, accuracy, and complexity of their introspection of the psychic elements that make up this image.

1st Best Fit	2nd Best Fit	3rd Best Fit	Characteristic Self-Image
1	2	3	**A. Complacent:** Reveals minimal introspection and awareness of self; seems impervious to the emotional and personal implications of his or her role in everyday social life (e.g., minimal interest in own personal life).
1	2	3	**B. Estranged:** Possesses permeable ego boundaries, exhibiting acute social perplexities and illusions as well as experiences of depersonalization, derealization, and dissociation; sees self as "different," with repetitive thoughts of life's confusions and meaninglessness (e.g., self-perceptions are haphazard and fragmented).
1	2	3	**C. Alienated:** Sees self as a socially isolated person, one rejected by others; devalues self-achievements and reports feelings of aloneness and undesirability (e.g., feels injured and unwanted by others).
1	2	3	**D. Inept:** Views self as weak, fragile, and inadequate; exhibits lack of self-confidence by belittling own aptitudes and competencies (e.g., sees self as childlike and/or fragile).
1	2	3	**E. Energetic:** Sees self as full of vim and vigor, a dynamic force, invariably hardy and robust, a tireless and enterprising person whose ever-present energy galvanizes others (e.g., proud to be active and animated).
1	2	3	**F. Gregarious:** Views self as socially stimulating and charming; enjoys the image of attracting acquaintances and pursuing a busy and pleasure-oriented social life (e.g., perceived as appealing and attractive, but shallow).
1	2	3	**G. Admirable:** Confidently exhibits self, acts in a self-assured manner, and publicly displays achievements, despite being seen by others as egotistic, inconsiderate, and arrogant (e.g., has a sense of high self-worth).

Table 1.4 (*Continued*)

1st Best Fit	2nd Best Fit	3rd Best Fit	Characteristic Self-Image
1	2	3	**H. Inviolable:** Is highly insular, experiencing intense fears of losing identity, status, or powers of self-determination; nevertheless, has persistent ideas of self-reference, asserting as personally derogatory and scurrilous entirely innocuous actions and events (e.g., sees ordinary life events as invariably referring to self).
1	2	3	**I. Autonomous:** Values the sense of being free, unencumbered, and unconfined by persons, places, obligations, or routines; sees self as unfettered by the restrictions of social customs and the restraints of personal loyalties (e.g., values being independent of social responsibilities).
1	2	3	**J. Combative:** Values aspects of self that present tough, domineering, and power-oriented image; is proud to characterize self as unsympathetic and unsentimental (e.g., proud to be stern and feared by others).
1	2	3	**K. Worthless:** Sees self as valueless, of no account, a person who should be overlooked, owing to having no praiseworthy traits or achievements (e.g., sees self as insignificant or inconsequential).
1	2	3	**L. Undeserving:** Focuses on and amplifies the very worst features of self; judges self as worthy of being shamed, humbled, and debased; has failed to live up to the expectations of others and, hence, should be reproached and demeaned (e.g., sees self as deserving to suffer).
1	2	3	**M. Discontented:** Sees self as unjustly misunderstood and unappreciated; recognizes that he or she is characteristically resentful, disgruntled, and disillusioned with life (e.g., sees self as unfairly treated).
1	2	3	**N. Uncertain:** Experiences the marked confusions of a nebulous or wavering sense of identity and self-worth; seeks to redeem erratic actions and changing self-presentations with expressions of contrition and self-punitive behaviors (e.g., has persistent identity disturbances).
1	2	3	**O. Reliable:** Sees self as industrious, meticulous, and efficient; fearful of error or misjudgment and, hence, overvalues aspects of self that exhibit discipline, perfection, prudence, and loyalty (e.g., sees self as reliable and conscientious).

Table 1.5 *MG-PDC* V. Mood/Affect DOMAIN

Few observables are more clinically relevant than the predominant character of an individual's affect and the intensity and frequency with which he or she expresses it. The meaning of extreme emotions is easy to decode. This is not so with the more subtle moods and feelings that insidiously and repetitively pervade the patient's ongoing relationships and experiences. The expressive features of mood/affect may be revealed, albeit indirectly, in activity level, speech quality, and physical appearance.

1st Best Fit	2nd Best Fit	3rd Best Fit	Characteristic Mood
1	2	3	**A. Apathetic:** Is emotionally impassive, exhibiting an intrinsic unfeeling, cold, and stark quality; reports weak affectionate or erotic needs, rarely displaying warm or intense feelings, and apparently unable also to experience either sadness or anger (e.g., unable to experience pleasure in depth).
1	2	3	**B. Distraught or Insentient:** Reports being *either* apprehensive and ill at ease, particularly in social encounters; anxiously watchful, distrustful of others, and wary of their motives; *or* manifests drab, sluggish, joyless, and spiritless appearance; reveals marked deficiencies in emotional expression and in face-to-face encounters (e.g., highly agitated and/or affectively flat).
1	2	3	**C. Anguished:** Vacillates between desire for affection, fear of rebuff, and numbness of feeling; describes constant and confusing undercurrents of tension, sadness, and anger (e.g., unusually fearful of new social experiences).
1	2	3	**D. Pacific:** Quietly and passively avoids social tension and interpersonal conflicts; is typically pleasant, warm, tender, and noncompetitive (e.g., characteristically timid and uncompetitive).
1	2	3	**E. Mercurial:** Volatile and quicksilverish, at times unduly ebullient, charged up, and irrepressible; at other times, flighty and erratic emotionally, blowing hot and cold (e.g., has marked penchant for momentary excitements).
1	2	3	**F. Fickle:** Displays short-lived and superficial emotions; is dramatically overreactive and exhibits tendencies to be easily enthused and as easily bored (e.g., impetuously pursues pleasure-oriented social life).

Table 1.5 (*Continued*)

1st Best Fit	2nd Best Fit	3rd Best Fit	Characteristic Mood
1	2	3	**G. Insouciant:** Manifests a general air of nonchalance and indifference; appears coolly unimpressionable or calmly optimistic, except when self-centered confidence is shaken, at which time either rage, shame, or emptiness is briefly displayed (e.g., generally appears imperturbable and composed).
1	2	3	**H. Irascible:** Displays a sullen, churlish, and humorless demeanor; attempts to appear unemotional and objective, but is edgy, touchy, surly, quick to react angrily (e.g., ready to take personal offense).
1	2	3	**I. Callous:** Exhibits a coarse incivility, as well as a ruthless indifference to the welfare of others; is unempathic, as expressed in wide-ranging deficits in social charitableness, human compassion, or personal remorse (e.g., experiences minimal guilt or contrition for socially repugnant actions).
1	2	3	**J. Hostile:** Has an overtly rough and pugnacious temper, which flares periodically into contentious argument and physical belligerence; is fractious, willing to do harm, even persecute others to get own way (e.g., easily embroiled in brawls).
1	2	3	**K. Woeful:** Is typically mournful, tearful, joyless, and morose; characteristically worrisome and brooding; low spirits rarely remit (e.g., frequently feels dejected or guilty).
1	2	3	**L. Dysphoric:** Intentionally displays a plaintive and gloomy appearance, occasionally to induce guilt and discomfort in others (e.g., drawn to relationships in which he or she will suffer).
1	2	3	**M. Irritable:** Is often petulant, reporting being easily annoyed or frustrated by others; typically obstinate and resentful, followed in turn by sulky and grumpy withdrawal (e.g., impatient and easily provoked into oppositional behavior).
1	2	3	**N. Labile:** Fails to accord unstable moods with external reality; has marked shifts from normality to depression to excitement, or has extended periods of dejection and apathy, interspersed with brief spells of anger, anxiety, or euphoria (e.g., mood changes erratically from sadness to bitterness to torpor).
1	2	3	**O. Solemn:** Is unrelaxed, tense, joyless, and grim; restrains overtly warm or covertly antagonistic feelings, keeping most emotions under tight control (e.g., affect is constricted and confined).

Table 1.6 *MG-PDC* VI. Intrapsychic Mechanisms DOMAIN

Although mechanisms of self-protection, need gratification, and conflict resolution are consciously recognized at times, they represent data derived primarily at the intrapsychic level. Because the ego or defense mechanisms are internal regulatory processes, they are more difficult to discern and describe than processes that are anchored closer to the observable world. As such, they are not directly amenable to assessment by self-reflective appraisal in their pure form but only as derivatives that are potentially many levels removed from their core conflicts and their dynamic resolution. Despite the methodological problems they present, the task of identifying which mechanisms are most characteristic of a patient and the extent to which they are employed is extremely useful in a comprehensive clinical assessment.

1st Best Fit	2nd Best Fit	3rd Best Fit	Characteristic Mechanism
1	2	3	**A. Intellectualization:** Describes interpersonal and affective experiences in a matter-of-fact, abstract, impersonal, or mechanical manner; pays primary attention to formal and objective aspects of social and emotional events.
1	2	3	**B. Undoing:** Bizarre mannerisms and idiosyncratic thoughts appear to reflect a retraction or reversal of previous acts or ideas that have stirred feelings of anxiety, conflict, or guilt; ritualistic or "magical" behaviors serve to repent for or nullify assumed misdeeds or "evil" thoughts.
1	2	3	**C. Fantasy:** Depends excessively on imagination to achieve need gratification and conflict resolution; withdraws into reveries as a means of safely discharging affectionate as well as aggressive impulses.
1	2	3	**D. Introjection:** Is firmly devoted to another to strengthen the belief that an inseparable bond exists between them; jettisons any independent views in favor of those of another to preclude conflicts and threats to the relationship.
1	2	3	**E. Magnification:** Engages in hyperbole, overstating and overemphasizing ordinary matters so as to elevate their importance, especially features that enhance not only his or her own virtues but those of others who are valued.
1	2	3	**F. Dissociation:** Regularly alters self presentations to create a succession of socially attractive but changing façades; engages in self-distracting activities to avoid reflecting on/integrating unpleasant thoughts/emotions.
1	2	3	**G. Rationalization:** Is self-deceptive and facile in devising plausible reasons to justify self-centered and socially inconsiderate behaviors; offers alibis to place self in the best possible light, despite evident shortcomings or failures.

Table 1.6 (*Continued*)

1st Best Fit	2nd Best Fit	3rd Best Fit	Characteristic Mechanism
1	2	3	*H. Projection:* Actively disowns undesirable personal traits and motives and attributes them to others; remains blind to own unattractive behaviors and characteristics, yet is overalert to and hypercritical of the defects of others.
1	2	3	*I. Acting Out:* Inner tensions that might accrue by postponing the expression of offensive thoughts and malevolent actions are rarely constrained; socially repugnant impulses are not refashioned in sublimated forms, but are discharged directly in precipitous ways, usually without guilt.
1	2	3	*J. Isolation:* Can be cold-blooded and remarkably detached from an awareness of the impact of his or her destructive acts; views objects of violation impersonally, often as symbols of devalued groups devoid of human sensibilities.
1	2	3	*K. Asceticism:* Engages in acts of self-denial, self-tormenting, and self-punishment, believing that one should exhibit penance and not be rewarded with life's bounties; not only is there a repudiation of pleasures but there are harsh self-judgments and minor self-destructive acts.
1	2	3	*L. Exaggeration:* Repetitively recalls past injustices and seeks out future disappointments as a means of raising distress to troubled homeostatic levels; misconstrues, if not sabotages, personal good fortunes to enhance or maintain preferred suffering and pain.
1	2	3	*M. Displacement:* Discharges anger and other troublesome emotions either indirectly or by shifting them from their true objective to settings or persons of lesser peril; expresses resentments by substitute or passive means, such as acting inept or perplexed, or behaving in a forgetful or indolent manner.
1	2	3	*N. Regression:* Retreats under stress to developmentally earlier levels of anxiety tolerance, impulse control, and social adaptation; is unable or disinclined to cope with responsible tasks and adult issues, as evident in immature, if not increasingly childlike behaviors.
1	2	3	*O. Reaction Formation:* Repeatedly presents positive thoughts and socially commendable behaviors that are diametrically opposite to his or her deeper, contrary, and forbidden feelings; displays reasonableness and maturity when faced with circumstances that normally evoke anger or dismay in most persons.

Table 1.7 *MG-PDC* **VII. Intrapsychic Content DOMAIN**

Significant experiences from the past leave an inner imprint, a structural residue composed of memories, attitudes, and affects that serve as a substrate of dispositions for perceiving and reacting to life's events. Analogous to the various organ systems in the body, both the character and the substance of these internalized representations of significant figures and relationships from the past can be differentiated and analyzed for clinical purposes. Variations in the nature and content of this inner world, or what are often called *object relations*, can be identified with one or another personality and lead us to employ the following descriptive terms to represent them.

1st Best Fit	2nd Best Fit	3rd Best Fit	Characteristic Content
1	2	3	**A. Meager:** Inner representations are few in number and minimally articulated, largely devoid of the manifold percepts and memories, or the dynamic interplay among drives and conflicts that typify even well-adjusted persons.
1	2	3	**B. Chaotic:** Inner representations consist of a jumble of miscellaneous memories and percepts, random drives and impulses, and uncoordinated channels of regulation that are only fitfully competent for binding tensions, accommodating needs, and mediating conflicts.
1	2	3	**C. Vexatious:** Inner representations are composed of readily reactivated, intense, and anxiety-ridden memories, limited avenues of gratification, and few mechanisms to channel needs, bind impulses, resolve conflicts, or deflect external stressors.
1	2	3	**D. Immature:** Inner representations are composed of unsophisticated ideas and incomplete memories, rudimentary drives and childlike impulses, as well as minimal competencies to manage and resolve stressors.
1	2	3	**E. Piecemeal:** Inner representations are disorganized and dissipated, a jumble of diluted and muddled recollections that are recalled by fits and starts, serving only as momentary guideposts for dealing with everyday tensions and conflicts.
1	2	3	**F. Shallow:** Inner representations are composed largely of superficial yet emotionally intense affects, memories, and conflicts, as well as facile drives and insubstantial mechanisms.
1	2	3	**G. Contrived:** Inner representations are composed far more than usual of illusory ideas and memories, synthetic drives and conflicts, and pretentious, if not simulated, percepts and attitudes, all of which are readily refashioned as the need arises.

Table 1.7 (*Continued*)

1st Best Fit	2nd Best Fit	3rd Best Fit	Characteristic Content
1	2	3	**H. Unalterable:** Inner representations are arranged in an unusual configuration of rigidly held attitudes, unyielding percepts, and implacable drives, which are aligned in a semidelusional hierarchy of tenacious memories, immutable cognitions, and irrevocable beliefs.
1	2	3	**I. Debased:** Inner representations are a mix of revengeful attitudes and impulses oriented to subvert established cultural ideals and mores, as well as to debase personal sentiments and conventional societal attainments.
1	2	3	**J. Pernicious:** Inner representations are distinguished by the presence of aggressive energies and malicious attitudes, as well as by a contrasting paucity of sentimental memories, tender affects, internal conflicts, shame, or guilt feelings.
1	2	3	**K. Forsaken:** Inner representations have been depleted or devitalized, either drained of their richness and joyful elements or withdrawn from memory, leaving the person to feel abandoned, bereft, discarded.
1	2	3	**L. Discredited:** Inner representations are composed of disparaged past memories and discredited achievements, of positive feelings and erotic drives transposed onto their least attractive opposites, of internal conflicts intentionally aggravated, of mechanisms of anxiety reduction subverted by processes that intensify discomforts.
1	2	3	**M. Fluctuating:** Inner representations compose a complex of opposing inclinations and incompatible memories that are driven by impulses designed to nullify his or her own achievements and/or the pleasures and expectations of others.
1	2	3	**N. Incompatible:** Rudimentary and expediently devised, but repetitively aborted, inner representations have led to perplexing memories, enigmatic attitudes, contradictory needs, antithetical emotions, erratic impulses, and opposing strategies for conflict reduction.
1	2	3	**O. Concealed:** Only those inner affects, attitudes, and actions that are socially approved are allowed conscious awareness or behavioral expression, resulting in gratification being highly regulated, forbidden impulses sequestered and tightly bound, personal and social conflicts defensively denied, kept from awareness, all maintained under stringent control.

Table 1.8 *MG-PDC* VIII. Intrapsychic Structure DOMAIN

The overall architecture that serves as a framework for an individual's psychic interior may display weakness in its structural cohesion, exhibit deficient coordination among its components, and possess few mechanisms to maintain balance and harmony, regulate internal conflicts, or mediate external pressures. The concept of intrapsychic structure refers to the organizational strength, interior congruity, and functional efficacy of the personality system, a concept almost exclusively derived from inferences at the *intrapsychic* level of analysis. Psychoanalytic usage tends to be limited to quantitative degrees of integrative pathology, not to *qualitative variations* in either integrative structure or configuration. Stylistic variants of this structural attribute, such as the following, may be employed to characterize each of the personality prototypes.

1st Best Fit	2nd Best Fit	3rd Best Fit	Characteristic Structure
1	2	3	**A. Undifferentiated:** Given an inner barrenness, a feeble drive to fulfill needs, and minimal pressures to defend against or resolve internal conflicts, or to cope with external demands, internal structures may best be characterized by their limited coordination and deficient organization.
1	2	3	**B. Fragmented:** Coping and defensive operations are haphazardly organized in a fragile assemblage, leading to spasmodic and desultory actions in which primitive thoughts and affects are directly discharged, with few reality-based sublimations, leading to significant further structural disintegrations.
1	2	3	**C. Fragile:** Tortuous emotions depend almost exclusively on a single modality for their resolution and discharge, that of avoidance, escape, and fantasy; hence, when faced with unanticipated stress, there are few resources available to deploy and few positions to revert to, short of a regressive decompensation.
1	2	3	**D. Inchoate:** Owing to entrusting others with the responsibility to fulfill needs and to cope with adult tasks, there is both a deficit and a lack of diversity in internal structures and controls, leaving a miscellany of relatively undeveloped and immature adaptive abilities and elementary systems for independent functioning.
1	2	3	**E. Fleeting:** Structures are highly transient, existing in momentary forms that are cluttered and disarranged, making effective coping efforts temporary at best. Affect and action are unconstrained owing to the paucity of established controls and purposeful goals.

Table 1.8 *(Continued)*

1st Best Fit	2nd Best Fit	3rd Best Fit	Characteristic Structure
1	2	3	**F. Disjointed:** A loosely knit structural conglomerate exists in which processes of internal regulation and control are scattered and unintegrated, with few methods for restraining impulses, coordinating defenses, and resolving conflicts, leading to broad and sweeping mechanisms to maintain psychic cohesion and stability and, when employed, only further disarrange thoughts, feelings, and actions.
1	2	3	**G. Spurious:** Coping and defensive strategies tend to be flimsy and transparent, appear more substantial and dynamically orchestrated than they are, regulating impulses only marginally, channeling needs with minimal restraint, and creating an egocentric inner world in which conflicts are dismissed, failures are quickly redeemed, and self-pride is effortlessly reasserted.
1	2	3	**H. Inelastic:** A markedly constricted and inflexible pattern of coping and defensive methods exists, as well as rigidly fixed channels of conflict mediation and need gratification, creates an overstrung and taut frame that is so uncompromising in its accommodation to changing circumstances that unanticipated stressors are likely to precipitate either explosive outbursts or inner shatterings.
1	2	3	**I. Unruly:** Inner defensive operations are noted by their paucity, as are efforts to curb irresponsible drives and attitudes, leading to easily transgressed social controls, low thresholds for impulse discharge, few subliminatory channels, unfettered self-expression, and a marked intolerance of delay or frustration.
1	2	3	**J. Eruptive:** Despite a generally cohesive structure of routinely modulating controls and expressive channels, surging, powerful, and explosive energies of an aggressive and sexual nature produce precipitous outbursts that periodically overwhelm and overrun otherwise reasonable restraints.
1	2	3	**K. Depleted:** The scaffold for structures is markedly weakened, with coping methods enervated and defensive strategies impoverished and devoid of vigor and focus, resulting in a diminished if not exhausted capacity to initiate action and regulate affect.
1	2	3	**L. Inverted:** Structures have a dual quality, one more or less conventional, the other its obverse—resulting in a repetitive undoing of affect and intention, of a transposing of channels of need gratification with those leading to their frustration, and of actions that produce antithetical, if not self-sabotaging consequences.

(continued)

Table 1.8   *(Continued)*

1st Best Fit	2nd Best Fit	3rd Best Fit	Characteristic Structure
1	2	3	**M. Divergent:** There is a clear division in the pattern of internal elements such that coping and defensive maneuvers are often directed toward incompatible goals, leaving major conflicts unresolved and psychic cohesion impossible, as fulfillment of one drive or need inevitably nullifies or reverses another.
1	2	3	**N. Split:** Inner cohesion constitutes a sharply segmented and conflictful configuration with a marked lack of consistency among elements; levels of consciousness occasionally blur; a rapid shift occurs across boundaries separating unrelated memories/affects, results in schisms upsetting limited extant psychic order.
1	2	3	**O. Compartmentalized:** Psychic structures are rigidly organized in a tightly consolidated system that is clearly partitioned into numerous distinct and segregated constellations of drive, memory, and cognition, with few open channels to permit any interplay among these components.

On the basis of your knowledge of the person you have evaluated, using the domain categories listed in Tables 1.1 through 1.8, summarize your judgments by making an overall first-, second-, and third-best-fit personality spectrum diagnosis on Table 1.9. If you wish, before you proceed to Table 1.9, you may want to go back to review your eight domain best choices and *double encircle* the three that you judge most important to be therapeutically modified.

Table 1.9   Spectra that Best Characterize the Person

1st Best Fit	2nd Best Fit	3rd Best Fit	Normal to Abnormal Personality Spectrum
1	2	3	Retiring—Schizoid
1	2	3	Eccentric—Schizotypal
1	2	3	Shy—Avoidant
1	2	3	Needy—Dependent
1	2	3	Exuberant—Hypomanic
1	2	3	Sociable—Histrionic
1	2	3	Confident—Narcissistic
1	2	3	Suspicious—Paranoid
1	2	3	Nonconforming—Antisocial

Table 1.9 (*Continued*)

1st Best Fit	2nd Best Fit	3rd Best Fit	Normal to Abnormal Personality Spectrum
1	2	3	Assertive—Sadistic
1	2	3	Pessimistic—Melancholic
1	2	3	Aggrieved—Masochistic
1	2	3	Skeptical—Negativistic
1	2	3	Capricious—Borderline
1	2	3	Conscientious—Compulsive

As earlier, we would like you to further evaluate the person you have just rated using the preceding eight domain characteristics. In Table 1.10 please assess his or her current overall level of social and occupational functioning. Make your judgment using the 7-point continuum, which ranges from Excellent to Markedly Impaired. Focus your rating on the individual's present mental state and social competencies, overlooking where possible physical impairments or socioeconomic considerations. Circle the number on the chart that closely approximates your best judgment.

Table 1.10   Overall Level of Social and Occupational Functioning

Judgment	Rating Number	Description
Excellent	1	Clearly manifests an effective, if not superior level of functioning in relating to family and social peers, even to helping others in resolving their difficulties, as well as demonstrating high occupational performance and success.
Very Good	2	Exhibits considerable social and occupational skills on a reasonably consistent basis, evidencing few if any major areas of interpersonal stress or occupational difficulty.
Good	3	Displays a higher than average level of social and occupational competence in ordinary matters of everyday life. He or she does experience intermittent difficulties in interpersonal relationships and in efforts to achieve work satisfaction.
Fair	4	Functions about average for a typical patient seen in outpatient clinical work. Although able to meet everyday family, social, and occupational responsibilities adequately, there remain problematic or extended periods of occupational stress and/or interpersonal conflict.

(*continued*)

Table 1.10   (*Continued*)

Judgment	Rating Number	Description
Poor	5	Able to be maintained on an outpatient basis, but often precipitates severe conflicts with others that upset his or her equanimity in either or both interpersonal relationships and occupational settings.
Very Poor	6	There is an inability to function competently in most social and occupational settings. Difficulties are precipitated by the patient, destabilizing job performance and upsetting relationships with significant others. Inpatient hospitalization may be necessary to manage periodic severe psychic disruptions.
Markedly Impaired	7	A chronic and marked disintegration is present across most psychic functions. The loss of physical and behavioral controls necessitate extended stays in residential or hospital settings, requiring both sustained care and self-protection.

General Methods and Goals of Personalized Psychotherapy

We will return to many of the numerous guiding principles and issues touched on in this extensive chapter as we proceed to the following chapters of this and subsequent books in the three-part personalized psychotherapy series. Many themes characterizing our rationale for personalized psychotherapy have been presented and argued in the preceding pages. It is hoped that these themes and justifications will become more clearly evident to the reader as we move forward to the next chapters and books.

Potentiated Pairings and Catalytic Sequences

What procedures contributed to making personalized therapy individualized and synergized rather than eclectic?

To restate from earlier paragraphs, there is a separateness among eclectically designed techniques, just a wise selectivity of what works best. In personalized therapy there are psychologically designed *composites* and *progressions* among diverse techniques. In an attempt to formulate them in current writings (Millon, 1988), terms such as "catalytic sequences" and "potentiated pairings" are employed to represent the nature and intent of theory-based polarity- and domain-oriented treatment plans. In essence, they comprise therapeutic arrangements and timing series that will resolve each patient's distinctive polarity imbalances and effect targeted clinical domain changes that would otherwise not occur by the use of several essentially uncoordinated techniques.

The first of the *personalized procedures* we recommended some years ago (Millon, 1988, 1990) was termed "potentiated pairings"; these are treatment methods that are *combined simultaneously* to overcome problematic characteristics that might be refractory to each technique if administered separately. These composites pull and push for change on many different fronts, so that the therapy becomes as multioperational and as tenacious as the disorder itself. A recent and popular illustration of treatment pairings is found in what has been referred to as cognitive-behavior therapy, one of the first of the combinatorial therapies (Craighead, Craighead, Kazdin, & Mahoney, 1994; Rasmussen, 2005).

In the second personalized procedure, termed "catalytic sequences," one might seek first to alter a patient's humiliating and painful stuttering by *behavior modification* procedures, which, if achieved, may facilitate the use of *cognitive or self-actualizing* methods to produce changes in self-confidence, which may, in its turn, foster the utility of *interpersonal* techniques in effecting improvements in relationships with others. Catalytic sequences are timing series that should optimize the impact of changes that would be less effective if the sequential combination were otherwise arranged.

A more recent example has begun to show up in numerous clinical reports this past decade (Slater, 1998). It relates to the fact that patients with depressive personalities or long-term dysthymic disorders have their clinical symptoms markedly reduced by virtue of pharmacologic medications (e.g., selective serotonin reuptake inhibitors [SSRIs]). Although these patients are greatly comforted by the reduction of their clinical symptoms, "depressiveness" has over time become a core part of their overall psychological makeup. Because their depressiveness is no longer a part of their everyday experience, many may now feel empty and confused, not knowing who they are, not knowing to what they may aspire, or how to relate to the world. It is here where a catalytic sequence of psychotherapies may come into play constructively. Patients may no longer be depressed, but they may require therapy for their new self-image and its valuation. No less important to their subsequent treatment will be opportunities to alter their formerly habitual interpersonal styles and attitudes, substituting in their stead social behaviors and cognitions that are more consonant with their current state. Former cognitive assumptions and expectations will no longer be infused with depressogenic elements calling for substantial psychic reformulations.

As the great neurological surgeon and psychologist Kurt Goldstein (1940) stated, patients whose brains have been altered to remedy a major neurological disorder do not simply lose the function that the extirpated area subserved. Rather, patients restructure and reorganize their brain capacities so that they can maintain an integrated sense of self. In a similar way, when one or another major domain of patients' habitual psychological makeup is removed or diminished (e.g., depression), the patients must reorganize themselves, not only to compensate for the loss, but also *to formulate a new self.*

Similarly, the neurologist Oliver Sacks in his 1973 book *Awakenings* describes what happens to patients who had been immobile for decades by encephalitis lethargica who suddenly "unfroze" when given the drug L-Dopa. Although these patients were restored to life, they had to learn to function in a world that had long passed them by. For them, their immobile state had an element of familiarity in which they had learned to cope, miserable though it was, for 10, 20, or 30 years. With the elimination of their adaptive lifestyle, they now had to deal with the new world in which they found themselves, a task that rarely can be managed without considerable guidance and encouragement. Catalytic sequences represent the steps that should be employed in succession to facilitate these relearning and reintegrative processes.

There are no discrete boundaries between potentiated pairings and catalytic sequences, just as there is no line between their respective pathological analogues, that is, adaptive inflexibility and vicious circles (Millon, 1969/1985). Nor should therapists be concerned about when to use one rather than another. Instead, they are intrinsically interdependent phenomena whose application is intended to foster increased flexibility and, hopefully, a virtuous rather than a vicious circle. Potentiated pairings and catalytic sequences represent the logic of combinatorial therapies. The idea of a potentiated sequence or a catalytic pairing recognizes that these logical composites may build on each other in proportion to what the tenacity of the patient's interwoven disorder domains require.

One question concerns the limits to which the content of personalized therapy can be specified in advance, that is, the extent to which specific potentiated pairings and catalytic sequences can be identified for each of the typical complex syndromes and personality disorders that exist. Many of the chapters of this and later texts of this series contain charts that present the salience of each of the clinical domains for that syndrome or disorder. To the extent that each patient's presentations are prototypal, the potentiated pairings and catalytic sequences that may be used should derive from the more or less typical modality tactics that are optimal for their problematic domains, for example, pharmacology for mood/affect. That, however, probably represents the limits to which theory or "therapies that work" can guide clinical practice, that is, without knowing anything about the history and characteristics of the *specific individual case*. Patient individuality is so rich and special that it cannot fit into any ideal taxonomic schema; personalized therapy, properly practiced, is full of specificities that cannot readily be resolved by classification generalities. Potentiated pairings, catalytic sequences, and whatever other higher order composites therapists may evolve are best conducted at an idiographic person level rather than at a nomothetic taxonomic level. Accordingly, their precise content is specified as much by the logic of the individual case as by the logic of the syndrome or disorder. At an idiographic level, each of us must ultimately be artful and open-minded therapists, using simultaneous or alternately focused methods. The synergism and enhancement produced by such catalytic and potentiating processes is what constitute genuinely innovative personalized treatment strategies.

Personalized therapists will be more efficacious if they think about the likely utility of treatment choices in probabilistic terms; that is, they should make concurrent and sequential modality arrangements, knowing that the effectiveness of each component is only partial, and that the probability of success will be less than perfect. To generate a high-probability estimate, therapists must gather all available assessment information and, as do mathematicians, calculate which combination of modalities will have the highest overall probability of being effective. Note that no combinational approach can automatically be judged "best." With each new patient, a therapist should recognize that he or she is dealing with a person whose composite of dispositions and vulnerabilities has never before existed in this exact form. Moreover, it is important that the personalized therapist never think in treatment absolutes, or in black-and-white results; all treatment modalities have reasonable probabilities of success.

There will be many cases in which the pattern of a patient's characteristics does not lend itself to an intelligent estimate of treatment success probabilities. Under such circumstances, therapists should not feel that they must create a long-term or overall plan. Available options in the early stages of treatment may not provide a good, no less an excellent, course of action. Such indeterminate states favor selecting a rather tentative or conservative course—until such time as greater clarity emerges. It should be evident from the foregoing comments that a personalized therapist will be challenged to make a series of difficult judgments, one more demanding and possibly with less assurance as to outcome than if the therapist routinely selected a specific modality for all or most of his or her cases. The latter course will be easier for the therapist, but not necessarily best for the patient. The remainder of this and other books of this series will seek to make the probabilistic task less indeterminate and less onerous. We will attempt to provide a rationale for which modalities and which combinations are likely to be most effective, given the pattern of the patient's clinical syndromes and personality disorders.

Theory-Based Polarity Goals

Among the points stated earlier in the book, we should select our specific treatment techniques as tactics to achieve polarity-oriented goals. Depending on the pathological polarity, the domains to be modified, and the overall treatment sequence one has in mind, the goals of therapy should be oriented toward the improvement of imbalanced or deficient polarities by the use of techniques that are optimally suited to modify their expression in those clinical domains that account for the imbalance or deficiency.

Therapeutic efforts responsive to problems in the *pain-pleasure polarity* would, for example, have as their essential aim the enhancement of pleasure among schizoid, avoidant, and depressive personalities (+ pleasure). Given the probability of intrinsic deficits in this area, *schizoids* might require the use of pharmacologic agents designed to activate their flat mood/ temperament. Increments in pleasure for *avoidants,* however, are likely to depend more on cognitive techniques designed to alter their alienated self-image and behavioral methods oriented to counter their aversive interpersonal inclination. Equally important for avoidants is reducing their hypersensitivities, especially to social rejection (− pain); this may be achieved by coordinating the use of medications for their characteristic anguished mood/temperament with cognitive methods geared to their desensitization. In the *passive-active* polarity, increments in the capacity and skills to take a less reactive and more proactive role in dealing with the affairs of their lives (− passive; + active) would be a major goal of treatment for schizoids, depressives, dependents, narcissists, masochists, and compulsives. Turning to the *other-self* polarity, imbalances found among narcissists and antisocials, for example, suggest that a major aim of their treatment would be a reduction in their predominant self-focus and a corresponding augmentation of their sensitivity to the needs of others (+ other; − self).

To make unbalanced or deficient polarities the primary aim of therapy is a new focus and a goal only moderately tested. In contrast, the clinical domains in which problems are expressed lend themselves to a wide variety of therapeutic techniques, the efficacy of which must, of course, continue to be gauged by ongoing experience and future systematic research. Nevertheless, our repertoire here is a rich one. For example, there are numerous cognitive-behavioral techniques, such as assertiveness training, that may fruitfully be employed to establish a greater sense of autonomy or an active rather than a passive stance with regard to life. Similarly, pharmaceuticals are notably efficacious in reducing the intensity of pain (anxiety, depression) when the pleasure-pain polarity is in marked imbalance.

Selecting Domain Tactics

Turning to the specific domains in which clinical problems exhibit themselves, we can address dysfunctions in the realm of interpersonal conduct by employing any number of family or group therapeutic methods, as well as a series of recently evolved and explicitly formulated interpersonal techniques. Methods of classical analysis or its more contemporary schools may be especially suited to the realm of object representations, as would the methods of Beck and Ellis be well chosen to modify difficulties of cognitive beliefs and self-esteem.

Tactics and *strategies* keep in balance the two conceptual ingredients of therapy; the first refers to what goes on with a particular focused intervention, and the second refers to the overall plan or design that characterizes the entire course of therapy. Both are required. Tactical specificity without strategic goals implies doing without knowing why in the big picture, and goals without specificity implies knowing where to go but having no way to get there. Obviously, one uses short-term modality tactics to accomplish higher level strategies or goals over the long term.

Psychotherapies seem to vary in the amounts of tactical specificity and strategic goals they prefer. This is not often merely an accident of history, but can be tied back to assumptions latent in the therapies themselves. Historically, a progression seems to be toward both greater specificity and clearer goals. More modern approaches to psychotherapy, such as the cognitive-behavioral, put into place highly detailed elements (e.g., agreed upon goals, termination criteria, and ongoing assessments) in which therapy itself becomes a self-regulating system. Ongoing assessments ensure the existence of a feedback process that is open to inspection and negotiation by both therapist and patient. The mode is one of action rather than talk. Talk is viewed as incapable of realizing possibilities in and of itself, but is merely a prerequisite for action, used to reframe unfortunate circumstances so that obstacles to action are removed or minimized. Action is more transactive than talk, and therapy is forward-looking and concentrates on realizing present possibilities as a means of creating or opening up new possibilities. Persons are often changed more through exposure and action than by focusing and unraveling the problems of the past. Insight may be a useful, even necessary but limited goal in itself.

It must be remembered that the primary function of any system is homeostasis. In an early book (Millon, 1981), personality was likened to an immune system for the psyche, such that stability, constancy, and internal equilibrium become the goals of a personality. Obviously, these run directly in opposition to the explicit goal of therapy, which is change. Usually, the dialogue between patient and therapist is not so directly confrontational that it is experienced as particularly threatening. When the patient does feel threatened, the personality system functions for the patient as a form of passive resistance, albeit one that may be experienced as a positive force (or trait) by the therapist. In fact, the structural grounding of a patient's self-image and object representations are so preemptive and confirmation seeking that the true meaning of the therapist's comments may never reach the level of conscious processing. Alternatively, even if a patient's equilibrium is initially up-ended by a particular interpretation, his or her defensive mechanisms may kick in to ensure that a therapist's comments are somehow distorted, misunderstood, interpreted in a less threatening manner, or even ignored. The first is a passive form of resistance, the second an active form. No wonder, then, that effective therapy is often considered anxiety provoking, for it is in situations where the patient really has no effective response, where the functioning of the psychic immune system is temporarily suppressed, that the scope of his or her response repertoire is most likely to be broadened. Personality goes with what it knows, and it is with the unknown where learning is most possible.

If the psychic makeup of a person is regarded as a system, then the question becomes: How can the characteristics that define systems be co-opted to facilitate rather than retard change? A coordinated schema of strategic goals and tactical modalities for treatment that seeks to accomplish these ends are what we expect to achieve in personalized psychotherapy. Through various coordinated approaches that mirror the system-based composition of the patient's complex clinical syndrome and personality disorder, an effort is made to select domain-focused tactics that will fulfill the strategic goals of treatment.

If interventions are unfocused, rambling, and diffuse, the patient will merely lean forward a little, passively resisting change by using his or her own weight, that is, habitual characteristics already intrinsic to the system. Although creating rapport is always important, nothing happens unless the system is eventually shook up in some way. Therapists should not always be toiling to expose their patient's defenses, but sooner or later, something must happen that cannot be readily fielded by habitual processes, something that often will be experienced as uncomfortable or even threatening.

In fact, personalized therapy appears in many ways to be like a "punctuated equilibrium" (Eldridge & Gould, 1972) rather than a slow and continuous process. This evolutionary insight argues for periods of rapid growth during which the psychic system reconfigures itself into a new gestalt, alternating with periods of relative constancy. The purpose of keeping to a domain or tactical focus, or knowing clearly what you are doing and why you are doing it, is to keep the whole of the therapeutic enterprise from becoming diffused. The person-focused systems model runs counter to the deterministic universe-as-machine model of the late nineteenth century, which features slow but incremental gains. In the prepunctuated evolutionary model as applied to therapy, moderate interventions become an input that is processed gradually and homeostatically, producing minor, if not zero change. In these earlier procedures, conservation laws play a prominent role; mild interventions produce small increments of change, with the hope that therapeutic goals will be reached, given enough time and effort. In contrast, in a focused, "punctuated" personalized model, therapeutic advances may clearly be spelled out to have genuine transformational potential, a potential optimized through procedures such as those we have termed potentiated pairings and catalytic sequences.

Tactical specificity is required in part because the psychic level in which therapy is practiced is fairly explicit. Most often, the in-session dialogue between patient and therapist is dominated by a discussion of specific domain behaviors, specific domain feelings, and specific domain cognitions, not by an abstract discussion of personality disorders or clinical syndromes. When the latter are discussed, they are often perceived by the patient as an ego-alien or intrusive characterization. A statement such as "You have a negativistic personality that should be changed" conceives the patient as a vessel to be filled or altered by some noxious substance. Under these conditions, the professional is expected to empty the vessel and refill it with something more desirable; the patient has relinquished control and responsibility and simply waits passively for the therapist to perform some mystical ritual, one of the worst assumptive sets in which to carry out psychotherapy.

For the therapist, operationalizing clinical syndromes and personality disorders as domain clusters of expressive behaviors or cognitive styles can be especially beneficial in selecting tactical modalities. The *avoidant's* social withdrawal can be seen as having enough pride in oneself to leave a humiliating situation. The *dependent's* clinging to a significant other can be seen as having the strength to devote oneself to another's care. Of course, these reframes will not be sufficient in and of themselves to produce change. They do, however, seek a bond with the patient by way of making positive attributions and thereby raising self-esteem, while simultaneously working to disconfirm or make the patient reexamine other beliefs that lower esteem and function to keep the person closed off from trying on new roles and behaviors.

Understanding traits as domain clusters of behaviors and/or cognitions is just as beneficial for the therapist as for the patient when it comes to overturning the medical model of syndromal and personality pathology and replacing it with a personalized model. One of the problems of complex syndromes and personality disorders is that their range of attributions and perceptions is too narrow to characterize the richness that in fact exists in their social environment. As a result, they end up perpetuating old problems by interpreting even innocuous behaviors and events as noxious. Modern therapists have a similar problem, in that the range of paradigms they have to bring to their syndromal and disordered patients is too narrow to describe the rich set of possibilities that exist for every individual. The belief that mental difficulties are medical diseases, monolithically fixed and beyond remediation, should itself be viewed as a form of iatrogenic pathology.

As has been noted previously, there are *strategic goals* of therapy, that is, those that endure across numerous sessions and against which progress is measured, and there are specific *domain modality* tactics by which these goals are pursued. Ideally, strategies and tactics should be integrated, with the tactics chosen to accomplish strategic goals, and the strategies chosen on the basis of what tactics might actually achieve, given other constraints, such as the number of therapy sessions and the nature of the problem. To illustrate, intrapsychic therapies are highly strategic but tactically impoverished; pure behavioral therapies are highly tactical but strategically narrow and inflexible. There are, in fact, many different ways that strategies might be operationalized. Just as diagnostic criteria are neither necessary nor sufficient for membership in a given class, it is likely that no technique is an inevitable consequence of a given clinical strategy. Subtle variations in technique and the ingenuity of individual therapists to invent techniques ad hoc assure that there exists an almost infinite number of ways to operationalize or put into action a given clinical strategy.

Individuals should be viewed as system units that exist within larger ecological milieus, such as dyads, families, communities, and, ultimately, cultures. Like the personality system, these higher level systems contain homeostatic processes that tend to sustain and reinforce their own unique patterning of internal variables. The fact that the ecology of complex clinical syndromes and personality disorders is itself organizational and systemic argues for another principle of therapy: Pull as much of the surrounding interpersonal and social context into the therapeutic process as possible, or risk being defeated by them. Where ecological factors are operative, therapeutic gains may be minimized and the risk of relapse increased. In the best-case scenario, family members can be brought into therapy as a group or as needed; if no latent pathologies exist, the family will cooperate in discussing characteristics of the status quo that perpetuate pathology and explore alternatives that might promote change. In the worst-case scenario, family members will refuse to come into therapy under some thin rationale, probably because nonparticipation is one way to passively undermine a change they in fact fear. If family members are not motivated to assist in the therapeutic process, it is likely that the individual is in therapy either because he or she must be, as in cases of court referral, or because family members do not want the burden of guilt that would accrue from actively refusing assistance.

Procedural Caveats and Considerations

All personalized therapies must consider several factors following the implementation of the general plan. First, progress must be evaluated on a fairly regular basis; second, problems of resistance and risk should be analyzed and counteracted; and third, efforts should be made to anticipate and prevent relapsing.

In personalized therapies, where things hopefully will change rapidly, treatment review should be a continuous process, every few sessions or so. The purpose of evaluating the plan is to ensure that progress is directed to achieving its strategic goals. Part of the evaluation process is intended to give the therapist a rough sense of how long treatment will be. Should progress be delayed or fail to reach a reasonable level, then it is clear that some rethinking of goals and strategies is called for. Evaluating the progress of therapy is difficult when treatment is unstructured or when the time commitment is limited. Personalized therapy may begin with a series of explicit goals and modalities; however, these may change over time, especially if treatment is open-ended (Bergin & Lambert, 1978).

Originally planned strategies and modalities are periodically found lacking. Therapies start with a limited set of impressions and with only a rough notion of the more complex elements of the patient's makeup. As treatment proceeds and knowledge of the patient grows and becomes more thoroughly understood, this new information may strengthen the original plan and strategy; on the other hand, as the assessment process continues, so may the conception of the patient's psychic difficulties be altered. A fine-tuning process may be called for. The overall configuration of syndromes and disorders may require a significant shift toward the use of different domain-oriented modalities. Hence, both strategies and tactics may have to be modified to accord with this new information.

There are numerous issues that arise with patients as therapy progresses. Some patients are highly resistant to the probing and psychic dislodging they experience in treatment. Others feel they have become free from their original constraints, employing treatment as a rationale to engage in increasingly risky activities. Therapeutic resistance derives from the patient's defensive armor, usually indicating a reluctance to voice his or her feelings and thoughts to the therapist. Most *resistances* manifest themselves in a number of well-known ways: silence, lateness, becoming helpless, missed appointments, having significant memory lapses, or simply paying later and later each month. On the other hand, *risky* behaviors are likely to show themselves in a tendency to act out, to be open with regard to expressing resentments, proving the therapist is wrong, exhibiting parasuicidal behaviors, and engaging in irrational behaviors. As Messer (1996) has noted, however, resistances are not the enemy of therapy but an informative expression of the way patients feel, act, and think in everyday life.

There are several choices when resistances or risks present themselves. We can insist on continuing with the original plan; we can interpret the meaning of the resistance and point out the consequences of risky behaviors; or we can alter aspects of the overall treatment strategy. Whatever the choice will be, it should be formulated as a positive and active decision. Otherwise, the whole structure of the treatment plan may be seriously compromised.

Despite substantial progress over the treatment course, patients should leave therapy in a better state than when they entered. A worst-case scenario is when certain fundamental aspects of the patient's psychic makeup have remained unresolved at the point of treatment termination. Whether it is the patient's decision that he or she has had enough therapy, or the therapist believes that there will be diminishing returns for continuing further, it may be advisable at some point to terminate treatment.

It is the task of the good personalized therapist to help the patient anticipate potential setbacks, to avoid stressful situations in which the patient may be highly vulnerable, and to assist him or her to develop problem-solving skills, as well as to strengthen his or her more constructive potentials. It is not uncommon to have patients develop new psychic symptoms during the treatment process. More typically, many patients experience a reassertion of pathological thoughts and feelings following termination. We strongly encourage therapists to stretch the time between sessions as therapy progresses. This enables the therapist to determine which aspects of the treatment strategy have been resolved adequately and which remain vulnerable and potentially problematic. It is our general belief that adequate therapy should continue over these periodic sessions to ensure that substantial relapses will not occur. The reemergence of certain symptoms does not mean that the patient has deteriorated, but that the more complex elements of the patient's psyche have come together with life circumstances in an especially troublesome way. Such symptoms serve as clues to both the therapist and the patient, enabling them to learn and anticipate what will continue to be troublesome in the future.

The system we have termed personalized therapy has raised concerns by some as to whether any one therapist can be sufficiently skilled, not only in employing a wide variety of therapeutic approaches, but also to synthesize them and to plan their sequence. As the senior author was asked at a conference some years ago: "Can a highly competent behavioral therapist employ cognitive techniques with any measure of efficacy; and can he or she prove able, when necessary, to function as an insightful intrapsychic therapist? Can we find people who are strongly self-actualizing in their orientation who can, at other times, be cognitively confronting? Is there any wisdom in selecting different modalities in treating a patient if the therapist has not been trained diversely or is not particularly competent in more than one ore two therapeutic modalities?"

It is our belief that the majority of therapists have the ability to break out of their single-minded or loosely eclectic frameworks, to overcome their prior limitations, and to acquire a solid working knowledge of diverse treatment modalities. Developing a measure of expertise with the widest possible range of modalities is highly likely to increase treatment efficacy and the therapist's rate of success.

In the following chapters and books of this series, we provide an initial framework for utilizing the personalized approach in a wide range of clinical syndromes and personality disorders. The next section of this text addresses those difficulties that are assigned to Axis I of the *DSM-IV,* primarily simple reactions and clinical syndromes, the latter signifying the interaction of the multiple domains, especially as they constitute personality styles. The second and third books of this series will address each of the prototypal personality disorders covered in Axis II of the *DSM-IV.* Not only will a mix of therapeutic modalities be described to help disentangle and treat each of these prototypal disorders, but illustrations will be presented for many personality subtypes.

PART **TWO**

CHAPTER 2

Personalized Therapy of Mood-Related Syndromes: Dysthymic, Major Depressive, and Bipolar Disorders

The history of depression in its manifold forms has been known to mankind since earliest recorded history. It has remained an enigma, however. The overt manifestations of the disorder are obvious to even the simplest of minds. Yet its underlying causes and shifting expressions are debated to the present time, as evident in intense discussions during the most recent *DSM* and *ICD* formulations. Does it covary with mania? Is there an irritable, explosive component associated with it? Does it wax and wane? Is there a continuous chronic state with moments of greater and lesser intensity? Is it an adaptive reaction to life circumstances, or a constitutionally based temperament with genetic origins? It is questions such as these that clinicians, theorists, and empiricists have sought answers to through the ages (Millon, 2004).

Hippocrates gave the first formal medical description of depression, referring to it as *melancholia.* The four-elements model that served as the basis of the physiological doctrines of Hippocrates was initially proposed by Empedocles. These four elements—fire, water, air, and the earth—were manifested in many spheres of life. As expressed in the human body they became the groundwork for the four humors—heat (blood), dryness (phlegm), moisture (yellow bile), and cold (black bile)—found respectively and most prominently in the heart, brain, liver, and spleen. When these humors were balanced, the individual was in a healthful state; when unbalanced, illness occurred.

It was the predominance of black bile that served as the substrate for melancholia. Although Hippocrates may have been the first to provide a medical description of depression, it was Aretaeus who presented a complete and very modern portrayal of the disorder. Moreover, Aretaeus proposed that melancholia was best attributed to psychological causes, having nothing to do with bile or other bodily humors. Further, he was the first to recognize the covariation between manic behaviors and depressive moods, antedating the views of many clinical observers in the sixteenth century and the seventeenth. Aretaeus wrote as follows:

> The characteristic appearances, then, are not obscure; for the patients are dull or stern, dejected or unreasonably torpid, without any manifest cause: such is the commencement of melancholy. And they also become peevish, dispirited, sleepless and start up from a disturbed sleep. . . . But if the illness becomes more urgent, hatred, avoidance of the haunts of men, vain lamentations are seen; they complain of life and desire to die. (Quoted in Lewis, 1934)

Although preceded by other works on melancholia in the sixteenth century, it was a layman, Robert Burton (1624), who wrote a most impressive, if wandering work entitled *Anatomy of Melancholy.* Sir William Osler judged Burton's immense and erudite work the most significant medical treatise written by a layman. It served as a guide to understanding melancholia for the next 2 centuries. As we note in later discussions of the borderline personality, it stimulated ideas concerning several variants of depressive disorder, most notably the writings of Bonet, Schacht, and Herschel, who, in turn, laid the groundwork for nineteenth-century French and German clinicians such as Baillarger, Falret, Feuchtersleben, Greisinger, and Kahlbaum. To illustrate, Feuchtersleben (1847, p. 135) wrote:

> Here the senses, memory, and reaction give way, the nervous vitality languishes at its root, and the vitality of the blood, deprived of this stimulant, is languid in all its functions. Hence the slow and often difficult respiration, and proneness to sighing. . . . When they are chronic, they deeply affect vegetative life, and the body wastes away.

Kahlbaum (1874) was firm in the belief that mania and melancholia were a single disease that manifested itself in different forms and combinations over time. He termed the milder variant of these patterns *cyclothymia.*

Kraepelin (1896) borrowed heavily from his German predecessor Kahlbaum's formulations but separated the "personality" and "temperament" variants of cyclothymia from the manifest or clinical state of the disease. Nevertheless, he proposed the name *maniacal-depressive insanity* for "the whole domain of periodic and circular insanity," including such diverse disturbances as "the morbid states termed melancholia" and certain slight colorings of mood, some of them periodic, some of them continuously morbid (p. 161).

In this chapter, we address the various forms in which mood disorders express themselves in periodic and relatively transient form: dysthymia, major depression, and bipolar disorders. We leave to another volume of the series on personalized psychotherapy a discussion of the more enduring and characterologic style of the depressive personality. Also of interest to the reader is a recent book by Bockian (2006) entitled *Personality-Guided Therapy of Depression.*

Dysthymic Syndromes

Dysthymic patients often alter their more intense feelings for fear that they might provoke social rejection and rebuke if openly expressed. Forbidden feelings are moderated in such ways as to recruit attention, support, and nurture instead of reproach and condemnation. Although their play for sympathy may be seen through by some, these patients convey their sad plight with such genuineness or cleverness as to evoke compassion and concern from most.

General Clinical Picture

Officially, dysthymia signifies the presence of a chronically but moderately depressed mood that is present more days than not over a period of at least 2 years. Certain symptoms are to be expected, such as feeling down in the dumps, having a poor appetite, experiencing insomnia and diminished energy, expressing low self-esteem, and having feelings of hopelessness. Also notable is the presence of self-criticism and self-devaluation. According to the official system, the diagnosis should not be made if the patient has ever experienced a manic episode. As will be seen when we discuss associated personality traits, these patients commonly report feelings of inadequacy, a loss of social interest, a tendency to withdraw and to feel guilt, and a brooding preoccupation about past troubling events.

The precipitants and manifest form in which dysthymia is expressed depend largely on the premorbid personality of the patient. Some exhibit their depressive mood with displays of dramatic gesture and pleading commentary; others are demanding, irritable, and cranky. Some verbalize their thoughts in passive, vague, and abstract philosophical terms. Still others seem lonely, quiet, downhearted, solemnly morose, and pessimistic. Common to all, in our judgment, is the presence of self-deprecatory comments, feelings of apathy, discouragement, and hopelessness, and a marked decline of personal initiative. Their actions and complaints usually evoke sympathy and support from others, but these reassurances provide only temporary relief from the prevailing mood of dejection.

All persons succumb, on occasion, to periods of gloom and self-recrimination, but these feelings and thoughts are usually prompted by conditions of objective stress and tend to pass as matters take a turn for the better. In contrast, dysthymia, as a pathological disorder, appears either as an uncalled for and intense response of despondency to rather trivial difficulties or as an unduly prolonged period of discouragement following an objective distressful precipitant.

A distinction must be made between the complex syndrome of dysthymia, to be described in this section, and the psychotic-level disorder termed major depression, to be discussed later in the chapter. This distinction is largely a matter of degree. No sharp line can be drawn to separate what is essentially a continuum. Nevertheless, when the patient's moods and oppressive thoughts are so severe as to preclude meaningful social relationships, or to foster total invalidism and dependency, or to be accompanied by delusions and grossly bizarre behaviors, we may justly categorize the disorder as a major depression (Bockian, 2006; Gotlib & Colby, 1987).

What aims are served by the patient's symptoms of morose hopelessness, ineffectuality, and self-recrimination?

First and foremost, the moods and complaints of the dysthymic person summon nurturing responses from others. He or she recruits from both family and friends reassurances of lovability and value to them and gains assurances of their faithfulness and devotion. As with other complex clinical disorders, the dysthymic syndrome may serve also as an instrument for avoiding unwelcome responsibilities. Dysthymia with its attendant moods and comments is especially effective in this regard as the patient openly admits his or her worthlessness and demonstrates his or her state of helplessness for all to see.

Along similar lines, some of these patients develop their impairment as a rationalization for indecisiveness and failure. Here, their complaints are colored with subtle accusations, claims that others have not supported or cared for them, thus fostering their sense of futility and their ineffectuality. Overt expressions of hostility, however, are rarely exhibited by these patients, as they fear that these actions will prove offensive and lead others to rebuke or reject them. As a consequence, feelings of anger and resentment may be discharged only in subtle or oblique forms. This often is done by overplaying their helplessness and futile state. Their sorrowful plight may not only create guilt in others, but cause them no end of discomfort as they attempt to fulfill the patient's "justified" need for attention and care.

These coping maneuvers may prove fruitless or may evoke exasperation on the part of others. Under these circumstances, patients may discharge their tensions and also solicit the sympathy they otherwise failed to achieve by turning their anger upon themselves and condemning their own behaviors. It is at these times that protestations of guilt and self-reproach come to the fore. These patients voice a flood of self-deprecatory comments about their shortcomings, the inordinate demands they have made of others, their irresponsibility, unworthiness, evil thoughts, and so on. Through self-derision and thinly veiled suicidal threats, they not only discharge their tensions, but manage to get others to forgive them and, once more, assure them of their lovability and worthiness.

Prevailing Treatment Options

Treatment of dysthymic disorders are not different from those recommended for major depressions, to be discussed shortly, other than the fact that the latter may require a period of inpatient observation and treatment. For the most part, cognitive and behavior methods have been shown to be reasonably effective, as is the prescription of one or another of the SSRI medications. An interpersonal strategy, designed to achieve problem resolution or social skills, such as assertiveness and decision making, may also prove to be beneficial (Bockian, 2006; Markowitz, Kocsis, Bleiberg, Christos, & Sacks, 2005; Roth & Fonagy, 1996). Important in the cognitive approach are efforts to undo cognitive misinterpretations and to develop attitudes that may overcome the patient's feelings of hopelessness (Markowitz, 1994; McCullough, 2003; Seligman,

1998). Well-planned maintenance therapies should be considered to reduce the likelihood of relapse. The continued use of medication is often advisable, as long as there is ongoing physician monitoring. It seems evident that a combinational approach that encompasses both medication and psychological intervention is likely to be both effective and sustaining.

Personalized Psychotherapy

The varieties of dysthymia exhibited in these patients reflect the particular sensitivities and coping strategies they acquired in the past. To better grasp these distinctions we must turn to the different personality backgrounds conducive to this syndrome.

The common theme unifying many clinical syndromes is the fear of behaving or expressing thoughts and emotions that might provoke social condemnation. In addition, most of these patients seek to solicit attention, sympathy, and nurture. Patients attempt to avoid events that might precipitate a disordering of their precarious equilibrium. Toward this end also, they utilize intrapsychic mechanisms to keep disruptive and forbidden impulses from conscious awareness. Where feasible, these mechanisms are used in the service of venting these tensions and impulses in camouflage form. The strategies employed to achieve these aims are determined largely by a patient's central past experiences and learnings. In the following paragraphs we survey the aims and coping styles of several of the patterns most vulnerable to dysthymia.

It is important that we restate a central principle in planning personalized psychotherapy: Causes need not correspond to therapies. For example, although the underlying origins and elements of a syndrome may be largely intrapsychic and biologic, the best treatment may prove to be procedures that are cognitive or behavioral. The person is a composite of many different psychic and biologic systems. What generates and sustains a clinical syndrome may be treated best and most efficaciously by an approach that reflects only one or two parts of the overall system, ones that operate in different spheres than where the pathogenic source may stem from. To illustrate, a toothache may best be treated initially by aspirin, but the toothache may stem from a physiological infectious process; treatment may best be dealt with by relieving the symptom directly and effectively by employing the aspirin medication. If the body resolves the infection on its own, the problem has been satisfactorily dealt with. However, if the problem (the infection) persists and recurs frequently, then treatment will have to continue, perhaps in a more intense biological manner, such as being surgically cleansed. So, too, in dealing with mood disorders: Cognitive and behavioral techniques, or cognitive/pharmacologic interventions, may prove all that is necessary, and the evidence is strong that these techniques are often capable of settling the problem on their own. Similarly, extensive interpersonal and intrapsychic procedures may be called for when the mood disorder has failed to be sufficiently undermined and dispersed by simpler and more direct procedures. As stated previously, there is no single "cause" for Axis I syndromes, even in patients with highly similar personality patterns; moreover, not only do depressive precipitants differ from patient to patient, but different sensitivities may take precedence from time to time within a single patient. Let us proceed with these cautions in mind.

The cases presented here, as well as those in later chapters, represent actual patients treated or supervised by Millon in the past 50+ years, as well as recent cases treated or supervised by Grossman, applying tenets of what we now term personalized psychotherapy. Graduate students, interns, and residents contributed to a significant degree to these formulations, as well as implementing their therapeutic goals. All cases have been substantially camouflaged; changes were made to age, gender, and vocation. It should be noted that many cases precede the development of the personalized psychotherapy model, and original treatment procedures were not as comprehensive as we would have preferred. In those cases, to illustrate personalized case conceptualization and treatment, we have logically inferred some aspects of treatment, while attempting to remain as true to the nature and character of the original case as possible. We discuss a number of the features of the mood disorder syndromes as they may be elicited and coped with by different personality patterns, that is, personality styles and disorders.

Dysthymia among Needy/Dependent and Aggrieved/Masochistic Personality Patterns

These personalities are especially susceptible to separation anxiety. Feelings of helplessness and futility readily come to the fore when they are faced with either burdensome responsibilities or the anticipation of social abandonment. The actual loss of a significant person almost invariably prompts severe dejection, if not psychotic depression.

Anticipation of abandonment may prompt these patients to admit openly their weaknesses and shortcomings as a means of gaining reassurance and support. Expressions of guilt and self-condemnation typically follow as these verbalizations often successfully deflect criticism from others, transforming their threats into comments of reassurance and sympathy.

Guilt may arise as a defense against the outbreak of resentment and hostility. Dependents and masochists usually contain their anger because they dread provoking the retribution of abandonment and isolation. To prevent this occurrence they turn their aggressive impulses inward, discharging them through self-derisive comments and verbalizations of guilt and contrition. This maneuver not only tempers the exasperation of others, but often prompts them to respond in ways that make the patient feel redeemed, worthy, and loved.

Case 2.1, Marcela N., 44

Presenting Picture

Marcela had dreamed of becoming a broadcast journalist since moving to the United States from Ecuador as a young child and pursued this line of work through college and into adulthood, but she could not seem to get hired in a position beyond peripheral assistantships. Although highly intelligent and facile in expressive abilities, Marcela, unfortunately, had a rather abrasive presence in both voice and appearance, which routinely cloaked an otherwise pleasant and agreeable personality. Clinical features of dysthymia pervaded Marcela's overall psychic makeup. Often notably downhearted and blue, her sorrowful and disconsolate demeanor was apparent even in better times, for feelings of dejection and self-defeating attitudes were intrinsic to her life. She routinely voiced concerns over her social adequacy and personal worthiness, made repeated self-deprecatory and guilt-ridden comments about her failures and unattractiveness, and regularly complained about her inability to do things right. Her troubled self-view extended to many aspects of her life, not the least of which was the romantic. Having announced her bisexuality in her late 30s following both of her parents' deaths, she found herself frequently conflicted while dating, prone to sabotaging seemingly healthy beginning relationships, while being drawn in by disingenuous or malevolent partners. Although Marcela reported being aggrieved and mistreated by others, she also claimed to deserve the anguish and abuse she received, an admission consonant with her self-image as an unworthy and undeserving person.

Initial Impressions

In concert with her innate dynamics, Marcela not only accepted interactions that aggravated her misery but also precipitated conditions and events that perpetuated it. True to her core motivating aims, which clearly reflected a self-defeating (masochistic) personality pattern, Marcela found ill-fitted life and career aspirations that set up inevitable letdowns, as well as social transactions and personal situations that she seemed to repeatedly undermine. Her ability to gauge and mediate *pain* (i.e., life-preserving tendency) was transposed, leaving her with a consistent tendency to find fulfillment and reinforcement in distress, ostensibly to ward off harsher treatment by others. Further perpetuating this tendency was Marcela's seeming refusal to change course or modify circumstances, despite many opportunities to do so. From her daily, repetitive interactions in which she attempted to overingratiate herself with colleagues, to her reluctance to address identity issues, she found herself continually challenged and belittled, resulting from overinvestment in her established modus operandi. This was indicative of a kind of *passivity,* a general reluctance to attempt to create better circumstances or take alternative actions. What was interesting, however, was that there did seem to be a great deal of ambivalence in this passive trend, indicated by sporadic bouts of active and unrestrained, almost over-the-top sociability. Marcela was deeply invested in this self-imposed state of helplessness, as it provided a modicum of comfort, if only for the perceived safety of the status quo. Initial therapeutic relationship building, to be successful, needed to emphasize the safe environment, one in which Marcela could, over time, begin to take risks, allowing herself to see different tactics to achieving her needs.

Domain Analysis

Marcela's MCMI-III and Grossman Facet Scales revealed an unusual and unanticipated combination of a primary masochistic pattern, with histrionic (i.e., *active-dependent*) traits. Although she did not meet criteria for a diagnosable personality disorder on these measures or in clinical judgment, an analysis of her significantly troubling domains underscored the manner in which her characteristic tendencies repeatedly facilitated her anguish:

Discredited Objects: This was clearly her most troubling domain, although not her most overt. Marcela expected cruelty from everyone, although she was only scarcely aware of this tendency. Reflecting her verbal report of ill treatment by everyone who had known her in any capacity, she saw all current and potential future associations (inclusive of her therapist) as potential for "justified and deserved" malice toward her.

Interpersonally Attention Seeking: Marcela frequently stumbled over herself to please others, and did so in a manner that became truly notorious among her peers and associates. Her awkward efforts to gain attention paradoxically distanced herself from others or made her subject to repeated derision.

Undeserving Self-Image: Marcela's self-abasement was in harmony with her overt attention-seeking tendencies, providing thereby a veritable storehouse of premises for "falling short," "needing to try harder," and the like, as well as a penchant for accenting her worst possible attributes in the least favorable light.

Therapeutic Steps

Predictably, Marcela demonstrated the three aforementioned qualities quite openly. Although not as actively as a *negativistic* personality pattern may have sought to "prove" that the therapist would reject her ("just like everyone else who's let me down"), she did seem to more clearly display her least favorable qualities, as if to say, "See, even someone I'm paying to talk to me won't like me." This frustrated the therapist, who was an intern, nearly to the point of asking for a reassignment after 2 sessions, but she was asked to persevere so as not to reinforce Marcela's *undeserving self-image.* Her supervisor monitored this dynamic closely, orienting the therapist toward a synergy of humanistic and short-term dynamic (e.g., Horowitz et al., 2001) methods to work at disentangling Marcela's *discredited objects* and undeserving self-image. These tactics could be described as understanding and unconditionally accepting, but holding expectations (i.e., "reparenting") for generating new directions and actions. This process also included preliminary exploratory work done to uproot her habit of undoing herself, but the brunt of this work needed to wait until later stages. Central to Marcela's dysphoric feelings and negative thoughts were her intense negative self-appraisals; a major theme, after establishing her initial level of comfort and ability to challenge herself safely, was to remedy these harsh judgments of self. Considerable attention was given to correcting cognitive distortions of her achievements and the harsh manner in which she perceived others' criticisms. As she began reflecting on herself in a more deserving light and began to recognize a more realistic view of the intents of others (i.e., a fuller spectrum of malevolence and benevolence from people), she and the therapist, now perceived as a tough but caring and benevolent figure, began to implement behavioral procedures designed to expand her social and interpersonal repertoire beyond simple (and often coarse) *attention-seeking* strategies.

Marcela opted to continue treatment for several sessions after her Axis I complaints had subsided. During this time, she sought to understand more about how she undermined herself, creating worse situations than were necessary. An example of these tactics was her reluctance to address her sexual orientation: She feared the anticipated reaction of family and friends to such a degree that she preferred instead to deepen her ambivalence about herself. Already facing the challenge of dual-minority status, identifying as both Hispanic and bisexual (Collins, 2004), she identified this confusing aspect of self as something that drove even more self-denigrating thoughts, and continued to make her feel at odds with herself. Continued intrapsychic exploratory measures helped her feel more of a sense of control by virtue of having logical explanations for current stresses.

Dysthymia among Skeptical/Negativistic Personality Patterns

These patients display an agitated form of dejection; they characteristically vacillate between anxious futility, despair, and self-deprecation on the one hand, and a bitter discontent and demanding attitude toward friends and relatives on the other. Accustomed to the direct ventilation of impulses, these patients restrain their anger and turn it inward only when they fear that its expression will result in total rejection. One senses a great struggle between acting out and curtailing resentments. They exhibit a grumbling and sour disaffection with themselves and with others. Moody complaints and an attitude of generalized pessimism pervade the air. These serve as a vehicle of tension discharge, relieving them periodically of mounting inner- and outer-directed hostilities. Instrumentally, the sour moods and complaints of these patients tend to intimidate others and enable patients to gain partial retribution for past disappointments by making life miserable for others.

Dysthymia among Shy/Avoidant Personality Patterns

These personalities are not viewed by most theorists as being among those who explicitly display a dysphoric mood. This contention reflects, no doubt, the characteristic effort of these patients to flatten their affect. For purposes of self-protection, they suppress or otherwise interfere with the experience of any and all emotions. Despite the validity of this analysis, there are times when these patients sense genuine feelings of emptiness and loneliness. Periodically, they express a vague yet hopeless yearning for the affection and approval they have been denied. Adding to this mood are the contempt these patients feel for themselves, the self-deprecation they experience for their unlovability, and their failure to assert themselves and stand up for their rights. Though hesitant to express this self-contempt before others, lest it invite a chorus of further derision, close inquiry or tactful probing will frequently elicit both the self-deprecatory comments and moods of futility and dejection that we more commonly associate with other patterns.

Case 2.2, Bennett H., 36

Presenting Picture

Bennett, a socially awkward and generally introverted man, experienced chronic, characterological dysphoric patterns for as long as he could remember, but never admitted these feelings beyond a wide-ranging apprehensiveness and a vexatious view of people's core intentions. He sometimes forced himself to be sociable, offering learned but transparent pleasantries that others grew weary of after brief interactions. For a period of time in his mid-20s, according to his report, Bennett had a few close friends and a fairly active social life, but, as he put it, "I was pretending. I think everyone knew it was fake." These days, he exhibited a persistent level of downheartedness that was consistent with dysthymic symptomatology. He owned a small watch repair business inherited from his uncle and dreamed of evolving it into a full jewelry store, but never took the initiative to learn what was necessary for the transition. In fact, he admitted during the intake that he had barely mastered watch repair, much less the nuances of running a small business, and relied on his sole long-time employee, who wished to retire but promised to stay on until Bennett felt more capable. Preoccupied with fleeting, rapid thoughts revolving around personal inadequacy, plagued with self-doubts, and feeling useless most of the time, he was bothered, especially, by his perception that he was socially and physically unattractive; to compensate, he began working out vigorously, but despite getting into nearly ideal shape, he never felt satisfied. Periodically sad, empty, and lonely, he had deep and frustrated yearnings for social acceptance. Because of his defensive efforts to flatten his emotions as well as to hide feelings of despair, his depressive pathology was contained sufficiently to fade into his typical bland presence.

Initial Impressions

Bennett's apprehension, not surprisingly, extended to the therapeutic relationship. He was among the most guarded of individuals seen by his therapist, and it took very skillful interviewing to elicit his more self-deprecatory thoughts and attitudes of futility. Bennett was masterful at pain evasion, as is typical of a shy (avoidant) pattern. Indeed, his MCMI-III scores reflected a moderate elevation on the Avoidant scale, with a mild Dependent elevation, indicating problematic active–pain personality attributes in a personality that perpetually felt ill-equipped to function independently of others. His immediate environs were highly insulated from possible derision from others; ironically, of course, this trend promoted his loneliness and unhappiness. As noted, Bennett was deeply defended, especially when it came to more powerful emotional content. To minimize Bennett's trepidation, his therapist approached initial interviewing tasks by encouraging him to voice and answer fears about disclosing difficult information in session, while eliciting difficult emotional content. This allowed Bennett to create his safe environment, while the therapist began examining important and otherwise inaccessible personal dynamics.

Domain Analysis

Although not presenting with a diagnosable Axis II disorder, Bennett evidenced several characteristics of both avoidant and dependent patterns, as just described. Domain analysis, as outlined by the MG-PDC, noted the following crucial trends:

Vexatious Objects: No one was really "safe," according to Bennett. Despite reassurances and repeated interactions to the contrary, Bennett not only viewed people as malicious toward him, but also internalized the view that he was unworthy of more positive interactions, to the end that he may even deserve pernicious treatment by others.

Alienated Self-Image: Bennett saw himself as entirely awkward and socially disabled. At a time of slightly higher self-esteem, he was able, as he put it, to "fake my way through a party," but as self-esteem became depleted, he viewed his efforts as progressively more futile, ending with a firm view that he had committed social suicide in those happier days.

Expressively Incompetent: Nearly devoid of confidence, Bennett considered himself weak and incapable. He invariably acquiesced to others in most all social and business exchanges, and often created losses by this strategy; paradoxically, this made him feel even more inferior and ill-equipped to manage his life.

Therapeutic Steps

Approximately 1 month was necessary to establish a modicum of therapeutic rapport with Bennett, during which time, as indicated previously, he was given free rein to voice concerns and question the therapist's intentions. Gradually, as he was satisfied with the therapeutic relationship's dynamics, he began to dread outside judgment less. This improvement in his tendency to expect all others to be troublesome (*vexatious objects*), stemming from a relational approach emphasizing new interpersonal experiences rooted in psychodynamic constructs (e.g., Curtis & Hirsch, 2003; Magnavita, 2000), gradually set the stage for further improvements in new social interactions. Although his distrust of others and his expectation that others would ("justly") treat him with contempt became much less pronounced, this remained a hurdle he would trip over throughout treatment. However, Bennett's persistent feelings of inadequacy (*expressive incompetence*) lessened, as a catalytic sequence of allowing him to gain new experience implicit in answering his own fears, with the support (rather than the "doing") of the therapist. In this new experience came a new level of confidence. He gradually released concerns about his perceived physical and social unattractiveness, and efforts toward the latter end of treatment began introducing an existentially based therapeutic paradigm. This approach began focusing on his strengths in individual differences, wherein he learned that it was important, in social settings, to have people who took on more of an "observer" role; his hyperconcern over harsh judgments of others relieved, Bennett started to explore more genuine attitudes and approaches with others, occasionally feeling vulnerable, but more frequently alleviating his *alienated self-image*. His shy personality pattern was moderated, not to an ideal level, but enough to allow his generally negative, grim worldview to brighten and to allay his chronic dysthymic state, which had persisted over the many prior months, if not years.

Dysthymia and Brief Manic Episodes among Capricious/Borderline Personalities

Overt and direct expressions of hostility tend to be exhibited only impulsively by borderlines because they fear these actions will lead others to reject them. A major form of anger control is to turn feelings of resentment inward into mild depressive episodes. Not only may they overplay their helplessness and futile state, but the borderline's sorrowful plight may create guilt in others and cause them no end of discomfort as they try to meet the borderline's "justified" need for attention and care. Of course, devious coping maneuvers such as these often prove fruitless and may evoke exasperation and rebuke from others. Should such a course prevail, borderlines may turn their anger on themselves even more intensely. Protestations of guilt and self-reproach come to the fore as they voice a flood of self-deprecatory comments about their own personal shortcomings, the inordinate and despicable demands they have made of others, their history of irresponsibility, unworthiness, evil actions, and so on. Self-derision and thinly veiled suicidal threats not only discharge borderlines' anger but manage to get others to forgive them and offer assurances of their devotion and compassion.

Some borderlines display periods of *Bipolar Disorder* similar to *schizoaffective* states, displaying a scattering of ideas and emotions and a jumble of disconnected thoughts and aimless behaviors. In some cases, there may be an exuberance, a zestful energy and jovial mood, that is lacking among other psychotic types. Although the ideas and hyperactivity of these borderlines tend to be connected only loosely to reality, they have an intelligible logic to them and appear consonant with the predominant mood. In other cases, behaviors and ideas are fragmented, vague, disjointed, and bizarre. Here, the borderlines' moods are varied and changeable, inconsistent with their thoughts and actions, and difficult to grasp and relate to, let alone empathize with. Albeit briefly, some borderlines successfully infect others for short periods with their conviviality and buoyant optimism. They may become extremely clever and witty, rattling off puns and rhymes and playing cute and devilish. This humor and mischievousness rapidly drains others, who quickly tire of the incessant and increasingly irrational quality of the borderlines' forced sociability. In addition to their frenetic excitement and reckless race from one topic to another, they may display an annoying pomposity and self-expansiveness. Boastfulness becomes extremely trying and exasperating, often destroying what patience and goodwill these patients previously evoked from others.

Dysthymia among Conscientious/Compulsive Personalities

These personalities exhibit a pattern of tense and anxious dejection that is similar to, but more tightly controlled than, that of their negativistic counterparts. Faced with difficult decisions but unable to obtain either clear direction or approval from others, these patients experience a strong upsurge of anger and resentment toward themselves for their weakness and toward others for their unyielding demands and their unwillingness to provide support. They are fearful, however, of exposing their personal shortcomings and hostile feelings to others. On the other hand, they have been trained well to express self-reproach and feel guilt. Thus, rather than vent their resentments toward others and suffer the consequences of severe social rebuke, these patients discharge their anger toward themselves. Severe self-reproach serves as a form of expiation for their forbidden contrary thoughts and feelings. Moreover, by being contrite they hope that no one will be so unkind as to attack and abandon them. Unfortunately, this hope rests on a poor foundation. Compulsives have experienced severe condemnation in the past for signs of weakness and incompetence. Thus, they cannot escape the bind they are in, cannot free themselves from the fear that their sorrowful state ultimately will provoke rejection. Their agitated and apprehensive dejection reflects, then, both their struggle to contain the expression of resentments and their fear that weakness and contrition will prompt derision and abandonment.

On occasion, compulsives display a benign and reflective moroseness. This may arise when they realize how empty their lives have been, how much they have denied themselves, and how much they have given up as a consequence of external pressures. These calm periods of dejection are often interrupted by brief episodes of assertive self-determination. However, old feelings of anxiety are reactivated during these episodes, making them rather short-lived. Almost invariably, these patients revert quickly to their established rigidly conforming ways.

Dysthymia among Sociable/Histrionic Personalities

These personalities overplay their feelings of dejection, expressing them through rather dramatic gestures and in fashionable jargon. This contrasts to the flat and somber picture of the dependent, and the tense, guilt-ridden and agitated quality seen in the negativists and compulsives. The histrionic coloring of their mood is a natural outgrowth of their basic coping style of actively soliciting attention and approval.

Episodes of dejection in these patients may be prompted to some degree by a deep fear of abandonment, but more likely by a sense of inner emptiness and inactivity. It arises most often when they feel stranded between one fleeting attachment and another, or between one transitory exciting preoccupation and the next. At these times of noninvolvement, they sense a lack of direction and purpose and experience a fearful void and aloneness.

Dejection in many of the histrionics tends to be expressed in popular jargon. The patient may philosophize about his or her "existential anxiety" or the alienation that one must inevitably feel in this "age of mass society." Their use of fashionable terms provides them with a bridge to others. It gives them a sense of belonging during those moments when they feel most isolated from the mainstream of active social life in which they so desperately crave to be. Moreover, their pseudo-sophistication about up-to-date matters and terminology not only enables them to rationalize their sense of emptiness and confusion, but also allows them to maintain their appeal in the eyes of "interesting" people. By attaching themselves to currently popular modes of group disenchantment, they reinstate themselves as participants of an "involved" cultural subgroup and manage, thereby, to draw interested attention *to* themselves. These expressions of social dissent also provide an outlet for venting some of their resentments and tensions. However, should these feelings of hostility be discharged without group support, they are quickly rescinded and replaced by dramatic expressions of guilt and contrition.

Case 2.3, Nora J., 32

Presenting Picture

Dysphoric symptoms were not readily admitted by Nora, a woman described by most people she knew as characteristically "outgoing," "bubbly," and "fabulous," according to her report. Generally inclined toward denial in self-disclosure, she whispered to the therapist, in something of a dramatic aside, the following: "I can't really say too much because I have a reputation around here, but I'm not doing so hot." As it turns out, recent setbacks and the deprivation of her usual support sources (in this case, her friends who had "let her down") prompted Nora to succumb to dormant patterns of fearfulness of standing on her own. Increasingly preoccupied with matters of personal adequacy or attractiveness, she was both sad and irritable, self-debasing and demanding, guilt-ridden and manipulative. Shamed over humiliating outbursts, evidence of deficits, and other perceptions of failures on her part, Nora felt an inner emptiness, devoid of the stimulation or support to which she was accustomed. Also noteworthy was her tendency to overplay her troubled feelings by expressing them in dramatic gestures or fashionable jargon.

Initial Impressions

Quite theatrical in her revelation of her dynamics, Nora clearly demonstrated a propensity for soliciting attention from anyone she encountered. Actively seeking visibility by all, she was most comfortable when admired by others. Perhaps more accurately, though, this trend may have been described as her being able to avoid her more difficult and personal subjects when reassured of her worthiness by her "bevy of onlookers." She described her friends as her "Nora's fans," and given her sense of humor, it was difficult to detect whether she was joking. When her therapist responded to this self-reference with "You're pretty funny!" it cut to the essence of this tendency; she immediately responded with "I don't really feel that's funny, per se." Indeed, she was quite serious and seemed slightly taken aback by the comment, but did follow up with "You think I'm funny?" Her therapist decided to indulge her basic *active—other* motivations in this regard by effectively becoming her audience. In this venue, Nora began reporting more as a soliloquy, which gave her license to gradually allow herself to be vulnerable. She even initiated the idea that the therapist could act as her critic "and let me know whether I'm being real or not." This began as their joke but fully catalyzed their relationship. Before long, and with Nora encouraged to drop her more melodramatic posturing in favor of a more humble, reflective rapport, the guises of "actress and critic" were dropped spontaneously and replaced with a much more honest working mode of treatment.

Domain Analysis

As anticipated, Nora's profile from the MCMI-III had a primary elevation on the Histrionic scale, with accompanying Narcissistic features. These scores were moderately elevated, indicating that global personality dysfunction was unlikely, although facets of the personality appeared to create recurrent problems, the most recent of which, of course, being her current disappointments with her support system. The Grossman Facet Scales revealed the following salient domains:

Interpersonally Attention Seeking: Nora actively solicited praise, sometimes in a seductive manner, to establish herself as an entity among her peers. As is frequently typical of this domain characteristic, however, maintaining this level of interpersonal interest becomes arduous and, ultimately, fleeting. Notably, a second facet elevation in this same domain was revealed on the Narcissistic scale: Interpersonally Exploitive. Nora appeared to demonstrate both of these interpersonal qualities to a degree.

Dramatic Expressive Behavior: Ranging in her emotional response from impulsive and volatile to perceived slights, to provocative and flirtatious in responding to compliments, Nora was capricious in her mannerisms and expression of feelings. Although this quickly engaged others, it was also tiring and had the ultimate effect of alienating her from her support network.

Expansive Cognitive Style: Often, Nora seemed determined in her quest to express her unbridled savvy and superior essence in all matters of concern to her, and this took on a nearly fantastical quality, especially in her thought process and rationalizations. Anything questioned was rapidly reframed by her as a tremendous success, an undeniable truth, and so on.

Therapeutic Steps

The early stages of treatment for Nora were most encouraging. She spoke of the fulfillment of her desire for interest when she learned that her "famous" therapist was in the process of writing a therapy book, and she asked if her case would be featured. She also felt that the "theatrical" approach that cemented the therapeutic relationship was "brilliant enough for a writer's award.... Will you get one?" Her motivation being high from this stimulation, she began encouraging a "more critical view" from her therapist, and she became more open to questions aimed at introspection. At this point, a rational-emotive behavioral therapy (REBT; e.g., Ellis, 1970) approach was employed to enable Nora to recognize that her *cognitive expansiveness* was not sustainable. This reflection brought her mood to a lower point for a time, which appeared at first to scare her into feeling that her dysphoric symptomatology was growing worse, but then opened the door to more pronounced changes. So much of her dysthymic syndrome derived from the loss of significant others (some brought on by her self-alienating behaviors) or the fear that more would abandon her. Her desperate search for approval and attention stemmed in part from the feeling of emptiness she experienced throughout her life. Here, her therapist employed methods to construct new cognitive beliefs and more sustaining relationships. Pairing up REBT with an interpersonal approach (Klerman, Weissman, Rounsaville, & Chevron, 1984) she learned to be effective not only in dealing with her depressive feelings, but in developing sustaining relationships with new interpersonal strategies other than *dramatizing* and active *attention seeking*. In addition to individual therapy, it was recommended that Nora participate in a group treatment setting. Interaction with members of this group proved to be highly useful and informative, providing Nora with an opportunity to understand how others see her and react to her. The emotional support she received from these peers, along with the opportunity to try on new behaviors that were more effective and less provocative and *exploitive,* carried her through initial self-doubts and planted a seed for lasting developments, a greater sense of self, and richer relationships.

Dysthymia among Confident/Narcissistic Personalities

Dysthymic Disorder is perhaps the most common symptom disorder seen among narcissists. Faced with repeated failures and social humiliations, and unable to find some way of living up to their inflated self-image, narcissists may succumb to uncertainty and dissatisfaction, losing self-confidence and convincing themselves that they are, and perhaps have always been, fraudulent and phony. Kernberg (1975, p. 311) has described this process of self-disillusionment well: "For them, to accept the breakdown of the illusion of grandiosity means to accept the dangerous, lingering awareness of the depreciated self—the hungry, empty, lonely primitive self surrounded by a world of dangerous, sadistically frustrating and revengeful objects."

Because dysthymia is not experienced as consonant with the narcissist's self-image, it rarely endures for extended periods unless the psychic blow is irreparable. More typically, we observe rapid shifts in the character of the depressive symptomatology as narcissists succumb at first to their feelings of apathy and worthlessness, and then abruptly seek to retrieve their grandiose self-confidence and reassert themselves. At one time, they may express their depressive mood dramatically; at other times, in a cranky and irritable manner; and at yet another, in a dreamy, vague, and philosophically abstract way. Often, narcissists will utilize their mood as a rationalization for their increasing indecisiveness and failures. Here, their complaints are likely to be colored with subtle accusations and claims that others have not supported or cared for them, thus fostering their growing sense of futility and ineffectuality. As is more characteristic of the negativistic personality, narcissists may vacillate for a brief period between anxious futility and self-deprecation, and bitter discontent and a demanding attitude.

A struggle ensues between venting and curtailing the rage felt toward others simply for being witness to their shame and humiliation. Moody and pessimistic complaints are not only genuinely expressed but are a useful outlet for mounting resentments. Moreover, depressively toned hostility often serves to intimidate others, and it thereby functions as a form of retribution or vengeance for their failure to rescue the narcissist from his or her own deficiencies.

Major Depressive Disorder

Numerous interpretations regarding the causes and dynamics of these severe depressive episodes have been formulated since the early work of Emil Kraepelin. As would be expected, those of the *psychoanalytic* school interpret depression as a symbolic loss of a significant or loved object, usually followed by an inward turning of anger that is felt toward the abandoning person. To analysts, self-valuation depends on the receipt of constant signs of nurturance and care on the part of others; depression results in part owing to the reality of abandonment (Blatt, 2004). *Cognitivists,* in general, interpret depression as stemming from reality misinterpretations and a faulty logic that derives from a persistent pessimistic orientation. *Behavioral theorists,* by contrast, see depression as incorrectly reinforced responses; in their view, secondary gains outweigh the painful depressive experience. *Interpersonal* thinkers consider depressed individuals to have deficient social skills, hence preventing them from experiencing positive social reinforcements. To them, depressives are unusually dependent on others and have poor communication abilities in relationships. Thinkers with a *developmental* perspective see depressives as persons who experienced parental discord in childhood or insufficient levels of maternal care, or to have been constrained by controlling parents. The more *biologically oriented* thinkers view depression to be a consequence of neurochemical dysfunctions of one of the major neurotransmitters (Atwood & Chester, 1987; Seligman, 1998; Tafet & Bernardini, 2003).

General Clinical Picture (Subdued and Agitated Depression)

There are similarities among patients with Major Depressive Disorder, but significant differences as well. Most depressed patients exhibit a generalized psychomotor deceleration, for example, heavy and lugubrious movements, slow or dragged-out speech, and an ever-present air of fatigue and exhaustion. Clinical observation, however, will uncover areas of considerable difference, even at the gross clinical level. The *DSM-IV* has delineated several specifiers that provide valuable information regarding the clinical status of depressed patients; it is advisable to utilize these criteria in case conceptualization and treatment planning, as they provide important information regarding etiology, history, and symptomatology. As our emphasis in this personalized psychotherapy series is focused on the personality patterns that interact with Axis I syndromes, we will be using slightly more general distinctions for simplicity and illustrative purposes. These distinctions coincide in great measure to the *DSM*'s "melancholic" and "atypical" specifiers, but are not intended to be exclusive to others (e.g., postpartum, catatonic), as is the case with official *DSM* specifiers. Our goal is to capture the most common general colorizations of the syndrome in a manner to which most clinicians may relate. The principles described and illustrated may be applied to other depressive disorder variants.

The first of these two is what we term the "subdued" depressed patient; this variant is closest to what most clinicians and laypeople alike associate with the term "depression." Many subdued-depressed individuals experience deep and heavy feelings; gloom and profound dejection are clearly conveyed through a furrowed brow, stooped body, and head turned downward and away from the gaze of others, as though hauling a burdensome weight. In other cases, however, a kind of apathy may take the place of this deep-feeling state, as the subdued-depressed patient experiences a disconnection from feeling, severe amotivational states, intellectualization of affect, and pronounced neurovegetative signs. Various physical signs and symptoms further enable us to identify subdued patients. They may often lose weight and look haggard and drained. In their nighttime habits they follow a characteristic pattern of awakening after 2 or 3 hours of sleep, turn restlessly, have oppressive thoughts, and experience a growing dread of the new day. Notable also is the content of their verbalizations, meager though they may be. They report a vague dread of impending disaster, feelings of utter helplessness, a pervasive sense of guilt for past failures, and a willing resignation to their hopeless fate. As will be noted shortly, subdued depression occurs most often among dependent, avoidant, depressive, and masochistic personalities.

The features of the "agitated" depressive, by contrast, are rather mixed and erratic, varying in quality and focus in accord with the patient's basic personality patterns. In many respects, it is a composite of what we have termed subdued depression and "hostile manic" bipolar disorders, although not as extreme as either when their respective dominant characteristics are prominent. In some cases, they may also resemble those diagnosed with Cyclothymic Disorder, though they present more consistently with one predominant characteristic over the other. In all cases, there is an incessant despair and suffering, an agitated pacing to and fro, a wringing of hands, and an apprehensiveness and tension that are unrelieved by comforting reassurances. In many cases, the primary components are angry depressive complaints and a demanding and querulous irritability in which the patient bemoans his or her sorry state and desperate need for attention to the manifold physical illnesses, pains, and incapacities that consume existence. In other cases, the agitated depressive picture is colored less by critical and demanding attitudes and more by self-blame and guilt; here we see anxious self-doubting, expressions of self-hate, a preoccupation with impending disasters, suicidal thoughts, feelings of unworthiness, and delusions of shame and sin (PDM Task Force, 2006).

Prevailing Treatment Options

The treatment of Major Depressive Disorder establishes positive effects for a number of antidepressant medications (tricyclics, SSRIs). The efficacy of these medications, as well as other SSRIs coming on the market every day, are very well accepted. Safety is often an issue with these pharmaceuticals (e.g., monoamine oxidase inhibitors [MAOIs]); here again, the SSRIs have a wide margin of safety over the long run. Electroconvulsive therapy should be considered among patients who are refractory to all forms of pharmacologic and psychotherapeutic techniques.

Equally efficacious as medications for depressives are psychological treatment techniques such as behavior therapy (Bellack, Hersen, & Himmelhoch, 1981, 1983; Lewinsohn & Gotlib, 1995; Nathan & Gorman, 2002), cognitive-behavioral therapy (Beck, Rush, Shaw, & Emery, 1979; Hollon, Stewart, & Strunk, 2006), and interpersonal psychotherapy (de Mello, de Jesus, Bacaltchuk, Verdeli, & Neugebauer, 2005; Klerman, Weissman, Rounsaville, & Chevron, 1984). Despite its utility as an explanatory schema, intrapsychic therapies have not proven to be comparatively more effective than these (Covi & Lipman, 1987; Levinson, 2004; McLean & Hakstian, 1979; Steuer et al., 1984).

Combinational approaches that begin to approach synergistic treatment programs have also been recommended, albeit without the reference base of differences among patients' personality styles or disorders (Bond & Perry, 2006; Sperry, 1995). Included in these proposals are the use of medications and group treatment (Salvendy & Joffe, 1991). Comparisons of psychotherapy and psychopharmacology suggest that combinations have the greatest efficacy (Bond & Perry, 2006; Manning & Frances, 1990; Wexler & Cicchetti, 1992). According to Manning and Frances, for example, there appears to be a U-shaped relationship between the use of combined modalities and the severity of depression. As they see it, combinational treatment is likely best for those in the midrange of depressive severity. Those with mild depression are likely to respond best to psychotherapeutic approaches such as cognitive-behavioral or interpersonal techniques. Those with very severe depression are best treated by hospitalization and medication, until the severity abates substantially.

As to be expected, medications appear to work more rapidly than most psychotherapies. On the other hand, cognitive and interpersonal psychotherapy encourage a broad base of changes that go beyond that generated by medication alone (Hollon & Fawcett, 1995; Hollon et al., 2006). Owing to the prevalence of these disorders and their impact on family life, patients should be guided to opportunities for psychoeducation, family therapy, and homogeneous medication groups (Bond & Perry, 2006; Sperry, 1995).

Personalized Psychotherapy

In this section we rank the personalities that are vulnerable in approximate order of their susceptibility to depression.

Subdued Depression among Needy/Dependent Personalities

Dependents are especially susceptible to this disorder; histrionic, borderline, and depressive personalities are only slightly less vulnerable. Each pattern manifests these symptoms in response to essentially similar precipitants, notably a loss or the anticipated loss of an important source of their dependency security, for example, the death of a parent or spouse or dismissal from a steady job. Their depression often represents a logical but overly extreme response to real or potentially threatening events. However, there is no question that the reaction is pathological; the depth of the response and the disposition to succumb to profound dejection, even before difficulties have arisen, clearly point to the presence of an unusual personality vulnerability.

Despite the genuineness of the depressive mood, dependent personalities do not forgo their coping aims in their disordered state. Their displays of contrition and the deep gravity of their mood solicit attention, support, and nurture from others. Moreover, their coping aims enable them to avoid unbearable responsibilities and provide them with the comforts and security of dependent invalidism. Aspects of this syndrome are depicted in the following brief example.

Case 2.4, Liane B., 37

Presenting Picture

Liane was admitted to the psychiatric wing of a general hospital with her third depressive episode in 8 years. When admitted this time, she was markedly underweight, had been "unable" to eat for weeks, and sat limply at the edge of her chair, weeping quietly and asking, over and over again, "What have I done to my family?" She was entirely inconsolable for the first 24 hours. After the first day, Liane was observed, at times, to be quiet, although severely downcast when left alone. However, as soon as someone appeared, she would again begin to moan aloud, deprecating herself for the harm and shame she had brought to her family. Needless to say, these lamentations evoked sympathetic and reassuring responses from others.

Initial Impressions

It was of paramount importance to allow for reassurances and sympathy in Liane's initial days in the hospital. Her very fragile state did not allow for significant inroads, therapeutically, for some time. During these early days, however, it was possible for her therapist to engage Liane in simple activities, such as learning a card game, something she noted that she "just never had the knack for." Assuring her that they would stop at the first sign of discomfort, the therapist, in effect, began pulling her out of a chronic state of passivity, giving her some assurance that she was not entirely incompetent. A conversation regarding music followed, and it was discovered that Liane had been a fairly adept clarinetist in high school. This approach, encouraging more activity and self-orientation, took place as her antidepressants, prescribed in the first days of admittance, began to take effect. Within the first few weeks, Liane began her therapeutic opportunities in a more invigorated and socially relevant manner than before, and she was able to be released to the hospital's outpatient facility, where she was able to follow through with the same therapist.

Domain Analysis

As her therapist engaged her in early days of treatment, he utilized the MG-PDC to discover some of the underlying facets of Liane's personality. Highlights of this assessment clearly followed dependent personality traits, likely to a disordered degree, and were as follows:

Inept Self-Image: Consistently self-deprecating, and finding justifications to shy away from novel experiences or skill-building, Liane viewed herself as entirely incapable of managing anything from small tasks to adult life chores.

Interpersonally Submissive: This was a source of guilt for Liane, in that her "ineptness" from the previous domain "required" her to rely heavily on others, "yet I failed them and disappointed everyone." Unable to take initiative, Liane was entirely dependent on the whims and wishes of family.

Temperamentally Pacific: This domain was clarified after the initial dysphoric stage, where her affect was clearly melancholic. More characteristically, Liane was subdued, timid, peaceable, and quiet, but under duress she was able to admit pessimism and feelings of dejection.

Therapeutic Steps

As Liane became more engaged through minor experiences of success (e.g., the card games) and reflections on skills she may still have, this supportive milieu allowed her sense of *ineptness* to began to give way to a more realistic view—that is, of a person who had *allowed* herself to give up on personal skills and interests. Though this was a difficult revelation, it was one that encouraged a small amount of appropriate and functional anger (Tavris, 1989), which then served as invigoration to counterbalance her otherwise *pacific mood,* which was further modified through her pharmacologic treatment. These treatments began to prepare her to deal with difficulties that stemmed from her lifelong personality style. It was clear that her view of herself as an inadequate and fragile person, first addressed through simple engagement, could move on to more mature self-actualizing techniques that will help build her self-esteem and confidence. Likewise, her excessive dependence on those close to her called for behavioral and interpersonal efforts to overcome her *submissiveness*. With the addition of these general therapeutic approaches, the likelihood of counteracting a future relapse was likely. In the second half of her treatment, integrating her new discoveries and feelings in family therapy sessions proved useful in providing Liane not only with a sense of warmth and protection, but with new skills in self-expression and competency. Within some 3 months following admittance, she seemed well on her way to overcoming her depression and to face the problems that led to her prior despondency.

Subdued Depression among Conscientious/Compulsive Personalities

Both ambivalent personalities succumb with some frequency to depressions, although, more characteristically, they lean toward the agitated form of depressive expression, to he discussed later. In the subdued form, compulsives have managed to gain a measure of control over their inner conflicts and hostile impulses. This they have done by turning their feelings inward, that is, by taking out their hatred on themselves. Thus, they persist in voicing guilt and self-disparagement for their failures, antisocial acts, and contemptuous feelings and thoughts. In this self-punitive depressive disorder, they manage to cloak their "real" contrary impulses, seek redemption, and ask absolution for their past behaviors and forbidden unconscious inclinations. Moreover, their illness solicits support and nurture from others. In a more subtle way it also serves as a devious means of venting their hidden resentment and anger. Their state of helplessness and their protestations of self-derogation make others feel guilty and burden others with extra responsibilities and woes.

Subdued and Agitated Depression among Shy/Avoidant Personalities

Given their detached style, we might think that avoidants would not be among those who display affective disorders. As stated with regard to avoidants who experience dysthymia, this belief would be consistent with their characteristic effort to flatten emotions and suppress or otherwise interfere with feelings. Despite their efforts in this regard, these patients often experience *major depressions,* feeling a deep sadness, emptiness, and loneliness. Many express a yearning for the affection and approval they have been denied. Added to this melancholic tone is the contempt these patients feel for themselves and the self-deprecation they experience for their unlovability, weaknesses, and ineffectuality. Though hesitant to display this self-contempt before others, lest it invite a chorus of further derision, tactful probing will readily elicit both the self-deprecatory comments and the genuinely felt moods of futility and dejection.

Subdued Depression among Pessimistic/Depressive Personalities

As should be obvious by the commonality in their label, depressive personalities are difficult to differentiate from those with Dysthymic and Major Depressive Disorders; this is especially evident when the Dysthymic Disorder is of an extended duration. The essential distinction lies in the fact that the depressive personality should be demonstrated in childhood or adolescence; that is, the depressive symptomatology should be observable before it is manifested in adult pathology. Similarly, the personality disorder may be differentiated from major depressive episodes by virtue of the latter's rapid onset and intensity. Nevertheless, covariations are to be expected. Perhaps most important is the presence among depressive personalities of a wide range of characteristic cognitive, intrapsychic, and interpersonal traits that emerge as a consequence of long-standing periods of unhappiness and sadness. Hence, early onset, extended and moderate clinical symptomatology, and the presence of multiple trait characteristics should help in differentiating these disorders.

Subdued Depression among Aggrieved/Masochistic Personalities

Separating the depressive and *masochistic* individuals has been a clinical issue for many therapists and theorists. As noted previously, some authors refer to a constellation termed the "depressive-masochistic" character (Kernberg, 1988). Distinctions between them have been alluded to in earlier sections of the chapter. The prime differentiating element is the depressive's feeling of hopelessness and the inevitability of his or her affective state. By contrast, masochists, though evidently discontent and unhappy, take pains to participate in their environment, by seeking either to please or submit to others, or to manipulatively create their own misfortunes and misery.

It is almost redundant, as it would be in the case of the depressive personality, to state that the masochistic individual is subject to mood disorders. A prolonged *dysthymia,* in particular, is in great measure an intrinsic feature of the masochistic pathology, a chronic and long-standing disposition to express, as well as to feel, extended periods of deep melancholy and a gloomy sadness. More than is typical of most depressives, these unhappy mood states are part of the self-sacrificial instrumental strategy employed by the masochist, a tendency to publicly display dysthymia and subdued depression as vehicles to deflect serious condemnation, to evoke guilt in its stead, to elicit sympathy, and to avoid assuming onerous responsibilities.

Agitated Depression among Skeptical/Negativistic Personalities

These persons are especially prone to agitated depressions. Their disorders can be seen as an extension of their premorbid personality style, that is, complaints, irritability, and a sour grumbling discontent, usually interwoven with hypochondriacal preoccupations and periodic expressions of guilt and self-condemnation. Their habitual style of acting out their conflicts and ambivalent feelings becomes more and more pronounced, resulting in extreme vacillations between bitterness and resentment, on the one hand, and intropunitive self-deprecation, on the other. Self-pity and bodily anxieties are extremely common and may serve as a basis for distinguishing them from other agitated types. The following illustrates a typical case.

Case 2.5, Gladys R., 55

Presenting Picture

Gladys, a woman often described as "passive-aggressive" by coworkers, with a prior history of several psychotic breaks, became increasingly irritable, despairing, and self-deprecating over a period of 1 or 2 months; no clear precipitant was evident. At work as a data entry clerk, she paced back and forth, wringing her hands and periodically shouting that God had forsaken her and that she was a "miserable creature, placed on earth to make my family suffer." At times, Gladys would sit on the edge of a chair, nervously chewing her nails, complaining about the disinterest shown her by her children. Then she would jump up, move about restlessly, voicing irrational fears about her own and her husband's health, claiming that he was a "sick man," sure to die because of her "craziness." One day, her husband was called to pick her up from work after she was given a temporary suspension with pay while she sought help.

Initial Impressions

Gladys's agitated and fretful behavior took on a more contentious and hypochondriacal quality when she met the therapist to which she was brought. After several standard intake questions, which appeared to make Gladys more agitated, the therapist said, "Why don't we dispense with the paperwork and formalities for right now, and you can just tell me what you'd like to tell me." Assuming a nonthreatening posture and nonjudgmental ("not overtly clinical") attitude, Gladys stopped pacing and fidgeting, and said, "Okay, I know you're paid to listen to me, but even so, maybe you'll be the someone who finally *will* listen to me." Breaking up her characteristic active ambivalence regarding her needs versus others', which was a driving force in her agitation and is the cornerstone of negativistic personality patterns, was a matter of having a clearly empathic listener available, something she (justified or otherwise) did not feel she had anywhere in her life. "But how am I going to get others to do this? I can't pay 'em!"

Domain Analysis

After her two initial sessions, which were largely comprised of venting, with the therapist actively listening and reflecting with occasional clarifications, the MG-PDC and Grossman Facet Scales of the MCMI were utilized to uncover the following clearly problematic domains:

Expressively Resentful: Much of Gladys's manner, which may have been characterized by obstinacy and resistance in more functional times, now took on the quality of overt indignation. This was underscored by another important domain, an irritable temperament.

Discontented Self-Image: Gladys had internalized feelings of bitterness and saw herself as not only misunderstood, but intermittently *deserving* and *trapped by* misunderstandings, leaving her feeling at times unappreciated, at other times "having no choice but to do things that aren't appreciated."

Interpersonally Contrary: Overtly ambivalent regarding others, Gladys seemed tortured by her inconsistency that, by her description, "necessitates me constantly struggling to do what's right and never finding the answer." This course of action, not surprisingly, alienated her from important figures in her life.

Therapeutic Steps

Over the course of a regimen of antidepressant drugs and supportive, empathic therapy, Gladys's *irritability* gradually remitted. She continued, throughout treatment, to attend a once-per-week medication group, in addition to individual therapy. Of note here was the value of straightforward self-actualizing techniques (e.g., Rogers's person-centered therapy) designed to unravel and permit expression of her deep sense of *discontent,* not only with others, but with herself. Following this in a catalytic sequence was the addition of cognitive reframing techniques, combined with an interpersonal potentiated pairing, which was helpful in curtailing her tendency to view life from a skeptical point of view and stabilizing her *contrary* interactions. These efforts helped forestall her repetitive experiences of disillusionment and disappointment. Not to be overlooked were her self-perpetuating *resentful behaviors* which exasperated others and impeded progress. Her group therapy milieu for medication effects proved to be a useful setting in which she learned to perceive human interactions in a more constructive and cooperative fashion.

Agitated Depression among Conscientious/Compulsive Personalities

Compulsive personalities exhibit the more traditional form of agitated depression noted by diffuse apprehension, marked guilt feelings, and a tendency to delusions of sin and unworthiness. These patients exhibit some of the whining and querulous qualities seen in their negativistic ambivalent counterparts. However, they turn the aggressive component of their conflict toward themselves, claiming that they deserve the punishment and misery that they now suffer.

Agitated Depression among Capricious/Borderline Personalities

As is evident from the preceding, borderlines succumb frequently to *major depressions.* In the more subdued form of depression, borderlines gain some measure of control over their inner conflicts and hostile impulses. They do this by turning their angry feelings inward, that is, by taking out their hatred on themselves. Guilt and self-disparagement are voiced for their failures, impulsive acts, contemptuous feelings, and evil thoughts. Feelings of emptiness, boredom, and deadness also are frequently reported. In the more self-punitive depressions, borderlines manage to cloak their contrary impulses by seeking redemption and asking absolution for their past behaviors and forbidden inclinations. Not infrequently, this sadness and melancholy solicit support and nurture from others. As in other symptom disorders, this is a subtle and indirect means of venting hidden resentment and anger. Helplessness and self-destructive acts make others feel guilty and burden them with extra responsibilities and woes.

Agitated Depression among Sociable/Histrionic Personalities

Histrionics evidence agitated depression less frequently than negativists. In their case, the primary precipitants tend to be anticipated losses in dependency security. They generally wail aloud and convey feelings of hopelessness and abandonment, all in the hope of soliciting support and nurture. Their agitation does not reflect an internal struggle of hostility versus guilt, as in the case of the ambivalents, but a more direct and simple expression of worrisome apprehension.

Bipolar Syndromes

During their manic episodes, bipolar patients tend to be rather disorganized, scattering their ideas and emotions in a jumble of disconnected thoughts and aimless behaviors. There is an abnormally and persistently elevated mood, either of a euphoric (expansive) or hostile (irritable) character. According to the official classification system, the patient gives evidence of a number of key symptoms, such as inflated self-esteem or grandiosity, high levels of distractibility notable for flights of ideas and pressured speech, a high degree of psychomotor agitation, a search for risk-taking pleasurable activities, diminished judgment and impulse control, and a decreased need for sleep. Not uncommonly, bipolar patients will give evidence of mood-congruent delusions or hallucinations, resulting often in erroneous schizophrenic diagnoses. Dysfunctional episodes are typically from 2 to 4 months in length, but may occur in periods of appreciably shorter duration. Although no absolute rule exists in this regard, the initial episode for men is often of a manic nature, whereas those for women are more often depressive in character. Distinctions are made between Bipolar I and Bipolar II, the latter characterized by the interposition of one or more major depressive episodes.

General Clinical Picture (Euphoric and Hostile Types)

For those of the "euphoric" type, there is an exuberance, a zestful energy and jovial mood among euphorics that is lacking in schizophrenically fragmented patients. Furthermore, their ideas and hyperactivity, although tending to be connected only loosely to reality, have an intelligible logic to them and are colored by a consistent mood of affability and congeniality which evokes feelings of sympathy and goodwill on the part of others. In contrast, the behaviors and ideas of the disorganized schizophrenic patients are extremely vague, disjointed, and bizarre; moreover, their emotional moods are more varied and changeable, inconsistent with their thoughts and actions and difficult to grasp and relate to, let alone empathize with.

Euphorics tend, albeit briefly, to infect others with their conviviality and buoyant optimism. Many are extremely clever and witty, rattling off puns and rhymes and playing cute and devilish tricks. However, their humor and mischievousness begin to drain others, who quickly tire of the incessant and increasingly irrational quality of their forced sociability. In addition to frenetic excitement and their impulsive and reckless race from one topic to another, these patients often display an annoying pomposity and self-expansiveness. Their boundless conceit, pretense, boastfulness, and self-aggrandizement become extremely trying and exasperating and often destroy what patience and goodwill these patients previously evoked from others.

Hostile excitement, one variant of the bipolar syndrome, differs appreciably from the euphoric type of this syndrome. In contrast to the rather cheerful and buoyant hyperactivity seen in euphoric excitement, these patients move about in a surly and truculent manner and explode into uncontrollable rages during which they threaten and occasionally physically assault others with little or no provocation. They may unleash a torrent of abuse and storm about defiantly, cursing and voicing bitterness and contempt for all. Quite unpredictably, they may lunge at and assail passersby and shout obscenities at unseen hallucinated attackers and persecutors. It is this quality of irrational belligerence and fury, the frenzied lashing out, that distinguishes this disorder from others. We might note, parenthetically, that since the advent of the major psychopharmacological drugs, the incidence of such acting out in hospitalized patients has been markedly reduced.

Prevailing Treatment Options

There are several goals that should be kept in mind when treating Bipolar Disorder. The first task is to alleviate the patient's acute behavioral excesses, to remedy problems of life stemming from the disorder, and to seek to prevent future manic episodes. The behavior of bipolar patients during their manic episodes is frequently extremely severe and self-destructive; hospitalization is often called for, brief though it may be, so as to moderate the patient's erratic and intense moods.

Studies have been carried out to treat acute mania, to stabilize patients, and to prevent recurrences. Lithium (as well as valproate and its divalproex formulation) is clearly the standard mode of pharmacologic treatment today. Its efficacy is reasonably good (Nathan & Gorman, 2002; Rosenbaum, Fava, Nierenberg, & Sachs, 1995), although lithium does not achieve a sustained remission for many of these patients.

Although pharmacological interventions appear to be the primary treatment for Bipolar Disorder, psychotherapeutic methods are often effective in increasing compliance to the medication regimen, reduce hospitalizations and relapse, and strengthen the ability to cope with precipitants, as well as improve the quality of life. Although therapy can be problematic during a patient's manic episode, attention can be directed, as things come under a degree of control, to methods that seek to repair the difficulties the patient has created. In this regard, cognitive-behavioral approaches are often useful, as are interpersonal therapies (Nathan & Gorman, 2002; Rosenbaum et al., 1995; Roth & Fonagy, 1996). Where appropriate to the nature and severity of the syndrome, consideration should also be given to the use of psychoeducational, social, family, or group therapies (Dion & Pollack, 1992; Michels & Marzuk, 1993; Swan, Sorrell, MacVicar, Durham, & Matthews, 2004).

Personalized Psychotherapy

Euphoric excitement occurs with reasonable frequency in several pathological patterns; in most, it tends to last for periods of less than 2 or 3 months.

Euphoric Mania among Sociable/Histrionic Personalities

Histrionic patterns are particularly susceptible to this disorder because they are consistent with these personalities' characteristic gregarious style. Confronted with severe separation anxieties or anticipating a decline or loss of social approval, these personalities may simply intensify their habitual strategy until it reaches the rather forced and frantic congeniality we term "euphoric mania." Here we observe a frenetic search for attention, a release of tension through hyperactivity, and a protective effort to stave off an undercurrent of depressive hopelessness, as illustrated in the following case.

Case 2.6, Maya Z., 39

Presenting Picture

Maya had been on her own for almost a year following the ending of an affair with a married man that had lasted for 5 years. She had been mildly dysthymic for several weeks thereafter, but she insisted that she "was glad it was all over with." Her coworkers at the department store in which she was employed as a buyer began to notice a marked brightening of her spirits several weeks prior to her "breakdown." Maya's "chipper mood" grew with each passing day until it became overtly extreme and irrational. She began talking incessantly and inappropriately, which was especially noticeable during company meetings. She would skip from one topic to the next and be uncontainable when telling lewd stories and jokes. She sought attention from anyone who came near. This attention seeking eventually spread beyond fellow employees to customers. Her indiscretions and the frightening quality of her pseudo-exuberance prompted her supervisor to recommend that she be seen by the store medic, who subsequently referred Maya for psychiatric treatment.

Initial Impressions

Maya exhibited a primary histrionic personality with some antisocial features. The more antisocial aspects were seen through the quest for attention through exaggerated and often grotesque attempts to manipulate others and "get a rise" through shock value. Always active in her interactions with her environment, her stable source of shock value (i.e., the affair) had been effectively dislodged, which appeared to threaten her ability to gain the attention to which she had become accustomed, and her uncertainty and emptiness appeared to fuel her energized quest to be center-stage. Response in the initial session required this tendency to be countered through a steadfast demeanor on the part of the therapist. Attempts at provocations were allowed to pass without incidence, but he did place emphasis on understanding her emotive experience by reflecting aspects of her interpersonal frustration, as evidenced by her flighty and fickle affect, as well as her current sense of emptiness having experienced a loss "maybe greater than you'd want to admit."

Domain Analysis

Maya was administered the MCMI and was prescribed Depakote after her first session. Results of the Grossman Facet Scales of the MCMI noted the following problematic domains:

> *Interpersonally Attention Seeking:* Maya was characteristically provocative and seductive in her interactions with others, but could always effectively market herself in better times (less appropriately/effectively during her current Axis I condition). She was especially adept at pushing buttons of others, knowing who might respond as she wished.

Expressively Dramatic: Known to be labile in expressed behavior, Maya not only was solicitous, but proudly proclaimed, "Believe me, I know where to put the exclamation point." The euphoric aspects of her condition took on the distinct quality of melodrama, as if she knew she was performing.

Acting-Out (Intrapsychic) Mechanism: Deep feelings of emptiness and desperation gave way in Maya to impulsive, precipitous, and unsuppressed discharges of inappropriate and aggravating exchanges and utterances. Some of these appeared to be so inappropriate as to be under some conscious control.

Therapeutic Steps

As therapy began and her medication began taking effect, thus stabilizing her mood, Maya's hyperactive behavior gradually diminished, and discussions took on a supportive reassuring character, also including some gestalt techniques which gave her opportunities to ventilate. That is, she was able to speak more freely of her concerns and disappointments through the "empty chair" and other techniques, allowing her to gain insight in the moment. Support and ventilation together appeared to be quite beneficial for Maya, who began to verbalize her desires to "be the bad girl," thus providing for her some explanation for her *acting-out defenses.* Following these revelations, it was important to initiate interpersonal measures (e.g., L. S. Benjamin, 2005) with her excessive dependence on the *attention* of others. Further techniques of cognitive reframing and altering interpersonal behavior proved useful in reducing her susceptibility to troublesome life situations and gave her strategies beyond *dramatic expression* to ward off frustrations in feeling noticed, appreciated, and understood. Flightiness and attention seeking, as well as her dramatic expressiveness, were also dealt with through a coordinated program of relevant cognitive-behavioral techniques aimed at reinforcing against possible relapses.

Euphoric Mania among Needy/Dependent Personalities

In the dependent pattern we see a marked, although usually temporary, reversal of these patients' more subdued and acquiescent coping style. Their effusive hyperactivity, their happy-go-lucky air, their boundless energy and buoyant optimism are a front, an act in which they try to convince themselves as well as others that all will be well; in short, it is a desperate effort to counter the beginning signs of hopelessness and depression, a last-ditch attempt to deny what they really feel and to recapture the attention and security they fear they have lost.

Euphoric Mania among Confident/Narcissistic Personalities

These personalities evidence a self-exalted and pompous variant of euphoric excitement. Faced with realities that shatter their illusions of significance and omnipotence, they become frightened, lose their perspective, and frantically seek to regain their status.

No longer secure in their image of superiority, they attempt through their euphoric behaviors to instill or revive the blissful state of their youth, when their mere existence was of value in itself. Thus, narcissists are driven into their excited state in the hope of reestablishing an exalted status and not to recapture support and nurture from others, as is the case among the dependents.

Euphoric and Hostile Mania among Shy/Avoidant and Retiring/Schizoid Personalities

These personalities exhibit brief and rather frenzied episodes of euphoric excitement in an attempt to counter the frightening anxieties of depersonalization. Here, for a fleeting period, they may burst out of their more usual retiring and unsociable pattern and into a bizarre conviviality. The wild, irrational, and chaotic character of their exuberance tends to distinguish their euphoric episodes from those of others.

These patients often experience brief hostile episodes, usually as a consequence of excessive social demands and responsibilities or events that threaten to reactivate the anguish of the past. As in the case of the ambivalent patterns, these patients often brutalize themselves during their aggressive fury as much as they do others.

Hostile Mania among Capricious/Borderline Personalities

The *mood* disorder features of the borderline are rather mixed and erratic, varying in quality and focus according to the patient's special vulnerabilities. It is essentially a composite of depression and hostility, although not as extreme as either when one of these is the predominant affect. Quite often we see an incessant despair and suffering, an agitated pacing, a wringing of hands, and an apprehensiveness and tension that are unrelieved by comforting reassurances. The primary components at these times are hostile depressive complaints and a demanding and querulous irritability. These patients may bemoan their sorry state and their desperate need for others to attend to their manifold physical ailments, pains, and incapacities. In other borderlines, the depressive picture is colored less by critical and demanding attitudes, and more by self-blame and guilt. In others still, we see anxious self-doubting, expressions of self-hate, a preoccupation with impending disasters, suicidal thoughts, feelings of unworthiness, and delusions of shame and sin. Borderlines are especially prone, however, to agitated depressions. These disorders are an extension of their personality style: unstable relationships and feelings, self-destructiveness, identity confusion, complaints, irritability, and grumbling discontent, usually interwoven with expressions of guilt and self-condemnation. Their habitual style of acting out their conflicts and ambivalent feelings becomes more pronounced at these times and results in vacillations between bitterness and resentment, on the one hand, and intropunitive self-deprecation, on the other.

Hostile Mania among Suspicious/Paranoid Personalities

These personalities are particularly prone to this disorder because they are hypersensitive to betrayal and have learned to cope with threat by acting out aggressively. Faced with repeated failures, humiliations, and frustrations, their limited controls may be overrun by deeply felt and undischarged angers and resentments. These forces, carrying with them the memories and emotions of the past, surge unrestrainedly to the surface and break out into wild and irrational displays and uncontrollable rage.

Hostile Mania among Conscientious/Compulsive Personalities

These persons may exhibit brief but highly charged hostile outbursts should adverse circumstances lead them to relinquish their normal controls. The buildup of repressed resentments, concealed for years under a veneer of conformity, occasionally erupts into the open when they have felt betrayed by those in whom they have placed their faith. During their rage, it is not unusual for these patients to brutalize themselves as well as others. For example, they may tear off their clothes, smash their fists and lacerate their bodies, thereby suffering more themselves than do their assailants and betrayers. Their violent discharge of pent-up animosity is usually followed by a return to their former controlled state. In many cases, however, these patients may begin to exhibit one of the other psychotic disorders following their hostile episode. Most common among these are the disorders labeled "motor rigidity" and "agitated depression."

Case 2.7, Alan M., 42

Presenting Picture

Alan's occasional experiences of hypomanic excitement were most uncharacteristic yet possibly understandable dynamically. He regularly looked composed, and even uptight, at the behavioral or motoric level; his thoughts and verbalizations, however, would quickly race ahead. During some occasions, he exhibited short spells of physical hyperactivity as well. This was, in most regards, a reversal of his acquiescent and subdued lifestyle as a loyal father and control room supervisor. However, Alan's most recent hostile manic episode was of a different breed. Walking calmly out of the control room one day, he snapped; that is, he experienced a temporary state by which he failed to deny and counteract sudden upsurges of troubling thoughts and feelings with which he feared he could not cope. The result was a series of smashed windows, incessant screaming, and an aftermath of berated employees now filing complaints. Alan left the office in a rage, squealing his tires as he drove off, and, in a huff followed by a sudden outburst of tears and contrition, he drove directly to the nearest emergency room asking desperately for a psychiatrist.

Initial Impressions

Never one to rock the boat, by his own admission, Alan felt utterly devastated by the explosion. "It's not that I don't get angry, it's that I don't fail to control for my anger." He noted that daily feelings of agitation "are always under control," and that though he feels many series of thoughts that are unpleasant, "I usually do my very best to keep them under wraps." Dedicated, loyal, and conscientious to a fault, Alan disallowed any thoughts of being overwhelmed by any circumstance. A therapeutic connection needed to be respectful of his boundaries on this; short-term exploration of deeper seated hostilities, at the outset, were rejected (see therapeutic steps). The initial session took on the qualities of a crisis intervention session, with the therapist playing an active-ally role; in essence, he took on the qualities of a parent to help Alan regain some of his characteristic defenses.

Domain Analysis

Following the administration of the MCMI with Grossman Facet Scales, as well as the clinician's MG-PDC, the following aspects of Alan's personality were uncovered as most salient:

Cognitively Constricted: Overly adherent to rules and regulations, Alan sought solace in established means of understanding the world. Novel ideas were notably upsetting to him; traditional values and customs, which determined his life roles, were much more comfortable than any means of self-expression.

Conscientious Self-Image: Perhaps the most troubling aspect of his "breakdown" was that Alan felt disengaged from the self for which he felt he was always known. He had done "unconscionable things" during his outbreak and felt that he needed some act of contrition.

Reaction-Formation (Intrapsychic) Mechanism: Alan's life may well have been defined by "doing the right thing." He was somewhat Pollyannaish in his typical positive spin on unpleasant feelings, fought against more dangerous impulses by engaging in upstanding behaviors, and dealt with hostility by working toward a supervisory position in his company.

Therapeutic Steps

As a matter of course with bipolar patients, pharmaceutical treatment (in this case, lithium treatment) was introduced, and Alan's hostile mania was then explored through reassurance and ventilation procedures. The use of ventilation proved counterproductive; essentially, Alan ardently denied and refused the distressing thoughts and impulses he had so well under control prior to his recent manic attack. This was an example of how a catalytic sequence, when not fully examined, may be ineffective: Although for optimal mental health, Alan would need to address his *reaction formations,* this timing (and even this intervention) was not the appropriate placement. A shift in strategy was made, directed at supporting his controls, enabling the therapist to make subtle modifications (adding only a modicum of flexibility) to Alan's *constricted cognitions,* leaving them largely unchanged but adding "only one alternative" to select cognitive strategies. In this manner, Alan was able to effectively gain control over that which was unleashed during his manic episode. With his jurisdiction restored, it was important, as a last stage of this brief therapy, to explore aspects of Alan's self-image, which had been depleted through his recent experience. A series of cognitive reframing and self-actualizing approaches were beneficial in restoring his perceptions of *conscientiousness*. This culminated in Alan's disorder appearing to resolve itself. Although further treatment was suggested, Alan preferred, at this point, to simply return to his formerly organized and systematic lifestyle. Had he the wherewithal and motivation to continue for an extended period, the methods of psychodynamic/object relations therapy would have been profitably employed to help him uncover his deeper conflicts, to develop alternative mechanisms to his reaction-formation, and to lend some flexibility to his tightly compartmentalized intrapsychic structure. Again, the process of unpacking these many layers of his conflicts and their resolutions would need to be done in a careful, step-by-step manner.

Hostile Mania among Skeptical/Negativistic Personalities

Negativists also exhibit brief episodes of hostile excitement, often associated with self-mutilation. Their behaviors, however, do not come as a total surprise to former associates because the symptoms of the disorder are but extreme variants of their lifelong pattern of hostile irritability and behavioral unpredictability. Not uncommonly, these hostile discharges covary with "agitated depressions."

Hostile Mania among Confident/Narcissistic Personalities

In these patients, we observe less of the physically vicious and cruel forms of excited hostility than is seen in the patterns noted previously. Rather, we observe an arrogant grandiosity characterized by verbal attacks and bombast. Anger and fury in these patients tend to take the form of oral vituperation and argumentativeness; there is a flow of irrational and caustic comments in which they upbraid and denounce others as inferior, stupid, and beneath contempt. This withering onslaught has little objective justification, is chaotic and highly illogical, often colored by delusions and hallucinations, and is directed in a wild, scathing, and hit-or-miss fashion in which they lash out at those who have failed to acknowledge the exalted status in which they view themselves.

CHAPTER 3

Personalized Therapy of Acute, Posttraumatic, and Generalized Anxiety Syndromes

Among the most unpleasant yet common experiences is that of anxiety in any of its diverse forms, as we elaborate in this and the next two chapters. Discomforting though it may be, anxiety plays a central role in the adaptive repertoire of all organisms; as a signal of danger, it mobilizes the individual's coping reaction to threat. Moreover, anxiety is involved in all forms of psychopathology, either as a symptomatic expression of psychological tension or as a stimulant either to adaptive or problematic coping. Because of its universality, however, we have restricted the usage of the term to the major conditions in which apprehension and emotional tension are prominent features of the clinical picture.

In the acute anxiety or panic syndromes, as we shall describe them, the utility of anxiety as a beneficial alerting signal has been undone. Anxious patients are often unable to locate the source of their apprehension; further, they often experience such unbearable distress that their coping efforts become disorganized. Thus, once these anxieties are aroused, they frequently continue to mount; unable to identify a reason for their fearful expectations, patients' anxiety generalizes and attaches itself often to entirely incidental events and objects in their environment. In this way, anxiety is not only disruptive in its own right, but it plants the seeds for its own perpetuation.

As will be evident in this chapter, pure or "simple" anxieties are a signal that patients have *not* been able to curtail the distress they feel. However, most patients do use anxiety's alerting signal to neutralize the feelings of stress. This is often done by focusing the stressful feeling on a specific external source (e.g., phobia) or transforming it into a bodily dysfunction (e.g., conversion). Anxiety syndromes, in contrast to mood disorders, *activate* the patient to seek relief. Mood disorders, such as the depressive syndromes, indicate a passive withdrawal from seeking a psychic resolution to one's difficulties, a "giving up" mentality, so to speak. Hence, there are few psychic transformations among the various mood disorders, but there are several neutralizing transformations in what we prefer to term "complex anxiety syndromes."

Even in the anxiety-driven syndromes, where rather distinctive and dramatic symptoms are often present (e.g., obsession or conversion), we note that in most cases there is a coexistence of several symptoms that covary and are interchangeable over time; these symptoms wax and wane in their potency and clarity during the course of a disorder, thereby complicating efforts to assign a single symptom label to the disorder. Thus, despite the long-established tradition of referring to a disorder in terms of its most dramatic symptom, most patients exhibit *intraindividual variability*, that is, display certain symptoms at one time and place and different symptoms at other times and places.

Two directions seem reasonable toward the goal of finding therapeutic solutions: systematic multivariate research designed to determine which symptoms covary or cluster together in the same patient, and systematic research to determine whether each of these multivariate symptom clusters are correlated with particular personality patterns whose basic traits (e.g., attitudes or coping strategies) could logically account for its correlated symptom cluster.

The clinical types described in this chapter, and their corresponding personality dispositions, represent the results of such an effort. Here we bring together the findings of multivariate cluster studies and the theoretical schema of pathological personality patterns described in Millon (1996a). As noted previously, although extensive research has not been done to validate the specific typology to be presented, it may serve as a useful model for further systematic studies.

Let us note before we proceed that investigators utilizing multivariate analysis have not uncovered identical symptom clusters. This lack of correspondence arises for a number of reasons: The factorial methods they have employed have differed; the populations they have used for their respective samples often were not comparable; and the measures on which they based their data tapped different clinical features. Thus, in the groupings presented in the previous chapter and in this one, we have taken a measure of liberty by selecting only those clusters that logically appear to correlate with established pathological personality patterns. It will be evident in the following discussion that we have *not* asserted that a one-to-one correspondence exists between a particular personality pattern and a particular complex syndrome; rather, as the evidence of our own research suggests, certain personality patterns are *more likely* to exhibit certain syndromes than they are others. This loosely fitting model of personality pattern–clinical syndrome correspondence is presented in the following discussion of the anxiety-related disorders; for example, we note that the Obsessive-Compulsive Disorder occurs not in one, but in several personality patterns, although with greater probability in some than in others.

As noted, simple anxiety reactions are relatively clear-cut and uncontaminated, and hence tend to be understandable and appropriate, given the nature of the external precipitant. Complex anxiety syndromes, in contrast, are often irrational, overdriven, and "symbolic"; they seem unnecessarily complicated and intricate and appear to bring surplus elements to bear on minimally troublesome situations. The reason, as in obsessions, phobias, and conversions, is the intrusion of deeply rooted clinically pathological adaptive strategies. Inner forces, biophysical or learned, override present realities and become the primary stimulus to which the patient responds. Anxious behavior, then, is less a function of present precipitants than of the chemical dysfunctions and/or the past associations they evoke. It is this primacy of either or both biological sensitivity or of reactivated past experiences that gives the complex syndrome patient's clinical picture much of its irrational and symbolic quality; the bizarre or "hidden meaning" of the patient's response can be understood if it is seen in terms of these inner-stimulus intrusions.

In addition to eruptions of past memories and biological emotions, patients' responses are distorted in accord with their habitual style of functioning. The behaviors that the patient exhibits are rational and appropriate if seen in terms of the emotions and memories that have been stirred up; however, they are quite bizarre and illogical if they are seen in terms of objective reality. In short, the patient's "symbolic" symptoms represent the direct consequences of intrusions of the past and of chemistry and the complicated strategies the patient employs to deal with them. These behavioral, cognitive, and intrapsychic convolutions contrast markedly with the relatively direct and simple responses that characterize simple anxiety reactions.

Complex syndromes represent different ways of handling anxious feelings by the use of various neutralizing methods; these methods are employed most often by persons who attempt to resolve their tensions internally, that is, by transforming them so that they are only partially distressful and do not elicit social shame or disapproval.

Mood syndromes comprised the general group of ailments that were discussed in chapter 2. There the patient's melancholic inclinations and psychic struggles could find neither internal resolution nor external expression; tensions remained bound up within the individual and continued to churn away until the patient gave up trying to resolve them. Chapter 6 discusses a group of Axis I clinical syndromes consisting of what we term the cognitive-dysfunction syndromes; they reflect either extreme intrinsic vulnerabilities or the consequences of ingesting substances that markedly reduce the individual's capacity to reason and think logically and rationally.

Acute Anxiety and Panic Reactions

We continue discussion of the Axis I syndromes with anxiety, as many other clinical syndromes are transformational maneuvers that patients utilize to control or diminish the experience of anxiety. In complex syndromes, patients utilize devious and often complicated behaviors or cognitions to maintain their cohesion against the upsetting and often disorganizing effects of anxiety. Should their defensive operations be deficient or without adequate compensatory measures, apprehension and tension will ensue and perhaps be accelerated.

Acute anxiety and panic attacks often are an initial reaction to impending threat; for most individuals, the precipitant subsides and the patient returns to normal functioning. However, should the source of anxiety persist, the individual will learn to cope with it in whichever way he or she finds possible and expedient; these ways of neutralizing anxiety often turn out to be the precursors of later complex syndromes. Depending on the severity and persistence of the stress patients face, and the coping methods that are available for them to learn, patients may acquire either healthy adaptive strategies or pathologically maladaptive ones.

Our attention in this section is directed to those cases of anxiety that arise relatively free of any maladaptive pattern of coping, that is, when the patient's style of functioning is relatively normal rather than routinely disrupted. Sources of environmental stress or neurochemical dysfunction that are normally under control have been activated and rise to the foreground. It is these cases of coping disorganization for which the *DSM-V* should reserve the term "simple anxiety reaction."

Acute anxieties and panic reactions are relatively episodic behaviors activated neurochemically or in response to a delimited class of ordinarily neutral stimuli; many tend to be both stimulus-specific and uniform in their expression as they are relatively free of maladaptive cognitive, interpersonal, and intrapsychic processes.

Although these simple, circumscribed, and episodic disruptions are acquired in response to the same determinants and in accordance with the same biophysical processes and learning principles as are complex syndromes, they lack the pervasiveness, generality, and complexities that characterize anxieties that are interwoven with problematic cognitive and interpersonal traits; that is, acute anxieties do not coexist with a number of traits that will permeate and color many aspects of the individual's functioning. Rather, they are a narrowly compartmentalized set of behaviors that are manifested in response to a restricted range of internal or external stimulus events.

Acute anxieties and complex anxieties are alike in that both are elicited in response either to biological dysfunctions or to external events. However, in the simple or acute anxieties, the internal or external stimulus precipitant is not merely a catalyst to activate a chain of complicating psychic processes, as it is in the more complex forms of the anxious syndrome. Rather, the stimulus evokes, directly and simply, just those responses to which it was connected by prior experiences. In other words, simple anxiety/panic syndromes are not contaminated by intervening psychic digressions and complications.

Several other types of anxiety should be distinguished. Some are transient situational anxieties which are immediate and short-lived responses to relatively brief but objectively stressful conditions. The patient may possess a notable vulnerability to feeling anxious or panicky; the source of this vulnerability may be biological or experiential. The second group differs on several counts. They are relatively ingrained or permanent states of anxiety that persist long after the conditions that gave rise to them have passed. They manifested in response to stressful but also to ordinarily neutral and trivial events. Thus, acute anxieties and panic reactions are emotionally charged responses precipitated by rather incidental and undramatic conditions and without evoking the intrusion of complicated cognitive and unconscious processes.

We need not elaborate the behavioral and phenomenological characteristics of acute anxiety and panic as they are well known. These syndromes are not considered pathological unless the response is entirely inappropriate or out of proportion to the objective seriousness of the stimulus that is associated with it, as, for example, in reacting fearfully to the sight of dirt on someone's dirty shoes or becoming panicky when seeing a group of Asians in a park.

As noted, there are many similarities and differences between acute anxiety and panic reactions; our elaboration of these distinctions may be instructive. Acute anxiety and panic are alike in that both are characterized by phenomenological tension and by a rapid increase in sympathetic nervous system reactivity (perspiration, muscular contraction, and rapid heartbeat). They differ from complex anxiety syndromes, which tend to be unanchored or free-floating, whereas simple anxieties are almost always focused on an identifiable stimulus.

Complex phobic syndromes and simple acute anxiety reactions are alike in that both tend to be focused on or anchored to a tangible external stimulus, leading many theorists to question whether any difference exists between them. As we conceive them, the difference is a matter of the degree and complexity with which cognitive, interpersonal, and other psychic domains contribute to shaping the pathological response. Phobias, as we define them, signify that intricate and highly convoluted psychic processes (self-image, cognitive style, object relations) play a determinant role in "selecting" a provocative stimulus that subjectively symbolizes but is objectively different from that which is actually feared; for example, agoraphobia, a panic response to open places, may symbolize a generalized feeling of inadequacy or a fear of assuming independence from others. In contrast, in what we conceive as a simple anxiety reaction, we observe behavior that is a direct and noncomplex response to an actual stimulus to which the patient is highly vulnerable or has learned to fear, for example, a fear of Asian persons that is traceable to distressing encounters in childhood with a Chinese teacher. Some measure of generalization occurs, of course, but the individual tends to make the anxious response only to objects or events that are essentially similar or closely associated with the original provocative stimulus; for example, learning to fear a cat in early life may be generalized into a fear of dogs as these are barely discriminable in the eyes of the very young. At most, then, acute and panic anxieties may include simple and uncomplicated generalizations based on specific earlier stressful situations. Although often appearing irrational to the unknowing outsider, they can be traced directly to a biologically based vulnerability or a well-circumscribed life experience.

As noted, this simple and direct linkage between internal or external stimuli and a response is *not* what is meant by the concept of a complex syndrome, be it anxiety-driven or depressive. As stated previously, an intricate chain of intervening processes is involved in what we have termed complex disorders. They usually occur in persons whose histories are replete with numerous instances of adverse experience. Given their repeated exposure to mismanagement and faulty learning experiences, these individuals have built up an obscure psychic labyrinth, a residue of cognitively complex, tangentially related, but highly interwoven memories and mechanisms, deeply activated emotions, and interpersonal behaviors that are easily reactivated under the pressure of stressful events. Because these incidental and comorbid psychic processes are stirred up under such conditions, no simple and direct line can be traced between the complex anxious or panic response and its associated precipitants. The final outcome, as in a phobia, appears as a symbolic rather than as a simple generalized fear because the associative route is highly circuitous, involving both the residuals of the past and a variety of psychic distortion processes. Complex anxieties are formed by the crystallization of diffusely anchored and psychically transformed past learnings acquired in response to a wide and diverse range of faulty experiences; this pervasively adverse background and the rather circuitous sequence of psychic distortions that are activated are frequently found among patients with personality disorders, rather than those with normal personalities. Because "normals" are not likely to have had such pervasively adverse experiences, they have little basis for developing a complex of associated psychic complications; as a result, what we observe in them are relatively clean, simple, and direct anxieties or panic reactions.

Let us briefly note a number of conditions that give rise to the acquisition of simple anxious and acute panic reactions.

The most basic of these are situations in which a previously neutral stimulus has been paired, either intentionally or incidentally, with a noxious stimulus. For example, an anxious response may be given naturally to the stimulus of a sharp noise. However, as in early experiments, this anxious response was conditioned to the evocative stimulus by the simple process of pairing the two stimuli through temporal contiguity.

Acute or panic reactions need not have been based on direct prior experience with a fear-producing stimulus. The basis of the panic reaction of many children may be a biochemical sensitivity, a disposition to experience as anxiety-producing that which is objectively neutral. Also, quite commonly, as in vicarious learning, children may have merely seen or read about the frightening qualities of certain stimuli; for example, a TV mystery in which a bloody murder occurs in a bathtub may build a persistent fear of taking a bath. In addition to visual pairings of noxious and neutral stimuli, children often acquire their anxieties through verbal association. For example, many youngsters who have never seen a snake have a dreadful fear merely of the thought of seeing one. They may have read about the "deadly poisonous" and "nauseatingly slimy" characteristics of these creatures, or may have been told, in a tense and agitated voice by a fearful parent, never to go near, let alone touch one. Along similar lines, children may acquire a variety of anxious attitudes simply by observing and imitating the behaviors, ideas, and emotions of an apprehensive parental model. Thus, even though parents may never have directly told their children to be afraid of certain objects or events, children vicariously soak in attitudes merely by incidental observation. Through indirect associations such as these, children may acquire within their behavioral repertoire a fearful expectancy of distress to stimuli that objectively are innocuous, despite the fact that they may never have had a direct or real experience with them.

If we think of the many incidental stimuli and chance-like conditions under which anxiety is learned, and add to it the effects of even a simple biological proneness or stimulus generalization, we may begin to understand why so many of these anxieties appear irrational and peculiar. Despite their strange, irrational, and often nonsensical quality, however, they are a simple product of learning, no more obscure in the manner of their acquisition than most of the attitudes and behaviors we take for granted as normal.

General Clinical Picture

Acute attacks of anxiety and panic are the most common of the simple anxiety disorders, characterized by prolonged periods of moderately intense and widely generalized apprehension and strain, followed by intense feelings of dyscontrol and impending doom. The coping patterns of these patients are barely adequate to the challenges and impulses they must handle. Most frequently, they seem on edge, unable to relax, are easily startled, tense, worrisome, irritable, excessively preoccupied with fears and calamities and prone to nightmares and insomnia, have poor appetites and suffer undue fatigue and minor, but discomforting, physical ailments. Many patients learn to adjust to their psychic state, but their lives tend to be unnecessarily limited and impoverished, restricted by the need to curtail their activities and relationships to those few that they can manage with relative comfort. In panic reactions, however, there are brief eruptions of extreme and uncontrollable emotion. For varied reasons, traceable to some biochemical susceptibility or coping inadequacy, these patients feel a sense of impending disaster; they feel that they are disintegrating and powerless against forces that surge from within them. These feelings often climax a period of mounting distress in which a series of objectively trivial events were viewed as devastating and crushing; at some point, patients' fears and impulses are reactivated, breaking through their crumbling controls and resulting in a dramatic upsurge and discharge of emotions. As the panic attack approaches its culmination, patients' breathing quickens, their heart races, they perspire profusely and feel faint, numb, nauseous, chilly, and weak. After a brief period, lasting from a few minutes to 1 or 2 hours, the vague sense of terror and its frightening sensations subside, and patients return to their more characteristic level of composure.

In those experiencing frequent panic attacks, especially those associated with open spaces (agoraphobia), there is a sweeping disorganization and an overwhelming feeling of terror. Controls completely disintegrate, and patients are carried away by a rush of irrational impulses and bizarre thoughts, often culminating in sprees of chaotic behavior, terrifying hallucinations, suicidal acts, even violent outbursts of hostility. These extreme behaviors are similar to, but briefer forms of, a number of psychotic states. Panic, however, refers to transitory states of severe anxiety and decompensation that terminate after a few hours, or at most after 1 or 2 days, following which patients regain their normal equilibrium. Should these shattering eruptions linger or recur frequently and their bizarre behaviors and terrifying anxieties persist, it would be proper to categorize the impairment as a psychotic disorder.

Let us turn to a more systematic analysis of the clinical signs of these acute anxiety and panic states.

Behavior

The overt actions of the anxious and panicky patient are easily observed. Most appear fidgety and restless, tend to pace excessively, engage in random movements, squirm in their seats, and are jumpy, on edge, irritable, and distractible. Others are overcontrolled, strained, muscularly tight; they bite their lips and exhibit minor hand tremors, facial tics, or peculiar grimaces. The tone of their voice may be tremulous and denoted by rapid shifts in tempo and loudness; speech may be voluble and hurried one time, and quavering, blocked, distracted, and paralyzed the next, as if extreme efforts at control have waxed and waned in their effectiveness.

Cognitive Reports

Apprehension is the most notable symptom reported by these patients; there is a vague and diffuse awareness that something dreadful is imminent, an experience compounded by the fact that they may not know what they specifically dread and from where the danger may arise. This feeling of impending disaster periodically reaches intense proportions, as in the acute and panic forms of anxiety.

Apprehension and fear of the unknown distract these patients from matters of normal daily routine; they often complain of their inability to concentrate and are unable to maintain interest in previously pleasurable activities and pursuits. No matter what they do, they cannot avoid this pervasive and interminable apprehension. They find themselves unable to distinguish the safe from the unsafe, the relevant from the irrelevant; they are increasingly forgetful and irritable and begin to view minor responsibilities as momentous and insurmountable tasks. Their distress really begins to mount when they become self-conscious of their growing incompetence and tension. As this self-awareness increases, it becomes a preoccupation. They experience tremors, palpitations, muscular tightness, butterflies in the stomach, cold sweats, a feeling of foreboding, and dreadful signs of imminent collapse. The fright of self-awareness not only perpetuates itself in a vicious circle, but feeds on itself and builds to monumental proportions. Unless patients are able to distract and divert their attention, their controls give way or feel torn apart; there is an upsurge of unconscious emotions and images that flood to the surface, further overwhelming the patient; at this point, we see an acute anxiety attack or panic.

Other Psychic Processes

Anxiety is experienced by all individuals. Why do some persons experience it more frequently and severely than others?

To answer this question fully, we must comment on phenomena that have become so automatic that they operate implicitly, or beneath the level of awareness.

Ineffective coping that leads to frequent anxiety and panic attacks is typical of the more complex forms of these disorders; they are essentially automatic and often beyond awareness, as well as deficient or adaptively inflexible. Complex anxieties typically possess implicit cognitive, interpersonal, or unconscious hypersensitivities to duplicates of a painful past. These coping inadequacies and reaction sensitivities contribute to the chronic, tenuous stability of these patients. If we extrapolate from three characteristics—coping deficits, biological and unconscious sensitivities, and tenuous stability—we may better understand why many personalities are disposed to anxiety syndromes.

First, because the coping strategies of these persons may be deficient or inflexible, they cannot mobilize themselves effectively to handle a wide range of objective environmental threats. Unable to shield themselves adequately from diverse sources of conflict and tension, patients must keep up their guard, remaining ever alert to dangers that may upset them; as a consequence, they may remain in a constant or chronic state of tension.

Second, the residues of past problematic experiences or distinct biological susceptibilities oversensitize persons to situations that are objectively insignificant. Because patients are generally unaware of the operation of these sensitivities, they find themselves unable to grasp the reason or source for their frequent apprehension. They know only that their distress is grossly disproportionate to reality conditions; they do not know that the basis for their response is to be found in chemical vulnerabilities or vaguely formed derivatives of past experience, now stirred up by objectively trivial events.

Third, once reactivated, these residuals upset the patient's tenuous controls; moreover, they, in turn, stimulate other emotions and impulses with which they were formerly associated. Thus, the individual not only feels a flood of seemingly unwarranted tension and fear, but also experiences a variety of other strange and unreasonable emotions, such as hostility and guilt.

Biophysical Factors

Individual patterns of somatic discomfort differ widely, but in anxiety most of these symptoms reflect sympathetic system hyperactivity. Cardiovascular signs predominate in many patients; they experience chest pains, palpitations, increased blood pressure, throbbing sensations, undue perspiration, and heat flashes. Among other visceral complaints are gastrointestinal symptoms such as nausea, vomiting, cramps, gas pains, and diarrhea. In other patients, a constriction of the musculature prevails; here we see signs of body tightness with occasional spasms, a shortness of breath, tension headaches, and wry necks. A generalized picture of fatigue and exhaustion is a common residual of daily tension and is often compounded by restless sleeping and insomnia.

Most mildly anxious states, and their associated bizarre thoughts and emotions, churn close to the surface but manage to be kept under control. If these feelings overpower the patient's tenuous controls, we will observe either acute anxiety or a panic attack. These attacks often exhibit a mixture of terror and fury. In the less severe acute attack, there is more terror than fury; violent and lascivious urges are partially controlled or neutralized in these eruptions. In panic, however, impulses rise to the behavioral foreground and account for the bizarre and turbulent picture seen during these episodes.

Although there is a marked loss of control during acute and panic episodes, these eruptions often serve as a useful safety valve. By discharging otherwise hidden and pent-up feelings, the patient's tensions may subside temporarily, and he or she may be able to relax for a while. For a fleeting moment, the patient has vented emotions and engaged in acts that he or she dares not express in the normal course of events. Chaotic and destructive as they often are, these temporary flings serve a minor adaptive function.

Some patients adaptively utilize their chronic moderate tensions as a source of surplus energy. These individuals may be characterized by their seeming indefatigability, their capacity to drive themselves tirelessly toward achievement and success. There are others, however, who draw on their tension surplus to intrude and disrupt the lives of their friends and families; they often become persistent and troublesome social irritants. Whether and how these tensions will be exploited depend on the overall pattern of psychic processes that characterize the patient.

Prevailing Treatment Options

Patients suffering from simple anxiety disorders should seek a focused therapy designed primarily for the purpose of relieving their distressing symptom. Should this be the central goal, sufficient in itself to reestablish the patient's disordered equilibrium, the therapist may focus his or her efforts appropriately, utilizing a variety of symptomatic treatment methods. Prominent among these are such psychopharmacological agents as alprazolam and diazepam. In conjunction with these, especially where objective precipitants are present, the therapist may engage in environmental manipulation, advising, where feasible, about changing jobs, taking vacations, moving, and so on. In addition, exposure procedures of behavioral and cognitive therapy may be especially effective as a means of modifying anxiety-producing reactions and attitudes; these techniques often achieve this goal in a relatively brief treatment course. Other pharmacological interventions for anxiety disorders, specifically Panic Disorder, include using a combination of benzodiazepine and SSRIs. Clinical trials have shown that a combination of clonazepam and sertraline are significantly more efficacious than the sole administration of benzodiazepines. The major benefit of such a combination includes a fast onset of panic symptom reduction (Goddard et al., 2001).

It appears fairly clear that in vivo exposure procedures are most effective when the anxiety source can be identified. Perhaps as many as 60 to 75% of patients benefit from this approach (Mattick, Andrews, Hadzi-Pavlovic, & Christiensen, 1990; McLean & Woody, 2001). In general, higher degrees of success were achieved for in vivo exposure in contrast to imaginal exposure techniques (Nathan & Gorman, 2002; Trull, Nietzel, & Main, 1988). The efficacy of cognitive therapeutic techniques indicates a moderate level of efficacy, perhaps equal to if not superior to medication (Nathan & Gorman,

2002; Roth & Fonagy, 1996). Several variations on the behavioral approach have been undertaken to evaluate their respective efficacies. Exposure treatments may be undertaken by therapists who accompany patients during their exposure experience; by contrast, exposure may be self-directed, that is, carried out by the patient himself or herself following a manualized set of instructions. In general, the results from both are highly favorable, but therapist-guided exposure experiences appear to be slightly superior.

Combination treatment of both behavioral exposure and various medications have been undertaken (Marks et al., 1993; Mavissakalian & Michelson, 1986; Nathan & Gorman, 2002). The results of these studies suggest that combination treatment does not enhance the effectiveness of in vivo exposure alone.

Applied relaxation methods contain both behavioral and cognitive elements. In general, the results suggest that modest levels of anxiety respond rather well to applied relaxation but have a lower level of efficacy among those patients with panic levels of the disorder (McLean & Woody, 2001; Ost, 1988).

As noted, straightforward cognitive techniques, though more limited in their efficacy than straightforward behavioral techniques, have nevertheless been packaged into a panic control treatment program (PCT; Beck & Emery, 1985; Hollon & Beck, 1994; Klosko, Barlow, Tassinari, & Cerny, 1990; Nathan & Gorman, 2002). The panic control program includes a cognitive reinterpretation of situations that are conceived as threatening, combined with an exposure to one's own interoceptive cues. Some 85% of those in the PCT combination approach proved to be panic-free, whereas those who received relaxation alone were only 60% improved. At a 2-year follow-up, 81% were still symptom-free with the PCT program.

Pharmacologic techniques do possess relatively rapid but temporary benefits for anxious and panicky patient populations; most notable in this regard is alprazolam. However, these medications are no more effective than psychological techniques, even for chronic and severe anxiety conditions. They should not be seen as alternatives that are preferred or can replace behavioral exposure, owing to the fact that their therapeutic effects tends to diminish rapidly when the drug is discontinued, resulting in a discomforting relapse. It should be noted that numerous other techniques, for example, self-actualizing and psychodynamic methods, may prove helpful, but at this stage of our knowledge, there are few data to support their efficacy.

Should any of the aforementioned measures of symptom removal prove successful, the patient is likely to lose incentive for further therapy; there is no reason to pursue treatment if the patient seems content and experiences no secondary complications. However, should the patient desire to explore associated roots of his or her disorder, or should symptom removal efforts have failed, it may be advisable to embark on more extensive and probing therapeutic techniques. Attention is directed here not to the relief of symptoms or to teaching patients to accept and utilize their anxiety; rather, the task is to uncover the residuals of the past that have sensitized the patient to anxiety (Taylor & Braun, 1998; Vassey & Dadds, 2001), and then to resolve or reconstruct these sustaining attitudes, relationships, and feelings. Here, therapists must proceed with caution, lest they release more of these feelings than the patient can tolerate;

severe panic attacks and psychotic disorders may not be an uncommon consequence of probing and releasing too much too fast.

Posttraumatic Stress Syndromes

Whereas many patients experience anxiety in conjunction with a concurrent stimulus situation, others manifest it sometime after the stressful event has occurred. In effect, the anxiety reemerges at a later time, a period often weeks or months after the distressing experience occurs. In the *DSM* these are designated as Posttraumatic Stress Disorder (PTSD).

General Clinical Picture

The *DSM-IV* has sought to explicate the PTSD category by noting clearly specified criteria, such as experiencing or witnessing an event involving actual or threatened physical harm, as well as events that precipitate intense fear or helplessness. Variations in the symptomatology are also noted. Some examples of this include having recurrent and unwanted recollections, having distressing dreams, and feeling and acting as if the event were reoccurring. Associated with these features is the need to avoid thoughts, feelings, and discussions about the trauma, or an inability to recall important details concerning the event. Also notable are two contrasting coping styles. For example, some patients adapt to their distressful memories by an emotional numbing and a restriction in the range of their affective sensitivities. Others exhibit hyperarousal symptoms such as difficulty in falling or staying asleep, difficulties in concentrating on the ordinary events of life, or an exaggerated startle response to modest everyday events, as well as persistent and repetitive dream flashbacks.

Traumatizing events include rape, natural disasters, and military combat in which the patient experiences or witnesses psychologically painful or physically harmful consequences. Those of a behavioral orientation speak of PTSD as a conditioned fear response that can be relieved by such methods as systematic desensitization. Cognitive and cognitive-behavioral theorists understand the patient's difficulties to be a consequence of misinterpretations or distortions of the trauma. Theorists of a cognitive persuasion, in contrast to those of a more psychodynamic orientation, see the traumatic event as the direct cause of the symptoms for the PTSD syndrome, whereas dynamic theorists see it as an expression of unconscious and symbolic significance, especially those underlying forces that represent deep conflicts or guilt feelings. Although the greatest efficacy has been achieved with behavioral and cognitive methods, there is no reason to assume that the PTSD syndrome could not be conceived of as a complex anxiety syndrome; that is, the cause of the disorder need not correspond theoretically with its most efficacious treatment. Many syndromes may be the result of complex psychological processes in the cognitive and intrapsychic realms, but treatment may be best achieved with behavioral procedures.

Along similar lines, there has been an increasing recognition of possible biological vulnerabilities to PTSD, suggesting that certain pharmacologic agents may be efficacious in reducing overt symptomatology. To date, there has been little progress in the use of medications. What has been indicated is the comparable success of SSRI use to psychotherapy in early acute stages of treatment, largely due to the proven efficacy of SSRI use in treatment of depression, a noted concurrent mood state associated with PTSD (McLean & Woody, 2001).

Prevailing Treatment Options

Pharmacologic approaches have not been notably successful in moderating the PTSD syndrome. These include double-blind studies of imipramine and amitriptyline, MAOIs, and SSRIs (Foa, Davidson, & Rothbaum, 1995).

Similarly, there appears to be limited support for the efficacy of psychoanalytically based treatment procedures. Although there is some evidence that short-term dynamic approaches result in modest improvements, the specific elements that provide for these small gains cannot be differentiated from those that are spurious (Gabbard, 1995).

It is primarily in the area of cognitive and behavioral therapy that the highest rates of success have been achieved. As with other therapeutic techniques, the exposure behavioral procedure has demonstrated a reasonably high level of efficacy (Cooper & Clum, 1989). Systematic desensitization would also appear to be useful in the PTSD syndrome. However, the limited research carried out with this treatment approach precludes definitive judgments concerning its efficacy.

Various combinations of treatment methodology have been developed, such as stress inoculation training (SIT) and anxiety management programs (AMP; Resick & Schnicke, 1992; Veronen & Kilpatrick, 1982). In studies employing the SIT model, elements of relaxation, role modeling, thought stopping, and guided self-dialogue are interwoven in an effort to overcome PTSD reactions to rape, with a modest level of efficacy achieved. Similarly, in AMP combination therapy where relaxation, biofeedback, and cognitive restructuring are employed, all facets of the PTSD syndrome have been shown to be diminished in their intensity, though only modestly. Foa et al. (1995) have sought to compare SIT alone, exposure alone, and SIT and exposure in combination. All procedures were equally effective, though the combination approach proved to be slightly more effective than those employing a single methodology. Rather interestingly, all three approaches achieved a very satisfactory level of success, but at follow-up the groups differed substantially in terms of their level of sustained recovery; the combination group achieved a 90% recovery rate as compared to 40% and 30% of those receiving SIT and exposure procedures, respectively.

Generalized Anxiety Syndromes

As an introduction to and perspective for the various subtypes of anxiety-related complex syndromes, it will be instructive to provide a brief comment concerning the concept of generalized anxiety.

Complex syndromes occur frequently in pathological personality styles and disorders because persons with these syndromes possess a variety of comorbid trait clusters, for example, cognitive assumptions, biophysical vulnerabilities, and self-image distortions. Each of these features adds forms of expression that go beyond the classical analytic view that persons with so-called neuroses possess primarily unconscious reaction sensitivities. Intruding in their responses are not only unconscious processes, but also habitual ways of relating socially and distortion-producing cognitive expectations employed in response to stressful experiences. Faced with stress—sufficient to upset or disorder their equilibrium—they repeatedly apply their multifaceted cognitive and interpersonal as well as intrapsychic strategies. Although these symptoms are similar to those seen in the simple reactions, those of complex syndromes are also a product of reactivated self-image difficulties, unconscious feelings, and habits beyond those stemming from direct biological vulnerabilities or narrowly circumscribed learnings.

There are other important differences between acute reactions and generalized anxiety syndromes. The latter usually signify a partial ability to control overt expressions of anxiety. Persons with generalized anxiety express some way, albeit indirect and symbolic, for discharging some of their felt or perceived tensions. In contrast, those with acute anxieties are unable to find internal or external measures to either control, neutralize, or vent their tensions. In simple and acute anxieties, tension is uncontrolled and consciously experienced, although its biogenic or psychogenic roots often remain either ambiguous or repressed. In complex syndromes, patients can often neutralize or camouflage the true character of their emotions so as to make them personally more tolerable and socially more acceptable.

We are now ready to survey the various complex disorders labeled as generalized anxiety. With minor exceptions, this grouping corresponds to the official *DSM-IV* classification of the Axis I syndromes. Points of difference, both substantive and semantic, will be specified as our discussion proceeds.

First, it should be noted that certain classical symptoms of "neuroses" appear less common today than when initially formulated a century ago. Moreover, a new set of syndromes seems to be supplanting the old. For example, fewer cases of conversion or dissociation are reported today, but there are more reports of what are termed "existential nonbeing," "alienation," and "identity diffusion." There is no way of knowing whether these changes in symptomatology are real or are linguistic and cultural, for example, changes due to new patterns of child rearing, a growing awareness of previously overlooked problems, social fashions, or theoretical interests of modern-day clinicians.

It seems to us that some of these changes are real and some are spurious. No doubt, there are differences in child-rearing practices and in the pressures and values of life, and between modern America and early twentieth-century Europe, to which early clinicians addressed their writings. We contend, however, that the basic processes and goals that underlie the formation of complex syndromes have not appreciably changed. It appears to us that the newer anxiety-related disorders are currently fashionable and acceptable ways of discharging anxieties and impulses. Symptoms such as conversion are outmoded, and perhaps even suspect, in our sophisticated post-Freudian age. Sufferers of these disorders may gain only minimal compassion and approval as a consequence of their impairment. In contrast, everyone today knows what a difficult world we live in and how hard it is to break out of the ruts of modern society; thus, symptoms of identity diffusion, feelings of meaninglessness and social alienation, and existential anxiety are likely to evoke approval and a sympathetic hearing, even though they may represent a subterfuge for dependency needs or overtly unacceptable aggressive impulses. In short, these new complex syndromes appear to reflect the same psychic maneuvers and goals as were found in more classical forms. They are expressed, however, in ways that are suitable to present-day values and conditions.

General Clinical Picture

What are the sources of generalized anxiety?

As was noted, the label "simple anxiety reaction" is reserved for those paniclike states found in otherwise essentially normal individuals. The primary distinction between simple and complex impairments is that the simple disorder is either stimulus-specific or chemically driven, whereas complex anxiety syndromes are precipitated also by distorted cognitions, problematic self-evaluations, or essentially unconscious processes. Thus, in complex syndromes, minor and objectively insignificant precipitants not only reactivate past memories and emotions, but stir up and unleash a variety of associated secondary thoughts and impulses. These learned or unconscious residuals of the past surge forward and become the primary stimulus that threatens the stability of the personality, giving rise to a pervasive state of chronic and diffuse anxiety.

Generalized Anxiety Disorders (GAD) are best characterized by an oversensitivity to worry about numerous and largely incidental life events. According to *DSM-IV*, the patient's worry is difficult to control, lasts at least 6 months, and is accompanied by a variety of characteristic symptoms, such as an inability to relax, the experience of tension, feelings of fright, a sense of jumpiness, and a general unsteadiness. The official manual specifies that three of the following six symptoms be present: feeling on edge, concentration difficulties, fatigability, irritability, muscle tension, and sleep disturbance. Although the clinician has little difficulty recognizing this syndrome, it has been a diagnosis with poor interrater reliability and with high rates of comorbidity. Debates in the literature exhibit conflict as to whether GAD is a distinct disorder or a subthreshold or residual state of other clinical or personality disorders. As will be noted shortly, anticipatory anxiety, or what has been termed anxiety sensitivity (Taylor & Braun, 1998), appears to be a central characteristic of GAD; it denotes the presence of a constant state of hypervigilance and overarousal in anticipation of potential psychic and physical threats.

As noted earlier, different theoretical schools advance different explanations for the causes of generalized anxiety. For example, psychoanalytic theorists propose that this ever-present anticipatory fear stems from internal impulses that evoke distress signals that punishment will be forthcoming should these impulses be expressed. Hence, patients are hyperalert to their own inner threats, which then become attached to the passing events of their life. By contrast, those of a cognitive and behavioral persuasion believe that it is the patient's belief in unrealistic sources of threat, that is, misinterpretations of reality, that produce the unjustified emotional reaction. According to them, these misinterpretations of external stimuli result from actual or generalized experiences in the patient's life, but now evoke unnecessary apprehension and behavioral avoidance that are inappropriate to current life situations. The existential view has proposed that a state of generalized anxiety reflects an awareness of life's inherent meaninglessness; similarly, those who are more biologically oriented interpret the psychic state as reflecting inner endocrine disturbances or minor cardiovascular dysfunctions. Barlow (1988), in his usual insightful way, proposes that biological and psychological vulnerabilities combine with problematic life events, thereby activating stress-related neurobiological reactions, and then producing repetitive and persistent levels of arousal that manifest themselves in unpredictable and uncontrollable states of generalized anxiety. It is this model that we will refer to shortly in noting which personality styles and disorders may be especially vulnerable to these neurobiological processes.

Generalized anxiety affects persons of both sexes, but is more frequently diagnosed in women. It frequently coexists with depression and dysthymia, and several antidepressants (SSRIs, tricyclics) appear to work well for patients with generalized anxiety.

Of course, no sharp line distinguishes normal styles from pathological personalities, but the differences in the pervasiveness and intensity of their respective painful past experiences make it less likely that normal personalities will subjectively distort reality or have disruptive past feelings reactivated by the presence of real threat. Relatively free of cognitive distortions and intrapsychic eruptions, normal persons rely on reality as the primary stimulus of their behavior; as a consequence, their responses are less everpresent and more anchored to objective reality than those seen as more pathological patterns.

Prevailing Treatment Options

In contrast to the simple anxiety and panic reactions, where behavioral exposure techniques appear to be maximally effective, GAD conditions seem to benefit substantially from cognitive procedures (Beck & Emery, 1985; Nathan & Gorman, 2002). In general, cognitive techniques, especially those with behavioral aspects added, have shown significant levels of efficacy, levels at which close to three-fourths of patients give evidence of improvement immediately upon the conclusion of therapy and at 6-month follow-up (Power, Simpson, Swanson, & Wallace, 1990). By contrast, those on pharmacologic medication improve reasonably well, but drop off in their effectiveness significantly and often relapse when medication is terminated (Lindsay, Gansu, McLaughlin, Hood, & Espie, 1987; McLean & Woody, 2001; Power et al., 1990). Nevertheless, a program including the benzodiazepines (e.g., Valium, Xanax) and/or the SSRIs (e.g., Prozac, Zoloft) for long-tem use may be quite helpful. Studies employing psychodynamic therapies have not been found to be especially efficacious (Durham et al., 1994; Vassey & Dadds, 2001), although the opportunity to explore childhood roots (fears, secrets) does appear to reduce anxious concerns for some patients. Moderate levels of success have been reported employing applied relaxation and nondirective or self-actualizing procedures. Though less effective in general than cognitive methods, these latter techniques appear to be sustained to a modest degree upon 6-month

(Nathan & Gorman, 2002) and 12-month (Borkovec & Costello, 1993) follow-up. Also of potential utility are a number of approaches that involve teaching patients how to manage a series of self-administered relaxation procedures and graded exposure, all combined with methods of cognitive distraction and the scheduling of pleasurable life activities (Butler, Cullington, Hibbert, Klimes, & Gelder, 1987; McLean & Woody, 2001).

It appears clear that there are numerous psychic and physical features involved in the chronic states of generalized anxiety; these encompass affective, cognitive, and intrapsychic processes. Cognitive-behavioral treatments appear to successfully tap into this mix of features.

Personalized Psychotherapy

As we have said, objective precipitants in complex syndromes play a secondary role to those that exist internally, either biological or learned. It is the patient's reaction sensitivities that dispose him or her to these syndromes; that is, the patient transforms essentially innocuous elements of reality so that they become duplicates of a problematic past; as in a vicious circle, these psychic intrusions and distortions stir up a wide range of comorbid clinical domains that feed and intensify the anxiety response. To specify the source of these complex anxieties, then, we must look not only to the objective conditions of reality, though these may in fact exist, but also to the deeply rooted and clinically relevant traits that compose the patient's personality sensitivities.

It should be noted that the task of identifying these correlated psychic and physical domains is a highly speculative one, as little research has been done to explore them empirically. Nevertheless, there is a rich clinical lore that can guide us (e.g., Millon & Davis, 1996). The best we can do is to make logical and clinically informed rationales as to which self-judgments and cognitive expectancies, for example, in each of the major personality styles and disorders are likely to give rise to anxiety proneness; these we provide in the following paragraphs.

We detail several of the personality patterns that appear susceptible to anxiety symptoms, and how the basic personality patterns interplay with the *DSM-IV* Axis I anxiety-spectrum disorders covered in this chapter. Where available, we highlight these descriptions with semifictionalized cases drawn from clinical experience. As always, note that some cases meet full criteria for Axis II diagnosis, whereas others present with problematic personality features and patterns but do not qualify for a full diagnosis.

Anxiety Disorders among Retiring/Schizoid and Eccentric/Schizotypal Personalities

These personalities are characterized by their flat and colorless style; intense emotions are rarely exhibited, and states of chronic anxiety are not frequently found. Two diametrically opposite sets of circumstances, however, may undergird a persistent anxious state: unrelenting and excess stimulation, or marked understimulation. These persons may seek treatment when they feel encroached upon or when they sense that they are being surrounded by oppressive social demands and responsibilities. Similar anxiety-sustaining consequences follow from marked understimulation; the patient experiences feelings of depersonalization, a frightening sense of emptiness and nothingness, a state of self-nonexistence, stagnation, barrenness, and unreality.

Case 3.1, Stan M., 45

Presenting Picture

Stan M. was a quiet and unassuming accountant who found contentment in a recent time-earned promotion that allowed him to work from home and, as he put it, "leave the people part of the job out of it." Stan was initially resistant to the idea of speaking with a therapist, but Stan's brother, with whom he shared a condominium, convinced him that he could receive help with his recent but recurrent troublesome "attacks." His typical surface appearance was one of somberness and control, albeit with some behavioral peculiarities (e.g., keeping even innocuous secrets from family, subscribing to fixed, eccentric personal "rituals"). In the past year, he began experiencing sudden attacks that manifested themselves in dizziness, overt bouts of worry, and psychosomatic problems (e.g., insomnia, cold sweats, muscular tightness). For a period of time, he was able to hide these panic episodes, but his brother eventually took notice.

Initial Impressions

Feelings of inferiority and/or guilt may have underlay and prompted Stan's discomfort. He may have perceived demands and expectations that exceeded his level of competence and tapped deeply rooted feelings of inferiority, opposition, and anger. Despite his statements of contentment in working from home in an isolated manner, Stan recognized, maybe realistically, that his isolative nature disconnected him from the interactive aspects of his work, affording him less relevance in his professional identity. Further, his personal quirks and poor self-definition appeared to create more depersonalization, which, he was able to identify after several sessions, seemed to be at the core of his panic episodes. This passivity and withdrawal, typical of retiring/schizoid personality patterns, combined with the cognitive non sequiturs and relational difficulties of eccentric/schizotypal patterns, could be seen as a driving force in what Stan began to call "my existential crisis." Indeed, MCMI-III scores reflected mild and nonpathological, but still elevated, scores on both Schizoid and Schizotypal scales.

Stan was loath to bring up his concerns in treatment, asking if there was simply a pill he could take to stave off the attacks. "Everything else is perfectly okay, I just want to get rid of the attacks." It was felt that rather than being a simple clinical reaction, this was more of a complex syndromal case, and Stan was encouraged to invest more in the therapeutic process, which began as a mix of support and reassurance, processed largely in a Rogerian self-actualizing paradigm. Clonazepam, a slower-acting agent than others in this class (Goddard et al., 2001), was employed along with this supportive therapeutic framework in an effort to equally emphasize humanistic and pharmacologic approaches, rather than giving a false impression of a "wonder" medication. In building rapport, it was important that the therapeutic relationship gradually build on Stan's increasing engagement in his own affairs; with a supportive approach, Stan began taking on more of an active role in determining what he wished to accomplish in treatment.

Domain Analysis

The MG-PDC highlighted several personality features that appeared to play a substantial role in perpetuating Stan's experience of panic episodes. Although these areas were not frequently troublesome, current stressors that were largely unacknowledged by him seemed to exacerbate these normally benign features. Highlights of this analysis are as follows:

Interpersonally Unengaged: Stan viewed himself as very much a "loner," unencumbered by close relationships. Normally an ego-syntonic feature, current demands and inner struggles regarding his relevance to his work, as seen in context with this feature, began to create a rift in his identity.

Estranged Self-Image: It is unlikely that Stan's usual self-view was that of this more schizotypal presentation; however, he did pride himself in "taking the unexpected path, and sometimes people think I'm a little weird." Combined with his disengagement, this feature served to further alienate him from his social context.

Intellectualization Mechanism: Detached from the more subjective and affect-driven aspects of his experience, Stan routinely perceived and experienced people and phenomena as simplified, objective matter in his world. Even when something appeared to bother him on more of a gut level, he explained the conflict logically, holding back any emotive aspect of his experience.

Therapeutic Steps

The initial supportive, humanistic approach was an important first step in giving Stan reason to invest in a psychotherapeutic process; although his *intellectualization mechanism* was largely an intrapsychic phenomenon, this Rogerian approach allowed him to feel safe enough to begin expressing more affective content and release some intrapsychic tension. Additionally, the choice of clonazepam, a slower-acting benzodiazepine, reinforced the idea that the medication was a part, and not the whole, of treatment, but he could feel safer against sudden panic onsets. Cognitive-behavioral strategies then helped Stan manage his *estranged self-image,* that is, his tendency to distort innocuous interactions with others as signifying pressure and demands, which led to a chain reaction of beliefs forming a self-perception of "weirdness." Altering this phenomenological view allowed Stan to reframe this self-imposed label to one more reflective of "uniqueness." This set the stage for *interpersonal* techniques employed to help him feel more socially *engaged* as he chose to do so, via such approaches as the *language of possibility* (Magnavita, 2000). As Stan's manifest symptomatology abated, he was taught methods such as desensitization and relaxation to moderate his distraught feelings and to begin replacing pharmacotherapy with these simple techniques.

Anxiety Disorders among Shy/Avoidant Personalities

These persons may experience generalized anxiety as a consequence of depersonalization and encroachment, in the same manner as do their schizoid counterparts. But, in addition, their histories have made them overly sensitized to social derogation and humiliation. They have acquired a cognitive distrust of others but lack the self-esteem to retaliate against insult and derision. When repeated deprecations occur, reactivating past humiliations and resentments, these patients cannot respond or fear responding as they would like; their frustration and tension may mount, spilling over into a generalized anxiety state.

The interpersonal abilities of avoidants are barely adequate to the social strains and challenges they must handle. As such, they characteristically seem on edge, unable to relax, easily startled, tense, worried, irritable, preoccupied with calamities, and prone to nightmares; they also have poor appetites and suffer fatigue and intangible physical ailments. Some avoidants adjust to the pervasively uncomfortable state of generalized anxiety, but their lives are thereby limited and impoverished, restricted by the need to curtail their activities and relationships to just those few they can tolerate or manage.

Phenomenological apprehension is the most notable symptom voiced by these patients. They often report a vague and diffuse awareness that something dreadful is imminent, an experience compounded by the fact that they are unsure as to what it is that they dread and from where the danger appears to arise. This persistent feeling of impending disaster periodically reaches intense proportions, often precipitated into acute states as a consequence of social encroachment. The histories of these patients have made them hypersensitive to social derogation and humiliation. Not only have they acquired a marked distrust of others, but they lack the self-esteem to retaliate against insult and derision. When repeated deprecations occur, reactivating past humiliations and resentments, avoidants are unable to respond or fear responding as they would like. As a consequence, their frustration and tension may mount beyond tolerable limits.

Case 3.2, Cory T., 29

Presenting Picture

Cory was employed as a mail sorter for a shipping company and was referred by the company's Employee Assistance Program (EAP) following an initial evaluation and preliminary brief treatment course which was deemed insufficient for his needs. Cory generally performed his work with competence and unobtrusiveness, keeping to himself and almost never speaking to anyone, even when greeted, with the exception of a muffled "Hi" accompanied by diverted eyes. From time to time, he would briefly disappear from the sorting line, first for 10 to 15 minutes, then for progressively longer. His coworkers covered for him until one morning, when a supervisor found him in his office, sitting and holding his head, unable to calm himself or to describe any reason for his behavior. His EAP counselor noted specific psychosomatic signs that were present in addition to the more general anxious state. These signs include fatigue, insomnia, headaches, and an inability to concentrate. With tenacious probing, the counselor was able to gather evidence to support a preliminary diagnosis of a generalized social phobia; however, Cory's long-standing hypersensitivity to incidental slights he had experienced in and outside of work, as well as his intense cognitive distractibility, spoke to more pervasive personality pathology accompanied by a generalized anxiety state.

Initial Impressions

Cory's presentation was marked with pervasive social disquiet, behavioral edginess, apprehensiveness over small matters, and worrisome self-doubts. These are fairly typical signs of a generalized anxiety, but it became obvious that perpetuation came from very deeply rooted tendencies. Early clues as to the nature of his insecurity were his subtle statements related to feelings of masculine inadequacy, his exquisite sensitivity to public reproach, and his lack of confidence in responding with equanimity. Long-standing patterns of interpersonal frustration began to give way to a persistent resentment and suspiciousness toward others with whom he would rather have maintained peace or a safe distance. In terms of his basic motivating aims, it became apparent that Cory's hypersensitivity to even the most innocuous slights, as well as his flights of solitude, were indicative of an exceedingly active-modifying tendency to avoid pain (harm); further, his self-protective tendencies across all polarities were becoming fixated and unalterable as his suspicions rose regarding the world around him. These features indicated a pattern described by Millon with Davis (1996a) as hypersensitive avoidant, or a blending of avoidant and paranoid characteristics. Scores on the MCMI and MG-PDC results were reflective of this pattern.

Even more than usual, an empathic, understanding approach in developing rapport was necessary. A traditional client-centered approach would have provided much of the basic supportive atmosphere; however, it was thought Cory may have become confused and overwhelmed, and possibly feel "abandoned as usual," by perceptions that he must take the lead in the traditional, nondirective Rogerian style. Instead, a sense of comfort was established by orienting dialogue toward the humanistic core condition of unconditional positive regard (Farber & Lane, 2002) framed within a motivational interviewing style, allowing for enhanced therapist direction within a client-centered paradigm. This approach allowed Cory to make small strides toward exploring ambivalent feelings (Hettema, Steele, & Miller, 2005), with considerable reassurance that his difficulties did not signify a problem of potentially psychotic proportions. From the outset, this supportive framework was supplemented by the use of the SSRI paroxetine, which has been shown to be effective in social anxiety and avoidant personality presentations (Koenigsberg, Woo-Ming, & Siever, 2002; Roy-Byrne & Cowley, 2002).

Domain Analysis

Cory's domain analysis, as measured by the MG-PDC, revealed several troublesome areas, which he was able to confirm as he gained a modicum of comfort within the therapeutic relationship. These areas may be described as consistent and deeply etched, causing repeated and perpetuated difficulties over long periods of time. These areas were further exacerbated by Cory's recent discovery that he had earned a teasing nickname at the office; what he neglected to note, however, was that his coworkers had all recently been given similar nicknames. Rather than being excluded, as was his perception, his peers had made an effort to include him, in spite of what they perceived as his standoffishness. Cory's domain analysis includes the following:

Expressively Fretful: Constantly searching for slights and derogations, Cory never let down his guard. He was always hyperaware of his behaviors, trying to assure himself that he wasn't doing anything "strange." This expressive style, of course, led to a good deal of awkwardness and inappropriate constraint.

Alienated Self-Image: Cory consistently thought of himself as "flawed beyond hope," and considered himself to be beneath others, unworthy of being part of any social circumstance. The possibility that his innocuous nickname was a sign of acceptance was entirely inconsistent with his view of self.

Mistrustful Cognitions: This domain, typical of the paranoid pattern, was evidence that Cory's personality structure was at risk of becoming more defective by virtue of greater inelasticity and compartmentalization. Cory's thought process had become unidimensional: Not only is the social world a frightening place, but it is specifically aiming to cause him harm.

Therapeutic Steps

As Cory gained trust through the supportive therapeutic environment combined with pharmacotherapy, he was able to begin work on the specific behavioral task of relaxation training in order to address *fretfulness* in his expression. At this early stage, it was important for the therapist to evidence understanding of Cory's fears and suspicions rather than attempt to dislodge them; with this approach, Cory began feeling that he was more effectively "armored" against perceived threats without having to cower in the face of antagonism. As he began to feel safer, he began to voice a desire to be closer with others. At this stage, a combination of cognitive-behavioral (e.g., Beck, Freeman, & Davis, 2004) and interpersonal (e.g., L. S. Benjamin, 2003) interventions served well to begin disputing dysfunctional belief systems and further examine effective social strategies. Through these methods, some of Cory's most salient *mistrustful beliefs* about himself and the world around him became less limiting, although he remained apprehensive when encountering those who seemed more malevolent. Symptoms of generalized anxiety became notably less frequent.

Had this not been limited to a very short-term intervention, further efforts would be focused specifically on Axis II patterns that gave rise to Cory's Axis I clinical condition. This treatment would have been likely to include an exploration of his deeper feelings of *alienation* in an effort to unburden him of his tendency to react to difficulties as intensely as he did. Self-actualizing and experiential methods would be employed to focus on affective feelings aroused in Cory when he contemplated potential problematic situations, as a likely prelude to deeper object-relations approaches (e.g., Kernberg, 1988).

Anxiety Disorders among Needy/Dependent Personalities

Dependent personalities are extremely vulnerable to anxiety disorders, especially those referred to as separation anxieties. Having placed their welfare entirely in the hands of others, they expose themselves to conditions that are ripe for generalized anxieties. There may be an ever-present worry of being abandoned by their primary benefactor and left alone to struggle with what they see as their meager competencies. Another factor that may give rise to periods of generalized anxiety is the anticipation and dread of new responsibilities. Their sense of personal inadequacy and the fear that new burdens may tax their limited competencies (thereby bringing disapproval from others) may precipitate a dramatic change from a state of pseudo-calmness to one of overt and marked anxiety. It should be noted, of course, that anxious displays often serve to evoke nurturant and supporting responses from others. Thus, the GAD syndrome may come to the foreground as a tool that enables the dependent to avoid the discomforting responsibilities of autonomy and independence.

Case 3.3, Karina L., 32

Presenting Picture

Karina, a world literature graduate student, was soon to be married to her professor, a strong-willed man some 20 years her senior whose wife had died several months earlier. Her symptoms began about 10 days after her fiancé asked her to marry him, which she quickly agreed to do on the advice of her aunt and uncle who had raised her since her parents died in an auto accident in her preteen years. During premarital counseling, she noted that she had been overprotected throughout her life, especially after her parents' death, and felt generally ill-equipped to assume the various roles of a wife. At first, she seemed to be suffering from an adjustment disorder, given her recent change in status and her anxious response to perceived new demands. However, the picture began to appear more complex as she disclosed further symptomatology. In recent weeks Karina was sporadically unable to sleep and woke up frightened, tense, and crying. She would wake, sit at home in her favorite chair, anxious and fretful, preoccupied with a variety of catastrophic thoughts, notably that her fiancé would die before the date of their wedding. She noticed that her hands trembled; she felt nauseated and had heart palpitations, feelings of dizziness, and irregularities in her menstrual cycle. Her rabbi, who had been conducting the premarital counseling, suggested more in-depth therapeutic work than could be provided for by his paradigm.

Initial Impressions

It was quickly evident on intake that Karina's presenting symptomatology matched *DSM* criteria for PTSD. Its manifestation was in the context of a person who had a more general fear of failure in independence and self-sufficiency, as she had never been compelled by need to develop vital independent living skills. When challenged to do so by her fiancé (via both direct and indirect expectations of her imminent new role as a wife), Karina invariably evidenced indirect anger and frustration while trying to do things that "are just not what I'm meant to do." While wishing to please others and simultaneously aggravated by her self-alleged incapacity to be useful to herself or anyone else, Karina's overall makeup appeared to resemble subclinical dependent and negativistic patterns, termed "cooperative" and "skeptical" in their nonpathological variants. Her basic needs were to bolster self-security through passive submission to others, while vacillating in an ambivalent manner regarding her self-expectations; clearly, there was some discord in terms of both her adaptation and replication personologic polarities. The approach to this therapeutic relationship needed to comprise and coordinate sensitivity to an overemphasized but ingrained self-perception of incompetence, along with an understanding but firm stance in addressing her tendency to confirm her ineptitude via expressions and setups of impossible situations.

Domain Analysis

In agreement with her clinician's impression of Karina's cooperative and skeptical personality patterns, the MG-PDC domain analysis revealed characteristics following nonpathological dependent and negativistic patterns, as follows:

Inept Self-Image: This domain was very clearly the most salient; Karina identified herself as weak, fragile, and susceptible to harm due to her inability to surmount even basic life demands. Understandably, a shift in roles, and a shift in caregiver (moving from her extended family to her fiancé), as abruptly as it happened, awakened many latent feelings regarding loss and abandonment.

Interpersonally Contrary: Although it is in the behavioral-interpersonal realm, Karina employed this characteristic almost as a defense mechanism. As demand required, Karina could vacillate between contrite acquiescence and resentful pseudo-independence, obstructing motion toward greater self-function by presenting evidence of her willingness to repeatedly try and fail.

Inchoate Organization: Fragility and undifferentiation characterized Karina's internal structure, and she had come to rely nearly exclusively on others to meet her needs and cope with adult expectations. Adaptation was best left to others, but this forced her to relinquish control, a matter for which she had deep ambivalent feelings.

Therapeutic Steps

Karina needed considerable reassurance that although her abandonment fears, expressed as PTSD symptoms, were based in real experience, they did not invariably apply to future relationships. Exploring these issues first in a supportive humanistic/existential framework, she began to reconceptualize her general attitudes toward anxiety-provoking feelings, as well as invest in the therapeutic relationship as a place where basic safety and trust may be built and enhanced (Maslow, 1970). This foundation laid the groundwork for a catalytic sequence to a cognitive approach, which fostered further phenomenological advances. After several cognitively oriented therapy sessions, Karina began to see that her anxiety was founded on her fear of losing the protective security of her family, first and foremost, and her dread that she would somehow fall short of her fiancé's expectations and lose him as well. During this process, elements of her *inept self-image* were addressed through behavioral and psychoeducational steps; as she became more confident, she began to challenge herself and build on basic independence skills. As she gained some understanding of the roots of her expressed symptomatology, and with adequate assurances of consistent affection, commitment, and support from her fiancé, her symptoms abated considerably. From here, Karina took it upon herself to pursue further counseling to explore the roots of her tendencies, the latent effect her parents' deaths had on her tendency to seek protection and be vigilant regarding possible losses, and her tendency to find herself in aggravating interpersonal scenarios. Both interpersonal (i.e., L. S. Benjamin, 1993) and insight-oriented intrapsychic (i.e., Binder, 2004) approaches were effective in resolving her *interpersonal contrariness* and previously foreclosed intrapsychic structure (i.e., *inchoate organization*). Notably, although the standard behavioral interventions for PTSD, such as overexposure or implosion therapy, were considered as therapeutic tools, they were not necessary, as working at the personologic level of intervention resulted in symptom abatement.

Anxiety Disorders among Dramatic/Histrionic Personalities

These persons are vulnerable to separation anxiety only to a slightly less extent than those with dependent personality traits; however, the specific conditions that precipitate these feelings are quite different. Histrionic personalities promote their own separation anxieties by their tendency to seek diverse sources of support and changing sources of stimulation; they quickly get bored with old attachments and excitements. As a consequence, they frequently find themselves alone, stranded for extended periods with no one to lean on and nothing to be occupied with. During these empty times they are at loose ends and experience a marked restlessness and generalized anxiety until some new excitement or attraction draws their interest. These patients experience genuine anxiety during these extended vacant periods, but they tend to overdramatize their distress as a means of soliciting attention and support; the use of anxiety histrionics as an instrumental tool of attention getting is most notable in these patients.

Case 3.4, Karla M., 37

Presenting Picture

Karla was a residence life director at a large university. Her coworkers lauded her as someone with boundless energy, but also noted that she was characteristically needy of stimulation and activity. Although easily agitated and sometimes demonstrating more than a little apprehensiveness when dealing with coworkers, Karla was routinely willing to don her professional demeanor and cheerlead and socialize as her job required. Recently, however, Karla had reported experiencing generalized anxiety symptomatology of an uncharacteristic nature. Following the latest breakup in a series of ill-fated relationships that she felt were marriage-bound, Karla began missing work, owing to a variety of complaints. She began reporting physical discomforts such as headaches, fatigue, and insomnia and, after leaving early on a few days, began calling in sick more than weekly. More along the lines of traditional GAD symptoms, Karla also experienced a number of behavioral signs such as jitteriness, diffuse fears, and ominous presentiments. Not surprisingly, her state seemed to be prompted by this recent relationship loss and the loss of a partner to depend on, and she now had a feeling of being "at loose ends." This was further complicated by the fact that she had, as with others before, latched onto her partner's interests and social milieu, and she now found herself at a loss as to defining her own interests and goals. In her words, "It's like he took away my whole life!"

Initial Impressions

Particularly notable to the therapist was that Karla routinely demonstrated a tendency to dramatize distress as an attention-getting maneuver, which both drew others in and repelled them, nearly simultaneously. As much as important people in her life were intrigued and entertained by her, Karla frequently frustrated them and created strained relationships in both friends and family, and seemed to nearly systematically alienate love interests, among others, according to her history. Constantly in search of stimulation and attention, she clearly demonstrated an active–other pattern associated with the Histrionic Personality Disorder, although she did not meet full criteria for an Axis II diagnosis. The therapeutic stance for a case such as this needed to balance delicately between nonthreatening and firm, reassuring Karla of unconditional regard while being gently confrontive of manipulative attempts to display symptomatology in a theatrical manner. It was important for the therapist to acknowledge that the symptomatology was entirely genuine. Any perception that the therapist was attempting to discredit the symptoms would very likely meet with considerable defensiveness.

Domain Analysis

Karla's MCMI-III confirmed a clear histrionic pattern with no significant secondary elevations, although neither her presentation nor her assessment score seemed to indicate an overall pathological personality structure; therefore, no Axis II diagnosis was given. Several domains/traits did surface, however, and were cross-validated on both the MCMI-III Grossman Facet Scales and the MG-PDC. They were as follows:

Interpersonally Attention Seeking: Karla actively sought reassurance and care by drawing attention to life stressors and interpersonal predicaments prior to experiencing physical symptoms, which later, of course, expanded to somatic complaints. Significantly, the nature of the complaint did not matter; it was simply important that there was invariably a reason for attention seeking, and it was usually used to elicit recognition or approval.

Gregarious Self-Image: Karla often joked that she was a "social butterfly" and that "this is the reason they hired me for my job!" She frequently referred to herself as the best person to "work a room," and that she knew her persona was that of a "cheerleader." Notably, she disliked job aspects that required her to work alone.

Expressively Dramatic: Karla's wide-ranging emotionality was instrumental in engaging others, and equally instrumental in pushing others away. Though many were intrigued and even enthralled by her frequent enthusiastic displays, she sometimes brought about derision with her rapidly shifting affect.

Therapeutic Steps

Despite being very sensitive regarding her attention-seeking style, the therapist was almost immediately trapped by Karla when, in an early session, he first attempted to redirect her away from overemphasizing a physical complaint. She nearly left the office, stating, "It figures, you don't believe me either. If you don't trust me, I suppose nobody will. Story of my life." She got as far as the elevator and turned around, noting that the therapist did not try to stop her. Upon returning, she attempted to continue the challenge, but the therapist remained matter-of-fact but supportive. In this manner, this exchange began a series of often challenging interventions aimed at modifying her *attention-seeking interpersonal style* through a social learning perspective. Although Karla sometimes tried to derail the therapeutic process in this manner, the therapist remained steadfast, demonstrating that he would not be overly affected by her *dramatic expression* but would respond well to her own attempts to talk through her needs. As she became reassured, she was better able to confront, in a cognitive manner, the fear that life "had ended," which was the major fuel for her anxious symptomatology. Sequencing interventions in this manner, Karla was better able to manage cognitive reevaluation techniques that were more directive than is usually employed with those who evidence generalized anxiety. As therapy progressed, it was possible to focus on this patient's high dependency needs, especially turning to others for constant approval and attention. Cognitive techniques were employed to assist Karla in recognizing her preoccupation with the judgments of others. Toward the later part of this intervention, which lasted approximately 18 sessions, it was appropriate to help instill a more genuine sense of positive self-esteem, rather than her façade of *gregariousness,* by moving toward a more person-centered approach, thereby enhancing an increased level of self-respect and self-confidence. This sequence decreased the likelihood that she would feel abandoned and lost whenever her interpersonal world proved problematic.

Anxiety Disorders among Confident/Narcissistic Personalities

These patients characteristically do not exhibit GAD; however, overt anxiety may be manifested for a brief period before these patients cloak or otherwise handle the expression of these feelings. The image of weakness conveyed in the display of this symptom is anathema to these persons; thus, it is rarely allowed to be manifested overtly, tending to be neutralized or expressed primarily in other domains.

The source of anxiety in these patients usually reflect matters such as failures to manipulate and exploit others or the growing disparity between their illusions of superiority and the facts of reality. Although they are not accustomed to inhibit emotions and impulses, their anxiety is manifested not in pure form but in an alloy of anxious hostility and resentment.

Generalized Anxiety among Nonconforming/Antisocial and Forceful/Sadistic Personalities

These persons experience appreciably greater and more frequent anxiety than is often claimed in the literature. The dread of attachment, of being controlled, punished, and condemned by others is intense, and events that reactivate these fears and memories evoke persistent mixtures of anxiety and hostility. Severe attacks of panic will occur if patients feel particularly powerless or at the mercy of the hostile forces they see about them; we might note that the perception of these sources of influence and persecution may become hallucinatory in patients disposed to paranoid traits, that is, projections on the environment of the patient's own aggressive and vindictive impulses. Also notable is the fact that these patients quickly find an external source to which they can ascribe their inner discomfort.

The surplus tension and energy generated by anxiety in these patients are often transformed and utilized to spur vigorous self-assertive action. Much of the drive and aggressiveness that characterize these patients reflect the exploitation of anxious energy in the service of their goals. Many, though not all, of these personalities possess what we have termed the "parmic temperament" (Millon, 1969), that is, a constitutionally based fearlessness or insensitivity to threat. However, despite their relative imperviousness to anxiety, they are human and therefore do experience intensely discomforting tensions. Nevertheless, their constitutional callousness decreases the probability of GAD.

Generalized Anxiety among Conscientious/Compulsive Personalities

The pervasive presence of chronic tension should be noted as a major feature of the Compulsive Personality Disorder; anxiety is so much a part of their everyday functioning that one cannot say where personality features end and where the generalized anxiety state begins.

Along with other ambivalents, obsessive-compulsive personalities are among the most frequent candidates for GAD. First, they experience a cognitive expectancy of social condemnation; every thought that may digress from an interpersonally straight and narrow path is subject to the fear of punitive reactions from external authority. Second, these cognitions and social behaviors are compounded by their deeply repressed hostile impulses, which threaten to erupt and overwhelm their controls; without these controls, the tenuous social façade and psychic cohesion they have struggled to maintain may be torn apart. Thus, ever concerned that they will fail to fulfill the demands of authority and constantly on edge lest their contrary inner impulses break out of control for others to see, these patients often live in a constant and generalized state of anxiety.

Many of these patients learn to utilize the excess energy they derive from their chronic tension to effective ends; the characteristic diligence and conscientiousness of the compulsive reflects, in large measure, the control and exploitation of anxious energy. However, should their tense and overcontrolled state be punctured, either by external social precipitants or by an acute vulnerability of internal impulses or biochemical dysfunctions, there is a high probability that a manifest anxious or panic attack will ensue.

Case 3.5, Brenda M., 38

Brenda M., a divorced Hispanic customer service manager, was diagnosed with GAD. She reported that under normal circumstances, she took pride in handling her emotions with balance and restraint; clinical impressions, however, indicated that this may have been characterized more as a "bottling up." More recently, Brenda had become intensely apprehensive, with diffuse worry and preoccupation and psychological and physical symptoms breaking through her intrapsychic controls and social proprieties. She began to experience regular catastrophic forebodings, would fidget uncontrollably, and found herself entirely unable to focus or concentrate. She also manifested gastrointestinal pains, as well as clear onset of fatigue, sleep disruption, and chronic exhaustion. Further exploration indicated that Brenda's manifest symptomatology may have been prompted by the reemergence of long-dormant fears of abandonment, wrought from recent interpersonal difficulties, or by the upsurge of strong oppositional impulses that threatened to overwhelm her controls.

Initial Impressions

Brenda regularly invested much of her efforts both in social mores and in service to key people in her life. In general, she appeared to favor a passive course in accommodating the world around her, always doing what she could to maintain devoted but "proper" relations with others. Additionally, she could be described as conscientious and duty-driven, loyally adhering to sociocultural, familial, and vocational demands. She conducted her life in this manner, almost always with a genuine but understated smile, yet her slightly exaggerated pride in maintaining her composure under any circumstance hinted at some ambivalence regarding her tendency to bypass her needs and desires. Although her personality pattern was considerably more adaptive than those diagnosed with Axis II pathology, Brenda evidenced several traits of both *compulsive* and *dependent* personality patterns. It was clear that for many reasons, social propriety and restraint were elements that contributed to her level of comfort. Among the reasons Brenda was comforted by clear, proper social guidelines was that this was aligned with cultural and familial gender expectations, although this was soon identified as a contributor to conflicting interpersonal ideas. Initially, maintaining this polite and somewhat passive conversational style was important to rapport development, as might be expected, and early sessions benefited from an air of professional decorum as she began to identify environmental causes of her agitation. As she was able to verbalize conflicts within her deferential style of interacting, it gradually became possible to utilize the therapeutic exchange itself as an example of how to gain more active self-direction. The therapist was able to graduate exchanges from a position of the expert or authority to that of a collaborator, as Brenda gained ability to balance assertions with accepting, rejecting, and/or negotiating therapeutic feedback without succumbing to guilt over what she previously labeled "unduly influencing things."

Domain Analysis

Brenda's MG-PDC assessment revealed several important domain characteristics that would become a focus of therapy. Examination of the MCMI-III Grossman Facet Scales and severity index of the MG-PDC, along with information gathered through clinical interview, revealed that these domains could be described as moderately to acutely troublesome in nature, but that in previous times, some were very adaptive. Highlights for therapeutic intervention were as follows:

Interpersonally Submissive: Brenda was very proud that she never made enemies and that important people in her life tended to protect her. However, she was at a loss to understand her ex-husband's departure several years earlier, and reported, "One day, he just said that he had enough and couldn't tell me why. I must have let him down but I can't understand what it could have been."

Constricted Cognitions: Brenda gave the impression of being very intelligent; however, her thought content could be characterized as linear. Although she could generate several explanations and plans for troubling aspects of her life, she quickly dismissed these alternative thoughts as intrusive and distracting from "what must be done."

Reliable Self-Image: Duty-bound and conscientious, Brenda took solace in her self-perception as unfailing and consistent. She was asked to describe a time when she felt she did not meet expectations; she replied, "I always seem to, but I'm never entirely satisfied—I can do more. Lately, that seems to be all the time."

Therapeutic Steps

The possibility of being anything other than unfailing was very painful to Brenda, and a supportive, humanistic/existential approach, validating her reliable identity, was a crucial first step. Cognitive approaches focused on alleviating her constricted beliefs would be important, but could not be implemented until she felt relaxed and secure enough to tolerate challenges to this well-ingrained system that, in better times, was adaptive and productive. Brenda needed a noticeable change in mood (which, at the outset, could be described as anguished), as well as a sense that she could handle discomfort and continue to function (lately, she attempted only very minimal tasks for fear of not being able to manage even routine demands). She was skeptical of medications, preferring initially to opt for behaviorally based relaxation techniques. In addition to psychoeducational training in progressive relaxation, she benefited from connecting meditation inherent in relaxation techniques with her spiritual beliefs, as well as learning to identify and moderate bodily signals of anxiety through several biofeedback sessions. These potentiated pairings of behaviorally based techniques proved fruitful in ameliorating immediate anxiety symptoms, but she noted that her worry was now manifesting more consciously. This indication signaled a good starting point for the introduction of other modalities (a catalytic sequence designed to capitalize on prior gains).

As Brenda became more cognizant of the content of her beliefs, therapy began taking on a more immediate and challenging tone. Confronting her decisions to cling tenaciously to her "tried and true" methods of problem solving was initially shocking and appeared to stifle some initial gains. However, with a moderately bolstered sense of self-efficacy wrought from her experience in controlling physical and acute psychological symptoms, she began to view these challenges as less threatening. At the same time, the indirect effect of the earlier behavioral tactics was to bolster her self-concept as a reliable person. As she utilized cognitive techniques, Brenda's self-concept became more fine-tuned, and she became capable of reducing the occurrence of absolutes in the process (e.g., Ellis, 1970). Through further thought modification, she gained awareness that some of her basic schemas needed slight modification (e.g., gender role, responsibility to others) but did not have to be discarded entirely (e.g., Beck, 1976). Through interpersonal techniques aimed at modifying her submissive tendencies (e.g., Benjamin, 2005; Kiesler, 1986), she was able to gain awareness that by allowing some self-serving activity, she was even better able to meet others' demands. Owing to this healthier and more ego-enhanced view of self, Brenda then expressed the need to modify some of her perceptions and interactions with important people. She initiated an examination of her former marriage and was able to note, "I didn't really bring too much uniqueness to the table, did I?" Through further interpersonal techniques, she was able to adopt a pattern that was less submissive and more confident. As this short-term therapeutic course came toward termination, Brenda reported greater mastery of important tasks, improved social patterns, and relative freedom from distractibility and loss of focus.

Generalized Anxiety among Skeptical/Negativistic Personalities

These patients experience frequent and prolonged states of anxiety. In contrast to their compulsive counterparts, for example, their discomfort and tension are exhibited openly and are utilized rather commonly as a means either of upsetting others or of soliciting their attention and nurture; which of these two functions takes precedence depends on which facet of their ambivalence comes to the foreground.

Typically, these patients color their apprehensions with depressive complaints, usually to the effect that others misunderstand them and that life has been full of disappointments. These complaints crystallize and vent their diffuse tensions and at the same time are subtle forms of expressing intense angers and resentments. Most commonly, these patients discharge their tensions in small and frequent doses, thereby decreasing the likelihood of a cumulative buildup and massive outburst; it is only when they are unable to discharge their angry impulses or experience the threat of separation that these generally anxious patients may be precipitated into an acute anxiety attack. Having learned to utilize anxiety as an instrument of subtle aggression or as a means of gaining attention and nurture, they often complain of anxiety for manipulative purposes, even when they do not genuinely feel it.

Case 3.6, Kevin O., 30

Presenting Picture

Kevin O., a police officer in a small city, had refused EAP services recommended by his department following an incident during his rookie year 4 years earlier. He had responded to a disturbance at an after-hours nightclub and witnessed one patron shoot another in the head at point-blank range. Even before the incident, Kevin's style could only be described as angry, irritable, and conflicted, but increasingly ever since, it had been complicated by sporadic periods of tension and apprehension complicated by acute physiological agitation. At the behest of his girlfriend of 1 year, he finally sought therapy independent of the police force, but he did not disclose the incident; therefore, the initial presentation seemed to suggest GAD. As he described his "episodes" with muscular tightness, headaches, perspiration, and palpitations, as well as ruminations about death, the therapist began to suspect differently. In a subsequent session, his girlfriend attended at Kevin's request, and she disclosed his midsleep waking pattern, at which time Kevin admitted to not really sleeping. Instead, he described recurring thoughts that would not allow him to sleep but that would sometimes get so intense as to make him tremble. Resentful of "having to disclose this," Kevin seized the opportunity to discharge his feelings regarding "being *ordered* to therapy," as well as his belief that psychology was nonsense and nothing would help.

Initial Impressions

Throughout his life, it seemed, Kevin felt trapped by what he saw as his inability to work through conflict in a way that would satisfy both his needs and those of others, as well as by his self-perception of powerlessness to face what he saw as uncontrollable forces all around him. At times he was acquiescent to authority and helpful to a fault, but more frequently he was angry at his "lot in life" as being "so insignificant I can't even make my own choices." These conflictual motivating tendencies (self-other conflict) were consistent with negativistic patterns, combined with some hints of the more overtly forceful and unpredictably explosive qualities of sadistic patterns. This pattern has been described elsewhere in the senior author's writings as the "abrasive negativist" pattern (Millon with Davis, 1996a; Millon, Grossman, Millon, Meagher, & Ramnath, 2004). Given his experience of recent years and his Axis I symptomatology, his anger and apprehensiveness had been very realistically reinforced. An initial approach with Kevin called for validation of those affective aspects of his experience, as well as a focus on the idea of hopefulness, but also carefully realistic feedback on his tendency to paint all things with a skeptical brush. An important perspective was to use the Rogerian tenet "You are your own best expert," but with the added direction of encouraging Kevin to generate alternative hypotheses to his very concrete, negative "truths" about the world in which he lived. In this manner, this otherwise untrusting man gradually gained respect for the therapist and the process, although he never became fully comfortable as a patient.

Domain Analysis

Kevin's MG-PDC indicated clear traits in line with both negativistic and sadistic personality patterns. Scores on the MCMI-III indicated that the negativistic pattern could likely be at a pathological level, whereas the sadistic pattern influenced his expression but did not appear to be highly dysfunctional. The major domains that emerged were as follows:

Cognitively Skeptical: Prone to distrust without question or reservation, Kevin readily assumed that nothing positive could be legitimate and nothing in his foreseeable future could improve. He openly criticized anyone who seemed content as "living in Disneyland."

Interpersonally Contrary: Kevin often vacillated between "doing well for others" and voicing hostile independence and resentment. He appeared to frequently introduce arguments of seemingly unrelated content, often during peaceful moments. Any frustration experienced by others in his life over his experienced symptomatology was interpreted by Kevin as a challenge to his trustworthiness.

Expressively Precipitate: There was very little predictability about Kevin; he seemed to respond with bitterness at innocuous statements, but sometimes appeared undaunted either by threats or by those stimuli that one might expect to trigger reactions (e.g., guns, dangerous police situations). In fact, those dangerous situations seemed to fill Kevin with hubris.

Therapeutic Steps

Kevin approached therapy with great trepidation. Recommendations were made at the outset for pharmacologic treatment (another problematic area was temperament/mood, which vacillated between simmering irritability and outright hostility, domains of both sadistic and negativistic patterns), along with a program of systematic desensitization. Both of these Kevin balked at. It was too early at this point for him to accept these more focal methods, for he was wary of "being manipulated by anyone or anything." Instead, his therapist began emphasizing a more humanistic approach, utilizing person-centered principles as described earlier in "Initial Impressions." By increasing trust and rapport and feeling legitimately accepted, Kevin began spontaneously voicing his very *skeptical* thought process; this created an opportunity to introduce cognitive methods to dispute the absoluteness of his perspective. With this seed planted, therapy moved toward reflecting on how his skepticism might impact therapy in a very immediate manner; interestingly, although he remained fairly guarded, he did voice appreciation for this immediacy and the therapist's willingness to fully understand and accept his doubt. These ideas were tied closely to the more behavioral domains, *precipitate expressive acts* and *interpersonal contrariness*. In fact, Kevin introduced his own tendency to create conflict in these regards. Efforts were directed at generating alternatives for his precipitate behaviors, which were really efforts to maintain a sense of efficacy and control, as well as beginning to resolve resentments giving rise to his contrary interactions. Unexpectedly, however, before more specific interventions were introduced for these issues as well as his Axis I PTSD presentation, he abruptly ended therapy at the fourth session. "I don't think I need this any more, Doc, I got it from here," were his parting words at the end of that session. Although it is possible that these adjustments in his personality constellation set positive trends into motion that would alleviate his overt symptomatology, Kevin would have likely benefited from further efforts to guard against recurrence and to more directly address presenting concerns.

Generalized Anxiety among Pessimistic/Depressive and Aggrieved/Masochistic Personalities

As part of the general dysphoric state that typifies these personalities, we often see a diffuse though usually moderate level of generalized anxiety. As with similar personalities, depressive and masochistic traits are associated with fears of loss and abandonment. The anticipation of such eventualities remains a persistent and underlying source of concern, leaving these persons vulnerable to the fear of finding that their desperate and self-sacrificial efforts will not suffice to protect them against personal loss. States of panic may also emerge under these conditions, especially when the attachments needed to maintain their equilibrium are in serious jeopardy.

Case 3.7, Arnold H., 28

Presenting Picture

Arnold, an aggrieved and unhappy man, experienced GAD symptomatology, which was hardly unexpected. He lived much of his life in this state, and viewed his run-of-the-mill existence, fraught with discontent, suffering, diffuse fears, mental distractibility, and fatigue, as the "normal state of things." Plagued by doubts, expecting the worst, and repeatedly undoing opportunities to better his circumstances, Arnold routinely created life stressors that promoted this characteristic anguished condition. At several previous times in his life, he had sought the help of a therapist but generally remained in treatment for only a few sessions, usually stating some variant of the statement, "The worst is over. I don't want to waste your time." Most recently, however, he was brought in by his father, who stated, "It's about time you shrinks did what you say you can do. He's really gone off the deep end this time." Indeed, Arnold was in the midst of an acute panic attack of unknown origin, unable to calm himself, evidencing a number of cognitive and somatic symptoms, and continually agitated by even the most benign help or intervention.

Initial Impressions

Arnold presented with a mix of both Generalized Anxiety and Panic Disorder, as well as some depressive signs. A suicidality risk assessment indicated a lack of self-worth, explicit future despair, and general hopelessness, but the presence of social support (i.e., his father, with whom he lived) and a pronounced religious mandate against self-harm prevented immediate hospitalization. Nevertheless, pharmacologic medication for dysphoric symptomatology and panic was in order, and Arnold was prescribed the SSRI paroxetine, one of the faster-acting antidepressant agents also approved for panic (Lecrubier & Judge, 1997).

Approaching Arnold for treatment was a difficult task, in that he evidenced deeply ambivalent thoughts regarding his lot in life. He was highly submissive toward his father, a retired Navy officer, and the dynamic between these two men seemed to give rise to rigid beliefs regarding Arnold's need for direction and his "attachment to a fault" to established rules and guidelines, even to his own detriment. Paradoxically reassured by criticism and deprecation, Arnold evidenced a pronounced passivity in dealing with others, although his constant deference (which was by no means limited to interactions with his father) did appear to give rise to his presenting anxiety. These passive-other tendencies, combined with ambivalent feelings regarding his needs and his seemingly favorable responsiveness to personal slights, constituted a clear profile of what Millon with Davis (1996a) described as the virtuous masochistic subtype, an amalgamation of masochistic and compulsive personalities. As the therapist began to see this pattern, a moderate shift in approach was fruitful: She maintained an accepting, empathic demeanor (until this time, she had been unsuccessfully employing a traditional person-centered Rogerian stance), but began to pepper her comments with supportive but demanding directives, such as "Arnold, you're more than due to take control of things." This intrapsychic reparenting seemed to be a very effective motivator for Arnold, and he began to make spontaneous efforts at challenging himself.

Domain Analysis

Arnold's MCMI-III profile very clearly indicated both masochistic and compulsive patterns; both the Grossman scales of the MCMI and the MG-PDC highlighted several exceedingly troubling domains, as follows:

Discredited Representations: Although he asserted a self-protectiveness and pride that he "only lets good people in," Arnold acknowledged that he consistently allowed others to label him as incapable, shameful, disgraceful, and "less than." That others might see him as any bit worthy was a foreign notion.

Constricted Cognitions: Arnold had been taught that looking at the world in terms of shades of gray was asking for trouble, and that clear, good decisions were simply a matter of following what was already established. This constricted view was helpful in maintaining safety and perceived security, but Arnold's innate curiosity was squelched by this tendency.

Undeserving Self-Image: No praise could be accepted by Arnold. He constantly sought the homeostasis inherent in the belief that he was more trouble than he was worth. In fact, at one point during the risk assessment, he muttered, "I wouldn't want to kill myself, then everyone else would have to clean up the mess I'd left behind."

Therapeutic Steps

The initial task of crisis intervention and risk reduction was followed, as mentioned before, by a nondirective Rogerian paradigm. Although this approach was not contraindicated, Arnold did not engage well with the nondirective therapeutic stance and open-ended statements inherent in a pure person-centered approach. Rather, he subsequently connected to therapeutic tasks via statements reminiscent of admonishing voices in his past, although the statements were more benevolent and supportive than those to which he had become accustomed. In a subtle manner, this healthy transference, aimed at connecting with and subsequently modifying his *discredited representations,* encouraged him to begin accepting more compassionate feedback and to begin questioning his deeply rooted view that all others would be malevolent. Simultaneously, a potentiated pairing of cognitive-behavioral therapy (e.g., Beck, Emery, & Greenberg, 2005) was utilized as a means of reorienting his expectations of his relationships and his personal future, which planted a seed for releasing his more black-and-white *constricted cognitions*. The focus of treatment from that point moved into the interpersonal domain (although this modality was also used to address the *discredited representations* domain noted earlier) and turned toward misinterpretations concerning people in his life, his belief that he must "do the bidding" of others, and his tendency to self-handicap and view himself as unworthy of carrying out his own wishes in ways that would potentially bring him success. Following this groundwork, rather than preceding it, were self-actualizing approaches such as humanistic and experiential therapy that were then optimal in contradicting his *undeserving self-image*. Finally, it was important to introduce Arnold's new perspective into his social support system. Family therapy sessions were employed, incorporating his father, to help Arnold with his interpersonal attitudes and difficulties, and his father in establishing a more equilateral stance with his son.

Generalized Anxiety among Capricious/Borderline Personalities

Brief eruptions of uncontrollable emotion occur in borderline patients, who often experience states of generalized anxiety. For varied reasons, traceable to particular biologic vulnerabilities or coping inadequacies, these patients repeatedly fear the omnipresence of an impending disaster, or feel that they are being overwhelmed or will disintegrate from the press of forces that surge within them. A generalized anxiety may follow a period of mounting stress in which a series of objectively trivial events cumulate to the point of being experienced as devastating. At other times, it is when patients' unconscious impulses have been activated and break through their controls that we see an upsurge of diffuse feelings, followed by an emotional discharge. After a few minutes (or at most 1 or 2 hours), the diffuse sense of fear, with its concomitant physical symptoms, begins to subside, and the patient returns to a more typical level of minor discomfort. There are other, more intense periods when a sweeping disorganization and overwhelming panic reaction may take hold. In this case the patient is carried by a rush of irrational impulses and bizarre thoughts that often culminate in a wild spree of chaotic behavior, violent outbursts, terrifying hallucinations, and suicidal acts. These extreme behaviors may be justly diagnosed as a brief psychotic disorder, a category listed under the Schizophrenia classification. In either case, we see transitory states of both intense anxiety and ego decompensation that terminate after a few hours, or at most no more than 1 or 2 days, following which the patient regains his or her normal equilibrium. Should these eruptions linger for weeks or recur frequently, with bizarre behaviors and terrifying anxieties persisting, it would be more correct to categorize the impairment as a specific psychotic disorder.

Generalized Anxiety among Suspicious/Paranoid Personalities

Severe GAD may take the form of diffuse apprehensions or fears of the unknown, often distracting the patient from dealing effectively with matters of daily routine. Paranoids may complain of their inability to concentrate and of being unable to enjoy previously pleasurable activities and pursuits. No matter what they do, they feel unable to avoid pervasive and interminable apprehension. They sense themselves incapable of distinguishing the safe from the unsafe. Some become notably irritable and view minor responsibilities as momentous and insurmountable tasks. Distress mounts when they become aware and self-conscious of their growing incompetence and tension. Soon this self-awareness becomes a preoccupation. Observing themselves, paranoids sense tremors, palpitations, muscular tightness, butterflies in the stomach, cold sweats, a feeling of foreboding, and, ultimately, the dread of imminent collapse. Their awareness of their own frailty has not only perpetuated their fright but feeds on itself until it builds to extreme proportions. Unless they can distract or divert their attention elsewhere, paranoids' controls may give way. The upsurge of otherwise controlled fears and images that flood to the surface may inundate and overwhelm them, resulting in an acute anxiety attack or panic reaction.

CHAPTER 4

Personalized Therapy of Anxiety-Related Psychological Syndromes: Phobic, Dissociative, and Obsessive-Compulsive Disorders

To discharge anxieties while at the same time being unclear about or blocking awareness of their true sources, avoiding social rebuke, and evoking social approval and support in their stead is a task of no mean proportions. It requires the masking and transformation of one's true thoughts and feelings by the intricate workings of several domains of psychic functioning, including the cognitive, unconscious, and interpersonal. The resulting complex syndrome represents the interplay and final outcome of these conscious and unconscious maneuvers. Not only have the patient's emotions been disguised sufficiently to be kept from everyday awareness, but he or she often manages to solicit attention and nurture and achieve a measure of tension discharge.

According to traditional Freudian theory, the primary function of complex, or what Freud (1900) termed "psycho-neurotic" symptoms is the avoidance, control, and partial discharge of anxiety. Complex syndromes also may produce certain positive gains; that is, as a consequence of his or her symptoms, the patient may obtain *secondary* advantages or rewards. For example, a woman's phobic symptom may gain positive rewards above and beyond the reduction and narrowing of anxiety precipitants; in the role of a sick and disabled person, she may solicit attention, sympathy, and help from others, as well as be freed of the responsibility of carrying out many of the duties expected of a healthy adult. In this fashion her phobic symptom not only controls and partially vents her otherwise more diffuse anxieties, but enables her to gratify her basic dependency needs.

The distinction between primary gains (anxiety reduction) and secondary gains (positive rewards) may be sharply drawn at the conceptual level but is difficult to make when analyzing actual cases as the two processes intermesh closely in reality. However, to those who subscribe to Freudian theory, the conceptual distinction is extremely important. As they view it, secondary gains play no part in stimulating the formation of the "neurotic" symptom. To them, patients are prompted to exhibit their syndrome *not* as a means of gaining secondary or positive reinforcements, but as a means of avoiding, controlling, or discharging the negative experience of anxiety.

This sharp distinction between primary and secondary gains seems rather arbitrary and narrow. Although it is true that anxiety reduction or neutralization is centrally involved in complex syndromal formations, this, in itself, could not account for the variety of complex syndromes that patients display. We may ask: Why are certain intrapsychic mechanisms, for example, employed by some patients and different ones by others, and why did certain cognitive beliefs rather than others emerge? If the sole purpose of complex symptom formation were anxiety abatement, a wide number of different intrapsychic mechanisms could fulfill that job.

This, however, is not the case. Only certain combinations of symptoms are displayed in complex syndromes, notably those that should neutralize or discharge anxiety, but do so *without provoking social condemnation* and quite often *managing to solicit support and nurture* as well. It would seem, then, that complex syndromes comprise a variety of psychic processes and coping maneuvers to reduce anxiety (primary gain) and, at the same time, achieve certain positive advantages (secondary gain). In contrast to traditional clinical theory, we believe that complex syndrome formation reflects the joint operation of both primary and secondary gain strategies. Moreover, a variety of trait clusters (what we call clinical domains) evolve as deeply embedded covariants of the primary or simple anxiety syndrome, notably interpersonal style, self-image, and cognitive beliefs.

As noted, complex syndromes display themselves to avoid social derogation and to elicit support and sympathy from others. For example, an agoraphobic patient manipulated members of her family into accompanying her in street outings where she gained the illicit pleasures of sexual titillation; through her unfortunate disablement, she fulfilled her dependency needs, exerted substantial control over the lives of others, and achieved partial impulse gratification without social condemnation. Let us look at two other examples. A female Axis I conversion patient with psychogenic visual impairments was not only relieved of family responsibilities, but through her troubling symptom made others feel guilty and limited their freedom while still gaining their concern and yet not provoking their anger. A somatoform woman who experienced diverse physical ailments precluded sexual activity; she not only gained her husband's compassion and understanding, but did so without his recognizing that her behavior was a subtle form of punishing him. She was so successful in her maneuver that her frustration of his sexual desires was viewed, not as an irritation or a sign of selfishness on her part, but as an unfortunate consequence of her physical illness. Her plight evoked more sympathy for her than for her husband.

Why do the symptoms of complex disorders take this particular devious route? Why are their hostile or otherwise socially unacceptable impulses masked and transformed so as to appear not only socially palatable but evocative of support and sympathy? To answer this question we must examine the various clinical domains and personality styles and disorders that tend to exhibit these symptoms. Moreover, what rationale can be provided for the correspondence between certain personality patterns and complex syndromes?

We previously stated that a full understanding of complex syndromes requires the study of a patient's pattern of involved traits. The complex symptom is but an outgrowth of, for example, various deeply rooted interpersonal sensitivities and cognitive beliefs. What events a person perceives as threatening or rewarding and what behaviors and mechanisms he employs in response to them depend on the entire history to which he was exposed. If we wish to uncover the reasons for the particular symptoms a patient exhibits, we must first understand the source and character of the aims he or she seeks to achieve. The character of the aims a patient chooses has not been a last-minute decision, but reflects a long history of interwoven biogenic and psychogenic factors that have formed his or her basic personality pattern.

Although each of these personality patterns has had different prior experiences, most share in common a hypersensitivity to social rebuff and condemnation, to which they hesitate reacting with counteraggression. In the *dependent and histrionic patterns,* for example, there is a fear of losing the security that others provide; these patients must guard themselves against acting in such ways as to provoke disapproval and separation; instead, where feasible, they will maneuver themselves to act in ways that evoke favorable responses. Patients with *obsessive-compulsive patterns,* particularly those in whom the dependency orientation is dominant, are similarly guided by the fear of provoking social condemnation. In patients with the *avoidant pattern,* where dependency is not a factor, as it is in other problematic personalities, there has been a painful history of social ridicule and humiliation, to which they feel incapable of responding. This prompts patients to restrain or dilute their aggressive urges so as to avoid further derogation. In all personality patterns, be they stylistic or disordered, behaviors and impulses that might provoke social disapproval must be reworked internally. They can be vented publicly only if they have been recast by psychic distortions and subterfuge.

Several observations may be drawn from the foregoing. First, complex syndromes do not arise in one personality pattern only, normal or otherwise. Second, we would expect, in many cases, the coexistence or simultaneous presence of several symptom syndromes that reflect the operation of the same basic coping aims and similar forms of expression. Third, we would assume that complex syndromes would be relatively transient because their underlying coping function would wax and wane as the need for them changes. And fourth, these symptoms will, in some measure, be interchangeable, with one symptom appearing dominant at one time and a different one at another.

Despite the fact that complex clinical syndromes may covary and be interchangeable, we would expect some measure of symptom dominance and durability among different personality patterns. No one-to-one correspondence should be expected, of course, but on the basis of differences in internal chemistry and lifelong habits, we would anticipate that certain personalities would be more inclined to exhibit certain symptoms rather than others. Thus, in the *obsessive-compulsive* personality, where ingrained intrapsychic mechanisms such as reaction formation and undoing have been present for years, we would expect the patient to display complex anxiety symptoms that reflect the operation of these mechanisms. Similarly, *histrionic* personalities should exhibit a more dramatic and attention-getting complex of symptoms because exhibitionistic displays have always characterized their stylistic behaviors. It seems reasonable, then, that despite the common functions achieved through symptomatic behaviors, differences will arise among personality patterns because patients will continue to draw on the habitual mechanisms they employed in the past.

There are reasons, however, not to overstate the precise correspondence between personality and specific complex symptoms. First, complex symptoms typical of those exhibited by pathological personality disorders also arise in healthy personalities. Second, there are endless variations in the specific experiences to which different members of the same personality have been exposed (Millon with Davis, 1996a). Let us compare, for example, two individuals who have been trained to become *compulsive* personalities. One may have been exposed to a mother who was chronically ill, a pattern of behavior that brought her considerable sympathy and freedom from many burdens. With this as a background factor, the person may be inclined to follow the model he observed in his mother when he is faced with undue anxiety and threat, thereby displaying hypochondriacal symptoms. A second compulsive personality may have learned to imitate a mother who expressed endless fears about all types of events and situations. In this case, there is a greater likelihood that phobic symptoms would arise in response to stressful and anxiety-laden circumstances. In short, the specific choice of the complex syndrome is not a function solely of the patient's personality pattern, but may reflect more particular and entirely incidental events of prior experience and learning.

Phobic Syndromes

Pathological fears were first reported in the writings of Hippocrates. Shakespeare referred to phobic reactions in *The Merchant of Venice* when he spoke of "Some, that are mad if they behold a cat." John Locke (1696/1956), in the late seventeenth century, speculated on their origin in his *Essays on Human Understanding*. In 1872, others reported on three cases of peculiar fears of open public places. It was not until the writings of Freud (1900), however, that the concept of phobia was presented, not as a simple although peculiar fear reaction, but as a displacement of a psychically based internal anxiety onto an external object. Phobias were seen by Freud as the outcome of transformations and symbolic externalizations of inner tensions, whatever its source, biological or psychological. Many experience intense fears of an object or situation that we consciously recognizes as of no real objective danger.

Different theoretical schools of thought have disagreed with the psychoanalytic model of phobic development. Biological thinkers stress the importance of certain chemical sensitivities and vulnerabilities that lead some people to avoid a wide range of the phobic objects (Atwood & Chester, 1987). In further contrast to the original Freudian interpretation, cognitive and cognitive-behavioral theorists believe phobias to be a result of cognitive distortions, selective and negative perceptions, overgeneralizations, and illogical thinking. Social learning theorists take a position incorporating both the notions of learning, such as conditioning and stimulus generalization, while at the same time recognizing the possibility that secondary gains may also play a part.

General Clinical Picture

Phobias are unrealistic fears; that is, they appear to be unjustified by the object or event that prompts them. For example, most people would agree on the inherent danger in and appropriateness of keeping distance from a large wild animal or a blaze in a building that had gotten out of control. But these are not the situations that evoke the phobic syndrome. Rather, anxiety is prompted by such innocuous events as crossing a bridge, passing a funeral home, or entering an elevator.

Specific phobias signify perhaps the most direct form of all complex syndromes and psychic transformations. Like other forms of pathological behavior, they enable the person to achieve several instrumental goals. Here, the patient does not neutralize or dilute the experience of anxiety but simply displaces it to a well-circumscribed and often quite manageable external source. In this way patients are able to control and focus any internal biological vulnerability or constrain an otherwise broad-based psychological basis for its presence. By the simple act of avoiding the substitute or phobic object, patients prevent the experience of a more widespread pattern of anxieties or panic attacks. As noted previously, in addition to mastering discomforting inner tensions, the behavioral symptom often achieves secondary gains such as avoiding responsibilities, gaining sympathy, controlling the lives of others, and finding rationalizations for failures.

As noted earlier, entirely incidental experiences of the past may determine the particular focus of a complex syndrome. Simple conditioned learning is not sufficient in itself to account for the presence of phobias, however. Phobias arise in both normal personality styles and in pathological personalities. The objects or events to which the phobic response is displaced often have a symbolic significance; that is, the external source of fear (phobic object) crystallizes a range of widely generalized and varied clinical realms of experience. The phobic object is merely an external symbol that condenses and focuses diffusely anchored domains that characterize the patient's total psychic structure. For example, through the processes of intrapsychic condensation and displacement, patients project their diversely rooted tensions onto a simple and tangible external source, enabling them thereby to cope with it by the direct act of physical avoidance.

Whereas specific phobias are attached to a particular event or object, for example, fear of animals, heights, flying, injections, and the sight of blood, they contrast with the category of *social phobias*. The latter signifies a repetitive fear of social and performance situations, especially those in which the person's actions are subject to the scrutiny of others. These social situational fears are problematic owing to the belief that the person will act in a way that will prove embarrassing.

It is not unlikely that social phobias are a facet of a wider *Avoidant Personality Disorder*, not only evidencing the problematic phobic response, but also displaying social skill deficits, distortions in cognitive beliefs, and a wide range of self-devaluations and interpersonal restrictions. Whereas specific phobias usually begin to develop in midchildhood, social phobias tend to start in adolescence and early adulthood.

Prevailing Treatment Options

It is nowhere more evident than in the phobias that causes and therapies are clearly separate. Despite a variety of insightful intrapsychic interpretations that help us explain the complexity of displaced symbolic objects, the facts clearly point to the distinctly superior role of a behavioral approach in remedying these phobic difficulties. All forms of phobia appear to respond best to *exposure* procedures, be they implosive, gradual, or imaginal. The intent here is to not only reduce the anxious phobic response, but to increase the patient's psychic comfort when facing the feared stimulus. Most behavioral therapists propose that patients must be exposed to the feared stimulus long enough for their fears to be activated and then reduced, often within a few sessions (Barlow, 1993; Kaplan, 2005). Of course, should their phobic anxiety become very intense, patients are encouraged to leave the frightening situations, but are requested to continue exposure treatment until a measure of comfort emerges. In these troublesome situations such medications as beta blockers and phenelzine may fruitfully be introduced to reduce the anxiety.

In addition to either in vivo or situational exposure therapy, there appears to be some value in utilizing supportive therapy and family counseling as strengthening elements, as long as the basic exposure procedure runs concurrently. The value of systematic desensitization should not be overlooked either (Maxmen & Ward, 1995; McGlynn, Smitherman, & Gothard, 2004). Here, the therapist helps the patient set up an anxiety hierarchy that reflects his or her fears in terms of their severity. Beginning with the lowest ranking of the feared objects, the therapist employs relaxation techniques to help the patient become comfortable with each level of exposure. The therapist progressively introduces higher ranking feared objects until the patient experiences comfort with each successive level. This use of an applied relaxation technique can be done with imaginal procedures (e.g., exposure to a photo) or in vivo, that is, in direct contact with the problematic stimulus.

Cognitive techniques have also been shown to be of value, but almost invariably when in combination with behavioral procedures. As noted earlier, the cognitive point of view interprets these fears as being inconsistent with reality conditions, as misinterpretations maintained by erroneous and distorted appraisals of life situations (Beck & Emery, 1985; McDermott, 2004).

Whereas behavioral exposure techniques for repeated phobic reactions is clearly the treatment of choice to overcome specific phobias (Kaplan, 2005; Schneier, Marshall, Street, Heindberg, & Juster, 1995), this approach is usually insufficient when dealing with the so-called social phobias; these latter disorders may be part of a larger constellation of psychological dysfunctions, such as is seen among Avoidant Personality Disorders. Although social phobias ostensibly signify a performance fear, and avoidant disorder a fear of intimate relationships, they are not distinct entities and, hence, often overlap in their symptomatology. Treatment for social phobias will therefore have to be multipronged, aiming to reduce the acute situational problem but also seeking to improve the patient's cognitive outlook, self-image, and interpersonal skills (Hofmann, 2004; Mattick & Peters, 1988). Optimal treatment results appear to call for a combination of in vivo exposure, cognitive reorientation, and social skill training (Chambless & Gillis, 1994).

Personalized Psychotherapy

Let us turn next to the personality traits and patterns most susceptible to phobic syndromes and explore the precipitants that give rise to them. As previously noted, different probabilities exist as to whom will exhibit these symptoms and why. The following paragraphs survey the typical phobic precipitants of those personality styles and disorders that have a high probability of evidencing a phobic syndrome. We present these personality contexts in descending order of symptom formation probability; for example, dependents and depressives are the most vulnerable to specific phobias; as far as social phobias are concerned, avoidants are most frequent, and so on. (These rankings are based on limited observations and deductions from clinical theory, not on systematic empirical research.)

Phobias among Needy/Dependent and Pessimistic/Depressive Personalities

These personalities develop phobic symptoms when their dependency security is threatened or when demands are made, especially those that exceed their feelings of competence; both syndromes dread responsibility, particularly responsibility that requires self-assertion and independence. For similar reasons of security, they are motivated to displace or transform any internal impulse that may provoke social rebuke.

Not only does the phobic syndrome externalize anxiety and avoid further threats to their security, but by anchoring tensions to tangible outside sources patients may prompt others to come to their assistance. Thus, phobias, as external threats, may be used to solicit protection. Dependents appear to be especially vulnerable to agoraphobic panic attacks. These anticipatory fears of leaving familiar and secure settings, most frequently one's home, serve well as a means of soliciting care and protection. Thus, the phobic maneuver achieves secondary gains that are fully consonant with the patient's basic orientation. In short, the phobic coping maneuver serves a variety of functions consonant with the patient's basic dependent or depressive orientation.

Although many of the clinical domains that compose a personality disorder should be addressed in planning a more synergistic treatment model, it is clear that the first order of business is to moderate the patient's phobic syndrome. Reducing that aspect of the patient's overall pattern of difficulties by exposure methods will often provide a means for exploring other, correlated difficulties that are part of these personalities' makeup, that is, cognitive distortions, interpersonal deficits, and difficulties stemming from their low self-esteem.

Phobias among Shy/Avoidant Personalities

Phobias (simple and social) among avoidant personalities tend to be private affairs. For them, the symptom does not serve as a means of evoking social attention, for they are convinced that attention will bring forth only ridicule and abuse. More commonly, it is a symbolic expression of feeling "surrounded" or of being pressured by excessive stimuli and demands. Crystallized in this fashion, the phobic source is identifiable and circumscribed; patients can actively avoid it, and hence achieve a feeling of competence. These features are illustrated in the following case.

Case 4.1, Jorge L., 26

Presenting Picture

Jorge L. described himself as a "loner" but wished to feel more capable and poised with others. He noted that he often felt uneasy even around family members and others who knew him very well; the idea of physical closeness to another human being instilled a sense of dread in him. Jorge had been living with these discomforting feelings as long as he could remember, although he noted that he remembered actually being "extroverted" and "a show-off" as a very young boy prior to approximately age 7. However, despite his desires for interpersonal comfort, he did not seek therapy for this reason. Instead, what had overcome him as of late was the experience of sudden surges of phobic anxiety whenever reference was made to the name of a major shopping center in his hometown. Although this was the most significant trigger, it was nearly as bad when anyone mentioned the word "mall"; further, this tendency generalized to most crowded areas, all of which made him feel insignificant and worthless, and sometimes stimulated frightening erotic and hostile impulses. For some unknown reason, shopping centers (one in particular) came to symbolize these unwanted feelings. By avoiding the shopping center, reference to its name, and references to other shopping centers or similar crowded places, he felt as if his fears and impulses could be kept in check.

Initial Impressions

Jorge would jump into an alert mode whenever he sensed those phenomena that would usually unnerve him (specifically, other people in close proximity) and broke into near panic when describing the shopping center in question. At other times, he seemed relaxed, but that appeared to be brought on only by rituals he had developed. Tentative when first meeting his therapist, he became more lucid and focused as he realized, in what appeared to be an established cognitive routine, the safety of the therapy office, that he would not be probed and "judged," and that the therapist would respect his boundaries regarding close contact. Primarily inhibited (avoidant) in his orientation, he could manage to elicit a modicum of personal safety by countering the many distracting thoughts and worries about himself in relation to his environment. The therapeutic question, at the outset, was "What if we could work to find this feeling of safety quickly and easily, in a lot of different situations?" In other words, the therapist sought to instill a basic wish of most inhibited/avoidant personalities: to feel interpersonally safe without having to exhaust oneself building buttresses. Most of the time, Jorge's method proved fruitful, albeit with too much trial and effort. As the therapist aligned with and encouraged Jorge's already established coping skills, temporarily tabling the most noxious stimuli, Jorge began feeling as though his problems were less insurmountable.

Domain Analysis

Utilizing the MG-PDC, several very problematic domains emerged, all of which were part of the avoidant pattern spectrum. These did not appear to be in place at all times, or under all circumstances, and Jorge was moderately successful in "surviving" (as he put it) most interpersonal interactions. Thus, his personality pattern did not fall into the disordered range, and these difficulties, acutely as they were sometimes experienced, were somewhat predictable and largely able to be modified:

> *Distracted Cognitions:* Jorge recurrently found himself under a deluge of intrusive, often painful thoughts regarding himself and his world; the content of this usually revolved around how he was a loathsome misfit, unworthy of close contact with others.

> *Interpersonally Aversive:* Although he sought acceptance, Jorge more actively sought assurance that he would be liked; this domain was intrinsically conflict-ridden and appeared to be the fuel for the phobic fire that was his Axis I complaint.

> *Vexatious Objects:* Deeply rooted in Jorge's psychic structure was a core belief regarding the problematic and unpredictable nature of all people and the lack of ability to find fulfillment in relations. In his perspective, most people were hypercritical and troublesome by nature.

Therapeutic Steps

Cognitive-behavioral methods made up the early components of treatment. Capitalizing on Jorge's established calming rituals, therapy concentrated on thought disputing and progressive relaxation combinations. In fact, Jorge was encouraged to hear that what he had begun doing instinctively was actually part of an established treatment modality. As a result, he was highly motivated to learn how to be even more effective and efficient with what he already knew. He was also happy to learn that confronting his phobic difficulties directly would not begin for a few sessions. The early cognitive-behavioral structure of therapy was soon combined with elements of psychodynamic methods into an effective time-limited approach emphasizing new experience, followed by new understanding (e.g., Binder, 2004; Levenson, 1995). These methods, combined, began to alleviate Jorge's tenacious *distractive cognitions* and *troubled objects* by means of self-soothing and active refuting and finding new experiences with people in more innocuous exchanges (the first of which was the therapeutic relationship). Only after moving through this corrective cognitive/intrapsychic experience was he fully ready to confront, with maximum efficacy, the more noxious, acute difficulties creating his phobic responses. Through standard phobia treatments of progressive relaxation and the imaginal use of systematic desensitization, Jorge's phobic anxieties diminished; however, he initially resisted any in vivo experiences at the shopping mall. Progressively, photos of the mall, starting with its parking lots and going to its entrance halls and then its walkways, were presented until he experienced a reasonable measure of comfort with each step in the sequence. After confronting resistance through a step back to the earlier brief dynamic model, Jorge was ready to confront, in vivo, his noxious stimuli. Levels of comfort and discomfort were carefully noted, but he was able to gradually place himself in this setting in a way that he could not before. As he was challenged with these exposure techniques, further cognitive modes began to resolve a wide band of erroneous assumptions that characterized his perceptions and thinking. Finally, as he began to gain awareness of his faulty assumptions about himself and his perceptions of the environment, interpersonal skill training was initiated to address his *interpersonal aversiveness*.

Social phobias are so deeply ingrained and pervasive a part of the avoidant personality that it is often difficult to say where the personality pattern ends and where the phobic symptom begins. Avoidant personalities may have phobic feelings about specific settings or persons that are of substantially greater magnitude than they possess toward other interpersonal situations. As noted, avoidants often keep their phobias to themselves. For them, the phobic symptom does not serve as a means of soliciting social attention, as it does in dependents or depressives, because they are convinced that such attentions will bring forth only ridicule and abuse. As with anxiety, phobias are an expression, albeit a symbolic one, of feeling encroached upon or of being pressured by excessive social demands. Crystallizing this feeling in phobic form may enable avoidants to redirect their feelings of resentment, feelings that they dare not express toward the true object of these feelings. Dreading social rebuke, avoidants will seek some innocuous external source to keep their resentments in check. Through various psychic means, the selected phobic object may come to represent a symbolic, yet real, basis for their anxieties and resentments.

Phobias among Sociable/Histrionic Personalities

Histrionic persons exhibit phobic symptoms somewhat less frequently than their dependent counterparts. Here, feelings of emptiness, unattractiveness, and aloneness, or the upsurge of socially unacceptable aggressive or erotic impulses, tend to serve as the primary sources for phobic transformations. These symptoms often are displayed exhibitionistically, utilized as dramatic vehicles to gain attention and support from others. In contrast to avoidant personalities, histrionics are quite open about their symptoms and try to get as much out of them as they can, as is evident in the following case history.

Case 4.2, Magda S., 36

Presenting Picture

Magda, a recently divorced woman, developed a phobic syndrome while driving alone in her car. She feared that she would miss her exit and be lost. At home, she spent her days with her mother and daughter; at work, she was busily engaged with fellow employees and customers. She was often "isolated," however, that is, without her characteristic need for attention and support met by others, such as when driving herself to and from work, which could sometimes be a commute of over an hour. To avoid her growing phobia about being alone, Magda managed to find a man whom she found "quite attractive" with whom she could ride. Her phobia appeared to symbolize her dread of aloneness; her solution not only enabled her to travel without anxiety, but brought her into frequent contact with an "approving" and comforting companion. Magda entered therapy after a recent intense phobic attack on a day when her friend called in sick. Fearing that she would frighten her newly found companion "on the first chance I have to blow it, like if he's on the cell phone and I start to feel lonely and get panicky," she began treatment in the hope that these fears could be curtailed, if not extinguished.

Initial Impressions

Magda thrived on the attention of other people and actively solicited it. To be alone or to have the feeling of loneliness or even the perception of "aloneness" was thoroughly discomforting, so much so that it had recently become the fertile soil for the budding phobic response she was experiencing. An initial assessment indicated that her personality dysfunction was mild, probably limited to the domain level, and included primary sociable/histrionic patterns with some dependent features. Her active–other polarity imbalance featured some flexibility, but also some conflict along the active–passive polarity. Initial therapeutic rapport was built by exploring her phenomenological view of herself and her environment, utilizing elements of humanistic/existential modalities (specifically, motivational interviewing techniques as described by Hettema et al., 2005). She began to point out these conflicts regarding her need to solicit attention versus perceptions of her inability to be effectively self-directed. By facilitating her self-discovery of "Magda's world in her own words," she came to appreciate and trust the therapy setting and the therapeutic relationship within 2 sessions, thereby setting the stage for maximizing work on her Axis I complaint.

Domain Analysis

Magda feared that "something really is wrong with me," and requested "considerable psychological assessment—poke and prod me as you need to!" Her therapist did consult for a full psychological battery, most of which corroborated the Millon domain measures (MCMI-III with Grossman Facet Scales, MG-PDC). Highlights of the domain measures were as follows:

Interpersonally Attention Seeking: Magda sought reassurance indiscriminately, focusing more on those who were more pleasing to her, but in no way limiting her pursuit of attention. She had learned to be seductive in gaining others' focus, but feared their adulation would be fleeting.

Temperamentally Fickle: Shifting from contentment, to excitement, to boredom, anger, and fear in relatively rapid sequence, Magda displayed variable emotions that seemed too closely tied with her immediate context.

Inept Self-Image: Magda was scared to be left alone, not only because of the lack of reinforcement, but because she deeply questioned her feelings of adequacy and self-sufficiency. This tendency had become more pronounced since her recent divorce.

Therapeutic Steps

Results of Magda's full battery assessment were catalytic and facilitative, as she used testing feedback to fully indulge in self-exploration and the voicing of her ambivalences regarding her feelings of initiative versus simple assimilation with her social context, as indicated previously. In reviewing the testing report, she began to notice that her other directedness took on a quality of self-identity through others, rather than being concerned with the needs of others, which is what she stated that she wanted. Addressing this *self-image* aspect (feelings of ineptitude, lack of efficacy) with humanistic approaches based on objective measures was fairly successful, but other processes were still unanswered. However, this appeared to be her "Aha!" moment and, prematurely, she felt "cured." In the later parts of this process, she began working with an exposure-based series of procedures, employed to help eliminate her phobic response while driving alone, as well as a number of other circumstances that reflected a generalized phobic anxiety response. Within a few sessions, she felt fully successful with these relaxation and desensitization procedures and decided to terminate prior to fully addressing underlying patterns that reinforced the initial phobias.

About 6 months later, Magda returned to therapy, this time feeling the need to find out why she was so vulnerable and troubled. The course of this second round of therapy more fully utilized the personalized therapy model; that is, it sought to weave together and in sequence a variety of treatment techniques to work primarily with her personality style, specifically her seemingly insatiable need for approval and her sense of insecurity, which (as something of a symptom) seemed to produce a very shallow and changeable *temperament*. Her social skills (*interpersonal attention seeking*) were of an affected nature, an aspect of her interpersonal style that was seen critically by her associates. Using cognitive methods to correct her miscalculations of how she would appear when doing this or that proved to be a helpful step in countering these personality tendencies.

Phobias among Conscientious/Compulsive Personalities

These patients develop phobias primarily as a function of three anxiety precipitants: stressful decision-making situations in which they anticipate being faulted and subjected to criticism; actual failures that they seek to rationalize or avoid facing again; and surging hostile impulses that they wish to counter, transform, or externalize lest they overwhelm their controls and provoke social condemnation.

Similar to avoidants, and in contrast to dependent or histrionic persons, these patients tend to hide their phobias, as their self-image would be weakened by such "foolish" and irrational symptoms. Similarly, they fear that these symptoms may provoke social ridicule and criticism. Thus, unbeknown to others, they displace their tensions onto a variety of external phobic sources. This enables them not only to deny the internal roots of their discomfort, but to make the discomfort tangible and identifiable, and thereby subject to easy control.

Phobias among Skeptical/Negativistic and Aggrieved/Masochistic Personalities

These personalities tend to be more open than other personality types about discharging their erratic feelings. This ready and diffuse discharge of anxiety and emotion has its self-defeating side. By venting tensions openly and generalizing them freely to any and all aspects of their lives, these personalities increase the likelihood that many formerly innocuous objects and events will become phobic-laden. To reduce the wide range of anxiety stimuli, negativists and masochists may anchor their floating quality to just a few clear-cut precipitants, thereby reducing the extent to which they are subject to a generalized state of anxiety. Moreover, and as with other personality patterns, these patients often utilize their phobic symptoms for secondary gain; they employ them to draw attention to themselves and as a tool to control and manipulate the lives of others, as portrayed in the following case.

Case 4.3, Colleen J., 32

Presenting Picture

Colleen was a social worker who had decided to defer her career in order to be "an acceptable mother and wife." She emphasized the word "acceptable," giving the impression of both striving and resentment. Prior to her current treatment, she had a history of two brief depressive episodes, one of which required emergency hospitalization. Just after her hospitalization, she developed an overwhelming dread of entering the kitchen of her home. At the initial clinical interview, it was clear that Colleen's phobia symbolized her growing feeling of incompetence as a wife and enabled her to avoid facing her general fear of failure. Moreover, the phobia seemed to be operational in that it brought her sympathy and served to punish her husband by forcing him to prepare most of the family's meals and to wash and dry the dishes, a chore he had made clear that he disliked.

Initial Impressions

The clinical interview proved very difficult. Having trained as a social worker and having been hospitalized twice before, Colleen was fairly well-versed as a therapeutic patient; she made it clear that she did not wish to, as she put it, "go mining around my childhood and all that personal baggage." She said that she had read empirical studies that stated that "in-depth psychobabble isn't necessary." Recanting this early attitude to an extent, she told the intern working with her, "I know, it's important to your training. Why don't you get my records from my hospitalization?" This back-and-forth style of responding to the therapeutic relationship, along with some expansiveness in her thought process, seemed to suggest to this intern's supervisor the active interpersonal ambivalence of the negativistic pattern with secondary narcissistic features. It was vital that this therapist understand, and not react to, the series of tests and resistances this patient would likely present. An approach to this person needed to be authoritative and clear but avoid contradictory or immediately confrontational dynamics. Consistency in response as well as clarity and nonreactiveness in helping Colleen recognize moments where she provokes others (thereby alienating herself from her social supports) were the most important directives for therapeutic rapport building.

Domain Analysis

Colleen did not want to share more in-depth information, and was even resistant to the clinical interview, despite her personal and professional experience with the mental health system. Her records from previous treatment indicated not only a recurrent agitated depression, which she did not seem to be acutely experiencing at the outset of this treatment, but what was noted as "Personality Disorder Not Otherwise Specified." Utilizing the MG-PDC, the treating psychology intern and supervisor were able to identify the following salient features, aligned with both negativistic and narcissistic personalities:

Vacillating Objects: Hugely contradictory feelings abounded in Colleen with respect to her relations with important figures in her life. Indirectly expressed resentments convoluted her relationships, and she frequently alienated herself from others via covert acts of aggression.

Interpersonally Contrary: Colleen wavered frequently between assuming the role of the agreeable spouse/friend/mother and expressing resentfulness (another important behavioral domain) that she was "pigeonholed by others." This domain was central to understanding her current phobic complaint.

Cognitively Expansive: Expanding on her education regarding mental health matters, Colleen often tried to disrupt the flow of the clinical interview, as well as subsequent treatment, with her unbridled knowledge of "how these things work." She hinted that this was not limited to therapy and that she often presented this attitude of "knowing better" in many of her relations.

Therapeutic Steps

Colleen wanted no more than "empirically validated procedures" to achieve relief of her phobic symptom, and the intern was left without a choice but to do just that. It required no more than 4 sessions of in vivo exposure for her to respond with relative comfort when entering her kitchen at home. She quickly learned a variety of techniques, such as systematic desensitization, a procedure that enabled her to deal with and confront other anxiety-based difficulties in her life. After 4 sessions she terminated therapy, simply not showing up for 2 sessions in a row and not responding to attempts at communication with her.

Not surprisingly, after a brief hiatus, Colleen decided to return to treatment, having concluded that her earlier period of therapy was incomplete, if not insufficient. The intern, who by then had graduated to a personality-specialized postdoc at the same facility, developed a more synergistic and personalized framework for her second therapeutic experience to focus more on personality traits in an effort to provide an intervention of more enduring value. Hence, a mixture of treatment techniques was employed to counteract Colleen's interpersonal defiance and resentful, fickle views of people. Utilizing interpersonal techniques inspired by Lorna Benjamin's Structural Analysis of Social Behavior (SASB/Intrex model; L. S. Benjamin, 2005), Colleen explored and gained greater understanding of her *contrary interpersonal interactions,* gradually unearthing experiences of anger from past relationships and viewing the repetitive nature of her current transactions. A major discovery was that since her phobia was successfully treated in the first series of sessions, her exacerbation with her husband increased, as it then had no symbolic means of anger expression. She was advised that at a later date, she might pursue couples counseling for greater communication capability with her husband, who, by the nature of the role he played, would inevitably make demands of her. By having this modality follow her discoveries in interpersonal techniques, a *catalytic sequence* was formed, allowing faster and more effective progression in the couples milieu to follow her individual treatment.

Potentiated pairings were integrated throughout Colleen's individual therapy. First, aspects of object-relational psychotherapy were interwoven into the therapeutic relationship, as her therapist, with whom she had developed a semi-long-term therapeutic relationship, took on a corrective-sisterly role, a model Colleen eventually internalized to combat her *vacillating objects*. Also employed were cognitively oriented efforts to undo her *expansive beliefs,* which really represented a deeper held schema of believing she was always unappreciated and misunderstood. Similarly, self-actualizing humanistic procedures were employed to moderate her feeling that she was always going to be a discontented person. Colleen continued in treatment for about 6 months, progressing in a highly satisfactory manner by the use of this combinational approach.

Dissociative Syndromes

Dissociation is closely linked to phobias; in fact, they are often subsumed under the more general label of "hysteria." Despite an overlapping in the personalities who exhibit them, as well as in the underlying strategies that give rise to them, these disorders are sufficiently distinct in other regards to justify their separation. For example, in phobias, inner tensions are displaced and discharged through a symbolic object or body part of which both the patient and others are fully conscious. In dissociation, however, patients neither crystallize their tensions into tangible forms nor give evidence of being conscious of their expression. Rather, they vent tension through transitory behavioral acts and do so in a dreamlike state, that is, while completely unaware of what they are doing.

Since the days of the early Greeks, observations have been made of individuals who seem to "drift off" and lose contact with their surroundings for varying periods of time. Some suffer total amnesia, forgetting who they are, what they have done, and where they have been. Others experience trance-like dream states in which they engage in activities of which they have no recall.

The concept of dissociation and the first understanding of the processes involved began with the inquiries of Charcot and Janet. It was Charcot (1885) in the early 1870s who suggested that the stream of consciousness breaks up into divergent paths in cases of hysteria. He believed that this "splitting" process was traceable to a hereditary degeneration of the nervous system. Janet (1901) pursued this theme in the late 1880s in his clinical investigations of states of amnesia and somnambulism. He coined the term "dissociation" to represent what he viewed as the central process in these disorders. As Janet conceived it, the mental energy required to bind the diverse elements of personality had deteriorated or had been "exhausted." As a consequence, certain thoughts, feelings, and memories, which normally cohere, drift apart and become lost to the principal core of the personality.

Janet's views were extended in 1905 by Morton Prince (1905/1978), an American psychologist who published a series of now famous inquiries into dramatic cases of "multiple personalities." Prince applied the term "co-consciousness" to represent aspects of thought that are not in the forefront of conscious attention. To him, hysteria, as found in cases of multiple personality, simply was an extreme example of independently acting co-conscious ideas.

Freud took exception to the views of both Janet and Prince, claiming that the mere process of "splitting" or "loosening" of associations, especially if attributed to neurological defects, was insufficient to account for both the timing and the content of the dissociative symptoms. He asserted that dissociation stemmed from an active process of repression in which forbidden impulses and thoughts are sealed into separate psychic compartments. These impulses are momentarily discharged during the dissociation state, providing the clinician with clues into the character of the patient's repressed anxieties and conflicts. Upon the patient's return to normal functioning, the memory of these ideas and emotions was again repressed and kept out of mind.

General Clinical Picture

For our purposes, the varieties of dissociation may be grouped into several categories: those that are relatively prolonged dreamlike states, such as events that are experienced as hazy or unreal; briefer states, such as when individuals seem divorced from themselves and their surroundings; and, among the major forms, cases in which there is a sweeping amnesia of the past and cases known as multiple personality, in which entirely different features of the individual's psychic makeup separate and become autonomous units of functioning.

Some include experiences of *estrangement* from self or environment. Here patients sense familiar objects and events as strange or foreign or view themselves as unreal or unknown (depersonalization). *Trance-like states* are akin to estrangement, but here patients' awareness is merely dimmed; they seem to be in a twilight dream world, totally immersed in inner events and entirely oblivious of their surroundings. *Somnambulism* refers to sleepwalking, a process of carrying out acts that are consistent with concurrent dream fantasies. In these states, individuals often search for desired objects and relationships or work out tensions and conflicts that normally are unconscious. For example, a young man wanders nocturnally to the foot of the bed of his sleeping parents, seeking comfort and security; a woman runs every so often to the basement of her home to escape a nightmare fantasy of being taunted by her neighbors; a wealthy and respected man gets fully dressed, strolls into neighboring streets looking into trashcans, and then returns home to sleep. Although somnambulists are able to get to wherever they are going, their thought processes tend to be hazy and incoherent during these episodes, and they rarely recall any of the events that happened. To be included also in these, more minor dissociations are *frenzied states,* in which sudden, brief, and totally forgotten bizarre behaviors erupt in the course of otherwise normal events. In these cases the person usually acts out forbidden thoughts and emotions that previously had been repressed.

The more major of the dissociative group include those experiencing total *amnesia;* here, patients usually forget both their past and their identity. This may occur in conjunction with a flight from their normal environment, an event referred to as a *fugue.* Whether or not physical flight occurs, amnesic patients have genuinely lost cognizance of their identities and the significant persons and places of their lives. Most amnesic episodes terminate after several days, although a few prove to be permanent. In *dissociative identity disorders,* we now include what was formerly called "multiple personalities"; these are extremely rare cases in which the patient's psychic makeup is reorganized into two or more separate and autonomously functioning units; the fictional characters of Dr. Jekyll and Mr. Hyde are a dramatic and simplified portrayal of the coexistence of diametrically contrasting features that often characterize the two personality units. In most cases, the patient's "normal self" is the dominant personality unit; it periodically gives way to, and is totally amnesic for, a contrasting but subsidiary unit of personality functioning. Appreciably less frequent are cases in which two equally prominent personality units alternate on a regular basis and with some frequency.

What gives rise to dissociative phenomena? To answer this question, it may be useful to go back first to Janet's original thesis: a lack of power for "psychic cohesion." Janet ascribed this deficiency to neural degeneration traceable either to hereditary weaknesses or to psychological "exhaustion." An alternative interpretation of Janet's thesis, one that is more consistent with current thinking, would assign the loss of psychic cohesion not to neural defects but to an acquired deficiency in cognitive controls. As a function of early training and experience, many individuals fail to acquire a coherent and well-integrated core of personality traits necessary for organizing their past and future experiences. We will note shortly that histrionic personalities lack an "inner identity," are largely empty and devoid of a past, tend to be overresponsive to external stimuli, and are deficient in self-controls. It would be consistent with their ingrained patterns for these patients to be subject to the splitting or disintegration of memories, impulses, and thoughts, as they lack the equipment to bind or cohere divergent elements of their psychic makeup.

Another cause or function of dissociation may be found in the writings of Freud (1900), who suggested that the disorder reflected the existence of strong and mutually incompatible elements of personality. Unable to contain these conflicting forces in a single cohesive unit, the personality is cleaved into separate systems, either with one system totally repressed (amnesia) or with two or more systems operating autonomously (multiple personality). This view, that dissociation reflects the preservation of the conscious self by banishing unacceptable traits from awareness, seems reasonable as another determinant of the disorder.

Not to be overlooked as a third factor are secondary gains. Janet's thesis, as modified, suggests the operation of deficient cognitive controls. The Freudian thesis focuses on primary gains, that is, the isolation of thoughts and impulses that provoke anxiety, should they coexist consciously. The third hypothesis asserts that the dissociative act may provide positive reinforcements in the form of advantages such as a new life, an escape from boredom, and the attraction of attention, affection, and nurture.

As in most pathologies, the dissociative symptom is likely to be overdetermined, an outcome representing a compromise of several determinants. Although the prevalence of dissociative disorders has demitted this past century, there is some indication that it increased in recent decades (probably owing to the growing literature on child abuse; Morrison, 1995). Various combinations of influence will be seen when we turn next to the personality background of dissociated patients.

Prevailing Treatment Options

Historically, work with dissociative amnesia occurred with high frequency during war time. Therapists were quite successful in relieving the disorder by removing those affected from the front lines and giving them a feeling of protection and nurturance (Kubie, 1943).

Most dissociative disorders are difficult to treat, yet are challenging to therapists who rarely become involved with such patients (Kluft, 1994; Turkus & Kahler, 2006). A series of studies by Coons (1986), employing general psychotherapeutic approaches over a $3\frac{1}{2}$-year period, indicated that two-thirds of patients were appreciably improved and one-fourth had satisfactorily integrated their diverse personality components. Coons used a variety of treatment procedures: social skill enhancements, constructive life management, and hypnosis and abreactions. Similarly, Kluft (1984, 1988) was able to move most of his patients toward a more integrated sense of self.

Research studies on dissociative identity techniques are quite modest in scope, owing to the fact that these disorders are infrequent, thereby precluding adequate numbers for statistical purposes. Nevertheless, researchers have employed with some measure of success *homogeneous group* techniques (Caul, 1984; Caul, Sacks, & Braun, 1988), *family therapy* (L. R. Benjamin & Benjamin, 1992), and several variants of *hypnosis* (Maldonado & Spiegel, 1995; Spiegel, 2003) as well as *narcosynthesis* (Baron & Nagy, 1988).

Personalized Psychotherapy

The personality patterns disposed to dissociative episodes are generally the same as those found in other anxiety-driven complex syndromes. The theme that unifies them in this regard is their common desire to avoid social disapproval. Other personalities, both pathological and normal, may exhibit dissociative symptoms, but the probability of such episodes in these cases is rather small. Our presentation proceeds in the order of the most to the least vulnerable of the persons in whom the disorder is most frequently exhibited.

Dissociation among Shy/Avoidant Personalities

These patients experience frequent and varied forms of dissociative phenomena. Feelings of estrangement may arise as protective maneuvers designed to diminish the impact of excessive stimulation or the pain of social humiliation. These symptoms may also reflect the consequences of the patient's devalued sense of self; without an esteemed and integrated inner core to which experience can be anchored, events often seem disconnected, ephemeral, and unreal. Self-estrangement, termed depersonalization, may be traced to a characteristic coping maneuver of cognitive interference, which not only serves to disconnect normally associated events, but deprives the person of meaningful contact with his or her own feelings and thoughts. Experiences of amnesia may occur as an expression of self-rejection. Forever to be oneself is not a cheerful prospect for these persons, and life may be started anew by disowning one's past identity. Frenzied states are a common dissociative disorder in these patients. For a brief period, patients may act out their frustrated and repressed impulses, as illustrated in the following case.

Case 4.4, Marla J., 23

Presenting Picture

Marla was hospitalized after a series of "hysterical fits" at home. She lived alone with an elderly mother, had been unemployed for several years, and spent most of her days sitting by the window, staring blankly. Her mother reported that Marla had always been a quiet girl and had never brought friends home. However, since her older brother left home some 2 years earlier, Marla almost never spoke to anyone, usually hiding in her room when visitors came. Her "fits" were repeated on an average of once a week while she was hospitalized. They would begin when Marla shouted aloud, "I don't want to, I don't want to"; she then fell on her bed, vigorously fighting an unseen assailant who, she believed, sought to rape her. As she fended off her hallucinated attacker, Marla would begin to tear at her clothes; finally, half denuded, she submitted to his desires, enacting a rather bizarre ritual of masturbation. After a brief period, mixed with tears and laughter, Marla became quiet and subdued. Conscious awareness gradually returned, with no recall of the episode.

Initial Impressions

Key issues in this case were Marla's shyness and social awkwardness, facets of her personality that she seemed keenly aware of, nearly to the point of its creating its own source of panic. Her mother mentioned that in her teens, Marla had adopted a manner of being extremely introverted, seemingly to the point of not even desiring company, much less seeking social outlets. Prior to this, she was more desirous of interaction, but also found many hours of contentment in solitary fantasy play. This, unfortunately, brought a good deal of shame and ridicule from her peers, an issue brought up by her teachers but never once mentioned by Marla. Increased safety, verbalizations by the therapist regarding "fears many people have" about talking about difficult things, and reassurances of confidentiality were vital to increase rapport for this terribly frightened young lady. Her primary pattern was avoidant, with secondary schizoid features. Helping answer her many questions of safety, motivated by her active–pain orientation, with very low to moderate expectations for disclosure, helped increase Marla's sense of freedom to speak about difficult subject matters. In this intervention, it was helpful at the outset to present intervention in terms of solutions rather than problems, utilizing techniques such as the "miracle" question suggested by solution-focused practitioners DeJong and Berg (2001). This less threatening approach helped Marla talk about desires rather than shortcomings, but opened the door to important information, as described in "Therapeutic Steps."

Domain Analysis

Marla's results on the MCMI-III, Grossman Facet Scales, and MG-PDC were consistent with strong avoidant qualities and supported the diagnosis of Avoidant Personality Disorder, with schizoid features. Her most salient domains included the following:

Temperamentally Anguished: More than anything, Marla seemed blunted by the confusing array of feelings, ranging from vice-like tension to mortifying embarrassment. Although she was good at hiding it in lucid moments, she often presented as someone who was about to burst into tears, though outside her fits she never did.

Fantasy Mechanism: Excessively aligned with a private world of her own creation, Marla seemed to get many of her emotional and interpersonal needs met through escapism and dissociation, discharging anger and affection needs privately. Her current hospitalization was closely related to this.

Interpersonally Unengaged: For nearly the past 10 years, Marla seemed to have given up on relating to the outside world, responding minimally even to close family members. At an earlier developmental stage, this domain may have been more aversive, as it would be with a prototypal avoidant, but Marla appeared to disengage as a defensive maneuver over time.

Therapeutic Steps

After initial exploration in solution-focused mode, Marla's treatment took on some psychoanalytic qualities in an effort to have her freely associate her thoughts and engage in semihypnotic sessions. Additionally, pharmacologic treatment was employed to afford a modicum of relief for her *anguished temperament*. It was soon uncovered that she was reenacting a number of sexual exploits with her significantly older brother over a period of many years, and only recently had her thoughts about these episodes taken the form of dissociative fits so pronounced as to catch anyone's attention. These were extremely distressful to her more conscious image of him. When the brother moved out of the region some years prior, Marla felt bereft and was extremely needy of the care and affection that he provided for her, a feeling that no one else, she believed, could furnish in her current state. Exposing these roots of her disorder, though the process was gradual and painful, began to release her from the powerful effects of her repressive behaviors and the acting-out *fantasy mechanism* that had become, in recent episodes, unbridled. Some 30 sessions were required to reintegrate fantasy and true history in a more realistic logic, and Marla began to express a greater desire to find fulfillment "outside of my own head."

Throughout this intervention, the approach taken with Marla infused a series of steps (e.g., L. S. Benjamin, 2005, Magnavita, 2000) that helped her not only resolve and reintegrate her intrapsychic conflicts and impulses, but learn social skills with which she could relate with more comfort to the real social world in a manner that would facilitate *interpersonal reengagement*. Many patients with dissociative disorders segment their self-awareness and their cognitions, leaving them lacking an appropriate range of interpersonal skills and knowledge. Although the therapist was fortunate in being involved with Marla for 30 sessions, the need to follow up was not taken advantage of; reintegration was a primary goal, but there were parts missing, so to speak. Bringing these parts (e.g., cognitions, interpersonal style) into therapy may have provided Marla with a wider range of competencies to create an extended psychic integration. The reader might find it useful to turn to Millon (1996a) which discusses the psychic needs of avoidant personalities.

It is only in accord with tradition that we view these frenzied dissociative states among the less severe syndromes. There is no question but that the bizarre behavior and loss of reality evident during these episodes are severe enough to merit viewing them as psychotic. Custom and perhaps the brevity of the eruption and the rapid return to former functioning are the only justifications for placing them in the moderately severe categories.

Dissociation among Needy/Dependent Personality Disorders

These persons may develop dreamlike trance states when faced with responsibilities and obligations that surpass their feelings of competence; through this maneuver they effectively fade out of contact with threatening realities. Amnesic episodes, however, are extremely rare as these would prompt or intensify separation anxieties. Repetitive somnambulistic states are not uncommon. The patient usually vents minor forbidden impulses or seeks to secure affect and nurture.

Brief frenzied states may arise at the moderately severe level if the patient experiences an upsurge of intense hostile impulses that may threaten his or her dependency security. In this way, contrary feelings may be discharged without the patient knowing it and therefore without having to assume blame. These irrational acts are so uncharacteristic of the patient that they tend to be seen by others as a sign of "sickness," often eliciting thereby nurturing and supporting responses.

Dissociation among Conscientious/Compulsive Personality Disorders

These persons succumb to dissociative episodes for a variety of reasons. Experiences of estrangement stem primarily from their characteristic overcontrol and repression of feeling. By desensitizing their emotions or withdrawing them as a part of everyday life these patients may begin to experience the world as flat and colorless, a place in which events seem mechanical, automatic, and unreal.

Episodes of total amnesia may occur if the patient is otherwise unable to isolate and control intense ambivalent feelings. The coexistence of conflicting habits and emotions may be too great a strain. Not only will the eruption of hostile and erotic impulses shatter the patient's self-image of propriety, but they may provoke the severe condemnation he or she dreads from others. Unable to restrain these urges, patients must disown their identity and in the process obliterate all past associations and memories. The following summarizes a typical case.

Case 4.5, Orlando F., 39

Presenting Picture

Orlando, a rather overrestrained and highly tense police officer, was mandated to counseling and given temporary suspension with pay by his precinct chief after a recent dissociative episode. One morning, he "forgot" who he was while driving to work, rode some 200 miles from his home town in his assigned police cruiser, and was found 3 days later in a motel room, weeping and confused as to his whereabouts. By his report, Orlando was "happily married 20 years without incident, and I still love my wife as much as the day we were married." However, in recent weeks he had become involved in an extramarital affair with a woman mistakenly arrested due to her physical similarity to a known felon. Grateful to Orlando, who was the processing officer and had noticed vital inconsistencies, she had offered "a cup of coffee after work" in gratitude. The affair started, unexpectedly, that night. After a few weeks, Orlando began to suffer marked insomnia and unbearable guilty feelings. Unable to share his thoughts and emotions and for the first time failing (and even refusing) to go to confession at his church, he became increasingly disconsolate and depressed, culminating in failing to report to work one morning. When he was found, he was initially hospitalized, then assigned to therapy after his acute dissociative state was resolved through psychodynamic/hypnosis methods.

Initial Impressions

By his own admission, Orlando was married to "established traditions and norms first, my wife second." He stated this half jokingly, but what was evident in this statement was that his marriage was, indeed, a source of ambivalence. Clearly, Orlando was never one to "rock the boat," and he sought solace, consistently, in the community organizations and societal expectations in which he was surrounded. Passively accommodating others, yet deeply conflicted over the lack of autonomy and unmet personal needs, he nearly always needed to clamp down on his anger, constantly reassuring himself that he was doing "the right thing, for the right reasons." There was no way, however, he could fit his transgression into this immovable, inflexible self-view. With clear ambivalence on both adaptation (active–passive) and replication (self–other) polarities, with most manifestations leaning toward a passive–other orientation, Orlando's overall personality patterns were a blend of a primary compulsive orientation with features of the negativistic style. Given his mature and ingrained, yet awkwardly rigid defenses, it was best to enter the therapeutic relationship not by addressing the affair, but by giving permission for him to explore these adaptive and interpersonal conflicts, as well as to allow him the freedom to recognize his anger and frustration emanating from these conflicts.

Domain Analysis

Badly shaken by feelings of embarrassment regarding both his transgression and his dissociative episode, Orlando was very compliant not only in faithfully completing all assessments, but in taking a proactive role in asking questions and attempting to understand "what I did to get here." Salient domains measured by the MCMI-III, the Grossman Facet Scales, and the MG-PDC were as follows:

Conscientious Self-Image: Very industrious and terrified of taking a wrong step, Orlando based his entire idea of self in the mantra "Do the right thing, always." This guided him as an officer, an upstanding citizen, and, with the exception of his transgression, as a husband.

Concealed Objects (Intrapsychic Content): Orlando had very little conscious awareness of any questions or conflicts he may have had regarding important figures of his life; as a consequence, his attitudes toward all others was guided by professionalism, unquestioned respect, and positive interaction, never bringing any part of anyone's character or motivation into question.

Temperamentally Irritable: One of Orlando's more interesting characteristics was that he was unwaveringly pleasant and professional, even when not on duty, and he evidenced kindness and helpfulness in all situations. However, he noticeably did so "through clenched teeth," according to the therapist, and it was apparent that there was a great deal of chronic hostility that was being suppressed.

Therapeutic Steps

As noted, therapy was guided initially by psychodynamic/hypnosis methods employed to help Orlando first regain coherence, then, as an outpatient, begin to reformulate an acceptable sense of identity. His therapist also suggested the use of SSRIs, particularly Paxil, to address Orlando's *irritable temperament.* Orlando was not fond of this idea, noting his dislike for foreign substances in his body as well as his belief that "my mood's actually pretty okay." He inquired about hypericum (or St. John's wort) as an alternative, which, upon his therapist's approval, he began. The combination of hypnotic-suggestion exercises (which, as a side benefit, had behavioral relaxation benefits) with the subtle mood-modifying qualities of the natural agent helped Orlando begin to recognize pockets of deep irritability, frustration, and even anger.

An insight-oriented intrapsychic approach tapped into the nature of his *object concealment;* that is, it helped him begin to allow for even good figures (objects), by any definition, to have their less positive qualities. Rather than compare himself to unrealistic ideals, Orlando could gradually begin to accept his less favorable qualities, at least in theory. Later stages of therapy would combine object relations with supportive and cognitive-reframing procedures to help him develop greater flexibility with his otherwise impenetrable *conscientious self-image.* During the early, gradual insight-raising procedures, he came to recognize his extreme self-harshness that culminated in his forgetting who he was. As he began to understand the basis of his amnesia, progress moved rather swiftly, enabling him to "fess up" to his transgressions and to resolve his difficulties through formal marital therapy techniques. To prevent risk of relapse, he voluntarily stayed with treatment for a short period of time; this was an opportunity for the therapist to introduce an existential paradigm to help Orlando integrate experiences of anger and conflictual feelings about himself and others into new meanings and expressions.

A frenzied state may be another form of discharge when tensions become unbearable. This allows patients to vent their contrary impulses without conscious awareness. Although infrequent, dissociative identity disorders may be formed, enabling patients to retain their "true" identity most of the time while gaining periodic release through their "other" self or selves.

Dissociation among Sociable/Histrionic Personality Disorders

These personalities generally lack an adequate degree of personality integration, making it difficult for them even in normal times to unify the disparate elements of their lives. At times of strain and discord, this integrative deficiency may readily result in a dissociative state.

Somnambulism, a nighttime phenomenon, is not uncommon and usually takes the form of a search for attention and stimulation when these patients feel otherwise deprived. Daytime trance-like episodes are rather unusual, however, as these patients desire to be alert to their environment. Also rare are amnesic fugues and multiple personality formations. When they do occur, they usually represent an attempt to break out of a confining and stultifying environment. Faced with internal poverty and external boredom or constraint, they may seek the secondary gains of a more exciting and dramatic life in which they can achieve the attention and approval they crave. These elements are nicely illustrated in the following brief history.

Case 4.6, Nadia F., 33

Presenting Picture

Over the past 2 years, Nadia had begun to feel "boxed in" by her suspicious husband. Around that time, her innocuous comment made to his best friend, "Wow, you look really delicious tonight," provoked his ruminations of her supposed infidelity. Although that was not the instigation of his jealousy, it served as "proof" to him that she was not trustworthy. After a year of fights over her extroverted mannerisms, with Nadia sometimes "purposely" being more outgoing "in order to teach him a lesson," she suddenly disappeared from her home and was not located for several months. She was found more than 1,000 miles away working in a run-down striptease bar, returning to her vocation prior to marriage 5 years earlier. Upon first questioning, she appeared to have "blacked out" her marital memories, to which her husband claimed, "It's just a ploy." Further interviewing revealed, however, that she was totally amnesic for her life since her marriage, but recalled with great clarity her activities and relationships prior to that time.

Initial Impressions

Nadia clearly demonstrated histrionic patterns, combined with some negativistic traits, although neither of these patterns proved to be disordered or overly pathological in their own right. Enigmatically, her former life fulfilled needs of both patterns. Not only was she able to actively seek and gain attention, but the environment reinforced her ambivalence regarding the attention that *was* paid to her. This attention, of course, came from the frequenters of lower-end strip clubs; "misogynistic" might be a rather mild adjective for these interactions. Only ambivalently contented with this life, Nadia began attending church, and it was there that she met her husband, a man with high moral values, a rather stilted worldview allowing for few gray areas, and more than a modicum of jealousy, which he termed "protectiveness." Attracted at first by what seemed to be the answer to her life (i.e., what appeared to be the opposite extreme of her life), she engaged him by talking about how she was now "finding her way" to being an upstanding woman. This case history drew attention to Nadia's continual wishing for her opposite, which was facilitative in helping her restore marital memories. This was done through relaxation and guided imagery exercises which asked questions such as "When you see your ideal life, tell me what you see" as well as "Describe what you're running from." Her answers began approximating the "very different" existence she hoped for with her husband, and memories of the 5-year marriage gradually returned.

Domain Analysis

The MG-PDC, which followed Nadia's reestablishment, revealed the following domain dysfunctions:

Vacillating Objects (Intrapsychic Content): Finding herself at odds with significant others (romantic as well as close associates) was the "way it always is" for Nadia.

Contradictory feelings regarding others were the norm, probably due to pervasively inconsistent familial transactions.

Dissociative Mechanism: Nadia had only limited ability for introspection, and concerned herself with external manners almost exclusively. Large chunks of unwanted memories escaped her awareness readily; not only was this element integrally involved in the presenting picture, but as treatment continued, more evidence of this trend was found throughout her history.

Interpersonally Attention Seeking: Actively solicitous of praise, Nadia demonstrated a clear ability to market and even change her persona as needed. Evidence of this was clear in the manner in which she initially attracted her husband.

At a later stage, the MCMI-III and Grossman Facet Scales were administered, and Nadia's interpretive report corroborated and helped confirm many of these elements.

Therapeutic Steps

Initial efforts, as indicated under "Initial Impressions," were focused on psychodynamic methods, not necessarily to explore the deeper regions of her intrapsychic world, but to access conflicts that appeared to ride just under the surface of awareness. This allowed access to information hidden by her *dissociative mechanism,* that is, self-reflections just slightly too difficult to acknowledge directly. Gaining insight in this manner began the process of making some of her conflictual feelings (*vacillating objects*) more accessible via a combination of these intrapsychic approaches and cognitive reframing techniques aimed at acceptance of non–black-and-white impressions of others. Her therapist, encouraged to explore these modalities that were outside his self-definition as a Rogerian therapist, also incorporated, by nature, a very caring manner, exhibiting genuine empathic sensitivity. He effectively evoked from Nadia a willingness to open up and overcome her repressive actions, thereby bringing her less attractive attitudes into full view. In later stages, therapy consisted of a combination of group treatment and marital therapy. Nadia was then able to openly discuss, in both venues, her sense of marital stultification, leading to a number of maritally constructive discussions with her husband, as well as feedback regarding her *interpersonal attention seeking,* which gradually gave her permission to be more herself rather than what she might think others expected of her. This final component had the benefit of further lowering resentful feelings, thus, also life dissatisfaction, and paved the way for her to more fully explore better, unique self-defining life activities.

Dissociation among Skeptical/Negativistic Personality Disorders

These individuals are accustomed to expressing their contrary feelings rather directly, and will exhibit dissociative symptoms only if they are unduly constrained or fearful of severe retaliation. Even under circumstances such as these, the frequency of these disorders is rather low. Temper tantrums, which approach dissociative frenzied states in their overt appearance, are rather common. However, in these eruptions patients do not lose conscious awareness and usually vent all the emotions that well up within them.

Dissociation among Capricious/Borderline Personality Disorders

Borderline personalities are likely to vent brief but highly charged and angry outbursts during psychogenic fugue states. Repressed resentments occasionally take this form and erupt into the open when these patients have felt trapped and confused or betrayed. Moreover, it is not unusual for borderlines to brutalize themselves, as well as others, during these fugues. They may tear their clothes, smash their fists, and lacerate their bodies, thereby suffering more themselves than do their presumed assailants. Most frequently, these violent discharges are followed by a return to their former state. In some cases, however, borderlines may disintegrate into one or another of the more prolonged psychotic disorders. Though strange and fearsome, fugues do not come totally unexpected to friends and family members of borderlines because the symptoms of this disorder are but extremes of their long-term pattern of impulsiveness, behavioral unpredictability, and self-damaging acts.

Obsessive-Compulsive (Axis I) Syndromes

Most people find themselves overly concerned and preoccupied when facing some real and troubling problem; they experience an inability to get their mind off it and turn to other matters. These events are similar to obsessive experiences, but in these cases the idea the person mulls over is rather picayune, absurd, or irrational, yet it intrudes with such persistence as to interfere with normal daily functioning. Compulsions are similar to obsessions; however, here patients cannot resist engaging in certain acts, in performing some trivial behavioral ritual that they recognize as ridiculous, humiliating, or disgusting, but which they must execute to avoid the anxiety they experience when they fail to do it.

Both obsessions and compulsions are similar to other complex syndromes in that they reflect the operation of numerous psychic domains and physiological vulnerabilities. Each complex disorder protects individuals from recognizing the true source of their upwelling anxieties, yet allows the anxiety a measure of release without damaging their self-image or provoking interpersonal rebuke. In phobias, the inner tension is symbolized and attached to an external object; in conversions, it is displaced and expressed through some body part; in obsessions and compulsions, tension is controlled, symbolized, and periodically discharged through a series of repetitive acts or thoughts.

Commonalities among diverse "neurotic" symptoms were first proposed by Charcot, 1885. However, it was his student Janet, 1901, who first made an effort to relate them systematically.

To Janet, all of these anxiety-neutralizing disorders were a consequence of a diminution of biological mental energies requisite to the integration of higher mental processes, a point of view that may be reexamined in light of the recent success of pharmacologic agents that help reduce the syndrome. Complex thoughts and emotions, which normally were connected and organized, drifted apart, according to Janet, into a chaotic mental anarchy when these energies diminished or were drained. As a consequence of this weakness, primitive and subsidiary forces took over the person and led to the scattering and disorganization of formerly coordinated thoughts and emotions. Obsessions and compulsions were seen in this light. They were merely incidental expressions of a basic disintegration of organized higher mental processes.

As noted earlier, Freud rejected Janet's thesis, claiming that both the timing and the choice of the symptom indicated the primacy of psychogenic rather than biogenic factors. All complex syndromes, then termed neuroses, stemmed from psychic mechanisms designed to control and alleviate anxieties traceable to early life experiences. The specific symptom reflected, symbolically, the character of the anxiety source, other facets of the patient's psychic makeup, and the maneuvers the patient employed to cope with it.

In current analytic theory, obsessions and compulsions symbolically represent the upsurging of sexual and aggressive impulses that the individual seeks to repress or inhibit. For example, the cleanliness seen in many compulsives is judged to signify a reaction formation, that is, an effort to constrain unacceptable "dirty" or aggressive impulses. Obsessions and compulsions indicated to Freud that previously repressed thoughts and feelings of hostility and guilt had been reactivated. To counteract, yet give partial ventilation to, these ideas and emotions, the patient employs several psychic mechanisms—namely, isolation, displacement, reaction formation, and undoing.

Through *isolation* the patient disconnects the association that previously existed between a forbidden thought and its accompanying feeling. For example, they might have obsessional thoughts of murder without being aware of or experiencing an appropriate parallel emotion; conversely, they may feel a frightening and intense murderous urge without knowing its cause. By isolating an affect from its associated thought, the patient avoids confronting the real connection between them. Isolation may not be completely successful, however, and some residuals of the forbidden feelings and thoughts may still be experienced as distressful. *Displacement* enables patients to find a substitute activity or thought to attach their tensions to, something that camouflages their real discomfort and serves to focus their attention elsewhere. Thus, they become obsessed with some trivial thought and thereby manage to divert themselves from true reflection. *Reaction formation* goes one step further toward self-deception; here, individuals think and behave in ways that are diametrically opposite to their "true" but forbidden ideas and impulses. Through this mechanism, not only are feelings and thoughts disconnected and displaced, but their content is twisted into its exact opposite. Thus, instead of expressing an urge to soil and be messy, the patient becomes compulsively clean and neat. *Undoing* parallels reaction formation. Having failed to reverse their attitudes and emotions beforehand, as in reaction formation, patients must rescind and gain forgiveness for their transgressions. Thus, they attempt symbolically to redeem themselves by various ritualistic acts. Through the undoing gesture, they not only pay penance for their forbidden thoughts, but seek in a magical way to restore themselves to a state of purity. For example, by compulsive hand washing, patients suffer the discomfort and embarrassment of the ritual and at the same time symbolically cleanse themselves of their past misdeeds and evil intentions. However, because the real source of the tension was not dealt with through the undoing maneuver, their relief is only temporary and they must repeat the ritualistic act time and again.

Recent research on obsessions and compulsions suggests that these symptoms reflect either or both a strong biological vulnerability and the simple overlearning of certain behaviors and thoughts. According to behavior theorists who eschew both neurochemical explanations and the role of unconscious processes, these acts stem from either a conditioning sequence, in which the behavior in question reduced anxiety effectively, or from repeated exposure to parental models. Learning theory, be it social or developmental, conceives obsessions and compulsions to be imitations of parental models that have been positively reinforced by virtue of their being successful in reducing anxiety. Along somewhat similar lines, interpersonal theorists suggest that obsessions may reflect underlying fears of embarrassment and humiliation; by contrast, they see compulsions as actions designed to enhance one's self-esteem. Others, viewing recent research, are disposed to support a biological basis for this disorder (Riggs & Foa, 1993).

Although learning is significantly involved in all forms of pathology, we focus our attention in this section on cases in which the symptom reflects the operation of more generalized personality traits, rather than being the direct and simple product of biochemical dysfunctions or overlearned behaviors. The distinction between these symptoms is a matter of the circumstances that give rise to them and the persons in whom they appear, rather than in biological processes or how they may have been acquired.

General Clinical Picture

As several features of the obsessive-compulsive syndrome have already been elaborated, we need only detail in more systematic fashion what has been said.

Obsessions tend to be exhibited in two forms. The first, *obsessive doubting,* represents a state of perpetual indecision in which patients interminably reevaluate a series of alternatives, rarely make a clear-cut choice, and if they do, rescind that choice, only to waver again. The uncertainty they feel leads them to brood about past actions and reexamine them endlessly, to believe that they were ill conceived or poorly executed, and then to undo or recheck them repeatedly; for example, a woman lies awake, uncertain whether she turned off the gas jets on the stove, proceeds to check them, finds them closed, returns to bed, thinks she may have inadvertently put them on, doubts that she could have done so, but must go and check again. *Obsessive thoughts* are intrusive ideas that the person cannot block from consciousness. Some are meaningless (e.g., "Where did I see a chair with one leg cut off?") and are experienced without emotion, but nonetheless are so persistent and distracting as to upset even the most routine of daily activities. Other recurrent thoughts are affect- and tension-laden, pertain to forbidden aggressive impulses or to prohibited sexual desires, and are experienced with shame, disgust, or horror. The more desperately patients try to rid themselves of these repugnant ideas, the more tormenting and persistent they become. For example, a passing thought of poisoning a wayward husband becomes fixed in a wife's mind; no matter how much she seeks to distract her attention from it, the thought returns to hound her at every meal.

Compulsions are behavior sequences, usually in the form of some ritual that is recognized by the patient as absurd or irrational, but which, if not executed, will provoke anxiety. These rituals express themselves most frequently as bizarre stereotyped acts, for example, touching one's nose with one's pinky before washing; repetition of normal acts, for example, tying one's shoelace exactly eight times before feeling satisfied with the outcome; or insisting on cleanliness and order, for example, being unduly concerned that ashtrays remain spotless or that one's books never be out of alphabetical sequence. The Freudian concepts of isolation, displacement, reaction formation, and undoing may be useful ways of referring to a principal psychic method by which the patient neutralizes his or her anxieties and forbidden impulses.

Obsessions relieve anxiety by isolating a thought from its associated feeling. In addition, by displacing the anxiety-provoking thought to a substitute and innocuous obsessional idea, patients distract themselves, as in phobias, from the true source of tension. Reaction formation enables them not only to disconnect, but to counteract their forbidden feelings. In addition, by thinking and acting in ways that are diametrically opposite to their dangerous impulses, they may be able to gratify these impulses with complete impunity; for example, by actively engaging in the censoring of pornography, patients provide themselves, through their careful "examination" of this "disgusting literature," with an acceptable rationale to ventilate their otherwise repressed hostile and erotic impulses.

Compulsions achieve similar coping aims. Patients' irresistible preoccupation with a variety of absurd but "safe" activities distracts them from confronting their real source of discomfort. Moreover, through reaction formation, they may be able to pursue activities that serve as a subterfuge for their socially unacceptable impulses. Symbolic acts traceable to undoing mechanisms serve not only to void past sins, but to ward off anticipated future punishment and social rebuke. Thus, the self-punitive and redemptive aspects of the undoing ritual often discharge and diminish the oppressive buildup of guilt feelings. In addition, patients' insistence on order and cleanliness and the self-righteous air with which they perform these acts evoke the secondary gains of attention and approval from others; for example, the compulsively orderly and "proper" high school student will be viewed, both by parents and teachers alike, as a fine, well-disciplined, and upright young man.

Prevailing Treatment Options

Despite the fact that complex psychological disorders play a distinct role in the etiology, content, and expressive forms of obsessions and compulsions, the research literature on the treatment of this syndrome has been most successfully achieved with behavioral treatment procedures and pharmacologic medications. Frequently employed are in vivo and imaginal exposure to the precipitants and maintainers of the anxiety precipitant. Response prevention methods (e.g., thought stopping) are also likely to be helpful in deterring troubling thoughts and actions. Exposure techniques are graduated such that low-anxiety associations are dealt with initially and higher levels of anxiety are introduced step by step. After a patient has developed a reasonable level of comfort, he or she may be encouraged to continue exposure opportunities at home and with the help of family or friends (Greist & Jefferson, 1996; Renshaw, Steketee, & Chambless, 2005).

In addition to exposure and response prevention techniques, a number of other treatment approaches also enhance therapeutic effectiveness. Notable among these are a variety of cognitive methods designed to alter erroneous beliefs and to stop intrusive ruminations (Kelly, 1996; Vogel, Stiles, & Götestam, 2004). Similarly, procedures of progressive relaxation, self-management, and assertion and social skill training have proven efficacious (Roth & Fonagy, 1996).

Not to be overlooked in the recent literature is the utility of certain pharmacologic agents (clomipramine and SSRIs) in amplifying the effectiveness of behavioral exposure and response prevention (Dattilio, 1993; Fineberg & Gale, 2005). Although best viewed as an adjunct to behavioral procedures, pharmacologic treatments appear to increase the overall effectiveness when approached in combination. Last, training in relaxation methods, perhaps augmented by biofeedback procedures, should deepen the patient's capacity to deal with life's stressors in a more manageable fashion. As noted, efforts should be expended, where appropriate, to facilitate the development of self-talk strategies to help diminish the patient's obsessive thoughts or compulsive behaviors (Pollard, 2005).

Personalized Psychotherapy

Despite the strong role that complex psychological factors play in the instigation and form in which the disorders are expressed, it is clear that many patients with this syndrome possess physiological weaknesses, as Janet argued. Identifying those disposed biologically will not be a simple task. We also know that there are intrapsychic dynamics involved in the creation of many obsessions and compulsions. Though they tend to be intellectually controversial, there is every reason to believe that they play a significant part in shaping the character and content of these disorders. Nevertheless, it is clear through research efforts that the most expedient techniques are a variety of behavioral procedures.

We turn next to the various personality styles and disorders that appear to be vulnerable to the development of obsessive-compulsive Axis I syndromes.

Obsessive-Compulsive Syndromes among Conscientious/Compulsive Personalities

These persons exhibit obsessive-compulsive symptoms with only a slightly greater frequency than most other pathological personalities. Apart from certain biochemical processes, the obsessive-compulsive symptomatology in these individuals is not so much a matter of disordered coping as it is a part of a deeply ingrained lifestyle strategy utilized to contain the upsurge of intense, socially forbidden impulses. By a pattern of widely generalized reaction formations, they have learned not only to control their contrary inclinations, but to present a front of complete conformity and propriety. Note should be made again of the success of a variety of pharmacologic agents (Fineberg & Gale, 2005; Rauch & Jenike, 1998) in curtailing these obsessive-compulsive symptoms, suggesting that a lower threshold may exist for certain persons in permitting their expression.

Obsessive doubting may also be typical of these patients' tendencies to reevaluate and reexamine even the most trivial decisions and acts. This excessive preoccupation with minor irrelevancies enables them to distract their attention from the real source of their anxieties. Although doubting is a habitual aspect of their daily functioning, it may become quite distinctive as a symptom if there is a sudden eruption of feelings that may give them away. Their pretense of equanimity and control is often disrupted by bizarre thoughts, usually of a hostile or erotic character. These stir up intense fears of social condemnation, which may be handled by a series of compulsive rituals. For example, each morning, by washing his face three times and knotting his tie five times, a patient assured himself of his purity; moreover, by repeating some insignificant act in which he feels competent, he strengthened his confidence in his ability to control his impulses.

Obsessive-Compulsive Syndromes among Shy/Avoidant Personalities

These persons develop symptoms for a variety of reasons. Obsessions may serve as substitute thoughts to distract these patients from reflecting on their true misery. Similarly, these thoughts may counter feelings of estrangement and depersonalization by providing avoidants with ideas and events that serve to assure them that life is real. Compulsive acts accomplish similar aims. They fill up time, diverting patients from self-preoccupations; moreover, these acts keep them in touch with real events and thereby help deter feelings of depersonalization and estrangement. Certain of these repetitive and superstitious acts may reflect attempts to cope with anticipated social derision. For example, a 30-year-old avoidant patient made a complete 360 degree turn each time prior to his walking through a door. This, he felt, would change his personality, which in turn would disincline those he subsequently met from ridiculing him. These ritualistic behaviors often signify also a bizarre method of controlling socially condemned thoughts and impulses. Thus, this patient put the index finger of his right hand to his lips, and then placed both hands in the back pockets of his trousers, whenever he felt the urge to shout obscenities or touch the breasts of women passersby.

Obsessive-Compulsive Syndromes among Needy/Dependent Personalities

These personalities are often preoccupied with obsessive doubts. These usually derive from reactivated feelings of inadequacy and are precipitated by situations in which they must assume independence and responsibility. They weigh interminably the pros and cons of the situation, thereby postponing endlessly any change in the status quo of dependency. Obsessional thoughts and compulsive acts frequently are manifested when feelings of separation anxiety or repressed anger come to the fore. Through mechanisms such as reaction formation and undoing, this psychic maneuver serves to counter tensions that would arise as a consequence of discharging their impulses. The symptoms displayed often take the form of sweet thoughts and approval-gaining acts, as illustrated in the following case.

Case 4.7, Joanna L., 34

Presenting Picture

Joanna entered therapy because she could not rid herself of the obsession about her husband's face being "the most beautiful image in the world." This was not an objectively harmful obsession, but she noted that she could not focus on other things when she perseverated on this thought, which was frequently. She also noted that she went to great lengths each night to painstakingly wash, iron, and prepare every item of clothing he planned to wear the next day, inclusive of examining each item for lint, dust, hair, and other particles. Upon clinical assessment, she revealed an intense fear that her husband might discover that she once allowed a neighbor to kiss her while he was away on an extended business trip. This had happened several years earlier, and her compulsions grew steadily since that time. It started as a desire to be helpful as her husband's business expanded, and culminated recently with these pervasive and repetitive behaviors. Joanna's obsessive symptom seemed to enable her to block any visualization of her neighbor's face. Her compulsive acts of caring for her husband were an attempt to prove her faithfulness and devotion to him.

Initial Impressions

The therapeutic interview, conducted by a particularly skilled intern, was able to easily uncover the moment of approximated infidelity and Joanna's striking fear of being left "to my own devices, if he would leave me." Joanna felt entirely helpless without a significant other; she had not been out of a relationship for more than a month since middle school, and she could recall that there had been only three relationships in those 20 or so years. Prior to middle school, she leaned heavily on her father, who was a widower; her mother had died unexpectedly of a rare heart defect when Joanna was 7. She had always found comfort in submitting to someone else in terms of creating direction in life, passing on any self-initiative, and taking on the role of the supportive, silent partner. For her, the simple act of expressing her fears and motivations without feeling judged or belittled (as she feared anyone would do, should she open her mouth) was sufficient for her to gain a healthy level of comfort in the therapeutic relationship. Experiencing, perhaps for the first time since childhood, the ability to direct a simple conversation was therapeutic in terms of her feelings of capability. This was important groundwork, as some of her anxiousness over potential loss was abated by simply feeling competent enough to find this mode of self-expression.

Domain Analysis

These three domains, each of them prototypal dependent domains, were found most salient by the MG-PDC:

Cognitively Naive: Easily persuaded by others, loath to take on a healthy skepticism regarding the word of others, and using strategies designed to gloss over difficulties, Joanna only vaguely thought through her idea that she could avoid trouble by simple overcompensation. Additionally, her fear of abandonment, stemming from an early loss, was an oversimplification of relational dynamics.

Introjection (Intrapsychic) Mechanism: Joanna felt that the more indispensable she was to her husband, the less likely he would leave her. Overdevoted, she acted in a manner that emphasized her perception of their inseparable bond, precluding differences and strengthening their union.

Inept Self-Image: Though not wholly inept in action, Joanna considered herself inadequate in many regards, which drove misguided fantasies about her being undeserving of the attention of another. She attempted to combat this instrumentally by doing all she could for him.

Treatment Steps

It was because her compulsive behavior abated her anxiety only minimally that Joanna sought to enter psychotherapeutic treatment. She was first given a prescription for anxiolytics, which, when combined with the inherently therapeutic act of client-directed therapy, helped her feel a modicum of competence and worthiness. She was able to sound out her feelings of incompetence (i.e., her *inept self-image*) and discover that much of what she feared was baseless. Cognitive-behavioral strategies (e.g., Beck, Freeman, & Davis, 2004) were employed, at times, during these early sessions; the focus of the cognitive-behavioral content was to help round out some of her rather 2-dimensional (*naive*) thoughts regarding the nature of close relationships. This was followed by an analytically oriented exploration of her wide-ranging fears and her marital concerns. Joanna came to recognize her intense dependency needs and her anticipations of loss and, through brief psychodynamic measures, was able to regulate her *introjections* in a more conscientious and balanced manner. Symptoms abated rather readily in this situation, but she felt uncertain, thinking that she could "far too easily relapse," and she requested a longer therapeutic course. A few sessions followed, in which a cognitive restructuring process was employed to help her realize the basis of several of these distorting beliefs; alternative attitudes were also encouraged. Further treatment may have proven paradoxical in one regard: She may have started to feel somewhat dependent on therapy. Because of this, she was invited to participate for several months in a weekly assertiveness training group program as an alternative wrap-up of treatment, with the invitation to return for a follow-up appointment with her individual therapist in a few weeks. She agreed with this treatment plan and followed through with the assertiveness program, but she did not return for individual follow-up.

Obsessive-Compulsive Syndromes among Sociable/Histrionic Personalities

These personalities are disposed to have their thoughts and emotions rather scattered and disconnected as a function of their general deficient personality integration. They characteristically exhibit dramatic emotional feelings over matters of minimal import and significance. Conversely, they may discuss serious topics and problems with a rather cool detachment. This ease with which affect and idea can be isolated from each other is a primary factor in contributing to their obsessive symptoms. Thus, with little strain or tension, they readily disconnect an emotion from its associated content.

Quite often, these patients experience a free-floating erotic emotion, that is, a sexual impulse without precipitant or focus. Conversely, hostile obsessive thoughts may preoccupy them, whereas the normally associated feeling of anger remains repressed. Which behavior or emotion is expressed and which is repressed is usually guided by their basic goal of gaining social approval and minimizing social rebuke; for example, they rarely vent hostile feelings but often manifest seductive emotions and behaviors.

Obsessive-Compulsive Syndromes among Skeptical/Negativistic Personalities

These personalities tend to vent their contrary impulses rather openly. However, these feelings may be transformed psychically into obsessions and compulsions if they are especially intense and likely to provoke either separation anxieties or severe social reproach. Obsessive thinking is a common resolution of this conflict. For example, a normally outspoken patient was quietly obsessed with the thought that her husband's clothes were stained with lipstick and sperm; this symbolized her fear that he was having an affair and that others would discover this "fact," much to her shame; she did not dare confront him with her obsessive suspicion, dreading that he would admit it and then leave her.

Obsessive-Compulsive Syndromes among Retiring/Schizoid Personalities

Extended social isolation, with its consequent periods of empty rumination, often results in obsessive thinking, which the schizoid may be unable to block from conscious intrusion. Most of these thoughts are meaningless (e.g., "Where did I see a chair with one leg?") and experienced without emotion but, nonetheless, may be so persistent and distracting as to upset the routine of daily activities. Some recurrent thoughts may become tension-laden, pertain to forbidden impulses or prohibited desires, and, hence, evoke feelings of shame, disgust, or horror. The more desperately these patients try to rid themselves of these repugnant ideas, the more persistent and tormenting they may become. For example, a passing thought of poisoning a wayward wife may become fixed in a husband's mind; no matter how much he seeks to distract his attention from it, the thought returns time and again.

Obsessive-Compulsive Syndromes among Suspicious/Paranoid Personalities

These patients will occasionally exhibit obsessive-compulsive syndromes, as seen in an irresistible preoccupation with some absurd but safe activity that serves to distract them from confronting more painful sources of discomfort. Also, through reaction formation, they may pursue these activities as a subterfuge for socially unacceptable impulses. Thus, symbolic acts of compulsive undoing serve not only to void past sins but to ward off anticipated future punishment and social rebuke. Moreover, the self-punitive and redemptive aspects of the undoing ritual often diminish the oppressive buildup of guilt. For example, insistence on order and cleanliness, not especially typical of the paranoid's characteristic behavior, and the self-righteous air with which he or she performs these acts, distract others from the paranoid's previous irrationalities and often evokes a number of secondary gains.

CHAPTER 5

Personalized Therapy of Anxiety-Related Physical Syndromes: Somatoform and Conversion Disorders

Interspersed between TV commercials for headache tablets, muscular relaxants, intestinal tonics, and the like, we manage to see a few of the other forms of entertainment provided to meet the public demand. It has often been noted that more ingenuity is invested in attracting the American populace to remedies for their nonexistent ailments than in filling their impoverished imaginations. There are many reasons for the vast and continuous commercial success of these nostrums. Primary among them is the need of millions of Americans to find magical elixirs and balms by which they hope, usually futilely, to counter their lack of energy and a bevy of minor physical discomforts. These perennial states of fatigue and the persistence of medically undiagnosable aches and pains signify another of the complex anxiety-related disorders, one that runs to endless expenditures for drugs and physicians and disables, in one form or another, a significant portion of our populace.

Although the clinical symptoms of a heightened sensitivity to somatic distress and/or fatigue were described in early Greek medical literature, it was not until P. Briquet (1859) and George Miller Beard (1869) that a specific theory was proposed to account for them. They described what we now call the Somatization Disorder, a stable and well-defined diagnostic category that has been recently introduced again in the formal literature (Guze, 1967). Beard coined the term "neurasthenia" to denote what he viewed to be the outcome of nervous exhaustion in these patients. His theory rested on the assumption that nerve cells operated like an electric battery; that is, they could run down or be depleted by overwork and inadequate psychic rest.

Somatoform Syndromes

In his early writings, Freud (1900) agreed with Beard that the neurasthenic syndrome represented a physiological dysfunction. However, he hypothesized that the difficulty lay not in the depletion of neural energy but in the cumulation of excess sexual energies, which failed to be appropriately discharged. Freud subsumed neurasthenia in a single broader syndrome, termed the "actual neuroses," which included anxiety neuroses, neurasthenia, and hypochondriasis. As he conceived it, these three disorders were, more or less, direct outcomes of undischarged or dammed-up physiological energies.

The actual neuroses were contrasted to the "psychoneuroses," whose origins lay in psychogenic trauma and whose tensions were transformed and discharged by the workings of various psychic transformations. Freud (1938) altered some of these views in his later writings, proposing that psychogenic factors could play a role in the actual neuroses as well as the psychoneuroses. However, he continued to speak of the actual neuroses as bound and undischarged sexual energies, but began to see them as sources of focal irritation that could serve as the base for associated symptoms. Specifically, he posited the view that neurasthenia (fatigue) might function as a somatic basis for a withdrawal from social and sexual life. Similarly, hypochondriasis, which he conceived to be a mixture of anxiety and neurasthenia, reflected the withdrawal of sexual energies from their normal external objects and their consequent attachment to narcissistically valued parts of the patient's own body.

More recent formulations of the somatoform syndromes have focused less on ostensive energy components and more on their cognitive and interpersonal roots. We base our presentation on these current viewpoints rather than on Freud's original thesis.

Somatization syndromes share with "real" medical disorders a common focus on bodily distress and discomfort. However, medical patients ostensibly have a demonstrable biological impairment that accounts for their physical discomfort; their symptomatology arises, in part, from a failure to discharge physical tensions, whereas the symptoms of somatoform patients reflect their way of discharging psychic tensions.

Somatoform patients divert part of their ambivalent feelings toward themselves, transforming their partially restrained emotions into bodily complaints. Instead of complaining directly to others about their psychic anger, for example, they camouflage and complain about it in the form of a physical substitute. By turning their anger inward, they are distracted from the reality of their hostile impulses; this psychic maneuver prevents undue condemnation by others.

It is our belief that the subvariants of the somatoform syndrome (e.g., somatization, hypochondriasis, pain) represent different facets of the same psychic process; in one, for example, the patient complains of specific bodily ailments, and in another he or she complains of pain or of a general bodily weariness. These symptoms often covary in a single patient because they serve essentially identical functions.

General Clinical Picture

The clinical features of the somatoform disorders are difficult to narrow down. Not only are the types of reported discomfort many and varied, but they almost inevitably combine with, complicate, and blend into several other domains of psychic functions (e.g., behavioral, self-image). They are given special note by the presence of prolonged periods of weariness and exhaustion, undiagnosable pain sensations, persistent insomnia, a state of diffuse irritability, and reported ailments in different, unconnected, and changing regions of the body. In general, this group of syndromes is characterized by somatic complaints or disease fears that are out of proportion to any specified medical evaluation; they likely suggest the presence of a heightened sensitivity to discomforting physical stimuli, an exaggerated fear of disease, and the possible secondary gains of adopting the patient role.

Several variants of the somatoform syndrome have been differentiated.

Somatization is the recurrence of multiple somatic complaints, often leading to frequent medical attention and treatment over a period of several years. No known general medical condition can account for the symptomatology. Somatization difficulties, previously noted as Briquet's syndrome, are not consonant with the results of physical examinations or laboratory tests; they must show up in at least four different physical locations, for example, head, abdomen, back, joints, in order to be diagnosed in this category.

As part of the overall somatoform group, *hypochondriasis* signifies a preoccupation with the idea that one has a serious disease, a fear based on misinterpretations of one's own bodily symptoms. Again, as with somatization, no general medical condition can fully account for the patient's worries. Fears persist despite medical reassurances.

Pain disorders signify that the symptom is the predominant focus of the patient's clinical state; it is usually of sufficient persistence and severity to warrant clinical attention. Although the pain is not intentionally produced and is not a necessary consequence of comorbid psychiatric disorders, it is judged to be experientially real but exacerbated by psychological factors.

Conversion Disorders are discussed separately owing to the authors' belief that conversions involve intrapsychic processes that are only tangentially seen in other disorders of the somatoform group.

Experientially, some patients speak of a heaviness and a drab monotony to their lives. Despite this lethargy, they are exquisitely attuned to every facet of their normal physiology and markedly concerned with minor changes in bodily functioning. Many patients, despite their preoccupation and concern with aches and pains, manage to function actively and with considerable vigor in the course of everyday life. Other patients, however, are easily exhausted and cannot perform simple daily tasks without feeling that they have totally drained their meager reserves. This state of perpetual weariness, unaccompanied by specific body anxieties or discomforts, is a very common complaint.

As has been stressed in prior chapters, anxiety-transformed symptoms reflect attempts to cope with overt anxiety and to achieve where possible a variety of secondary gains. Although coping efforts employed in these syndromes may sound as if patients plan them consciously, this is very rarely the case. Strategies of coping engage deeply ingrained interpersonal habits and cognitive attitudes. These habits automatically take over when the patient is confronted with current situations that he or she perceives as comparable to those of the past. They persist, in part, out of sheer inertia, if nothing else.

Among the principal goals of the somatoform strategy are these patients' desires to solicit attention and nurture from others and to evoke reassurances that they will be loved and cared for, despite their weaknesses and inadequacies. By their illness, patients divert attention from the true source of their dismay, usually the lack of interest and attention shown to them by others. Thus, without complaining directly about their disappointment and resentment, they still manage to rekindle their flagging interests and devotions. Moreover, these physical complaints are employed as a means of controlling others, making them feel guilty, and thereby retaliating for the disinterest and mistreatment these patients feel they have suffered.

Prevailing Treatment Options

Of all the pathologies described, we can see most clearly the close interweaving of biological and psychological functions in the somatoform disorders. Of course, every psychopathological ailment derives in part from the operation of both psychic and somatic factors; somatoform disorders are notable in this regard only because they give evidence of this inseparable fusion in manifest physical form. What distinguishes them as disorders is not the fact that physiological processes are involved— a fact true of all disorders—but that they represent a failure to find a means of curtailing or dissipating the cumulation of these physiological processes. In other disorders, physiological tensions cumulate less rapidly and are discharged more efficiently. Let us turn to the general therapeutic approaches that have been devised to alleviate them.

The somatic symptoms of these disorders either persist for long periods or recur at frequent intervals. This state of affairs reflects in part the occasional physical damage that occurs in conjunction with the disorder. In addition, unless the circumstances that led to the difficulty are resolved, tensions will continue to mount and disrupt normal biological functioning. Further complications arise because many of these patients fail to recognize the psychogenic roots of their disease, and some often adamantly refuse to admit that they suffer any psychological discomfort or discontent. (We must be reminded, in this regard, that not all patients exhibiting somatoform disorders suffer these ailments for psychogenic reasons; clinicians must not attempt to convince a patient that he or she may be emotionally troubled unless they have a sound reason for believing so.) Resistance to psychogenic interpretations is found among patients who fear to open up or to become conscious of their forbidden or repressed feelings. In these cases, the prognosis is extremely poor as patients will shy away from therapeutic involvements that threaten to expose their hidden emotions. Only if their physical symptoms become extremely discomforting, frightening, or painful will they allow themselves to be subjected to psychodiagnostic scrutiny.

Therapeutic attention must be directed first to remedying whatever physical impairments have occurred in conjunction with the disorder. Body pathology, as in ulcer perforations, should be dealt with promptly by appropriate medical, nutritional, or surgical means. When the physical disease process is under adequate control, attention may be turned to the management of environmental stresses and to the modification of detrimental attitudes and habits.

As we have said, somatic symptoms arise often as a consequence of these patients' inability to resolve their conflicts and discharge their tensions. Because of their dread that these emotions will overwhelm them if released, the therapist must move slowly before exposing these conflicting attitudes or opening the floodgates to the onrush of these repressed feelings. Quite evidently, these patients have been willing to suffer considerable physical discomfort as the price for containing their unacceptable conflicts and impulses. The danger of precipitating a crisis is great if patients gain insight too quickly or if their previously hidden feelings are uncovered and unleashed too rapidly. Such exposure and release must be coordinated with a parallel strengthening of the patient's capacity to cope with these feelings.

The warning just noted points to the important role of supportive techniques in the early stages of treatment. At first, care should be taken to diminish tension and to help dissipate the cumulation of past tensions. Anxiolytics may be useful in softening the response to tension precipitants. In addition, arrangements should be made where feasible to have the patient avoid those aspects of everyday living that prompt or aggravate unresolvable anxieties and conflicts.

Turning to formal psychotherapeutic measures, the procedures of behavior modification and cognitive reorientation may be used to extinguish attitudes and habits that have generated tensions, and to build in new ones that may facilitate discharging, avoiding, or otherwise coping with them (Nathan & Gorman, 2002; Tazaki & Landlaw, 2006). Group therapy often serves as a valuable adjunct to help pain patients explore their feelings, learn methods of resolving conflicts, and liberate their tensions (Arthur & Edwards, 2005; Turner, 1982). Hypochondriacal patients appear to benefit especially with group cognitive methods that set out to correct misinformation and exaggerated beliefs, especially those that maintain the disease fears (Barsky, Geringer, & Wood, 1988; Kellner, 1982; Wattar et al., 2005). As was noted earlier, the probing and uncovering methods of intrapsychic therapy should not be utilized in the early phases of treatment as they may prompt the upsurge of severely upsetting forbidden thoughts and impulses.

However, should other procedures prove unsuccessful in alleviating tension or in diminishing the disturbing symptomatology, it may be necessary to employ intrapsychic processes and to begin a slow and long-term process of reconstructing the patient's pervasive personality pattern.

Personalized Therapy

As with others, there is no specific formula to detect which personalities will develop which disorders. But there are proclivities for some patterns, due to their psychic structure and function, to be more or less prone toward specific expressions of difficulty. With this in mind, let us turn to the various personality patterns that are susceptible to somatoform syndromes.

Somatoform Syndromes among Pessimistic/Depressive Personalities

In certain cases, somatoform symptoms are a form of symbolic self-punishment, an attack on oneself disguised in the form of bodily ailments and exhaustion. The following case illuminates somatoform disorders among depressive personalities.

Case 5.1, Samir N., 42

Presenting Picture

Samir, a Lebanese immigrant who came to the United States in his late teens, had recently begun to feel that his work at the office was of "empirically lesser quality and quantity" than that of his colleagues and that his exhaustion at the end of the day prevented him from being a "proper" father and husband. Although Samir was able to voice guilt for his perceived failures, this was the extent of his ability to consciously focus on his difficulties. Essentially, he was unable to fully face the real sources of his recent distressing and depressing thoughts, which began with a single episode of his "faking" a data set at an important meeting to make it appear as though he was keeping up with his coworkers. Thus, he manifested some symbolic physical substitute to punish himself for his guilt: "arthritic" pains in his fingers that made it increasingly difficult to write or to operate a computer.

Initial Impressions

Of note in Samir's case was his pattern of giving up. Highly sensitive to criticism and unwilling to admit psychological symptoms, Samir effectively put himself in a place where he had no choice but to break down physically. He was unaware that his secondary gain here was to avoid responsibilities that could potentially threaten his life pattern. Clear also was the use of his physical illness as a rationalization for his perceived inadequacies. For Samir, it was easier to tolerate weakness in his body than in his mind, a fact that also needed to be handled delicately, as it was intrinsically tied to certain cultural expectations. The fact that he had sought help from a psychotherapist (although he was referred by a physician, which made the prospect somewhat more palatable) brought about a sense of shame that he had a great deal of difficulty facing. Further, his sense of responsibility (both to his work and to his family) was compromised. With a patient with more Westernized values, this man, who displayed some traits of compulsive ambivalence (specifically, the willingness to create inner conflict by neglecting self-interests in favor of others' needs) within the structure of the depressive's passive resignation to environmental malevolence, may have been challenged more directly to examine gains brought on by his physical difficulties (e.g., possibly with Glasser's [1965] reality therapy approach, or with Ellis's (1970) REBT). However, it was necessary, in this case, to steer away from these more direct approaches in favor of one that would acknowledge the loss of his role in a more empathic light. At the outset, an existential framework (e.g., Frankl, 1946/1984), allowed Samir to focus on what the losses *meant* and reorient himself to finding ways that would make him feel more relevant without ascribing as much meaning to his more narrowly defined role. In this way, he became engaged in a paradigm of fulfillment, without overemphasizing what he conceptualized as a physical trauma.

Domain Analysis

Psychological testing for Samir was framed in a manner that emphasized self-learning, as the therapist described how the tests could identify aspects of self that "could be problematic when out of check, but could be strengths when they are controlled." His most salient domains on the MG-PDC were as follows:

Worthless Self-Image: This aspect, the therapist explained, was related to many people's tendency to frequently be their own worst critic, whereas it may serve in better times to set reasonably high standards. Samir, however, seemed to allow specific examples to devalue his overall character.

Temperamentally Melancholic: Samir admitted to feeling dour much of the time, wrapped in a sense of gloom, and failing to approach challenges with good humor because of a sense of worry that difficult situations will bring only hardship and strife.

Cognitively Constricted: It was difficult for Samir, for most of his life, to define anything nontraditionally, especially his ordained roles as father, husband, provider, and protector. His world and his duties were wrapped in many shrouds of "shoulds" and "musts," and therapy was an eye-opening experience in that he had never acknowledged even the mere existence of any other acceptable male role forms.

Therapeutic Steps

Following the establishment of an existential framework, which engaged Samir in growth orientation, he became much more open to the notion that his physical difficulty may have had a psychological underpinning. He became open to the suggestion of an SSRI (in this case, Wellbutrin) to address his *melancholic* tone. As a first cognitive step in this framework, he was engaged in a series of dialogues that sought to overcome his preoccupation with his physical difficulty, followed by those that focused, more thematically, on his tendency to produce *constricted* schemas regarding himself and his world. With this greater sense of comfort, Samir was better able to handle more direct challenges to his world of rules (i.e., REBT). Although further intrapsychic probing may have uncovered more deeply seated aspects of his inferior feelings, the combination of medications and cognitive procedures helped Samir, first, overcome his disability, and second, begin rebuilding his sense of self-efficacy. In this regard, the existential, supportive framework worked more subtly at helping Samir modify his *worthless self-image* into one that balanced targeted self-criticisms with an ability for self-accolade. A great boon for this overall process was Samir's acknowledgment, during a later session, that his employer had defined his work as well-regarded and, in fact, superior on many occasions.

To recap, this approach began with efforts to moderate Samir's low sense of self-esteem and his self-derogation, as well as his troubled mood, which was of extensive value in carrying him forward more effectively into the use of other, more targeted and directive procedures.

Somatoform Syndromes among Shy/Avoidant Personalities

Avoidant personalities exhibit somatoform syndromes to achieve a variety of different coping goals, such as countering feelings of depersonalization. They may become alert to bodily sounds and movements to assure themselves that they exist as real and alive. In more severe states, and because of these patients' habitual social isolation and self-preoccupations, these bodily sensations may become elaborated into bizarre, if not delusional, experiences. Discomforting bodily sensations may be used also as a symbolic form of self-punishment, representing the disgust, and sometimes hatred, that some avoidants feel toward themselves. Fatigue in these personalities may be seen as an extension of the avoidant's basic detachment strategy. Thus physical inertia can serve instrumentally as a rationalization to justify withdrawal from social contact.

Case 5.2, Kimberly G., 35

Presenting Picture

Hesitant, shy, and moody, Kimberly was a troubled woman who kept her distance from people whenever possible, although her retail job at a rental car agency forced her to deal with the public on a daily basis. She was well-regarded for her ability to attend to detail, as well as her timeliness and overall job performance, inclusive of her willingness to take on extra duties outside her job description (e.g., cleaning cars). She did receive several complaints from customers, however, which focused largely on unfriendliness as well as occasionally forgetting to inform customers of fine print, additional charges, and so on. This led to a "promotion" of sorts, in that she was then granted the nonpublic office job of subrogation administrator, dealing with insurance claims. This was better suited to her, although Kimberly then found herself unhappy with her coworkers. She struggled with minor digestive system complaints for most of her adult life, but shortly after the promotion, she manifested much more severe symptoms and preoccupations of a somatoform disorder (e.g., gastrointestinal discomfort, pain). Highly sensitive to public reproach and humiliation, as well as often feeling mistreated and aggrieved, Kimberly experienced considerable bitterness toward others, which she could not express directly for fear of retribution. Hence, her inner turmoil remained bottled up, vented indirectly through multiple complaints of a physical nature as well as through hypochondriacal concerns over undefined and unconfirmed bodily diseases.

Initial Impressions

Kimberly's complaints served as an outlet for discharging her psychic discontent, and her concerns over her bodily defects served as a symbolic displacement of her feelings of low self-esteem and self-worth. In talking with Kimberly in the initial interview, it became apparent (though she hid this well from others) that she was deathly fearful of what others thought of her. She conducted herself aversively, evidencing discomfort when any attention was paid to her, whether positive or not (she generally interpreted all stimuli negatively). Additionally, she did not directly acknowledge driving people away, but she did admit to actions and expressed negative opinions that, as a secondary gain, had the effect of averting attention. Keeping herself virtually cocooned, Kimberly warded off potential "disaster" by very actively being closely aware of all those around her and creating just enough negativity and unpleasantness in her demeanor that people simply disregarded her but did not disparage her. She balanced this with a willingness to work hard and be valued for those work actions she *could* control, rather than draw attention to her physical and character flaws, which she felt were beyond control, though there was little more "imperfect" with her than a very minor weight-control issue. In short, her primary avoidant pattern was infused with aspects of the ambivalent and skeptical negativistic style. In Kimberly's case, it was most important to decrease *activity*, that is, to focus efforts on bringing to light and then to control her tendency to scan the environment for sources of discontent and disparagement.

Domain Analysis

Although very vocal in her doubt of the value of psychological measures, Kimberly acquiesced to a full assessment in an effort to address her somatic concerns. Her MG-PDC produced the following highlights:

> *Interpersonally Aversive:* Kimberly was quite creative in finding ways to avoid interactions with people, but was ill-equipped for inevitable transactions that arose out of circumstance. In these situations, her sympathetic arousal was pronounced, and she shied away from any extended exchange.

> *Alienated Self-Image:* Underlying much of her interpersonal discomfort was the nagging feeling that Kimberly simply didn't belong to, or relate to, anyone in her daily context, a feeling that she was always aware of, sometimes sorrowful for, but often denied.

Cognitively Skeptical: Prone to view most circumstances in an unfavorable light, Kimberly anticipated the worst, and directed most efforts to letting the worst happen, as a self-protective measure. Discontentment, understandably, brewed from this mind-set.

Therapeutic Steps

A pervasive quality for Kimberly was a great deal of sympathetic arousal and conscious scanning for trouble. It was explained to her that therapy would begin with some desensitization, in the form of relaxation and a biofeedback procedure, to reduce anxious response. Over the course of these treatments, Kimberly's somatoform ailments did recede in their prominence, but did not go away altogether. In continuing treatment, a nondirective, client-centered approach was employed to permit Kimberly to express her concerns and fears and to explore the possibility that they may be an expression of her general personality traits. Cognitive modes, inclusive of altering and reframing cognitive content, were employed to assist her in recognizing her tendencies to interpret most events negatively and to cast *skepticism* over all internal cues and external stimuli. Several additional therapeutic modalities were also helpful in overcoming Kimberly's negative approach to life. Most central were efforts in the context of a phenomenological approach (most notably, motivational interviewing) to modify her *alienated self-image,* that is, to help improve her self-valuation. Similarly, a series of interpersonal skill-building techniques followed in a catalytic sequence to overcome her pervasive *aversive interpersonal style.* In this regard, efforts were made to aid her in sorting her feelings about others so that they did not interfere with one another, to guide her into feeling calmer, and to utilize a slower and more deliberate style of communication, one in which the interference of miscellaneous thoughts could be reduced. It was the clustering of Kimberly's fragmented thoughts, emotional hypersensitivities, fearful behaviors, and social detachment that contributed significantly to her Axis I syndrome.

Somatoform Syndromes among Needy/Dependent Personalities

Dependent personalities may develop somatoform disorders as a means of controlling the upsurge of forbidden impulses. More commonly, these symptoms promote the avoidance of onerous responsibilities and help recruit secondary gains such as sympathy and nurture. By displaying physical helplessness, dependents often succeed in eliciting the attention and care they need. Somatoform symptoms may be a form of self-punishment for feelings of guilt and worthlessness. However, dependents tend not to be too harsh with themselves. Their somatoform symptoms are likely to take the form of relatively mild sensory anesthesias, such as a generalized numbness in the hands and feet. It is notable that their symptoms often are located in their limbs, a way perhaps of demonstrating to others that they are "disabled" and, therefore, incapable of performing even routine chores.

Among other principal goals are the dependents' desires to solicit attention and nurture from others and to evoke assurances that they will be loved and cared for, despite weaknesses and inadequacies. By their illness, dependents divert attention from the true source of their dismay, the feeling that others are showing little interest and paying little attention to them. Without complaining directly about their disappointment and resentment, dependents still manage through their physical ailments to attract and rekindle the flagging devotions of others. Not to be overlooked also is that illness complaints may be employed to control others, make them feel guilty, and thereby retaliate for the disinterest and mistreatment dependents may feel they have suffered. In some cases, pain and nagging symptoms represent a form of self-punishment, an attack on oneself that is disguised in bodily ailments and physical exhaustion.

Case 5.3, Melinda L., 46

Presenting Picture

Melinda had moved to a new city following her divorce several years ago. Her ex-husband, a surgeon, had "fallen in love with an intern" and left Melinda with little notice. She stated that she was never truly sure why the marriage had failed; her hunch was that he never really wanted to have children, and Melinda had started to press the issue in her late 30s. In her "new life," Melinda had made few friends and was experiencing considerable distress and poor luck in the dating world. In the past year, she thought she had found her "soul mate," a man she described as having "infinite kindness and patience." However, as she became more attached and emphatically expressed her love and commitment to him, this man rapidly grew distant and abruptly ended the relationship, noting that he felt he needed much more space than she could provide. Melinda had recently sought medical treatment after experiencing a pattern of hazily defined bodily symptoms and hypochondriacal preoccupations. Although no clear organic findings could account for the full range of her ailments, she could not acknowledge the possible role emotional factors played in aggravating them, although she humored her doctor's advice and sought psychotherapy.

Initial Impressions

It appeared clear from the outset that several intrapsychic processes were involved in maintaining Melinda's symptoms. She used the ailments to distract attention from recent losses to her self-esteem over matters related to her attractiveness. No less plausible was the role her symptoms played in accommodating her feelings of emptiness and aloneness by compensatory self-stimulation and self-ministration. Not to be overlooked, too, was the possibility that she used her symptoms to gain and wishfully maintain the attention of significant others. Melinda's presentation was clearly *passive* and submissive to *others,* as was clearly demonstrated in the first session with her therapist. In fact, she found it extremely difficult to fill out the necessary paperwork and repeatedly asked the advice of the therapist in completing even basic information. What was empowering, in this regard, was to remind Melinda that she had completed similar paperwork with her medical doctor and that similar answers to those she had already given were appropriate. Much of this approach was repeated throughout the initial interview with this dependent patient; skillful interviewing techniques applied by the therapist called on Melinda to recall times in her life when tasks were completed. Not surprisingly, many times this included descriptions of when decisions were made or tasks were undertaken only with the support of significant others. This continued until Melinda discovered the humor in the repetition and began to acknowledge her needs in this nonthreatening manner.

Domain Analysis

Despite Melinda's early admissions of her dependent nature, the MCMI-III turned out to be too much of an arduous task to produce a valid profile. She stopped and asked questions throughout the protocol, second-guessing most items. Her clinician, however, was able to note the following domain highlights on the MG-PDC:

Inept Self-Image: Clearly, Melinda's greatest difficulty revolved around feelings of incompetence and a constellation of self-reflections indicating weakness and inadequacy, coupled with inability to make decisions or initiate action.

Immature Objects: Melinda's internalized world and expectation of others involved poorly conceived models of interaction, where she invariably took on the childlike role and expected others to resolve conflicts and save her from inevitable life stressors.

Expressively Incompetent: Much of Melinda's dependent needs played out in an expressed inability to assume adult responsibilities, soliciting instead nurturance and help for even basic needs.

Therapeutic Steps

The context of this overall personalized treatment plan was one where the relationship served as an *object reorientation* exercise. The therapist, who achieved a successful male role model transference in this treatment, worked from a combined object-relations and interpersonal framework to model and achieve more *mature representations* within the therapeutic relationship. This insight-oriented approach helped Melinda begin to realign her social role less as an inquisitive child, and more as an adult with parallel assertions and responsibilities. Although individual therapy was imperative in this situation, Melinda's therapist also advised a concurrent treatment approach. This was a homogeneous group composed of other dependent personalities. Discussion centered on their tendency to develop symptoms that curtailed their capacity to function effectively. Some group members were hypochondriacal, others suffered severe and recurrent pain, and the remaining gave evidence of a long-term somatization difficulty. The presence of other group members with similar physical ailments, as well as the willingness of members to share the possible psychological basis of their physical disorder, proved to be very useful. Gradually introduced in overlapping form with the group approach were individual treatment sessions centered on reevaluating Melinda's persistent misinterpretation of her sensory signals and her irrational beliefs concerning health and illness. A high measure of success was associated with these treatment methods. Although problems of interpersonal habit were amply explored in the group format, concurrent individual treatment served to reinforce and amplify this social learning milieu. Perhaps most important in these sessions were efforts to strengthen Melinda's sense of self-esteem, that is, to overcome her *inept self-image.* Her general lack of self-confidence, added to her tendency to belittle her own competencies, had left her with the feeling that she simply could not deal with life's exigencies on her own. A sequence of self-actualizing and skill-training techniques, for example, client-centered and behavioral learning, was fruitfully synthesized to achieve this end. These behavioral steps introduced her to enhanced adult activities and responsibilities in an effort to introduce more *competent expression* in both words and actions.

Somatoform Syndromes among Sociable/Histrionic Personalities

Histrionics utilize hypochondriacal and somatization symptoms as instruments for attracting attention and nurture. To be fussed over with care and concern is rewarding for most individuals; in histrionics, it is like a drug that is needed to sustain them. When histrionics feel a sense of emptiness and isolation, they desperately seek a diet of constant concern and approval. To be ill is a simple solution as it requires little effort yet produces guaranteed attention. Thus, if nothing else works, created symptoms may be depended on as a means of achieving these ends. Moreover, if life becomes humdrum and boring, physical ailments not only evoke attention from others but provide a new preoccupation and a source of stimulation.

Psychogenic pain and aches are another form of preoccupation and stimulation to fill the empty moments. Only rarely, however, do histrionics display somatic fatigue, as this symptom runs counter to their active stimulus-seeking style. They prefer to use obvious and dramatic complaints to draw attention to themselves, for these behaviors enable them to continue to participate actively in social affairs.

Somatoform Syndromes among Retiring/Schizoid Personalities

Although only modestly prevalent, somatoform disorders will become prominent and salient features when they do occur in schizoids. Noted for having prolonged periods of weariness and exhaustion, undiagnosable physical sensations, and persistent insomnia, these patients may fall into a state of diffuse irritability and report pains in different, unconnected, and changing regions of the body. Cognitively, schizoids report experiencing a heaviness and a drab monotony to their lives. Despite this lethargy, they become fixated, exquisitely attuned to some facet of normal physiology, or uncharacteristically concerned with a minor change in their bodily functioning. These preoccupations seem to reflect a need on their part to latch onto something tangible about themselves, something that will assure them that they do, in fact, exist and are not insubstantial or disembodied.

Somatoform Syndromes among Confident/Narcissistic Personalities

There is a reasonable likelihood that narcissists will exhibit somatoform symptoms following the shame of a humiliating defeat or embarrassment. Unable to solicit the tribute they expect from others, narcissists become their own source of solicitude by nurturing their wounds symbolically. Their hypochondriacal concerns are a form of self-ministering, an act of providing the affection and attention they can no longer obtain from others. Not to be overlooked among the secondary gains of these symptoms is their use as a rationalization for failures and shortcomings. Discomforting though it may be to admit to any frailty, it impugns narcissists' competence somewhat less if they can ascribe their defeats to a physical illness rather than to a self-implicating psychological shortcoming. Additionally, physical complaints are often a useful disguise for discharging anger and resentment. Discontent over their own inadequacies and too ashamed to express anger directly, narcissists may cloak their resentments by using their physical impairments as an excuse. Thus, they may become household tyrants, not only by creating guilt in others for failure to attend to the needs of a sick person, but by demanding that their claims for special status be instituted once again.

Somatoform Syndromes among Skeptical/Negativistic Personalities

These personalities often display somatization symptoms in conjunction with genuine physical disorders. Discontent, irritable, and fractious, they often use physical complaints as a weak disguise for hostile impulses, a veil to cloak their deeply felt anger and resentment. Feelings of retribution for past frustrations often underlie the excessive demands they make for special treatment. They seek not only to create guilt in others but to control the lives of family members and to cause them grief and financial cost. Although a significant proportion of these personalities may have been subjected in childhood to inconsistent parental treatment, most learned that they could evoke reliable parental attention and support when they were ill or when they complained of illness. As a consequence, when they need care and nurture, they may revert back to the ploy of physical complaints. Some may be sufficiently aware of the maneuvers they engage in to be justly diagnosed as exhibiting a factitious disorder. Others, less successful in evoking the care and sympathy they desire, have learned to nurture themselves, that is, to tend symbolically to their own bodily needs. Disillusioned by parental disinterest or inconsistency, these patients have learned to provide a hypochondriacal ministering to themselves, ensuring thereby a consistency in self-sympathy and self-gratification that can be obtained from no one else.

Because these personalities express their feelings rather openly and directly, tension builds up more slowly than in their similarly conflicted counterpart, the compulsive personality. Moreover, when emotional tension is discharged, it is less likely to be camouflaged.

Case 5.4, Whitney W., 43

Presenting Picture

Whitney was a dance professor at a prestigious university drama department. After a reasonably successful career as a dancer on Broadway, she noted that she had become "blacklisted" and had trouble even getting further auditions. At that time, she decided to change career directions and pursue teaching, and was eagerly snapped up by a department that was in need of a new head of its dance division. As a teacher, she was demanding as well as demeaning, and she soon received multiple complaints from students. Soon after, she experienced an injury while teaching, not unlike the one she had described in her faculty interview a year or so earlier that had presumably ended her Broadway career. Whitney's moody and conflicted bodily preoccupations and concerns were produced by both physical and psychological factors, resulting in a syndrome of features suggestive of a somatoform disorder. Enmeshed in an erratic pattern of resentment and brittle emotions, her anxious concerns about her somatic state aggravated her characteristic sullenness and led her to demands for attention and special treatment.

Initial Impressions

Not only did she exploit her ailments to control the lives of others, but Whitney also liked to complain of her discomfort in ways that induced others to feel guilty. Continually employed by virtue of her acquiescence to attend EAP sessions with the university's provider, Whitney was notably hostile in her description of her peers, her students, and her department, but in an offhand and indirect manner. Clearly ambivalent regarding her feelings toward others and actively manipulative in her solicitation of guilt and sympathy, Whitney demonstrated clear negativistic patterns. In approaching her for treatment, her therapist began with a softer Rogerian approach that appeared ill-suited for this purpose; at her supervisor's suggestion, she then modified this approach slightly, emphasizing boundaries and protocol in a manner that emulated Whitney's description of her teaching environment (i.e., "firm but fair"). One adjustment was made, however: The therapist made this a clearly democratic process, involving Whitney in the selection and adjustment of therapeutic boundaries that would serve to create this firm/fair atmosphere. In this manner, interpersonal respect was enhanced for both therapist and patient, and a working atmosphere was fostered in which clear progress could take place.

Domain Analysis

Whitney's results on the MG-PDC and the Grossman Facet Scales of the MCMI-III revealed these most salient personologic domains:

Cognitively Skeptical: Cynical, distrusting, and pessimistic, Whitney viewed good intentions as false intentions and lived by the mantra "Wait for the other shoe to drop." She had grave difficulty seeing the good in anyone and actively short-circuited any exchange for which she had any mixed feelings.

Interpersonally Contrary: Whitney could be cooperative and contrite one minute, hostile and underhanded the next. Perpetually unpredictable, it was rarely clear as to what motivated her, and the uneasiness fostered in others served to maintain her assertions that friends, family, and colleagues could not be trusted.

Discontented Self-Image: Whitney fostered guilt that seemed to emanate from her self-view of being misunderstood and unappreciated, as well as being handed a sorrowful lot in life; this was reinforced in her somatic symptoms, as "What could be worse than a dancer with an injury?"

Therapeutic Steps

A rational-emotive cognitive procedure was employed early in treatment to guide Whitney into an awareness of her manipulative and *contrary interpersonal behaviors*. Particularly useful was her assumption that significant others would not likely come to her assistance should she need or desire support. Her physical ailments were seen as an instrumentality to evoke such nurturant behaviors, Similarly, she was guided into recognizing not only her fears, but the anger she felt toward those she believed should be more consistent in their caring and nurturant behaviors. An early gestalt technique was also employed to provide her with opportunities to better understand how others were likely to feel in response to her manipulations. Combined with the cognitive methodology, these "empty chair" techniques proved to be extremely helpful. Whitney decided to continue treatment after her physical symptomatology abated in order to continue to undo some of these more troublesome characteristics. A key element at this point was to alter her *skeptical attitudes* and contrary behaviors and also to guide her cognitively to modify her *discontented self-image*. Much of Whitney's diffuse unhappiness stemmed from her unhappiness about herself. Hence, a variety of self-actualizing methods were blended fruitfully in undercutting the psychic conflicts that inhered within her, especially those that were perpetually reinforced by her own actions and beliefs. Similarly, greater efforts were employed to undercut her anticipation of disappointments and to help her appraise the motives and behaviors of others more accurately. Though not explored in this intervention due to session-limit constraints, other insight-oriented methods would have proven fruitful in helping Whitney experience deeper psychodynamic adjustment. Owing to the largely intrapsychic nature of her conflicts, brief variants of psychodynamic therapy might also have been helpful, especially those of an object-relations variety. Also, had her family been intact, thought may have been given to the possibility of dealing directly with its members so as to reduce her manipulative behaviors.

As noted earlier, among the principal sources of somatoform disorders are repetitive upsets of the body's homeostatic balance and chronic failures to dissipate physiological tension. These problems arise most frequently in patients such as Whitney who repeatedly find themselves in unresolvable conflict situations, such as when the discharge of tensions associated with one side of a conflict only increases the tensions engendered by the other side. This state of affairs describes the typical experience of both negativists and compulsives. They are trapped between acquiescent dependency, on the one hand, and hostile or assertive independence, on the other. When they submit or acquiesce to the wishes of others, they experience resentment and anger for having allowed themselves to be "weak" and having given up their independence. Conversely, if they are defiant and assert their independence, they experience anxiety for having endangered their tenuous dependency security. Although negativists do periodically discharge both sources of tension, their repetitive and chronically irritable behaviors reactivate these troublesome conflicts time and again. As a consequence, they often generate and accumulate tension faster than they can dissipate it. Moreover, because of their constantly fretful behaviors, their body is subjected repeatedly to vacillations in mood and emotion. As they swing from one intense feeling to another, their homeostatic equilibrium, so necessary for proper physiological functioning, is thrown off balance again and again. Not only do they experience an excess of chronic tension, but their system rarely settles down into a smooth and regularized pattern. By keeping their body churning, they set themselves up for repeated bouts of psychosomatic discomfort.

Somatoform Syndromes among Conscientious/Compulsive Personalities

Compulsive personalities succumb to somatic disorders, albeit infrequently, as another means of containing the upsurge of forbidden impulses. Somatoform disorders are not an easy choice for these patients, however, for to be ill runs counter to their image of competence and self-sufficiency. Nevertheless—and in contrast to phobic symptoms, which are especially embarrassing in this regard—somatoform symptoms enable these patients to advertise their illness as one of physical origin. It allows them not only to achieve the important secondary gains of attention and nurture but also to continue their belief that they are basically composed and proper, merely unfortunate victims of a passing sickness. Despite these gains, however, compulsives will feel most comfortable if they underplay their ailment, acting quite indifferent about it.

Somatization and hypochondriacal disorders are also employed by compulsives as a way of rationalizing failures and inadequacies. Fearful that they will be condemned for their shortcomings, compulsives may seek to maintain self-respect and the esteem of others by ascribing deficiencies to some ill-defined ailment or "legitimate" physical illness. This maneuver may not only shield them from rebuke but may evoke praise from others for the few accomplishments they do manage to achieve. How commendable others must think they are for their conscientious efforts, despite their illness and exhaustion. Compulsives do frequently suffer real fatigue and pain symptoms as a consequence of their struggle to control undischarged inner resentments. Bodily ailments may also represent a turning inward of repressed hostile impulses. Frequently, ailments such as these function as a displaced and symbolic self-punishment, a physical substitute for the guilt they feel after having expressed condemned emotions. Suffering not only discharges tension but serves as a form of expiation.

As noted previously, compulsives keep under close wraps most of the tensions generated by their inner conflicts. Through various psychic mechanisms, their resentments and anxieties are tightly controlled and infrequently discharged. As a consequence, physiological tensions are not dissipated, tend to cumulate, and result in frequent or persistent real somatic ailments.

Case 5.5, George S., 65

Presenting Picture

George, a retired economics professor at a community college, was known as one of the most cooperative and productive members of his faculty and was beloved by students. If it was for the greater good of the school or a student's learning, he did it. Although he was a tough examiner with a reputation for "dreaded" midterms, finals, and essay papers, his students felt strongly that they had learned and grown as a result of being in his class. Shortly after retirement, he experienced a somatoform pain disorder. He could not understand where his shoulder pain came from, as he diligently went through several checklists with his doctor in terms of physical activity and sleep position patterns, and medical test results showed no clear etiology. He also tried a chiropractic approach, but to no avail. As a last course of action, he turned, at his son's behest, to psychotherapy. Although he had spent a lifetime making jokes about the psychotherapy profession and dissuading his oldest daughter, a medical student, from specializing in psychiatry, he was, as he put it, "desperate." No longer able to sleep or sit comfortably for any length of time, he noted, in corroboration with his children, that he was becoming irritable, short-tempered, and sometimes directly hostile. The last straw came when he received a friendly birthday call from his ex-wife, with whom he had managed to preserve a friendship. At her friendly jest about his age and condition, George fired off a slew of bitter and vitriolic statements (he had never before raised his voice to her, even during the divorce some 20 years prior).

Initial Impressions

Unable to express disappointment with others directly or with relative equanimity, George turned his frustration and anger inward, thereby generating a variety of mild psychosomatic symptoms (e.g., tension headaches) over the years, but nothing had disabled him like this latest disorder. Although a number of concomitant anxieties as well as dysthymia were evident, he resisted the suggestion that emotional factors lay at the root of his discomfort. Efforts to downplay the psychological significance of his difficulties were consistent with his *passive-ambivalent* compulsive personality style. He tended to overlook the possibility that his physical discomfort served as a form of self-punishment, a means by which he sought to expiate feelings of guilt or shame for his usually repressed oppositional and hostile urges. What was eye-opening to George, in the initial interview, was that his therapist did not respond with shock or judgment at his recent hostile exchange with his ex-wife. Rather, he was awed that the clinician asked sensitive questions to try to understand George's feelings about the encounter. For what seemed like the first time, George did not feel as though he was being held to some external standard, but rather, to his own gauge of appropriate behavior.

Domain Analysis

Despite his disbelief in psychological technique, George was a willing patient who seemed to take interest in objective personality measures. He was intrigued by the psychometric and theoretical approaches inherent in this methodology. In addition to several other measures, he was administered an MCMI-III, and his clinician completed the MG-PDC. Highlights of his domain analysis from the latter instrument, as well as the Grossman Facet Scales, were as follows:

Cognitively Constricted: George constructed his world only in terms of external rules, laws, and expectations, mostly centered around being a good and kindly person who works hard and does "what he's supposed to do" with a modicum of humor and grace.

Concealed Objects: George allowed only pleasant feelings and thoughts regarding others and the world around him to come into consciousness; others were sent to the deepest inner chambers, where they were safely wrapped away and out of awareness. This extended to negative and hostile self-impulses that he regarded as dangerous or forbidden.

Interpersonally Respectful: Unusually kind and courteous to all close friends and family, as well as acquaintances, George exhibited strong tendencies to follow social conventions unquestioningly and conscientiously.

Therapeutic Steps

For short periods of time before treatment, George would "minister" to himself, experiencing less pain throughout his body. However, these periods were brief and

George relapsed time and time again in rapid succession, although he insisted that there must be "some more scientific way to do this that you must know, doctor." With this lead, the therapist did employ common cognitive distraction and behavioral relaxation techniques, which furthered the dynamic set in the first session—that of George's taking a more internal locus of control over his experience of pain. This helped, albeit indirectly, with both the expressed symptom and to derail George's deeply held and *constricted belief* that only external rules and processes were relevant to progress, but more directive cognitive techniques were necessary, as he could tolerate them, to begin questioning absolutes in his judgment and worldview. Less directive therapeutic approaches, infused into this cognitive milieu, included insight-oriented intrapsychic techniques to help George deal with what he experienced as a sudden upsurge of his anger and resentment. Cognitive techniques were then adjusted to assist him in recognizing that much of his disorder reflected a form of self-punishment. Centrally involved in this procedure were efforts to explore his feelings of guilt and shame, and that these feelings stemmed in part from unconscious resentments and anger wrought from his *concealed objects*. In this realm, the intense conflict that George had felt between his own wishes and those imposed upon him by others began to get sorted out. He then began, spontaneously, to ask about *behavioral* and *interpersonal* approaches (he had done some psychotherapy research on his own, at this point!) to deal with, as he called it, "my tendency to be so damned nice all the time." These skill-building exercises served well to moderate his unquestioning *interpersonal respectfulness;* that is, he learned how to remain respectful, yet pursue courses of action with others that helped him assert more reasonable boundaries and expectations of his own.

Somatoform Syndromes among Aggrieved/Masochistic Personalities

As described in other sections of this chapter, somatoform disorders may be experienced and utilized by masochists as a decoy to diminish the likelihood that hostile actions on the part of others would be moderated in their intensity. Instrumentally, such ailments may also serve the unconscious purpose of self-depredation, a means of inducing suffering in oneself to accommodate feelings of guilt and to reflect acts of self-flagellation. Also notable is the fact that many have learned that illness is associated with genuine parental care and attention, an attitude on their part that would not otherwise be forthcoming.

Somatoform Syndromes among Capricious/Borderline Personalities

These syndromes have as their primary goal blocking from awareness the true source of the borderline's anxiety. Despite the price these patients must pay in diminished bodily functioning, they remain relatively free of tension when they accept their disability. The choice of the symptom and the symbolic meaning it expresses reflect the particular character of an individual's underlying difficulties and the secondary gains he or she wishes to achieve. Both the problems and the gains that borderlines seek stem from their basic vulnerabilities and habitual personal style. This interplay can be illustrated with three brief examples: One borderline patient, whose pattern of life has been guided by the fear of social rebuke, may develop a muscle weakness to control the impulse to strike someone whom he or she hates; another borderline may suddenly become extremely hoarse for fear of voicing intense anger and resentment; a third patient may lose much of his or her ability to hear as a way of tuning out contradictory voices, both real and imagined. Somatoform symptoms rarely are the end product of a single cause or coping function. Overdetermined, they reflect a compromise solution that blends several emotions and coping aims. Thus, a pained and immobilized arm may not only control an angry impulse but also may attract social sympathy, as well as discharge the patient's self-punitive guilt feelings.

Conversion Syndromes

The discovery of the psychic roots of complex conversion disorders, aligned now with the somatoform group of syndromes, was a turning point in the history of psychopathology. The concept of Conversion Disorder, in which physical symptoms serve as vehicles to discharge psychological tension, may be traced to the early Greeks and Egyptians. They identified a disease, termed "hysteria," that represented a malady they believed was primarily found in women, and which they attributed to abnormal movements of the uterus (*hystera* is Greek for "womb"). A wandering uterus, they believed, could result in either the total loss of sensation in any of several body regions or the experience of peculiar sensations and involuntary movements. Treatment in ancient times included the burning of incense or the rubbing of sweet-smelling ointments on the body in order to draw the uterus back into its proper anatomic position. Similarly, the *Corpus Hippocraticum* asserted that hysteria was more common in elderly virgins and widowers and was the result of a lack of intimate or sexual relationships; marriage was recommended for both groups. Hysteria remained in the medical literature through the medieval period, although at that time it was attributed not to physical sources but to the operation of demonic spirits. In the sixteenth century, Lepois suggested that the disorder should not be attributed either to evil forces or to the wandering of the uterus but rather to lesions in the brain. Given this etiology, he claimed that the ailment should be found in both women and men. In the ensuing 3 centuries, however, no evidence of a pathological lesion was discovered, and the view persisted that the disease was limited to the female sex.

As reported earlier, a major advance came in the late nineteenth century through the work of Charcot and the subsequent clinical studies of Janet, Breuer, and Freud. Charcot, the leading neurologist of his day, proposed that "conversion" symptoms were caused by a functional weakness in the brain of a vulnerable individual. Refining this view, Freud proposed the first entirely psychological theory of conversion symptom formation. On the basis of a few cases, he claimed that the symptom represented repressed emotions engendered by a traumatic incident, which failed to be discharged at the time of the trauma. These emotions and their associated thoughts were dammed up because they were morally repugnant to the patient's conscience. By disconnecting them from the mainstream of consciousness, the person was spared the pain of recognizing their contrary or immoral character. However, through the operation of several psychic mechanisms, these emotions could be vented in disguised form. Phobias were one outcome; here, emotional energy was detached from its original source or idea and displaced to some innocuous external object or event. In conversion hysteria, the affective energy was displaced, converted, and discharged through a body symptom; other symptoms, though often obscure in their psychic significance, do convey elements of the original unacceptable thought or impulse. To Freud, these symptoms also symbolically represented the repressed and forbidden idea.

Although Freud later altered his views on the central role played by traumatic episodes, substituting in its stead the notion of repressed sexual attachments to the opposite-sex parent (Oedipus complex), his basic formulation of the genesis of the conversion symptom remained essentially unchanged. His work on the dynamics of conversion disorders, presented at the turn of the century, became the cornerstone of his psychoanalytic contributions. About the only significant extension of his original theory of symptom formation was the concept of secondary gain, developed to account for the fact that symptoms persisted even after their repressed emotions had been ventilated.

General Clinical Picture

Among the major overt symptoms of these disorders are the following (rarely is more than one evident in any patient): loss of speech—persistent mutism or repetitive laryngitis or prolonged speech stammers; muscular paralyses—loss of voluntary control of major limbs or fingers; tactile anesthesias—total or partial loss of sensitivity in various external body parts; visual or auditory defects—total or partial loss of sight or hearing; and motor tics or spasms—eye blinks, repetitive involuntary grimaces and erratic movements or muscular or intestinal cramps. The list can be expanded exponentially as there is a tremendous number of body parts and functions that can be used as the focus of conversion. The few we have noted are the most common and distinctive of these transformations. Other, less frequent symptoms reflect the operation of the same coping processes. What is significant in these bodily ailments is the fact that there is no genuine physical basis for the symptom.

The primary gain of the conversion maneuver is the blocking from awareness of the true source of anxiety. Despite the price these patients must pay in diminished bodily functioning, they remain relatively free of tension by accepting their disability. The choice of the symptom and the symbolic meaning it expresses reflect the particular character of the patients' overall problem and the secondary gains they seek to achieve. Both the problem and the gains patients seek stem from their basic personality style.

It has often been reported in the literature that conversion patients evidence what is termed *la belle indifférence,* that is, a rather bland lack of concern about their bodily symptom. Although this indifference to illness is found in some cases of conversion, it is by no means typical of all. It would be expected to appear in patients who for some reason do not wish to draw attention to their ailment. Thus, it may be found in compulsive and avoidant personalities, both of whom have serious doubts as to how others might react to their infirmity. Other patients, however, voice open dismay about their impairment. Such public displays of discomfort would likely be exhibited among the dependent patterns, where the desire for sympathy and nurture may play a part. It should be especially noted also in histrionics, who characteristically seek to draw attention to themselves.

The view has often been expressed that the frequency of conversion symptoms has been on the wane in the past half century. Systematic research, limited though it is, seems to suggest, however, that the proportion of these cases in outpatient clinics has not changed during this period (Stephens & Kamp, 1962). If there is, in fact, a decline in the reporting of this complex disorder, it may reflect changing habits of clinical diagnoses (e.g., terming these cases Somatization Disorder) or changing theoretical interests of psychopathologists (e.g., focusing on more basic symptomatic features). Not to be overlooked, however, is the possibility that patients in modern-day America express their tensions in different ways than those exposed to cultures of a century ago. Given the currently popular theme of sexual abuse, there appears to be an increase in its associated comorbid disorders; in this regard, there has been an increment in the diagnosis of one or another of the "hysterical" symptom patterns.

Another often held belief, recently reaffirmed, is that conversion is a woman's syndrome. This view persists, despite the fact that the disorder was exhibited by hundreds of soldiers during World War II and is often found today among men. There is, however, a factual basis for the belief that women exhibit conversions to a greater extent than men. We are inclined to attribute this fact *not* to intrinsic physical characteristics that distinguish men from women but to the greater proportion of women who develop dependent personalities. Because conversions arise frequently among dependent patterns, it would follow that more women would be subject to this syndrome.

In recent decades, interpretations of conversion disorders have added possibilities other than the psychoanalytic conflict-resolution model. For example, interpersonal thinkers stress secondary gains, such as the opportunity to take advantage of the sick role, thus, enabling patients to be free of their social obligations (Taylor & Braun, 1998). Other recent interpretations relate to the signal conveyed by the conversion symptom. Here, the symptom signals a distress regarding emotional feelings that are culturally forbidden or that may provoke retaliation should they be vented directly. Other proposals are based on behavioral learning theory; in this approach, a conversion symptom, regardless of its original source in unconscious processes, may recur time and again if it is reinforced under certain conditions. For example, an accident that temporarily disabled an arm may become a pseudo-neurological conversion owing to the success with which the individual gains sympathy from others or is freed from physically unpleasant activities.

Prevailing Treatment Options

Any treatment for Conversion Disorder should encompass three elements. First, there is a possibility that certain predispositions may incline individuals to develop the syndrome, for example, underlying neurological disorders, personality traits, or impaired communication abilities. Second, an appraisal should be made of a precipitating event of a traumatic or distressing nature, for example, an unpromising marriage or anticipation of failure in a new job. Third, perpetuating factors should be noted to determine the possible presence of sustaining secondary gains. On the basis of this assessment, treatment may best be thought of either as the mere removal of a symptom, the resolution of a neurological dysfunction, or the reworking of intrapsychic processes.

There appears to be a minimal role for psychodynamically oriented treatment—this despite the intrapsychic part these processes frequently play in generating the syndrome. Patients who utilize the conversion symptom tend not to be psychologically minded, nor are most capable of handling the costs and time required of such treatment. There may be facets of the analytic model for procedures that facilitate emotional catharses so that repressed emotions can be expressed; these cathartic expressions should be set in a context of supportive methods to help patients orient themselves to problem solving. Other supportive and reassuring procedures may help patients recognize that their symptoms are essentially benign and are likely to be resolved with a variety of psychically oriented treatment techniques. Such supportive techniques may be used as a face-saving device so that patients may give up their symptoms with a measure of personal dignity.

Hypnosis can prove helpful for some conversion patients. The use of this altered state of consciousness may allow patients to relax their symptomatic state, be freed of their unconscious defenses, and provide useful information concerning the disorder's precipitating agent or underlying psychological conflict (Oakley, 2006; Swartz & McCracken, 1986). Cognitive-behavioral techniques, including positive reinforcement, have also been reported as beneficial (Lupu, 2005). Here, heavy portions of praise and approval are communicated as the patient makes increasingly successful efforts at improvement; together with a measure of cognitive reorientations, the strong praise may reinforce a more healthy behavioral style.

Chronic pain calls for a broad-based management procedure rather than one that seeks to extinguish or to cure the disorder. Patients must be guided to learn skills necessary to cope with the pain rather than being subjected to often fruitless and discomforting therapies. Cognitive-behavioral procedures, however, may prove helpful in reorienting the patient's preoccupation with his or her disability. Similarly, through behavioral conditioning procedures, efforts may be made to introduce reinforcements that differ from the usual responses that the patient's pain has elicited, for example, being excused from social and intimate activities. In its stead, the patient may be rewarded for attempts to engage in more constructive and active behaviors (Lupu, 2005). Group therapeutic methods, especially in inpatient programs, also lend themselves effectively to the treatment of a variety of pain syndromes (Turner, 1982), as do cognitive-behavioral family approaches (Lemmens et al., 2003; Spence, 1989).

Personalized Therapy

We are now ready to turn our attention to correlations between personality styles/disorders and conversion syndromes. We shall bypass extensive reference to the typical precipitants of conversion syndromes. The events that trigger conversions are no different from those found in most other complex syndromes. These have been amply referred to in prior discussions.

What does differentiate the Conversion Disorder from these other syndromes is the strategy the patient utilizes to deal with his or her distress. The discussion that follows focuses on psychic maneuvers and covariants that achieve significant positive gains. Which gains are sought and which strategies are used to attain them derive from a long history of experiences that have shaped the individual's overall personality pattern.

Conversion Syndromes among Needy/Dependent Personalities

These patients may develop conversions as a means of controlling an upsurge of forbidden impulses. However, more commonly, these symptoms serve to help patients avoid onerous responsibilities and to recruit the secondary gains of sympathy and nurture. By demonstrating their physical helplessness, these patients often succeed in eliciting attention and care. Conversion symptoms may also represent self-punishment in response to feelings of guilt and worthlessness. However, these patients tend not to be too harsh with themselves. As a consequence, their conversion symptoms often take the form of relatively mild sensory anesthesias such as a generalized numbness in the hands and feet. Also notable is the observation that their symptoms are often located in their limbs. As with somatoform syndromes, this may be a means of demonstrating to others that they are disabled and incapable of performing even the most routine chores.

Conversion Syndromes among Conscientious/Compulsive Personalities

These persons succumb to conversion symptoms primarily as a means of containing hostile or other forbidden impulses. The conversion syndrome is not an easy choice for these patients, because to be ill runs counter to their image of self-sufficiency. However, in contrast to phobic symptoms, which prove especially embarrassing in this regard, conversions enable patients to assume that their illness is of a physical origin. Thus, it not only allows them to achieve the important secondary gain of dependence and nurture, as in somatoform disorders, but it also enables them to continue to believe that they are basically self-sufficient, merely an unfortunate victim of a passing sickness.

As noted earlier, these patients tend to underplay their ailment, acting rather indifferent and even comfortable with it. However, because of their need to cloak the pleasure they gain in their surreptitious dependency and to rigidly seal off the intense but forbidden impulses that well up within them, the symptoms they exhibit tend to be rather severe. Thus, in these personalities we often find the *total* immobilization of some body function, for example, blindness, mutism, or complete paralysis of both legs. The severity of these symptoms not only reflects the sweeping nature of their habitual controls and the need to prove the seriousness and unequivocal character of their illness, but it frequently represents, in addition to self-punishment, intense guilt feelings. By becoming blind or disabling their limbs, they sacrifice a part of themselves as penance for their "sinful" thoughts and urges.

Conversion Syndromes among Shy/Avoidant Personalities

These personalities display a wide variety of conversion symptoms, ranging from minor tics, generalized sensory anesthesias, and motor paralyses to the total loss of vision or hearing. These symptoms are not frequent because these patients avoid situations that promote tension. Nevertheless, when they are unable to avoid censure or excessive social demands and fear expressing their tensions overtly, they may bind their anxieties in the form of a conversion symptom. These symptoms are especially likely if circumstances stir up strong impulses of counterhostility that must be contained.

The loss of vision and hearing in these patients may be seen as an extension of their habitual avoidance strategy. By eliminating all forms of sensory awareness, they no longer see or hear others deriding them. Suspension of body functions, by means of either sensory anesthesia or motor paralysis, may represent the condensation and displacement of depersonalization anxieties. Rather than experience a total sense of nothingness, patients may crystallize and contain this dreadful feeling by attaching it to one part of their body. Conversion symptoms may also reflect an act of self-repudiation. Because these patients tend to view themselves with derision and contempt, they may utilize conversion as an expression of self-rejection. By disconnecting some part of themselves, they symbolize their desire to disown their body. The following case illustrates some of these elements.

Case 5.6, Richard B., 19

Presenting Picture

Richard never felt as though he fit in anywhere and was frequently the butt of jokes in his childhood social encounters. Though not unattractive, he did have the unfortunate liability of a long, thin nose, which was an easy target for bullies in elementary and early secondary school. The teasing abated through high school (partially because physical maturation helped reproportion his facial features to a degree), but Richard's uneasiness and social difficulties did not. He was seen for several years by his family physician in conjunction with periodic complaints of breathing difficulties associated with numbness in the nasal region. Subsequent neurological examination proved negative, and he was referred on for psychiatric evaluation. The presence of an ingrained avoidant pattern was evident. The specific referring symptom of breathing difficulty remained a puzzle. Interviews revealed that he was extremely sensitive and, although he had not lately been taunted by his peers for his rather long and misshapen nose, he still anticipated derision and degradation as he met new people while starting college.

Initial Impressions

Richard had become a master at covering his insecurities with a quiet, calm façade, but he remained acutely aware of those around him. If anything, the new people he encountered at college may have perceived him as standoffish, perhaps even snobbish, but what became clear in the therapeutic interview was that hypervigilance permeated his conscious thought content. Additionally, his active withdrawal based on his need for self-sustaining protection (pain orientation) inadvertently but systemically created an air of self-alienation. By virtue of the comfort level he ostensibly created by remaining aloof, Richard also reinforced the belief that he had no personal value, that is, no intrinsic matter of any consequence. Somewhat paradoxically, Richard's therapist decided to emphasize this comfort zone he had created, essentially giving it her blessing to such a degree that two important things happened simultaneously: First, Richard immediately trusted the therapist because she validated his strategy; second, and more progressive therapeutically, he began his own questioning of his alienated self and, for the first time in years, acknowledged his growing discontent in an open manner.

Domain Analysis

Richard had understandable trepidation about uncovering some very difficult personal matters. However, he responded very favorably to the assessment measures, as a modicum of interpersonal embarrassment was alleviated. His Grossman Facet Scale scores from the MCMI-III, in conjunction with the MG-PDC, revealed these problematic areas:

Alienated Self-Image: Routinely devaluing himself, Richard sought to conceptualize himself consistently with the disparaging remarks he experienced in earlier years. By creating this consistency, he felt he had a greater handle on the harsh realities of his existence.

Interpersonally Aversive: In tandem with his creation of a comfort zone, Richard did his best to maintain a safe distance from any intimate personal relationships, as these were seen as inevitably self-damaging. He seemed to even perceive a moderate but unfulfilling interpersonal success by virtue of being a peripheral character in social circles.

Vexatious Objects (Intrapsychic Content): Richard experienced people negatively due to internalized representations that never afforded opportunities for positive self-reflection. Owing to the residue of past problematic relationships, he anticipated rejection in social situations.

Therapeutic Steps

As he began to trust his therapist, Richard voiced frequent derogatory remarks about his own unattractive physical appearance, particularly the humiliation he had experienced when his earlier classmates called him "the anteater," a term of derision designed to poke fun at his long nose. The basis for his nasal anesthesia and its attendant breathing difficulties became apparent quickly. The nose symbolized the source of both social and self-rejection. By conversion desensitization, he disowned it. Breathing difficulties naturally followed the failure to use his nasal musculature. As this personalized treatment went forward, several therapeutic conditioning sessions were infused with insight-oriented efforts to bring to light his *vexatious intrapsychic content,* and his conversion symptoms receded with some ease. However, to leave other features of his basic personality unmodified would have been a moderately successful intervention, at best, as Richard would likely relapse and manifest his symptoms in some other way, all the while remaining discontent with his view of self as a viable entity, as well as his social situation. Most significant in this respect were efforts to modify his *alienated self-image,* that is, his sense of isolation and his devaluation of self. Alone and feeling empty much of the time, Richard benefited substantially not only from the paradoxical intervention utilized at the outset, but also from the creation of a self-actualizing environment (e.g., Rogers, Maslow) which assisted him in viewing himself more positively. For Richard, this treatment was nearly sufficient in and of itself. Punctuating this modality with targeted desensitization for his conversion symptom and with interpersonal techniques (e.g., L. S. Benjamin, 2003; Kiesler, 1986) helped him adopt more constructive habits inconsistent with his *aversive interpersonal attitude.*

Conversion Syndromes among Sociable/Histrionic Personalities

These personalities openly and dramatically exhibit physical symptoms. This is consistent with their desire to attract attention to themselves. Among their more common conversions are mutism and persistent laryngitis; these usually serve to protect against an unconscious impulse to verbalize hostile thoughts that may provoke social rebuke. Moreover, dealing with these symptoms results in eye-catching displays and enables the patients both to dramatize their plight and to draw the total attention of others to their only means of communication: gesticulation and pantomime.

Conversion Syndromes among Skeptical/Negativistic Personalities

Because these personalities express their feelings openly and directly, tension builds up more slowly than in their ambivalent counterpart, the compulsive personality. Moreover, when emotional tension is discharged, it is less likely to be camouflaged. Thus, conversion symptoms among negativists are exhibited in fleeting or transitory forms such as intestinal spasms, facial tics, or laryngitis. Symptoms of this type often signify sporadic efforts to control anger and resentment. Trained to use physical ailments as instruments for manipulating others, their complaints of vague sensations and pains are designed to draw attention and nurturance, as well as to create concern and guilt in others. These behaviors, however, are often difficult to distinguish from the other complex anxiety syndromes.

Among the principal origins of their conversion disorder are repetitive upsets of the body's homeostatic balance and chronic failures to dissipate most of their physiological tension. These problems arise most frequently in patients who repeatedly find themselves in unresolvable conflict situations, such as when the discharge of tensions associated with one side of a conflict only increases the tensions engendered by the other side. This state of affairs describes the typical experience of ambivalent personalities. As stated previously, both compulsives and negativists are trapped between acquiescent dependency, on the one hand, and hostile or assertive independence, on the other. When they submit or acquiesce to the wishes of others, they become resentful and angry for being "weak" and giving up their independence. Conversely, if they are defiant and assert their independence, they experience anxiety for having endangered their tenuous dependency security. Although negativists do periodically discharge both sources of tension, their repetitive and chronically irritable behaviors reactivate these troublesome conflicts time and again. As a consequence, they often generate and accumulate tension faster than they can dissipate it. Moreover, because of their constantly fretful behaviors, their bodies are subjected repeatedly to vacillations in mood and emotion. As they swing from one intense feeling to another, their homeostatic equilibrium, so necessary for proper physiological functioning, is thrown off balance again and again. Not only do they experience an excess of chronic tension, but their systems rarely settle down into a smooth and regularized pattern. By keeping their bodies churning, they set themselves up for repeated bouts of somatic discomforts.

CHAPTER 6

Personalized Therapy of Cognitive Dysfunction Syndromes: Substance-Related and Schizophrenia Spectrum Disorders

This chapter covers schizophrenic and substance abuse syndromes, the former essentially of an *endogenous* origin, the latter resulting from *exogenous* sources. Both disorders arise as a function of brain disturbances, the former primarily built in, so to speak, the latter stemming from drug incursions into normal brain processes.

Substance-Related Syndromes (Exogenous)

The "addiction" label has been used rather freely to describe a number of diverse preoccupations with activities such as golf, TV, and gambling. There are similarities between these normal social absorptions and those traditionally subsumed under the substance-related label, for example, the needs they fulfill, but they differ in terms of the impact they have on normal brain functions. Hence, the official definition in psychopathology restricts the substance-related disorder to involvements with certain chemicals, notably alcohol and various legal and illegal drugs. We believe that the cognitive dysfunctions of the schizophrenic group are essentially generated internally; that is, they derive from natural chemical imbalances and anatomical abnormalities. By contrast, substance-related disorders induce similar cognitive dysfunctions, but result from the introduction of foreign chemicals and substances into the body.

The general literature dealing with alcohol and drugs has grown rapidly in recent decades owing to their increased use among high school and college students. Along with the marked concern of parents and authorities and the fascination and intrigue that young people exhibit with regard to newer drugs, these chemicals are of major interest to psychopathologists owing to their effects on the brain. Concern and fascination notwithstanding, however, we deal with these substances only briefly, allying them with Schizophrenia, to illustrate that similar brain pathogens can be induced by exogenous agents.

Alcohol-Related Syndromes

Although early civilizations used and identified alcoholic intoxication with religious fervor and ecstasy, persistent inebriation was almost invariably condemned as a sign of moral degradation. Nevertheless, numerous figures of historical eminence were plagued with extended bouts of alcoholic indulgence, an ailment that apparently must have aided as well as impaired their attainments.

General Clinical Picture

The question arises, given the devastating effects of alcoholic addiction, of why the habit persists; that is, what functions does it fulfill to compensate for its many inevitable and crushing losses? In contrast to other pathological habits and their disastrous consequences, the solution to the alcoholic habit is so simple and uncomplicated: Stop drinking. What propels the addict to persist in his or her "foolishness" with so simple a solution at hand? Does this perverse habit reflect a deeper and more pervasive pathology? A literature review provides us with an endless number of psychological functions associated with the use of alcohol. These varied and diverse aims of the alcoholic habit can be grouped into four categories: *self-image enhancement,* for example, providing a feeling of well-being and omnipotence and bolstering self-esteem and confidence; *disinhibition of restraints,* for example, allowing previously controlled impulses such as hostility or extramarital and homosexual inclinations to be released without feeling personal responsibility and guilt; *dissolution of psychic pain,* for example, alleviating the anguish of frustration and disappointment in a dead-end job or a hopeless marriage, or blotting out awareness of one's loneliness, meaningless existence, and feelings of futility; and *masochistic self-destruction,* for example, relieving one's sense of guilt and worthlessness by destroying one's career or breaking up one's family. It is evident, then, that there is no single purpose or function to which the alcoholic habit is directed; in fact, some of them, for example, dissolution of psychic pain and masochistic self-destruction, appear at odds.

Given this diversity in alcoholic coping functions, it is not surprising that no one has been able to pinpoint an "alcoholic personality type." Some alcoholics are impulsive, expansive, and hostile; others are withdrawn and introverted; still others are plagued with guilt, tension, and worry. Notable are such varied characteristics among alcoholics as schizoid traits, dependent traits, depressive traits, hostile and self-destructive impulses, and sexual immaturity. In short, research and clinical observation lead us to conclude that almost all forms of troubled and maladjusted personalities may be found among alcoholics, none of them distinctive or unique to alcoholism, and none of them necessarily a cause rather than a consequence of the habit. Moreover, no evidence has been adduced to tell us why alcohol rather than other means has become the primary instrument for adaptive coping in these patients.

Disentangling the web of interacting determinants in behavior habits that involve biochemical properties such as alcoholism is especially difficult. The interplay between predisposing constitutional factors and experiential determinants is so intricate and subtle that no one as yet has been able to trace their relations. Most studies seeking to implicate a role for biogenic influences either have been poorly designed or achieve results that lend themselves to psychogenic as well as biogenic interpretations.

Vicarious learning seems to be a universal source for the original acquisition both of drinking habits and of alcohol's use as a coping instrument. Most notable in this regard is exposure to parental models and to the well-advertised image of drinking as a social lubricant and dilutor of tension. Youngsters may learn to believe that drinking is sanctioned for purposes of coping with frustration or dissolving guilt and responsibility simply by observing similar uses on the part of their parents.

Not to be overlooked among the forces of vicarious learning and imitation are common social stereotypes regarding the drinking habits of certain ethnic groups. Thus, the popular image that "the Irish are drunks" may not only serve as an implicit model to copy for youngsters of Irish descent, but also be a form of encouragement and sanction for drinking. When faced with the normal strains of life, an Irish youngster may turn to alcohol rather than to other forms of coping because he or she feels that this course of behavior is not only expected, but inevitable among members of his or her ethnic background.

Once the practice of "normal" social drinking has become established, the powers of positive reinforcement become more significant than those of imitation. Given the presence of any of the various coping needs that alcohol can serve, drinking if practiced repetitively can become deeply ingrained as a habit. Alcohol not only serves as a useful source of reinforcement, but it is especially powerful in this regard because its effects are immediate, in contrast to the slow and delayed character of other, more complicated forms of coping. Because of this distinctive feature of immediacy, the drinking response may preempt all other coping methods. Progressively, then, the individual's alternatives for dealing with tension and discomfort are narrowed to this one preeminent response.

Of course, there are negative consequences of drinking (hangovers, spouse complaints, and loss of job), but these negative effects are not as immediately experienced as its positive rewards. Moreover, if the person pauses to reflect on these troublesome consequences, he or she can quickly turn off these thoughts simply by taking another drink.

The final stage of alcoholism follows a long-term psychological addiction. Ultimately, there are changes in the individual's cell metabolism that result in severe withdrawal symptoms (tremors, nausea, fevers, and hallucinations) when drinking is terminated. At this stage, alcohol has become more than a psychological habit; it is a substance that the alcoholic craves to ward off a physiologically induced suffering. Now, as the vicious circle expands, he or she drinks not only for psychological reasons, but to avoid the negative reinforcements of physiological withdrawal. The alcoholic is both a psychological and a physiological addict.

Prevailing Treatment Options

Alcohol-related disorders are ideally approached in a multipronged fashion. First, however, there is need to detoxify the patient and to outline both the goals and duration of therapy. As an initial effort, therapy should be used to increase the patient's motivations and to assess those social and interpersonal factors that sustain the continued use of alcohol. Although hospitalization may be helpful, this may be bypassed with patients who are properly motivated and can remain in their normal circumstances without drinking (Hester, Squires, & Delaney, 2005; McCrady, 1993).

Unless treatment is complicated by a variety of personality factors, the primary thrust of treatment is usually behavioral, especially treatment in like-minded groups (Carroll & Onken, 2005). Efforts here seek to extinguish impulsive behavior, to identify and cope with cues for drinking, to closely monitor drinking behaviors, and to reward abstinence (Kaskutas et al., 2005; Monti, Abrahams, Kadden, & Cooney, 1989). Although groups can function with patients alone, most are structured under the guidance of a professional counselor or therapist. This is especially the case when efforts are made to deal with the reduction of anxiety and the acquisition of decision-making and assertiveness training techniques. Family therapy is often advisable, especially in helping family members share their perceptions of the patient's difficulties, as well as to reinforce the patient's healthy habits.

Except for complicating personality elements, there is little indication that intrapsychic approaches are useful. Similarly, the use of disulfiram (Antabuse) as a method of aversion therapy has not proved effective (Emmelkamp, 1994; Roth & Fonagy, 1996). On the other hand, programs based on the 12-step procedure of Alcoholics Anonymous demonstrate a reasonably high level of sobriety over extended periods (Gabhainn, 2003; McCrady, 1993).

Personalized Psychotherapy

As before, it may be useful to illustrate some of the typical personality patterns that occur with a more than average frequency with alcohol problems, as well as how they may best be treated from a personalized psychotherapeutic framework.

Alcohol-Related Syndromes among Nonconforming/Antisocial and Assertive/Sadistic Personalities

These personality patterns are among the most frequent in individuals disposed to alcoholic addictions, as described in the following case.

Case 6.1, Tom S., 26

Presenting Picture

Alcoholism was part of a general substance abuse spectrum for Tom. He was currently "being forced" to finish college by his father, who had pulled him from his fifth year at a school several hours away, then enrolled him at a local university and arranged to have him live with his aunt. This arrangement was because, as Tom put is, "We totally clash and he figures he can hide me there and not have to see me, but still be able to micromanage everything." Tom's alcohol use, as he stated it, "is the root of everything; anything else is just dabbling." He said that he smoked pot socially "but could take it or leave it," and also "sometimes upped the ante with some club drugs," but "at least I didn't get addicted to coke, like my dad did in med school." Set within a broad framework of hedonistic and exploitive traits, his drinking started as an adolescent recreational activity, which proved consonant with his general pattern of self-indulgence and stimulus seeking. Beyond its compatibility with several of his fundamental traits, alcoholism provided an outlet for his oppositional and antiauthority attitudes; it served as a means of expressing his unwillingness to accept conventional social limits and as a way to directly flout family expectations and to exhibit his disregard and even disdain for his family's feelings. Over several years, though, what he called his ability to be "a functional alcoholic" had become an inability to meet even his own goals. His once expansive mood that typified his daily persona, largely as a function of being intoxicated most of the time, had turned toward dysphoria and inability to focus. Although pressured by family to seek treatment, he was able to admit, "I probably can't keep this up and even take any care of myself."

Initial Impressions

Actively independent and self-centered, yet sometimes evidencing concern and regard for family and others, Tom appeared to show moderate antisocial patterns, along with some negativistic traits. Although not personality disordered per se, these tendencies served as a good guideline for approaching, understanding, and communicating with Tom. It was clear that a simple, reflective stance would likely be seen as an invitation to manipulate. What was more effective, in this circumstance, was to listen openly and to reflect selectively, that is, to engage Tom at points where he was clearly not meeting his desires and was unable to actively seek out what he wanted owing to the "friction" created by his alcoholism. It was too early, at this stage, to attempt to bring focus to his ambivalence regarding his aims and the aims of others (which, in reality, were more aligned than he cared to admit). A focus on self, with the reality that he was not really *capable* of pursuing his aims in his current state, was what was necessary for Tom to connect with the therapeutic process on his own terms.

Domain Analysis

Resistant at first to any attempts at "psychoanalyzing me," Tom begrudgingly took the MCMI-III along with more unilateral substance measures. His low rate of disclosure and conflict between faking good and faking bad yielded a questionably valid profile. The MG-PDC, filled out by the clinician, was more fruitful and revealed the following problematic domains:

> *Autonomous Self-Image:* Disdainful of social customs and flagrantly disparaging of familial expectations, Tom's braggadocio, in more "functional" days, emphasized his "need of no one." Of course, as the substance effects increased, he found himself less capable of this autonomy.

Expressively Impulsive: Tom was fond of the saying "You think too much," and he evidenced almost none in his behavior. Little restraint was evident, and he frequently found himself entertaining and indulging any whim without regard for safety or the feelings of anyone else.

Vacillating Objects (Intrapsychic Content): Resentful of others, and quick to point out their inconsistencies and shortcomings, Tom's inconsistent perception of others seemed to initiate actions that had the consistent quality of covertly unnerving significant figures in his life.

Therapeutic Steps

Despite his antagonism toward his father's wishes, Tom was willing to be admitted to a 2-week inpatient alcohol treatment program. Primarily detoxification and psychoeducational methods were employed in this venue. Tom completed the program having learned, to a modest extent, some of the cues that stimulated his impulsive drinking. This course of therapy was not atypical, of course; most programs such as these are oriented to having the individual stop drinking and be exposed to an educational reorientation. Tom returned to individual treatment, saying that he had learned nothing he didn't already know, but told the therapist, "Where you're coming from seems like it makes more sense." Clearly, a greater effort needed to be expended to expose Tom to a realistic/control program such as Glasser's (1965) reality therapy. The initial interview was conducted with elements of this style, and his therapist was inclined to continue this modality, also offering aspects of cognitive-behavioral, interpersonal, and self-actualizing approaches. Aspects of interpersonal approaches (e.g., L. S. Benjamin, 2005; Kiesler, 1986) encouraged Tom to examine his patterns of oppositional interpersonal interactions stemming from his inconsistent and *vacillating objects* (intrapsychic content); it was more fruitful to explore transactions from an interpersonal perspective, rather than adopting a more psychodynamic approach, as it was felt that Tom would become resistant to deeper explorations. His *impulsiveness* was addressed with cognitive-behavioral techniques, as suggested by Beck, 2005; in this manner, he not only learned alternative behaviors, but came to understand that his *lack* of thought regarding actions stemmed from illogical thought sequences, which he would rather dispose of than critically address. Finally, as some of these disparate elements came together in a more integrated sense of self, the reality therapy framework utilized throughout this intervention began to move toward an existential framework (e.g., Frankl's, 1946, logotherapy). Evidence was now available that there were resources within Tom, as alternatives to his drinking, that would serve the functions he wished (such as a striving for independence). Through this modality, his overemphasis on his *autonomous image* began approximating more of what one would call an "interdependent" self-image. Somewhat more agreeable with family matters and reoriented to curtail his substance proclivities, Tom began taking greater control of matters in his life without the dependence on exogenous resources.

Alcohol-Related Syndromes among Skeptical/Negativistic Personalities

Another frequent personality pattern found among alcoholics is the ambivalent struggling negativistic person, as in the following case.

Case 6.2, Wanda C., 39

Presenting Picture

Wanda came from a wealthy family and was able to live in a comfortable manner
without working. Family money paid for her luxurious condominium, replete with any
service she would possibly need, yet she disliked most of the other inhabitants. She
was intermittently subject to periods of alcoholism, provoked, by her admission, by
loneliness, disappointment, and resentment. Generally disposed to vent her brittle
emotions, she was prone to create and then escalate stormy scenes with destructive
consequences when she was drinking heavily. When sober, she was sometimes
contrite and very often isolative, sometimes spending entire weekends in the
bedroom of her condo, which she had painted a dark navy blue, with the lights on
very low or off. Although her discontent and dissatisfaction were entwined with
voiced guilt and contrition, her anger and reproach subsided only infrequently, and
remained, seething under the surface, even in those isolated times. When more
flagrant, her resentments often were aired in accusatory statements, irrational
jealousies, and harsh recriminations that intimidated members of her family. Added
to these denunciations was a self-destructive element that compelled Wanda to
undermine not only her good fortune, but also that of others whom she saw as
having frustrated and disillusioned her.

Initial Impressions

Wanda was quite used to the "drill" of therapy; she had been through five or six
clinicians since late childhood and couldn't remember a time when she was not in
therapy. In most previous situations, she remained in treatment until challenges
arose; claiming that her therapist had "lost all credibility," she sought our another.
As she entered therapy this time, this clinician took note of Wanda's history and was
careful to establish therapeutic rapport, yet not create "too cozy" an atmosphere.
One of her first statements to Wanda was "Therapy is not always comfortable,"
adding, "It is always safe, but not always comfortable." This was a very different
expectation than Wanda had experienced with others. Keeping a clear professional
relationship helped develop a boundary distinguishing the therapeutic relationship
from friendship or something more familiar. This is often a fuzzy boundary (at times,
for sound therapeutic reason), yet it is especially important given negativists' active
ambivalence, that is, their active conflict of self versus other, to maintain a visible
distinguishing structure in the relationship. Wanda's other therapists had made the
mistake of eventually resembling friends, which may even sometimes be

therapeutically appropriate, given needs, but not here. Carefully creating a safe atmosphere with Wanda, but precluding any opportunity for her to expect that she could back out of conflictful therapeutic material ostensibly for the sake of the relationship, encouraged her to open up while discouraging her from attempting interpersonal manipulations or vacillations. These challenges did arise, but they were more easily dealt with, and she did not attempt to flee therapy prematurely.

Domain Analysis

The MG-PDC identified the following domain dysfunctions, consistent with a prototypal negativistic personality disorder presentation:

Cognitively Skeptical: Cynical and untrusting and filled with pessimism, Wanda doubted good news, the intentions of others, and perhaps even her own forthrightness. "Nothing gold can stay" was a favorite quote, and she was fond of saying this about her own and others' fortunes.

Interpersonally Contrary: Unclear whether she wished to be "a better family member" or to continue to be, as she put it, "the thorn in everyone's side," Wanda would unpredictably shift attitudes, catching others off guard, and create "impossible" situations for those around her.

Vacillating Objects (Intrapsychic Content): Deeply ambivalent, both loving and hating close figures with no integration of conflicting feelings, Wanda's vacillations fueled her anger as well as her escape into bouts of alcoholism.

Therapeutic Steps

It hardly is worth pointing out both the expressed and unexpressed anger emanating from Wanda. However, it was worth pointing it out to her. Although she was able to admit resentments, loneliness, and extreme interpersonal disappointments, she had, surprisingly, never really felt herself to be an angry person, nor conceptualized herself in this manner. Rather, she felt everyone else had anger issues. But in the therapeutic environment created this time, Wanda eventually felt safe enough to begin to peruse this self-aspect. She had been in alcohol treatment programs numerous times before. Periods of improvement occurred for briefer and briefer time spans, despite her effort to become involved in Alcoholics Anonymous and other community-based therapeutic programs. Owing to her resistance and to her family's disinclination to explore more long-term programs, thus "wasting money" on nonsense, Wanda failed to improve in any significant and enduring way. What was clear this time was that she would likely improve if she were exposed to methods that would integrate her alcoholic behaviors with deeper personality styles of contrariness and resentfulness. She benefited from cognitive methods designed to overcome her anger and self-perpetuating *cognitive skepticism*. Similarly, a mix of behavioral and interpersonal procedures helped her deal with her covertly hostile ways of relating to others (*interpersonal contrariness*). Self-actualization procedures followed these techniques and provided Wanda with the opportunity to further explore her inner discontents and her feelings of being unappreciated and disillusioned. In later sessions, as she became much more productive, had resolved many of her immediate discontents, and had learned a variety of alternative copings skills, aspects of Kernberg's (1988) object-relations approach were introduced to further expose her more unconscious ambivalences, that is, the conflicts that she felt between a desire to be cared for and loved, and her need to assert her own independent impulses (her *vacillating objects*).

Alcohol-Related Syndromes among Conscientious/Compulsive Personalities

Alcoholism in compulsive personalities runs counter to their habitual pattern of propriety. They usually signify a developmental sequence of imitative learning or the need to break free of the shackles they have placed on themselves, as noted in the following.

Case 6.3, Sheila R., 49

Presenting Picture

Sheila was a pillar of her community. In the public eye, she was beyond reproach. She was a devoted mother, a dedicated volunteer at her temple's underserved outreach organization, a school board member, and a supportive wife. She performed her duties, in this regard, without a hitch. Schooled as a lawyer, she felt it appropriate to forgo her career for the sake of her husband's professorship, as well as for the sake of being a full-time mother to three children. Most people said of Sheila and her family, "It just seems too good to be true. No one's family unit works that well," which was true. There was a dark secret: Sheila experienced repeated periods of alcoholism that both reflected and engendered concealed family tensions. She expressed genuine regret and self-reproach over her recurring drinking, and she made many concerted efforts to resolve the habit, but she would be only marginally successful over the course of several years. Each relapse, however, seemed to be more troublesome than the previous. More tensions arose each time, the children started to respond with poor school performance, and there was even a threat of divorce. The final straw came about when Sheila's oldest child was suspended from high school for possession of a marijuana joint. Sheila decided that she could not possibly be effective in any role without professional help.

Initial Impressions

Despite her passive denial, Sheila's recurrent alcoholism was sustained and reinforced by the psychological needs it fulfilled for her. True to her compulsive personality pattern, she appeared caught in an unsolvable conflict between wishing to maintain her sense of propriety and responsibility and wanting to display strong resentment toward those she felt no longer valued her dutiful efforts. She would not openly admit the latter aspect, as she appeared to be unaware of the effects of this lack of appreciation. This underappreciation despite her devotion and conscientiousness left her highly disappointed and resentful, but without an acceptable outlet. Alcohol not only served to dissolve her restrictive conscience but also enabled her to discharge negativistic impulses and embittered feelings while displacing responsibility for their consequences elsewhere. To develop rapport with Sheila and instill a modicum of safety, language in the therapeutic setting took on the quality of hypotheticals, for example, "How do you imagine a less tolerant person might respond to . . . ?" The therapist remained nondirective at this stage, but gently prompted Sheila to add flexibility to her overconscientiousness. As a result, Sheila voiced not only more alternatives to drinking, but her perceived resistance to those alternatives.

Domain Analysis

In addition to substance screening instruments (e.g., Substance Abuse Subtle Screening Inventory—SASSI) and a clinical interview, Sheila was administered an MCMI-III along with the clinician's MG-PDC. Domains from these latter instruments revealed the following problematic domains, consistent with compulsive and negativistic tendencies:

Cognitively Constricted: Sheila's cognitive content was notably narrow in its focus, resistant to thinking about less traditional or possibly unacceptable thoughts, feelings, or behaviors regarding her role as a parent and member of the community.

Conscientious Self-Image: It was painful for Sheila to think of herself in any other way than as dutiful, hard-working, and focused on always "doing the right thing." This regularly played out in her tendency to be *expressively disciplined,* in itself not problematic but too closely tied to her self-perception to be comfortable.

Interpersonally Contrary: In this domain, Sheila played out resentments. Vacillating between being "perfectly respectful" while sober and sharply resentful when drinking (represented by semiconcealed jabs and barbs at important figures in her life), Sheila could allow only covert expression of any hostility.

Elsewhere (e.g., Millon with Davis, 1996a; Millon et al., 2004) this particular compulsive and negativistic pattern has been referred to as the "bedeviled compulsive," although this refers to a more pathological variant. Sheila did not qualify for an Axis II diagnosis in this regard, but demonstrated specific domain dysfunction, which appeared to be the catalyst for her alcohol abuse.

Therapeutic Steps

Sheila wanted to stop drinking altogether, and felt that she could do so quickly, with appropriate support. Her therapist began by combining use of Antabuse with a Rogerian self-actualizing orientation; Sheila concurrently joined Alcoholics Anonymous, incorporating many of the techniques and philosophy guiding that group. The combination appeared to be successful in that Sheila's alcoholism was sharply reduced within a brief period, and then given up altogether. Not unexpectedly, she adhered to this regimen that had been constructed for her, and was most appreciative of the acceptance she received from her therapist. But this also left her with several aspects of her psychic makeup unresolved and with her resentments now more pronounced and without outlet, despite greater hopefulness owing to her rapid success over her alcohol use. Her world was *constricted cognitively,* which required more directive cognitive-behavioral methods than were introduced at the outset of treatment. A linguistic change occurred at this point, changing hypotheticals to more direct questions, such as "What can you do differently?" Sheila was forced to make more *active, conscious* decisions without the use of alcohol. With newfound confidence, her decisions were not only self-directed but were in line with what was more broadly acceptable. She had been overly disciplined in her behavior and was dependent on rules and regulations to keep her behavior within acceptable bounds; now she found that she could sensibly adjust societal rules without threatening her *conscientious self-image.* What remained were her resentments, and rarely were these emotions brought to the surface. At this point it was beneficial to change modes to family therapy, to assist her in recognizing her deep antagonisms and resentments, the source of her *interpersonal contrariness,* and to do so without resulting in an emotional explosiveness or alcoholic acting-out.

Alcohol-Related Syndromes among Shy/Avoidant Personalities

Involvement with alcohol is not unexpected among avoidant personalities owing to their anguishing life experiences and the desire to obliterate their reality and its residues.

Case 6.4, Roland G., 45

Presenting Picture

Roland, a slight, thin man, lived in the same small, one-bedroom apartment through college and for all of his adult life. Although he lived in this same community, he knew very few people, spent most of his adult days alone, and experienced repeated, intermittent episodes of alcohol abuse. A repair supervisor at the same electronics franchise store in which he took a part-time job in college, Roland was capable of directing his small department only by relying heavily on his title, earned more as an accolade for time on the job than for any particular leadership or supervisory ability. He had extreme difficulties once outside of that familiar environment. Anxiously troubled, lonely, and socially apprehensive much of the time, he turned to alcohol to fulfill a number of otherwise difficult to achieve psychological functions, most notably socialization necessitated by coworker activities, official company events, and casual get-togethers. Alcohol not only served to medicate his social anxiety and thereby enhance his confidence but also helped him relate more comfortably to others by bolstering his feelings of self-esteem and well-being. Beyond that, however, he had also taken to drinking alone, spending most nights with a six-pack of beer and his television set. For him, alcohol provided a quick dissolution of psychic pain and a method for blotting out awareness of his loneliness and troubled existence.

Initial Impressions

Roland fought hard to escape what he saw as his dismal plight in life, in which he had no choice but to "grin and bear" the many disappointments and seeming injustices life doled out. He had graduated with honors from his university with a degree in electronics engineering, but he declined to ever put his talents on the market, instead settling for what was essentially an unintentional management track in retail. Numerous other examples of his *active* orientation toward self-protection (i.e., *pain avoidance*) abounded in his existence, inclusive of his refusal to allow his parents or extended family members to know his whereabouts, his frequenting of noisy bars in which he could "just disappear" into the background, and his apprehensiveness when meeting new people, even new employees of the electronics store joining as rookie salespeople. Roland clearly demonstrated an *avoidant* personality, nearly prototypal in his presentation, and his use of alcohol served a protective role, ensuring the status quo of his life while dulling sensations that would otherwise serve to create self-effacing ruminations and beliefs that others serve no purpose other than to ridicule and harm him. Approaching Roland for treatment required strong understanding, an empathic response oriented to his view of the world as a hostile and cut-throat place for which he was not cut out. This is not to say that the therapist would enjoin him to take on a defeatist attitude, but rather, to allow Roland freedom to express these fears without the subsequent fear of repercussion in the form of dispute (to be read by Roland as ridicule). The framework required that in preparation for forward motion, Roland would view any therapeutic step as a challenge, and he alone would dictate what steps, and at what rate, goals and treatment plans would progress.

Domain Analysis

Scores on his MCMI-III and MG-PDC reflected Roland's prototypal avoidant pattern, as follows:

> *Alienated Self-Image:* Roland suffered tremendously from feelings of inferiority and consistently devalued his achievements and personal qualities, opting to place himself on the fringe of his community and expect rejection at any attempt to engage with others.

> *Cognitively Distracted:* Constantly "on the lookout" for potential slights and threats, rarely would Roland allow himself moments of relaxation, much less a break in the continuum of constant interruptive and intrusive thoughts about his lack of worthiness.

Interpersonally Aversive: Although surrounded by people daily, Roland made it a point to remain at a safe distance from all others, distrusting even family members looking out for his best interest, as well as those who made explicit overtures of friendship.

Therapeutic Steps

In his initial treatment (prior to the current personalized course), Roland was encouraged to simply join a hospital-based alcohol treatment program. From a therapeutic viewpoint, efforts were designed to teach him the cues that precipitated his drinking behaviors and to have him participate in a daily group session composed of others who possessed alcohol-related problems. On completion of his outpatient protocol treatment at the hospital, Roland joined Alcoholics Anonymous, but found the setting discomforting. He noted that with new and inconsistent people joining and leaving the group at each session, he was once again intimidated, fearful, and aversive—the very feelings that had perpetuated his behavior. He then sought additional individual treatment. In his new personalized psychotherapy course, a broader perspective was taken than to simply address his drinking behavior. He was encouraged to continue the AA meetings and, just as that milieu allows, remain silent and listen until he felt he had something to say. Given that he fit the classic pattern of an avoidant personality, an initial effort was directed at increasing his awareness of the functions served by alcohol. Allowing Roland permission to simply observe, as he had done previously in the noisy bars, provided fodder for the initial individual therapy conversations. Reflecting on his experience in those meetings, he found awareness and insight into the origins of his escapist behaviors and came to a fuller understanding that he had utilized alcohol to reduce his social anxieties and intrapsychic tensions. This was achieved not only by examining similar statements of others, but by reflecting on his immediate early experience in that environment. A potentiated pairing was created here: Not only did Roland gain the insight that he was not alone in his insecure feelings and was not the only person to use a substance to attempt to self-medicate, but he also found his wandering, threat-bearing thoughts to be incompatible with the reality surrounding him. In other words, he felt less *alienated,* in that men and women at this meeting who were seemingly respectable shared this awful plight! At the same time, thought disputing (e.g., Beck, 2005) was used against his tendency toward troublesome *distractible cognitions* that had him looking for slights, as the people around him were just as vulnerable. This provided a foundation for moving into other matters of significance to him. These first two milieus required several sessions of follow-up work, and his sense of alienation required a bit more; thus, it was possible to begin efforts in the *interpersonal* realm beyond that already provided by his presence in the group. To combat *aversive* interpersonal feelings, Roland progressively worked through assertiveness and social skills training, gradually making connections with other group members, and eventually finding himself with enough sense of support to begin speaking at the meetings.

Drug-Related Syndromes

Alcohol has not been the only instrument for facilitating people's need to relieve pain and monotony. Drugs also have served since ancient times to moderate the discomforts of life and to expand its illusory possibilities.

Alcohol is a drug, although Western customs have guided our thinking otherwise. There are as many differences in chemical composition and effects between drugs as there are between alcohol and most drugs. In short, were it not for our customary practices, alcohol would be viewed as just one of a number of chemical substances to which people become habituated and addicted. Viewed in this way, the preceding discussion on alcohol-related syndromes applies in large measure to drug-related syndromes.

Because of condemnatory attitudes toward and laws against drugs in this country, the incidence of drug abuse is somewhat less than that found with alcohol. However, in recent decades there has been a marked rise in the usage of certain hallucinogens and stimulants, especially among adolescents of all socioeconomic groups. This increased evidence has given rise to a flood of public concern and consternation.

General Clinical Picture

Broadly speaking, two groups of patients misuse drugs: those who are in psychological or physical pain and who employ drugs as a form of self-medication, and those who use drugs for recreational purposes and appear to enjoy the experience generated by drugs (Leigh, 1985). Those who misuse drugs come from a wide range of psychological backgrounds, but most present themselves with a variety of interpersonal and occupational problems. Difficulties with impulse control is very common, particularly among those who readily experience boredom and have a need to seek excitement. We shall not go into the many varieties of drug disorders in this chapter, but touch on a few of the more prevalent in use today.

Marijuana and cocaine are among the oldest and best known drugs used to induce temporary euphoria and relaxation (cocaine or "coke" has been listed in some quarters as an addictive drug, but it does not fulfill the criteria of physiological dependence and withdrawal symptoms). In recent years, marijuana, better known as "pot" or "grass," has attained great popularity among "liberated" high school and college students. Here, it is used as a means of "cooling it," that is, gaining a pleasant interlude of mild euphoria to block out what are felt to be the absurd values and oppressive regulations of a dehumanized and bigoted society. This drug has no known harmful physical effects, but it often serves as a prelude to the use of other, less benign agents.

As was stated earlier, drugs and alcohol appear to fulfill essentially similar purposes, although perhaps in somewhat different population groups. Thus, we would include self-image enhancement, disinhibition of restraints, dissolution of psychic pain, and masochistic self-destruction among the various coping aims of drug use.

Etiological factors conducive to the development of drug habits appear, essentially, to be the same as those found in alcoholism: imitation as the source of habit origination; positive reinforcement of coping aims as a means of strengthening the habit; and body chemical changes resulting in physiological addiction. Narcotic and sedative addictions often have their origin in medical treatment; thus, morphine may have been prescribed to relieve pain, and Seconal recommended to counter insomnia. The hallucinogenic habit is most commonly acquired as an incidental by-product of peer group involvement; thus, smoking pot or tripping with coke has come to be expected of everyone associated with the "alienated" adolescent subculture.

Next, we may ask if there are differences between those who become addicted to alcohol rather than to drugs. There is a considerable overlap, of course, but it appears that drug involvement, with the exception of sedative addictions, is primarily a problem of the young. Relatively few people over 50 are frequent users of narcotics, hallucinogens, and stimulants. This difference between age groups reflects in part the relative recency and popularity of certain drugs. Thus, older people who were addictively disposed years ago could not have been exposed to these agents until well after they had been hooked on something else, in all likelihood alcohol. Moreover, until fairly recently, the image of the drug addict was that of a lower-class degenerate, hardly an inviting model for the young of the past to identify with. This contrasts with the rebellious juvenile or alienated intellectual hippie images associated with current-day users, an attractive model to be emulated by ingroup high school and college students.

Prevailing Treatment Options

There is no single approach that works with all varieties of drug-involved patients. If appropriate, initial steps should be taken to detoxify the patient. A basic program of drug education may also be helpful in the early phase of treatment. Where available, a measure of environmental management should be considered as a means of diminishing the number of opportunities conducive to continued drug intake. Various behavioral therapy methods should be explored to promote impulse control (e.g., reinforcement withdrawal, aversive learning). Group treatment settings, composed of a number of peer-level fellow drug patients, may be highly useful to explore their thoughts and plan methods of remediation. In these settings, styles of thought and behavioral experiences can be openly shared *without* the presence of the authority of a professional leader, hence, avoiding the oppositional feelings that characterize many drug patients. Involvements with family members may be helpful, where support and reassurance may be conveyed. In general, formal cognitive and intrapsychic therapies that focus on insight have not achieved desirable levels of success.

Personalized Psychotherapy

Are there differences in personality among those who use different drugs? No clinical research or data have accumulated to provide an answer to this question. From the few unsystematic studies available, it would appear that drug choice may be influenced in part by the characteristic coping style of the individual. In other words, addicts may select a drug that is consonant with and facilitates their preferred mode of dealing with stress. If there is merit to this speculative hypothesis, we would expect to find a disproportionate number of schizoid and avoidant personalities among narcotic users, as these drugs would facilitate their tendencies to social withdrawal and indifference. Similarly, sedatives might be preferred among the dependent and compulsive personalities to aid in controlling impulses that can upset their equanimity and protected status. Hallucinogens, to extend this series of conjectures, might be found more commonly among narcissistic types, who characteristically turn inward to enlarge their world of experience. Stimulants may be preferred by histrionics, who seek excitement, change, and adventure, and by sadists and antisocials, who not only dread feelings of weakness, but desire energy to act out their resentments and aggressive impulses.

There is a major degree of overlap between antisociality and substance-related disorders. In great measure, this covariation can be attributed to economic influences and social dynamics rather than to intrapsychic processes that are distinctive to any specific personality. Among antisocials, the opportunities for material gain (at least for those who deal in drugs) and status enhancement are a powerful draw. For others, there are elements of dissolving feelings of guilt and self-destructiveness that may contribute some share to their intrapsychic motivation.

There is also a strong association in contemporary society between borderline personality characteristics and heavy involvement in substance abuse. The association does not appear to be an intrinsic element of these disorders, but appears to signify borderlines' desire to experience varied forms of reality and an effort to search for an identity that may give structure to their divergent impulses and confusions. Hence, borderlines are inclined to be abusers of many different substances, including alcohol, as well as cocaine, speed, and crack.

Schizophrenic Syndromes (Endogenous)

Schizophrenic disorders are extremely severe forms of psychopathology and normally require periods of inpatient or hospital treatment. The rather baffling symptoms we observe in these patients represent extreme brain impairments plus the bizarre efforts on their part to cope with the disintegration of their thinking processes. These disorders contrast with the severe personality patterns, such as the schizotypal, in which corrosive pathological processes have permeated the entire personality structure. In Schizophrenia the pathology tends to be episodic and reversible and not as permanent and ingrained as the personality patterns.

We refer to the schizophrenic syndromes as "endogenous" because it is our belief that this complex cluster of severe behaviors, thoughts, and feelings stem largely from internal or biological deficiencies and dysfunctions. They contrast with the substance-related disorders in that external forces serve to induce the disturbed cognitive processes of individuals in the latter group. In both, we see potential thought disturbances as well as irrational emotions and behavior.

General Clinical Picture

Patients are described as schizophrenic when their mental functioning is sufficiently impaired to interfere grossly with their capacity to meet the ordinary demands of life. The impairment may result from a serious distortion in their capacity to recognize reality. Hallucinations and delusions, for example, may distort their perceptions. Alterations of mood may be so profound that the patient's capacity to respond appropriately is grossly impaired. Deficits in perception, language, and memory may be so severe that the patient's capacity for mental grasp of his or her situation is effectively lost.

The range and variety of clinical features associated with schizophrenic pathology cannot be encompassed by a summary listing. Equally difficult and problematic are attempts to classify the complex and infinitely diverse clusters into which these symptoms may form. We will address some of the issues connected with specific symptom clusters in conjunction with our later presentation of personality dispositions. For the present, we note in general several features that justify the schizophrenic disorder label. The two distinguishing characteristics of these markedly severe states are a *diminished reality awareness* and a *cognitive and emotional dyscontrol.*

As the tide of uncontrollable neurochemicals and psychic impulses surges forward, schizophrenic patients begin to sink into a hazy and phantasmagoric world of fleeting, distorted, and dreamlike impressions in which subjective moods and images become fused with, and ultimately dominate, objective realities. Overt behaviors, stimulated primarily by internal biological vulnerabilities, appear purposeless, disjointed, irrational, stereotyped, and bizarre. There is a disunity and disorganization to their communications. Ideas and thoughts are conveyed in an inchoate and jumbled fashion, often taking the form of delusions or projected onto the world as hallucinatory perceptions. Controls are rendered useless or are abandoned as emotions break loose. There is no instrumental purpose or goal other than the ventilation of impulse and anxiety. Unable to grasp objective reality or coordinate feelings and thoughts, these patients regress into a totally helpless state of social invalidism.

Before we describe the various clinical types of Schizophrenia, we must point out that it is extremely difficult to predict the *particular* symptoms a patient will manifest when he or she succumbs to a psychotic level. The first complication we face in this regard is the fact that the experiences of each individual are unique. Thus, the specific content and form of patients' symptoms will reflect the idiosyncratic character of their learnings. As a consequence of this individuality, no two persons will exhibit identical psychotic features. This presents a problem in organizing a classification system, for some reliable basis must be found to group together individuals who are, at least in part, dissimilar.

Certain *general* and fundamental traits gave rise to similar, but in their details often overtly different, behaviors and attitudes. Enough flexibility should be built into each category to allow for considerable variability. Thus, no single behavioral symptom should be viewed as the sine qua non of Schizophrenia. References are made to specific symptoms only to illustrate the likely presence of certain fundamental characteristics.

In some cases, the schizophrenic designation does *imply* the preeminence of a *particular* clinical feature, a singular symptom that emerges in clear fashion. However, the inevitable individual variability in the symptomatic picture of these cases produces a blurring of the preeminent symptom on which the category label is based. For example, we noted in an earlier chapter that even in anxiety-based complex syndromes, where rather distinctive and dramatic symptoms are often present (e.g., obsession or conversion), there is a coexistence of several symptoms that covary and are interchangeable over time; these symptoms wax and wane in their potency and clarity during the course of a disorder, thereby complicating efforts to assign a single syndrome label to the disorder. Thus, despite the long-established tradition of referring to a disorder in terms of its most dramatic symptom, most patients exhibit intraindividual variability, that is, display certain symptoms at one time and place and different symptoms at other times and places. Nevertheless, tradition suggests the following broad categories of schizophrenic subtypes:

1. Most striking among *withdrawn catatonic* types is their lethargy and seeming indifference to their surroundings. They move listlessly, are apathetic and even stuporous. Clothes are drab and their face appears lifeless and masklike. Speech is slow, labored, and often blocked, whispered, or inaudible. They seem passively withdrawn and unresponsive to their environment, cannot participate or feel involved, and tend to perceive things about them as unreal and strange. There is an emotional poverty, a dreamy detachment, a tendency to stand immobile or fixed in one place for hours. They habitually sit in cramped, bent over, and peculiar positions, to which they return repeatedly if they are distracted or dislodged. Some not only show a total lack of initiative, but display an automatic obedience to the requests of others, even when these directives could result in severe physical discomfort or danger. Others are so profoundly detached that they fail to register reactions of distress to painful stimuli such as a slap or a pinprick.

All these behaviors signify a protective withdrawal, a retreat into indifference, and a purposeful uninvolvement and insensitivity to life so as to avoid the anguish it has produced. By disengaging themselves totally, they need no longer feel the painful emotions they experienced before, no longer suffer the discouragement of struggling fruitlessly, and no longer desire and aspire only to be frustrated and humiliated again. Faced with a sense of hopelessness and futility, they have given up, become uncaring, neutral, flat, impassive, and dead to everything.

2. Cases of *rigid catatonic* disorders are likely to display the following four dominant features: mannerisms and posturing, emotional withdrawal, motor retardation, and uncooperativeness. These patients exhibit minimal motor activity and often appear to be totally withdrawn and stuporous. (It may be of interest to note that these disorders occur primarily in individuals with passive personality patterns.) The feature that distinguishes the rigidity disorder from the others lies in the patient's purposeful recalcitrance and manifest uncooperativeness; one senses that beneath the quiet and restrained exterior lies a seething but controlled hostility. The patient is not only mute and immobile, but bullheaded and adamant about remaining in certain fixed and preferred positions, opposing all efforts to alter them. This rigidity and restiveness are manifest in body tension. For example, a patient's fists may be clenched, teeth gritted, and jaw locked tight and firm. Breaking periodically through this physical immobility,

however, are stereotyped repetitive acts, bizarre gestures and grimaces and peculiar tics, grins, and giggles. It appears that every now and then these patients' inner impulses and fantasies emerge briefly to be discharged or enacted through strange symbolic expressions. Quite evidently, there are active although confused thoughts and emotions churning beneath the passive exterior. Periods of motor rigidity may be exhibited, in passing, by all personality patterns, but they occur rather infrequently and arise as a dominant symptom primarily in several personality types.

3. *Disorganized schizophrenic* patients are identifiable by their incongruous and disoriented behavior. They seem lost, scattered, confused, and unclear as to time, place, and identity. Many exhibit posturing, grimacing, inappropriate giggling, mannerisms, and peculiar movements. Their speech tends to ramble into word salads composed of incoherent neologisms and a chaotic mishmash of irrelevancies. The content of their ideas is colored with fantasy and hallucination and scattered with bizarre and fragmentary delusions that have no apparent logic or function. Regressive acts such as soiling and wetting are common, and these patients often consume food in an infantile or ravenous manner. For most patients, schizophrenic disorganization signifies a surrendering of all coping efforts. Thus, every pathological pattern may exhibit the disorder. In some personalities, however, disorganization may be an active coping maneuver, thereby increasing the likelihood of its occurrence in these types. Furthermore, some patterns are more disposed than others to surrender their controls and thus collapse into a disorganized state. In short, although all personalities may succumb to the disorganized disorder, some are more likely to do so than others.

4. *Paranoid schizophrenics* exhibit prominent delusions and auditory hallucinations, despite only a partial loss of cognitive and affective functions. Delusions are usually persecutory or grandiose and tend to be organized around a particular theme (e.g., jealousy, religiosity, or somatization). Although the delusions may be multiple in form, they usually have a central and coherent theme to them. Many such individuals, as with their parallels among paranoid personalities, have an air of superiority and a socially patronizing style that is often formal and stilted as they interact with others. Violent possibilities exist among these schizophrenics, especially when persecutory and grandiose delusions are present. Most paranoid types tend to have an onset later in life than the other schizophrenias.

The *DSM* also includes a variety of mixed and short-term schizophreniclike states: the undifferentiated type, the residual type, Schizophreniform Disorders, Schizoaffective Disorders, and Delusional Disorders. Not to be overlooked also are schizophrenic-related syndromes such as Brief Psychotic Disorders, Shared Psychotic Disorders, and substance-induced psychosis.

The various schizophrenic disorders differ in their prognoses and in their therapeutic management, but an extended discussion of these distinctions is beyond the province of this book. As a consequence, we mention only a few points applicable to the psychoses in general, and report some minor observations regarding schizophrenic disorders.

Before we proceed, let us again be reminded that the descriptive label given to each of the schizophrenic disorders is misleading in that it suggests that a single symptom stands alone, uncontaminated by others. This is not the case. Although a particular symptom may appear dominant at one time, it coexists and covaries with several others, any one of which may come to assume dominance. As a further complication, there is not only covariation and fluidity in symptomatology, but each of these disorders may arise in a number of different personality patterns.

Prevailing Treatment Options

Psychotics usually are hospitalized, remaining as inpatients for periods as wide-ranging as 2 to 3 days for some, and several years for others. Generally, schizophrenic syndromes run through the full course of an episode in less than a year, with a large proportion of patients returning to their prepsychotic levels within a matter of a few months. The determination of the length of hospitalization depends, in large measure, on a variety of factors that are not intrinsic to the disorder, for example, the administrative efficiency and policies of the institution and the willingness of the patient's family to accept his or her return home. One finds all too often that patients who have recovered from their schizophrenic episode remain institutionalized because no one has made proper efforts to arrange their treatment or discharge. Many become immersed for months in the routine of the hospital as a consequence of institutional oversight or family disinterest. Today, however, approximately two-thirds of all schizophrenic patients return to live with their families after a first psychotic episode.

Practically every therapeutic modality and technique has been employed in the service of rehabilitating schizophrenic patients. In the following discussion we note some of the measures that have been used and comment briefly on their respective merits.

Environmental management is a necessary step in the handling of schizophrenic disorders. This should consist of more than the mere removal of adverse conditions in life. Proper institutional placement should provide patients not only with a refuge from environmental stress, but also with opportunities to resolve their tensions and programs to reorient them toward social recovery. In what is termed "milieu therapy," the patient's daily routine is scheduled to maximize both emotional support and the acquisition of attitudes and skills conducive to a better social adjustment than existed previously.

Pharmaceutical treatment methods can be of particular value in several disorders. Antipsychotic and antidepressant medications may fruitfully be utilized to stabilize patients suffering these disorders. Notable in this regard are new antipsychotic drugs, such as clozapine, risperidone, and olanzapine. Other medications are now under evaluation; progress owes to advances in our knowledge of the brain's neurochemical transmitters and receptor sites (Heresco-Levy, 2003; Penn & Mueser, 1996). Each of these pharmaceutical tools is of value not only in its immediate and direct effects, but in bringing the patient to a state in which other therapeutic measures may be employed; for example, a lethargic and unresponsive patient who has been activated by drugs may now be disposed to communicate in verbal psychotherapy.

Psychological therapeutic measures have not been especially successful in the early phases of schizophrenic disorder. Cognitive and intrapsychic methods cannot be used effectively until the patient possesses a modicum of intellectual clarity and emotional quietude. Nevertheless, the sympathetic attitude, patience, and gentle manner that these procedures employ may serve to establish rapport and build a basis for further therapy.

Behavior modification techniques appear especially promising as instruments for extinguishing or controlling specific symptoms, as well as shaping more adaptive alternative responses. Especially useful are methods oriented to strengthen patients' social skills and to help them understand why they must take their drugs on a regular basis. Also useful are steps to teach them how to take appropriate self-care and to secure housing and suitable jobs by such procedures as model imitation and selective positive reinforcement (McKinney & Fiedler, 2004; Penn & Mueser, 1996). In this approach, patients observe others as models and repeatedly rehearse appropriate behaviors. Acquiring these very basic competencies have clearly reduced relapse rates. Although the durability of and the ability to generalize from these beneficial effects have not been adequately researched, these techniques are among the most encouraging.

Group therapeutic methods are especially efficient and adaptable to hospital settings, given the shortage of professional institutional personnel and the ease with which sessions can be arranged. They are particularly valuable as vehicles for resocializing patients and enabling them to express their confused attitudes and feelings in a highly controlled yet sympathetic environment. Family approaches can be extremely important as vehicles of resocialization and psychic stability, if the family system can be adequately empathic and supportive.

Personalized Psychotherapy

We subdivide this section to highlight several classical variants of Schizophrenia and those personality patterns in which they most frequently occur.

An intrinsic deterrent to progress may be the schizophrenic's basic personality. Certain of the personalities possess attitudes and coping styles that undermine chances for recovery; some resist therapeutic rapport, whereas others are difficult to motivate. For example, schizoid and schizotypal personalities frequently deteriorate rapidly despite all treatment efforts. These personalities often succumb to catatonic states, with their flat and difficult to activate qualities, or to disorganized disorders, which, given their characteristic cognitive disorganization, are highly resistant to meaningful therapeutic communication. Other patterns are conducive to better prognoses because they provide a handle that the therapist can use to relate to and motivate the patient. For example, dependent and histrionic patients are desirous of social approval and can be motivated by therapeutic attitudes of gentility and nurture during their treatment periods. For different reasons, notably the drive to assert themselves and to reestablish their autonomy, antisocial and narcissistic personality patterns, despite delusional episodes, have less than promising prognostic pictures.

Catatonic Withdrawal among Retiring/Schizoid and Shy/Avoidant Personalities

Catatonic withdrawal can occur in all personality patterns. The shutting off of emotions and the retreat into indifference are protective devices that can be employed easily by all individuals who have been overwhelmed by a sense of hopelessness and futility. Despite its ease as a coping maneuver, it appears with greater frequency among patients whose lifelong strategies dispose them to emotional detachment and social isolation. As a logical extension of their personality style, we find the catatonic withdrawn pattern arising often in avoidant and schizoid personalities. Unable to handle even minor degrees of overstimulation, be it from unexpected responsibilities, objective threat, or reactivated anxiety, they may overemploy their coping strategies and withdraw into an impassive, unresponsive, and unfeeling state. These cases can usually be identified by their total muteness and their complete tuning out of the world, traits that result in an inner void and a picture of masklike stupor, as portrayed in the following.

Case 6.5, Manny K., 31

Presenting Picture

Manny had always been known as a loner, eschewing normal interpersonal exchanges and activities for those requiring, by their nature, a certain kind of shutting out of the rest of the world. A mechanic and fancier of classic cars, though not an owner himself, he would travel alone to various conventions and auto shows, spending many hours transfixed by the classic machines, studying what he called the "flow of energy" through the restored, shiny motors. It was here where he experienced his first psychotic break at the age of 31, which came in the form of a catatonic withdrawal. Manny was admitted to the psychiatric section of a general hospital after being found by a hotel chambermaid as he sat on the edge of the bed in his room, staring vacantly at a wall. When brought to the ward, he sat impassively in a chair and was unresponsive to questioning, indifferent to his surroundings and well-being, disinterested in food, and unwilling to feed himself. He remained mute, withdrawn, and close to immobile for several days, following which he slowly began to take care of himself without assistance, although he failed to speak to anyone for almost a month.

Initial Impressions

As Manny was unresponsive, little initial information was available aside from that uncovered by his mother and father when they were identified and brought to the hospital. They both described Manny's history as one devoid of much social contact, despite their many attempts to introduce him to various social milieus. Entirely *passive* in most environments, Manny would occasionally find solace in solitary activities, which is what eventually got him oriented to learning auto mechanics.

When he found such an activity, he would become nearly obsessed with it, spending days, and sometimes weeks, studying all aspects of his new pursuit and talking about nothing but the minute details of his interest, though only in response to questions posed by others. Notably, he would also become discomforted, to a degree, when in social situations removed from a current avocation, evidencing distress and difficulty verbalizing even basic needs or social graces. This began to paint the picture of a basic schizoid presentation, with minor avoidant characteristics. Reengagement by his therapist required a supportive approach emulating some of the qualities of these earlier scenarios, eliciting interest regarding his avocations. Automobiles, however, did not immediately interest him; it was surmised that Manny had become somehow overwhelmed by his most recent experience. Instead, family members offered suggestions of past interests.

Domain Analysis

At first Manny was not capable of sitting for psychological assessment. However, his family members were willing to assist the clinician in piecing together the more troublesome domains by reviewing the MG-PDC. The most problematic domains uncovered were as follows:

Interpersonally Unengaged: Manny was characteristically removed from most social situations, seeming to, at most times, be aloof to the interactions of others, not wishing to join or pursue any more intimate connections, even with family members.

Temperamentally Apathetic: Unexcitable, stark, and cold in his usual demeanor, Manny generally seemed devoid in range of human emotions, only showing sympathetic engagement when turned on by a solitary interest, and responding with indifference to events and circumstances that entice most people to arousal.

Alienated Self-Image: Interestingly, there was a great deal of consensus that Manny never thought of himself as capable, viable, or skilled, especially when it came to cooperative efforts, even in many isolated challenges. When he did find something he felt some skill with, he attended to it to the exclusion of everything else.

Therapeutic Steps

The essential format for treatment was short term. A modicum of time was allotted to provide Manny with a supportive approach that, albeit slowly, brought him partially out of his shell. The reassurance and empathy of his therapist and the beneficial effects of the primary medication employed to combat his psychotic state helped Manny become *reengaged* in the world of people around him, as well as helping him reconnect emotionally with his former interests in an effort to combat *temperamental apathy*. As a beginning stage in helping Manny acquire a more *capable self-image*, the development of basic social competencies may have also reduced the likelihood of periodic relapses. The task of resocializing a patient such as Manny is especially problematic, however, owing to his intrinsic interpersonal deficiencies. As many clinicians are aware, large numbers of patients are turned around within a few days of their admittance to a managed care hospital program, and this, unfortunately, was no exception. Had time permitted, behavioral methods designed to help Manny comply with long-term pharmaceutical treatment should have been an essential element in this endogenously generated syndrome.

Catatonic Withdrawal among Needy/Dependent Personalities

These personalities succumb on occasion to catatonic impassivity, but here we often see a coloring of sadness, a tone of inner softness, an inclination to be nice and to acquiesce in the wishes of others in the hope of maintaining some measure of affection and support from them. It is in these patients that we often observe a cataleptic waxy flexibility, that is, a tendency to maintain bodily positions into which others have placed them. This willingness to be molded according to the whims of others signifies their total abandonment of self-initiative and their complete dependence and submission to external directives. At the heart of their acquiescent impassivity is the deep need to counter their separation anxieties and to avoid actions that might engender disapproval and rejection.

Catatonic Withdrawal among Sociable/Histrionic Personalities

In histrionic patients, the catatonic psychosis usually reflects a collapse of their lifelong style of actively soliciting attention and approval. Rather than face failure and rejection, these patients may retire from their habitual strategy, disown their need for stimulation and excitement, and temporarily reverse the course of their lifestyle. Catatonia is usually of short duration in these patients, and can be relieved by genuine assurances from others of their care, interest, and affection.

Catatonic Rigidity among Conscientious/Compulsive Personalities

These personalities are especially subject to this form of psychotic disorder. Their physical uncooperativeness is a passive expression of their deeply felt resentments and angers. Their body tightness reflects an intense struggle to control against the outbreak of seething hostility, and their physical withdrawal and obduracy help them avoid contact with events that might provoke and unleash their aggressive impulses. Thus, motor rigidity both communicates and controls their anger without provoking social condemnation. It may be viewed as a bizarre extension of their habitual coping style, a means of controlling contrary impulses by protective restraint and rigid behaviors. The stereotype gestures and grimaces seen in these patients usually convey symbolically an abbreviated and immediately retracted expression of their intolerable aggressive and erotic urges. Features of this disorder are illustrated in the following case history.

Case 6.6, Howard C., 39

Presenting Picture

Howard's wife found him one morning "staring in a funny way" out his bathroom window. Not only did he refuse to reply to her concerned questions regarding his health, but he remained in a rigid position and refused to budge; no amount of pleading on her part was adequate to get him to relax or lie down. A physician was called to examine him shortly thereafter, but he was equally unable to penetrate Howard's mutism or to alter his taut and unyielding physical posture. Although Howard did not resist being carried into an ambulance, he refused to change the body position in which his wife found him that morning.

Initial Impressions

Howard's wife provided the initial interview information, noting that he had recently seemed slightly "out of sorts," and that he would occasionally mutter obscenities under his breath when leaving for his work as an assistant manager of a franchise hardware store. Prior to recent weeks, however, she stated that he was generally cheerful and cooperative, rarely complaining even when there were significant demands. She did note, however, that there was some strife in the marriage, in that they had never agreed on the issue of children, and their only child, a daughter, was born a year earlier. She wanted to have several children; Howard did not want more than one. Howard had come from a family of eight children and, being the oldest male, he was charged with being an assistant parent to many of his siblings. According to his wife, Howard seemed somewhat resentful about the responsibility, especially because he often had to fill the father role while his own father was out of town on business. He took pride in handling responsibility well and fulfilling expectations, but she wondered "how anyone can just take on so much, always smiling." These qualities seemed to match the compulsive pattern, although the description felt more in line with a healthier, conscientious style through much of his life. It is possible, though, that recent events, most notably the introduction of a child, brought more deep-seated ambivalence to the surface.

Domain Analysis

It was several weeks before Howard sat for more comprehensive evaluation. When he regained lucidity, he was administered the MCMI-III, which indicated moderate compulsive and dependent elevations. Responses on the MG-PDC, filled out by his clinician after several individual sessions, revealed several salient domains:

> *Temperamentally Pacific:* Generally warm and avoiding of social tension, Howard worked fastidiously to maintain equilibrium and the status quo in his environment; however, this conciliatory manner seemed to be cracking near the time of his break.

Reaction-Formation Mechanism: Howard displayed only positive thoughts and behaviors, sending any negative qualities or nuances to the deep unconscious, where they would be entirely out of awareness and unable to cause difficulty.

Conscientious Self-Image: Generally industrious and notably task-oriented, Howard seemed to invite others to rely on him, to the extent that he routinely placed any self-need behind what was needed by others.

Therapeutic Course

Howard's physical rigidity gave way under sedation and he spoke during these periods in a halting and confused manner. As soon as the effects of the drug wore off, however, he again was mute and resumed his immobile stance. Only after several weeks did he loosen up and begin to divulge his thoughts and feelings and was able to handle a more comprehensive evaluation. As he disclosed information, it became clearer that his cognitive and affective processes both indicated a struggle to contain the rage he felt toward his father and his wife for the excessive demands he believed they imposed on him. Efforts then were made to help Howard recognize that many of his difficulties stemmed from his deep-seated ambivalence toward significant others. Hence, insight-oriented and humanistic procedures were utilized in tandem to provide Howard with a basis for recognizing both the character of his ambivalences and his tendency to categorize his relationships in a black-and-white manner. Gradually, through growing awareness of his predicament, he learned the interrelationship of his overreliance on his view of himself as a *conscientious* person, always looking to do right by everyone but himself, and his tendency to cloak bitter or otherwise negative feelings about immediate demands from people ("concealed" objects, to examine his personality constellation further), and to change these, in an automated way, to their overtly positive counterparts (an example of his *reaction-formation mechanism*). As this more unconscious and preconscious material came to light, it was necessary to elicit behavioral and interpersonal changes, all the while keeping part of the focus on more immediate feelings. Not surprisingly, this disrupted his *pacific mood,* although this was therapeutically beneficial. He was taught anger management techniques geared toward effectively utilizing anger for its assertive, communicative qualities (Tavris, 1989). Bringing him into family therapy as he learned more effective communication measures also enabled Howard to deal with these complex feelings. Not to be overlooked, as he completed treatment, were procedures to enable him to reduce provocative sources of anxiety, especially those that he had formerly employed as excessive and rigid psychic controls.

Catatonic Rigidity among Shy/Avoidant Personalities

These personalities exhibit catatonic rigidity for reasons similar to those found in the catatonically withdrawn. Here, patients are motivated more by their desire to withdraw from external provocation than by the need to control their aggressive impulses, not that the latter is to be overlooked as a factor. Faced with unbearable derogation and humiliation, they withdraw into a shell, resistant to all forms of stimulation that may reactivate past misery. The grimaces and giggling often observed in these patients clue us to their rather chaotic fantasy world.

Disorganized Type among Shy/Avoidant Personalities

These personalities are especially inclined to this disorder, not only because they can easily be overwhelmed by external and internal pressures, but because psychic disorganization is an extension of their characteristic protective maneuver of interfering with their own cognitive clarity. By blocking the normal flow of thoughts and memories, they distract themselves and dilute the impact of painful feelings and recollections. Thus disorganization may arise as a direct product either of intolerable pressures, self-made confusion, or both. What we see as a result is a picture of forced absurdity and incoherence and a concerted effort to disrupt cognitive clarity and emotional rationality. The following portrays such an episode.

Case 6.7, Martha R., 21

Presenting Picture

Martha was a once precocious and outgoing child, but almost overnight, according to her mother, began displaying terribly fearful withdrawal, starting in late elementary school. She became shy and fearful of all people, even those she had known all her life. She found herself devoid of friendships and activities, preferring to spend her days at home helping her mother cook and clean for her father and younger brothers. Despite graduating from high school with honors and being accepted to prestigious universities, she chose to attend the local community college, dropping out halfway through the semester. One morning she became "silly and confused," began to talk "gibberishly," as her mother put it, became incontinent, and grimaced and giggled for no apparent reason. She then grabbed a cooking knife her mother was using and began dancing around the kitchen with it, making self-threatening gestures in what seemed to be almost an interpretive dance. As her mood deflated, Martha placed herself into a series of contorted positions on the floor, sang incoherent songs, and cried fitfully for brief periods. She continued this behavior, although more sporadically, after her involuntary commitment, following which she became quiet and withdrawn.

Initial Impressions

Upon admission, Martha was administered antipsychotic medication and participated in thrice-weekly group sessions of a supportive nature, for a very brief course. After this time, she returned home and resumed her normal pattern of behavior, but her family insisted that she continue outpatient treatment, which is where a more personalized psychotherapy was initiated. Through a nonintrusive and supportive therapeutic approach, Martha began speaking about her personal social history. As a young child, she felt she had "everything," inclusive of a supportive family life, the attention and admiration of peers, and a feeling of self-efficacy. Her family came into some money in her mid-elementary school years, and there was a substantial move from rural to metropolitan life; this event set the course for dramatic social changes. At once, she lost her peer group, was exposed to a much more hostile and competitive social milieu, and was tormented by peers as not only the new kid, but the "country bumpkin." She was ill-equipped to deal with these changes; what made matters worse was that her well-intentioned parents stepped in and defended her against bullying peers. These events prompted a shift inward, as well as a hard self-protective shell with pervasive sensitivities to possible slights. Further, Martha had learned that there was solace in allowing stronger others to protect her, but there was even greater solace in avoiding difficult exchanges altogether. In essence, she had adopted the *active–pain* orientation of the avoidant pattern, as well as some dependent characteristics.

Domain Analysis

The MCMI-III Grossman Facet Scales, as well as the MG-PDC, uncovered these highlights in Martha's domain-salience analysis:

Cognitively Distracted: Martha scanned the environment obsessively, even when there were no palpable threats (e.g., at home with family), for signs of possible slights. She also feverishly created distractions to moderate the salience of malevolent thought content.

Alienated Self-Image: Martha felt that she did not fit in *anywhere,* even in those few places where she sought comfort (although these were the least difficult). A "sore thumb" in any crowd, she sulked in loneliness but felt there was no hope for connections.

Expressively Incompetent: This dependent domain spoke to Martha's feelings that she needed to be taken care of, to be guided, and to be protected, as she could never act on her own initiative or assertively self-protect.

Therapeutic Steps

Given the support of her family and the general efficacy of her medications, her initial brief treatment regimen in the hospital sufficed to stabilize her. Further serious efforts, however, were necessary in individual personalized therapy to reduce Martha's intense anxieties and her self-made cognitive confusions. A potentiated pairing of a supportive, Rogerian approach, combined with a slow, behavioral progressive relaxation technique (ventilation/reassurance) worked on two aspects. First, it gave Martha the feeling of self-efficacy in response to her overt and not so overt assertions of "I can't!" (i.e., her *expressive incompetence*). Second, the client-centered, genuine stance of the therapist allowed Martha to explore and clarify her *alienated* introspections and to find those more troubling aspects of those feelings inconsistent with newer feelings of self-efficacy brought about by the aforementioned behavioral techniques. This newfound state of deeper overall relaxation naturally decreased her *distracted cognitive style*. Martha further cognitively explored both her social fears and her defensive need to undermine the clarity of her thinking through aspects of Ellis's (1970) REBT, at this later stage where she could find enough self-assurance to discover humor in her self-presentation. This acquisition of an enhanced sense of self-worth and interpersonal competencies contributed measurably to her overall movement toward enhanced mental health.

Disorganized Type among Needy/Dependent Personalities

Dependents are disposed to fragmentation when faced with situations that seriously tax their limited capacity to function independently. Without external security and support and lacking a core of inner competence and self-determination, they may easily crumble and disintegrate, usually into regressive or infantile behaviors. Beneath their confusion and bizarre acts we often see remnants of their former coping strategies. For example, their regressive eating and soiling may reflect a continued seeking of care and nurture. Their stereotyped grimacing and giggling may signify a forced and pathetic effort to capture the goodwill and approval of those on whom they now depend.

Disorganized Type among Conscientious/Compulsive Personalities

Disorganization among compulsives follows the shattering of controls previously employed to restrain deeply repressed conflicts. Unable to keep these divisive forces in check, these patients are torn apart, engulfed in a sea of surging memories and contrary feelings that now spew forth in a flood of incoherent verbalizations and bizarre emotions and acts. In their case, stereotyped grimacing, posturing, and mannerisms often signify feeble efforts to contain their impulses or to dampen the confusion and disharmony they feel.

Disorganized Type among Eccentric/Schizotypal Personalities

Particularly subject to *disorganized schizophrenic* disorders, schizotypals are identifiable by their incongruous and fragmented behaviors. At these times they seem totally disoriented and confused, unclear as to time, place, and identity. Many will exhibit posturing, grimacing, inappropriate giggling, and peculiar mannerisms. Speech tends to ramble into word salads composed of incoherent neologisms and a chaotic mishmash of irrelevancies. Ideas are colored with fantasy, illusion, and hallucination and scattered with bizarre and fragmentary delusions that have no apparent logic or function. Regressive acts such as soiling and wetting are not uncommon, and these patients often consume food in an infantile or ravenous manner.

As described earlier in the chapter, these psychotic states may occur after a period when the tide of unconscious anxieties and impulses have surged forward, overwhelming these patients and sinking them into a hazy world of fleeting and dreamlike impressions. Subjective moods and images become fused with, and ultimately dominate, objective realities. Overt behaviors are distorted and guided by primary process thinking and thereby appear purposeless, disjointed, irrational, stereotyped, and bizarre.

Paranoid Type among Confident/Narcissistic Personalities

Under conditions of unrelieved adversity and failure, narcissists may decompensate into paranoid disorders. Owing to their excessive use of fantasy mechanisms, they are disposed to misinterpret events and to construct delusional beliefs. Unwilling to accept constraints on their independence and unable to accept the viewpoints of others, narcissists may isolate themselves from the corrective effects of shared thinking. Alone, they may ruminate and weave their beliefs into a network of fanciful and totally invalid suspicions. Delusions often take form after a serious challenge or setback in which their image of superiority and omnipotence has been upset. They tend to exhibit compensatory grandiosity and jealousy delusions in which they reconstruct reality to match the image they are unable or unwilling to give up. Delusional systems may also develop as a result of having felt betrayed and humiliated. Here we may see the rapid unfolding of persecutory delusions and an arrogant grandiosity characterized by verbal attacks and bombast. Rarely physically abusive, anger among narcissists usually takes the form of oral vituperation and argumentativeness. This may be seen in a flow of irrational and caustic comments in which others are upbraided and denounced as stupid and beneath contempt. These onslaughts usually have little objective justification, are often colored by delusions, and may be directed in a wild, hit-or-miss fashion in which the narcissist lashes out at those who have failed to acknowledge the exalted status in which he or she demands to be seen.

Paranoid Type among Assertive/Sadistic Personalities

Acute delusional episodes characterized by hostile excitement may be displayed by these personalities. Particularly prone to this disorder as a result of their hypersensitivity to betrayal, they have learned to cope with threat by acting out aggressively and, at times, explosively. Faced with repeated failures and frustrations, their fragile controls may be overwhelmed by undischarged and deeply felt angers and resentments. These hostile feelings, spurred by the memories and emotions of the past, may surge unrestrained to the surface, spilling into wild and delusional rages.

Paranoid Type among Suspicious/Paranoid Personalities

Paranoid personalities develop *delusional* paranoid disorders and paranoia insidiously, usually as a consequence of anticipating or experiencing repeated mistreatment or humiliation. Acute paranoid episodes may be precipitated by the shock of an unanticipated betrayal. In these acute phases, previously repressed resentments may surge to the surface and overwhelm the patient's former controls, quickly taking the form of a delusional belief, usually persecutory in nature. During these episodes, typically brief and rather chaotic, patients both discharge their anger and project it on others. Note that the resentments and suspicions of the paranoid usually do not cumulate and burst out of control. Rather, these patients continue to be persistently touchy, secretive, and irritable, thereby allowing them to vent their spleen in regular, small doses. Only if their suspicions are aggravated suddenly do they take an explosive or irrational form.

REFERENCES

Alexander, F. (1930). The neurotic character. *International Journal of Psychoanalysis, 11,* 292–313.

Arkowitz, H. (1992). Integrative theories of therapy. In D. K. Freedhein & H. J. Freudenberger (Eds.), *History of psychotherapy: A century of change* (pp. 261–303). Washington, DC: American Psychological Association.

Arkowitz, H. (1997). Integrative theories of therapy. In P. L. Wachtel & S. B. Messer (Eds.), *Theories of psychotherapy: Origins and evolution* (pp. 227–288). Washington, DC: American Psychological Association.

Arthur, A., & Edwards, C. (2005). An evaluation of support groups for patients with long-term chronic pain and complex psychosocial difficulties. *European Journal of Psychotherapy, Counselling, and Health, 7*(3), 169–180.

Atwood, J. D., & Chester, R. (1987). *Treatment techniques for common mental disorders.* Northvale, NJ: Aronson.

Barlow, D. H. (1988). *Anxiety and its disorders: The nature and treatment of anxiety and panic.* New York: Guilford Press.

Barlow, D. H. (1993). *Clinical handbook of psychological disorders* (2nd ed.). New York: Guilford Press.

Baron, D. A., & Nagy, R. (1988). An amobarbital interview in a general hospital setting: Friend or foe? A case report. *General Hospital Psychiatry, 10,* 220–222.

Barsky, A., Geringer, E., & Wood, C. A. (1988). A cognitive-educational treatment for hypochondriasis. *General Hospital Psychiatry, 10,* 322–327.

Beard, G. M. (1869). Neurasthenia, or nervous exhaustion. *Boston Medical and Surgical Journal, 80,* 217–221.

Beck, A. T. (1976). *Cognitive therapy and the emotional disorders.* New York: International Universities Press.

Beck, A. T., & Emery, G. (1985). *Anxiety disorders and phobias.* New York: Basic Books.

Beck, A. T., Emery, G., & Greenberg, R. (2005). *Anxiety disorders and phobias: A cognitive perspective.* New York: Basic Books.

Beck, A. T., Rush, A. J., Shaw, B. F., & Emery, G. (1979). *Cognitive therapy of depression.* New York: Guilford Press.

Beck, A. T., Freeman, A., & Davis, D. D. (2004). *Cognitive therapy of personality disorders* (2nd ed.). New York: Guilford Press.

Bellack, A. S., Hersen, M., & Himmelhoch, J. M. (1981). Social skills training compared with pharmacotherapy and psychotherapy in the treatment of unipolar depression. *American Journal of Psychiatry, 138,* 1562–1567.

Bellack, A., Hersen, M., & Himmelhoch, J. M. (1983). A comparison of social-skills training, pharmacotherapy and psychotherapy for depression. *Behavior Research and Therapy, 21,* 101–107.

Benjamin, L. R., & Benjamin, R. (1992). An overview of family treatment in dissociative disorders. *Dissociation, 5,* 236–241.

Benjamin, L. S. (1993). *Interpersonal diagnosis and treatment of personality disorders.* New York: Guilford Press.

Benjamin, L. S. (2003). *Interpersonal reconstructive therapy: Promoting change in nonresponders.* New York: Guilford Press.

Benjamin, L. S. (2005). Interpersonal theory of personality disorders: The structural analysis of social behavior and interpersonal reconstructive therapy. In M. Lenzenweger & J. Clarkin (Eds.), *Major theories of personality* (2nd ed.). New York: Guilford Press.

Bergen, A. E., & Garfield, S. L. (Eds.). (1994). *Handbook of psychotherapy and behavior change* (4th ed.). New York: Wiley.

Bergin, A. E., & Lambert, M. J. (1978). The evaluation of therapeutic outcomes. In S. L. Garfield & A. E. Bergin (Eds.), *Handbook of psychotherapy and behavior change* (2nd ed.). New York: Wiley.

Beutler, L. E., & Clarkin, J. (1990). *Selective treatment selection: Toward targeted therapeutic interventions.* New York: Brunner/Mazel.

Binder, J. L. (2004). *Key competencies in brief dynamic psychotherapy: Clinical practice beyond the manual.* New York: Guilford Press.

Blatt, Sidney J. (2004). *Experiences of depression: Theoretical, clinical and research perspectives.* Washington, DC: American Psychological Association.

Bockian, N. (2006). *Personality-guided therapy of depression.* Washington, DC: American Psychological Association.

Bond, M., & Perry, J. C. (2006). Psychotropic medication use, personality disorder and improvement in long-term dynamic psychotherapy. *Journal of Nervous and Mental Diseases, 194*(1), 21–26.

Borkovec, T. D., & Costello, E. (1993). Efficacy of supplied relaxation and cognitive-behavioral therapy in the treatment of generalized anxiety disorder. *Journal of Consulting and Clinical Psychology, 61,* 611–619.

Briquet, P. (1859). *Trait clinique et therapeutique a l'hysterie.* Paris: J. B. Balliere & Fils.

Burton, R. (1624). *Anatomy of melancholy: What it is.* Oxford, England: John Lichfield and James Short for Henry Cripps.

Butler, G., Cullington, A., Hibbert, G., Klimes, I., & Gelder, M. (1987). Anxiety management for persistent generalized anxiety. *British Journal of Psychiatry, 151,* 535–542.

Cameron, N. (1963). *Personality and psychological development.* New York: Houghton-Mifflin.

Carroll, K., & Onken, L. (2005). Behavioral therapies for drug abuse. *American Journal of Psychiatry, 162*(8), 1452–1460.

Caul, D. (1984). Group and videotape techniques for multiple personality. *Psychiatric Annals, 14,* 43–50.

Caul, D., Sacks, R. G., & Braun, B. G. (1988). Group psychotherapy in treatment of multiple personality disorder. In B. G. Braun (Ed.), *Treatment of multiple personality disorder* (pp. 145–156). Washington, DC: American Psychiatric Press.

Chambless, D. L., & Gillis, M. M. (1994). Cognitive therapy of anxiety disorders. *Journal of Consulting and Clinical Psychology, 61,* 248–260.

Charcot, J. M. (1885). *Oeuvres completes* [Complete Works]. Paris: Bureau du Progrès Mèdical.

Collins, J. F. (2004). The intersection of race and bisexuality: A critical overview of the literature and past, present, and future directions of the "borderlands." *Journal of Bisexuality, 4,* 99–116.

Coons, P. M. (1986). Treatment progress in 20 patients with multiple personality disorder. *Journal of Nervous and Mental Diseases, 174,* 715–721.

Cooper, N. A., & Clum, G. A. (1989). Imaginal flooding as a supplementary treatment for PTSD in combat veterans: A controlled study. *Behavior Therapy, 20,* 381–391.

Covi, L., & Lipman, R. S. (1987). Cognitive-behavioral group psychotherapy combined with imipramine in major depression. *Psychopharmacology Bulletin, 23,* 173–176.

Craighead, L. W., Craighead, W. E., Kazdin, A. E., & Mahoney, M. J. (Eds.). (1994). *Cognitive and behavioral interventions: An empirical approach to mental health problems.* Boston: Allyn & Bacon.

Curtis, R. C., & Hirsch, I. (2003). Relational approaches to psychoanalytic psychotherapy. In A. S. Gurman & S. B. Messer (Eds.), *Essential psychotherapies: Theory and practice* (pp. 69–106). New York: Guilford Press.

Dattilio, F. (1993). A practical update on the treatment of obsessive-compulsive disorder. *Journal of Mental Health Counseling, 15,* 244–259.

DeJong, P., & Berg, I. K. (2001). *Interviewing for solutions.* Pacific Grove, CA: Brooks/Cole.

de Mello, M. F., de Jesus, M. J., Bacaltchuk, J., Verdeli, H., & Neugebauer, R. (2005). A systematic review of research findings on the efficacy of interpersonal therapy for depressive disorders. *European Archives of Psychiatry and Clinical Neuroscience, 255*(2), 75–82.

Dion, G. L., & Pollack, W. S. (1992). A rehabilitation model for persons with bipolar disorder. *Comprehensive Mental Health Care, 2,* 87–102.

Drake, R. E., Merrens, M. R., & Lynde, D. (Eds.). (2005). *Evidence-based mental health practice: A textbook.* New York: Norton.

Durham, R. C., Murphy, T., Allan, T., Richard, K., Trevliving, R., & Fenton, A. (1994). Cognitive therapy, analytic psychotherapy and anxiety management training for generalised anxiety disorder. *British Journal of Psychiatry, 165*(3), 315–323.

Eldridge, N., & Gould, S. (1972). Punctuated equilibria: An alternative to phyletic gradualism. In T. Schopf (Ed.), *Models in paleobiology.* San Francisco: Freeman.

Ellis, A. (1958). *How to live with a neurotic.* New York: Crown.

Ellis, A. (1970). *The essence of rational psychotherapy: A comprehensive approach to treatment.* New York: Institute for Rational Living.

Emmelkamp, P. M. G. (1994). Behavior therapy with adults. In A. E. Bergin & S. L. Garfield (Eds.), *Handbook of psychotherapy and behavior change* (4th ed., pp. 247–379). New York: Wiley.

Eysenck, H. J. (1959). *The structure of human personality.* New York: Wiley-Interscience.

Farber, B. A., & Lane, J. S. (2002). Positive regard. In J. C. Norcross (Ed.), *Psychotherapy relationships that work: Therapist contributions and responsiveness to patients* (pp. 175–194). New York: Oxford University Press.

Feuchtersleben, E. (1847). *The principles of medical psychology: Vol. 14. Being the outlines of a course of lectures.* London: Sydenham Society.

Fineberg, N., & Gale, T. (2005). Evidence-based pharmacotherapy of obsessive-compulsive disorder. *International Journal of Neuropsychopharmacology, 8*(1), 107–129.

Fisher, J. E., & O'Donohue, W. T. (Eds.). (2006). *Practitioner's guide to evidence-based psychotherapy.* New York: Springer.

Foa, E. B., Davidson, J., & Rothbaum, B. O. (1995). Posttraumatic stress disorder. In G. O. Gabbard (Ed.), *Treatments of psychiatric disorders* (pp. 1499–1520). Washington, DC: American Psychiatric Press.

Frances, A. J., Clarkin, J. F., & Perry, S. (1984). *Differential therapeutics in psychiatry.* New York: Brunner/ Mazel.

Frank, J. D., & Frank, J. B. (1991). *Persuasion and healing.* Baltimore: Johns Hopkins University Press.

Frankl, V. (1984). *Man's search for meaning.* New York: Washington Square Press. (Original work published 1946)

Freud, S. (1900). *The interpretation of dreams.* New York: Norton.

Freud, S. (1938). *The basic writings of Sigmund Freud.* New York: The Modern Library.

Gabbard, G. O. (Ed.). (1995). *Treatments of psychiatric disorders.* Washington, DC: American Psychiatric Press.

Gabhainn, S. (2003). Assessing sobriety and successful membership of Alcoholics Anonymous. *Journal of Substance Use, 8*(1), 55–61.

Glasser, W. (1965). *Reality therapy: A new approach to psychiatry.* New York: Harper & Row.

Goddard, A. W., Brovelle, T., Almai, A., Morrissey, K. A., Clary, C. M., Jetty, P., et al. (2001). Early co-administration of clonazepam with sertraline: For panic disorder. *Archives of General Psychiatry, 58,* 681–686.

Goldstein, A. P., & Dean, S. J. (1966). *The investigation of psychotherapy: Commentaries and readings.* New York: Wiley.

Goldstein, K. (1940). *Human nature in the light of psychopathology.* Cambridge, MA: Harvard University Press.

Goodheart, C. D., Kazdin, A. E., & Sternberg, R. J. (Eds.). (2006). *Evidence-based psychotherapy: Where practice and research meet.* Washington, DC: American Psychological Association.

Gotlib, I. H., & Colby, C. A. (1987). *Treatment of depression.* New York: Pergamon Press.

Gottschalk, L. A., & Auerbach, A. H. (1966). *Methods of research in psychotherapy.* New York: Appleton-Century-Crofts.

Greist, J. H., & Jefferson, J. W. (1996). *Carbamazepine & Manic Depression: A Guide.* Madison, WI: Madison Institute of Medicine.

Grunbaum, A. (1952). Causality and the science of human behavior. *American Scientist, 26,* 665–676.

Guze, S. (1967). The diagnosis of hysteria: What are we trying to do? *American Journal of Psychiatry, 124,* 491–498.

Hempel, C. G. (1961). Introduction to problems of taxonomy. In J. Zubin (Ed.), *Field studies in the mental disorders.* New York: Grune & Stratton.

Heresco-Levy, U. (2003). Glutamatergic neurotransmission modulation and the mechanisms of antipsychotic atypicality. *Progress in Neuro-Psychopharmacology and Biological Psychiatry, 27*(7), 1113–1123.

Hester, R., Squires, D., & Delaney, H. (2005). The drinker's check-up: 12-month outcomes of a controlled clinical trial of a stand-alone software program for problem drinkers. *Journal of Substance Abuse Treatment, 28*(2), 159–169.

Hettema, J., Steele, J., & Miller, W. (2005). Motivational interviewing. *Annual Review of Clinical Psychology, 1,* 91–111.

Hoch, P. H., & Zubin, J. (1964). *The evaluation of psychiatric treatment: The proceedings of the fifty-second annual meeting of the American Psychopathological Association held in New York City, February, 1962.* New York: Grune & Stratton.

Hofmann, S. (2004). Cognitive mediation of treatment change in social phobia. *Journal of Consulting and Clinical Psychology, 72*(3), 392–399.

Hollon, S. D., & Beck, A. T. (1994). Cognitive and cognitive-behavioral therapies. In A. E. Bergin & S. L. Garfield (Eds.), *Handbook of psychotherapy and behavior change* (4th ed.). New York: Wiley.

Hollon, S. D., & Fawcett, J. (1995). Combined medication and psychotherapy. In G. O. Gabbard (Ed.), *Treatments of psychiatric disorders* (pp. 1222–1236). Washington, DC: American Psychiatric Press.

Hollon, S. D., Stewart, M. O., & Strunk, D. (2006). Enduring effects for cognitive behavior therapy in the treatment of depression and anxiety. *Annual Review of Psychology, 57,* 285–315.

Horowitz, M., Marmar, C., Krupnick, J., Wilner, N., Kaltreider, N., & Wallerstein, R. (2001). *Personality styles and brief psychotherapy.* Northvale, NJ: Aronson.

Janet, P. (1901). *The mental state of hystericals* (C. R. Corson, Trans.). New York: Putnam.

Kahlbaum, K. L. (1874). *Die katatonie, oder das spannungsirresien.* Berlin, Germany: Kirschwald.

Kaplan, D. A. (2005). One-session treatment of a patient with specific phobia. *Journal of Cognitive Psychotherapy, 19*(1), 85–87.

Kaskutas, L., Ammon, L., Delucchi, K., Room, R., Bond, J., & Weisner, C. (2005). Alcoholics Anonymous careers: Patterns of AA involvement 5 years after treatment entry. *Alcoholism: Clinical and Experimental Research, 29*(11), 1983–1990.

Kellner, R. (1982). Psychotherapeutic strategies in hypochondriasis: A clinical study. *American Journal of Psychotherapy, 36,* 146–157.

Kelly, K. R. (1996). Review of clinical mental health counseling process and outcome research. *Journal of Mental Health Counseling, 18,* 358–375.

Kernberg, O. F. (1975). *Borderline conditions and pathological narcissism.* Northvale, NJ: Aronson.

Kernberg, O. F. (1984). *Severe personality disorders.* New Haven, CT: Yale University Press.

Kernberg, O. F. (1988). Object relations theory in clinical practice. *Psychoanalysis Quarterly, 57,* 481–504.

Kiesler, D. J. (1986). Interpersonal methods of diagnosis and treatment. In J. O. Cavenar (Ed.), *Psychiatry* (Vol. 1, pp. 1–23). Philadelphia: Lippincott.

Klerman, G. L. (1984). Ideologic conflicts in combined treatments. In B. Beitman & G. L. Klerman (Eds.), *Combining pharmacotherapy and psychotherapy in clinical practice* (pp. 17–34). New York: Guilford Press.

Klerman, G. L., Weissman, M. M., Rounsaville, B. J., & Chevron, E. S. (1984). *Interpersonal psychotherapy of depression.* New York: Guilford Press.

Klosko, J. S., Barlow, D. H., Tassinari, R., & Cerny, J. A. (1990). A comparison of alprazolam and behavior therapy in treatment of panic disorder. *Journal of Consulting and Clinical Psychology, 58,* 77–84.

Kluft, R. P. (1984). Aspects of the treatment of multiple personality disorder. *Psychiatric Annals, 14,* 51–55.

Kluft, R. P. (1988). The dissociative disorders. In J. A. Talbot, R. E. Hales, & S. C. Yudofsky (Eds.), *Textbook of psychiatry* (pp. 557–585). Washington, DC: American Psychiatric Press.

Kluft, R. P. (1994). Treatment trajectories in multiple personality disorder. *Dissociation, 7,* 63–75.

Koenigsberg, H. W., Woo-Ming, A. M., & Siever, L. J. (2002). Pharmacological treatments for personality disorders. In P. E. Nathan & J. M. Gorman (Eds.), *A guide to treatments that work* (pp. 625–641). New York: Oxford University Press.

Kraepelin, E. (1896). *Psychiatrie: ein lehrbuch* (5th ed.). Leipzig, Germany: Barth.

Kubie, L. S. (1943). Manual of emergency treatment for acute war neuroses. *War Medicine, 4,* 582–598.

Lazarus, A. A. (1981). *The practice of multimodal therapy: Systematic, comprehensive, and effective psychotherapy.* New York: McGraw-Hill.

Lazarus, A. A., & Messer, S. B. (1991). Does chaos prevail? An exchange on technical eclecticism and assimilative integration. *Journal of Psychotherapy Integration, 1,* 143–158.

Lecrubier, Y., & Judge, R. (1997). Long-term evaluation of paroxetine, clomipramine and placebo in panic disorder: Collaborative Paroxetine Panic Study investigators. *Acta Psychiatrica Scandinavica, 95,* 153–160.

Leigh, G. (1985). Psychosocial factors in the etiology of substance abuse. In T. E. Bratter & G. G. Forrest (Eds.), *Alcoholism and substance abuse* (pp. 3–48). New York: Free Press.

Lemmens, G., Verdegem, S., Heireman, M., Lietaer, G., Van Houdenhove, B., Sabbe, B., et al. (2003). Helpful events in family discussion groups with chronic-pain patients: A qualitative study of differences in perception between therapists/observers and patients/family members. *Families, Systems and Health, 21*(1), 37–52.

Levenson, H. (1995). *Time-limited dynamic psychotherapy: A guide to clinical practice.* New York: Basic Books.

Levinson, M. H. (2004). On the therapeutic action of SSRI medications. *Journal of the American Psychoanalytic Association, 52*(2), 483–486.

Lewin, K. (1936). *Principles of topographical psychology.* New York: McGraw-Hill.

Lewinsohn, P. M., & Gotlib, I. H. (1995). Behavioral theory and treatment of depression. In E. E. Becker & W. R. Leber (Eds.), *Handbook of depression* (pp. 352–375). New York: Guilford Press.

Lewis, A. (1934). The story of unreason. In A. Lewis (Ed.), *The state of psychiatry.* London: Routledge & Kegan Paul.

Lindsay, W. R., Gansu, C. V., McLaughlin, E., Hood, E. M., & Espie, C. A. (1987). A controlled trial of treatments for generalized anxiety. *British Journal of Clinical Psychology, 26,* 3–15.

Livesley, W. J., Jackson, D. N., & Schroeder, M. L. (1989). A study of the factorial structure of personality pathology. *Journal of Personality Disorders, 3,* 292–306.

Locke, J. (1956). *An essay concerning human understanding.* Chicago: Henry Regnery. (Original work published 1696)

Lupu, V. (2005). Cognitive-behavioral therapy in the case of a teenager with conversion disorder with mixed presentation. *Journal of Cognitive and Behavioral Psychotherapies, 5*(2), 197–205.

Magnavita, J. J. (2000). *Relational therapy for personality disorders.* New York: Wiley.

Maldonado, J. R., & Spiegel, D. (1995). Using hypnosis. In C. Classen (Ed.), *Treating women molested in childhood* (pp. 163–186). San Francisco: Jossey-Bass.

Manning, D. W., & Frances, A. (1990). *Combined pharmacotherapy and psychotherapy for depression.* Washington, DC: American Psychiatric Press.

Markowitz, J. C. (1994). Psychotherapy of dysthymia: Is it effective? *American Journal of Psychiatry, 151,* 1114–1121.

Markowitz, J. C., Kocsis, J. H., Bleiberg, K. L., Christos, P. J., & Sacks, M. (2005). A comparative trial of psychotherapy and pharmacotherapy for "pure" dysthymic patients. *Journal of Affective Disorders, 89*(1/3), 167–175.

Marks, I. M., Swinson, R. P., Basoglu, M., Kuch, M., Noshirvani, H., O'Sullivan, G., et al. (1993). Alprazolam and exposure alone and combined in panic disorder with agoraphobia. *Journal of Psychiatry, 162,* 776–787.

Maslow, A. H. (1970). *The farther reaches of human nature.* New York: Penguin.

Mattick, R. P., Andrews, G., Hadzi-Pavlovic, D., & Christiensen, H. (1990). Treatment of panic and agoraphobia: An integrative review. *Journal of Nervous and Mental Diseases, 178,* 567–576.

Mattick, R. P., & Peters, L. (1988). Treatment of severe social phobia: Effects of guided exposure with and without cognitive restructuring. *Journal of Consulting and Clinical Psychology, 56,* 251–260.

Mavissakalian, M., & Michelson, M. (1986). Two year follow-up of exposure and imipramine treatment of agoraphobia. *American Journal of Psychiatry, 143,* 1106–1112.

Maxmen, J. S., & Ward, N. G. (1995). *Essential psychopathology and its treatment* (2nd ed.). New York: Norton.

McCrady, B. S. (1993). Alcoholism. In D. H. Barlow (Ed.), *Clinical handbook of psychological disorders* (2nd ed., pp. 362–395). New York: Guilford Press.

McCullough, J. P. (2003). Treatment for chronic depression using cognitive behavioral analysis system of psychotherapy (CBASP). *Journal of Clinical Psychology, 59*(8), 833–846.

McDermott, S. (2004). Treating anxiety disorders using cognitive therapy techniques. *Psychiatric Annals, 34*(11), 859–872.

McGlynn, F., Smitherman, T., & Gothard, K. (2004). Comment on the status of systematic desensitization. *Behavior Modification, 28*(2), 194–205.

McKinney, R., & Fiedler, S. (2004). Schizophrenia: Some recent advances and implications for behavioral intervention. *Behavior Therapist, 27*(6), 122–125.

McLean, P. D., & Hakstian, A. R. (1979). Clinical depression: Comparative efficacy of outpatient treatments. *Journal of Consulting and Clinical Psychology, 47,* 818–836.

McLean, P. D., & Woody, S. R. (2001). *Anxiety disorders in adults: An evidence-based approach to psychological treatment.* New York: Oxford University Press.

Messer, S. B. (1986). Eclecticism in psychotherapy: Underlying assumptions, problems, and trade-offs. In J. C. Norcross & M. R. Goldfried (Eds.), *Handbook of eclectic psychotherapy* (pp. 379–397). New York: Brunner/Mazel.

Messer, S. B. (1992). A critical examination of belief structures in integrative and eclectic psychotherapy. In J. C. Norcross & M. R. Goldfried (Eds.), *Handbook of psychotherapy integration* (pp. 130–165). New York: Basic Books.

Michels, R., & Marzuk, P. M. (1993). Progress in psychiatry: II. *New England Journal of Medicine, 329,* 628–638.

Millon, T. (1969). *Modern psychopathology: A biosocial approach to maladaptive learning and functioning.* Philadelphia: Saunders. (Reprinted 1985, Prospect Heights, IL: Waveland Press)

Millon, T. (1981). *Disorders of personality: DSM-III, Axis II.* New York: Wiley-Interscience.

Millon, T. (1984). On the renaissance of personality assessment and personality theory. *Journal of Personality Assessment, 48,* 450–466.

Millon, T. (1986a). Personality prototypes and their diagnostic criteria. In T. Millon & G. L. Klerman (Eds.), *Contemporary directions in psychopathology: Toward the* DSM-IV (pp. 671–712). New York: Guilford Press.

Millon, T. (1986b). A theoretical derivation of pathological personalities. In T. Millon & G. L. Klerman (Eds.), *Contemporary directions in psychopathology: Toward the* DSM-IV (pp. 639–669). New York: Guilford Press.

Millon, T. (1988). Personologic psychotherapy: Ten commandments for a post eclectic approach to integrative treatment. *Psychotherapy, 25,* 209–219.

Millon, T. (1990). *Toward a new personology: An evolutionary model.* New York: Wiley-Interscience.

Millon, T. (1991). Classification in psychopathology: Rationale, alternatives, and standards. *Journal of Abnormal Psychology, 100,* 245–261.

Millon, T., & Davis, R. D. (1996a). *Disorders of personality:* DSM-IV *and beyond.* New York: Wiley.

Millon, T., & Davis, R. D. (1996b). *Personality and psychopathology: Building a clinical science.* New York: Wiley-Interscience.

Millon, T. (1999). *Personality-guided therapy.* New York: Wiley.

Millon, T. (2002). Assessment is not enough: The SPA should participate in constructing a comprehensive clinical science of personality. *Journal of Personality Assessment, 78,* 209–218.

Millon, T. (2004). *Masters of the mind: Exploring the stories of mental illness from ancient times to the new millennium.* Hoboken, NJ: Wiley.

Millon, T., Bloom, C., & Grossman S., (in press). *Personalized assessment.* New York: Guilford Press.

Millon, T., & Davis, R. D. (1996). An evolutionary theory of personality disorders. In J. Clarkin & M. Lenzenweger (Eds.), *Major theories of personality disorder.* New York: Guilford Press.

Millon, T., & Grossman, S. (2004). Psychopathologic assessment can usefully inform therapy: A view from the study of personality. In J. Magnavita (Ed.), *Handbook of personality disorders: Theory and practice.* Hoboken, NJ: Wiley.

Millon, T., & Grossman, S. D. (2006a). Millon's evolutionary model for unifying the study of normal and abnormal personality. In S. Strack (Ed.), *Differentiating normal and abnormal personality* (2nd ed., pp. 3–46). New York: Springer.

Millon, T., & Grossman, S. (2006b). Personology: A theory based on evolutionary concepts. In M. Lenzenweger & J. Clarkin (Eds.), *Major theories of personality disorder* (2nd ed., pp. 332–390). New York: Guilford Press.

Millon, T., & Grossman, S. (in press). *Millon-Grossman personality domain checklist.* Coral Gables, FL: Dicandrien.

Millon, T., Grossman, S., Millon, C., Meagher, S., & Ramnath, R. (2004). *Personality disorders in modern life* (2nd ed.). Hoboken, NJ: Wiley.

Millon, T., Millon, C., Davis, R. D., & Grossman, S. D. (2006). *Millon Clinical Multiaxial Inventory—III Manual* (2nd ed.). Minneapolis, MN: NCS Pearson Assessments.

Monti, P. M., Abrahams, D. B., Kadden, R. M., & Cooney, N. L. (1989). *Treating alcohol dependence: A coping skills training guide.* New York: Guilford Press.

Morrison, J. (1995). DSM-IV *made easy.* New York: Guilford Press.

Murray, E. J. (1983). Beyond behavioural and dynamic therapy. *British Journal of Clinical Psychology, 22,* 127–128.

Nathan, P. E., & Gorman, J. M. (2002). *A guide to treatments that work* (2nd ed.). New York: Oxford University Press.

Nathan, P. E., & Gorman, J. M. (2002). *A guide to treatments that work* (2nd ed.). New York: Oxford Press.

Norcross, J. C., & Goldfried, M. R. (Eds.). (1992). *Handbook of psychotherapy integration.* New York: Basic Books.

Oakley, D. (2006). Hypnosis as a tool in research: Experimental psychopathology. *Contemporary Hypnosis, 23*(1), 3–14.

Ost, L. G. (1988). Applied relaxation versus progressive relaxation in the treatment of panic disorder. *Behaviour Research and Therapy, 26,* 13–22.

Patrick, H. T., & Bassoe, P. (1912). *Occupational neuritis: The practice medicine series: Vol. 10. Nervous and mental diseases.* Chicago: The Year Book Publishers.

PDM Task Force. (2006). *Psychodynamic diagnostic manual.* Silver Spring, MD: Alliance of Psychoanalytic Organizations.

Penn, D. L., & Mueser, K. T. (1996). Research update on the psychosocial treatment of schizophrenia. *American Journal of Psychiatry, 153,* 607–617.

Pollard, C. (2005). Freedom from obsessive-compulsive disorder: A personalized recovery program for living with uncertainty. *Cognitive and Behavioral Practice, 12*(3), 371–372.

Power, K. G., Simpson, R. J., Swanson, V., & Wallace, L. A. (1990). A controlled comparison of cognitive-behavior therapy, diazepam, and placebo, alone and in combination, for the treatment of generalized anxiety disorder. *Journal of Anxiety Disorders, 4,* 267–292.

Prince, M. (1978). *The dissociation of a personality.* New York: Oxford University Press. (Original work published in 1905)

Quine, W. V. O. (1961). *From a logical point of view* (2nd ed.). New York: Harper & Row.

Rasmussen, P. R. (2005). *Personality-guided cognitive-behavioral therapy.* Washington, DC: American Psychological Association.

Rauch, S. L., & Jenike, M. A. (1998). Pharmacological treatment of obsessive compulsive disorder. In P. E. Nathan, J. M. Gorman (Eds.), *A guide to treatments that work* (pp. 358–376). New York: Oxford University Press.

Renshaw, K., Steketee, G., & Chambless, D. (2005). Involving family members in the treatment of OCD. *Cognitive Behaviour Therapy, 34*(3), 164–175.

Resick, P. A., & Schnicke, M. K. (1992). Cognitive processing therapy for sexual assault victims. *Journal of Sex and Marital Therapy, 7,* 184–194.

Riggs, D. S., & Foa, E. B. (1993). Obsessive-compulsive disorder. In D. H. Barlow (Ed.), *Clinical handbook of psychological disorders* (2nd ed., pp. 189–239). New York: Guilford Press.

Rosenbaum, J. F., Fava, M., Nierenberg, A., & Sachs, G. S. (1995). Treatment-resistant mood disorders. In G. O. Gabbard (Ed.), *Treatments of psychiatric disorders* (pp. 1275–1328). Washington, DC: American Psychiatric Press.

Roth, A., & Fonagy, P. (1996). *What works for whom? A critical review of psychotherapy research.* New York: Guilford Press.

Roy-Byrne, P. P., & Cowley, D. S. (2002). Pharmacological treatments for panic disorder, generalized anxiety disorder, specific phobia, and social anxiety disorder. In P. E. Nathan & J. M. Gorman (Eds.), *A guide to treatments that work* (pp. 337–365). New York: Oxford University Press.

Rubinstein, E. A., & Parloff, M. B. (Eds.). (1959). *Research in psychotherapy, proceedings.* Washington, DC: American Psychological Association.

Sacks, O. (1973). *Awakenings.* New York: Harper & Row.

Salvendy, J. T., & Joffe, R. (1991). Antidepressants in group psychotherapy. *International Journal of Group Psychotherapy, 41,* 465–480.

Schneier, F. R., Marshall, R. D., Street, L., Heindberg, R. G., & Juster, H. R. (1995). Social phobia and specific phobia. In G. O. Gabbard (Ed.), *Treatments of psychiatric disorders* (pp. 1453–1476). Washington, DC: American Psychiatric Press.

Seligman, L. (1998). *Selecting effective treatments: A comprehensive, systematic guide to treating mental disorders.* San Francisco: Jossey Bass.

Shlien, J. M. (1968). *Research in psychotherapy: Proceedings of the third conference, Chicago, IL, May 31–June 4, 1966.* Washington, DC: American Psychological Association.

Slater, L. (1998). *Prozac diary.* New York: Random House.

Spence, S. (1989). Cognitive-behavior therapy in the management of chronic, occupational pain of the upper limbs. *Behavior Research and Therapy, 27,* 435–446.

Sperry, L. (1995). *Handbook of diagnosis and treatment of the DSM-IV personality disorders.* New York: Brunner/Mazel.

Spiegel, D. (2003). Hypnosis and traumatic dissociation: Therapeutic opportunities. *Journal of Trauma and Dissociation, 4*(3), 73–90.

Stephens, J. H., & Kamp, M. (1962). On some aspects of hysteria. *Journal of Nervous and Mental Diseases, 134,* 305–315.

Steuer, J., Mintz, J., Hammen, C., Hill, M. A., Jarvik, L. F., McCarley, T., et al. (1984). Cognitive-behavioral and psychodynamic group psychotherapy in treatment of geriatric depression. *Journal of Consulting and Clinical Psychology, 52,* 180–192.

Stollak, G. E., Guerney, B. G., & Rothberg, M. (Eds.). (1966). *Psychotherapy research: Selected readings.* Chicago: Rand McNally.

Strupp, H. H., & Luborsky, L. (1962). *Research in psychotherapy: Proceedings of a conference, Chapel Hill, North Carolina, May 17–20, 1961.* Washington, DC: American Psychological Association.

Swan, J., Sorrell, E., MacVicar, B., Durham, R., & Matthews, K. (2004). "Coping with depression": An open study of the efficacy of a group psychoeducational intervention in chronic, treatment-refractory depression. *Journal of Affective Disorders, 82*(1), 125–129.

Swartz, M. S., & McCracken, J. (1986). Emergency room management of conversion disorders. *Hospital and Community Psychiatry, 37,* 828–832.

Tafet, G. E., & Bernardini, R. (2003). Psychoneuroendocrinological links between chronic stress and depression. *Progress in Neuro-Psychopharmacology and Biological Psychiatry, 27*(6), 893–903.

Tavris, C. (1989). *Anger: The misunderstood emotion.* New York: Touchstone.

Taylor, S., & Braun, J. D. (1998). Illusion and well-being. *Psychological Bulletin, 103,* 193–210.

Tazaki, M., & Landlaw, K. (2006). Behavioral mechanisms and cognitive-behavioral interventions of somatoform disorders. *International Review of Psychiatry, 18*(1), 67–73.

Tringone, R. (1990). Construction of the Millon Personality Diagnostic Checklist—III-R and personality prototypes. *Dissertation Abstracts International, 51*(10), 5045B.

Tringone, R. (1997). The MPDC: Composition and clinical applications. In T. Millon (Ed.), *The Millon Inventories* (pp. 449–474). New York: Guilford Press.

Trull, T. J., Nietzel, M. T., & Main, A. (1988). The use of meta-analysis to assess the clinical significance of behavior therapy for agoraphobia. *Behavior Therapy, 19,* 527–538.

Turkus, J., & Kahler, J. (2006). Therapeutic interventions in the treatment of dissociative disorders. *Psychiatric Clinics of North America, 29*(1), 245–262.

Turner, J. (1982). Comparison of group progressive-relaxation training and cognitive-behavioral group therapy for chronic low back pain. *Journal of Consulting and Clinical Psychology, 50,* 757–765.

Vassey, M. W., & Dadds, M. R. (2001). *The developmental psychopathology of anxiety.* New York: Oxford University Press.

Veronen, L. J., & Kilpatrick, D. G. (1982). *Stress inoculation training for victims of rape: Efficacy and differential findings.* Paper presented at the 16th Annual Convention of the Association for the Advancement of Behavior Therapy, Los Angeles, University of South Carolina, National Crime Victims Research and Treatment Center.

Vogel, P., Stiles, T., & Götestam, K. (2004). Adding cognitive therapy elements to exposure therapy for obsessive compulsive disorder: A controlled study. *Behavioral and Cognitive Psychotherapy, 32*(3), 275–290.

Wattar, U., Sorensen, P., Buemann, I., Birket-Smith, M., Salkovskis, P., Albertsen, M., et al. (2005). Outcome of cognitive-behavioral treatment for health anxiety (hypochondriasis) in a routine clinical setting. *Behavioral and Cognitive Psychotherapy, 33*(2), 165–175.

Westen, D., & Weinberger, J. (2004). When clinical description becomes statistical prediction. *American Psychologist, 59,* 595–613.

Wexler, B. E., & Cicchetti, D. V. (1992). The outpatient treatment of depression: Implications of outcome research for clinical practice. *Journal of Nervous and Mental Diseases, 180,* 277–286.

INDEX

Abrahams, D. B., 224

Abrasive (interpersonal conduct), 53

Abstinent (expressive behavior), 51

Acting out (intrapsychic mechanisms), 61, 109

Adaptation modes, 22

Admirable (self-image), 56

Aggrieved/masochistic personalities:
    in circulargrams, 28, 29, 30
    domain analysis (code L in tables), 49, 51, 53, 55,
        57, 59, 61, 63, 65, 66
    dysthymia in masochistic personalities, 41–42
    generalized anxiety among, 149–151
    polarities and, 27
    somatoform syndromes among, 210
    subdued depression among, 102–103

Agitated depression. *See* Major depressive disorder,
    agitated depression

Agoraphobia, 119, 121, 154

Alcohol-related syndromes, 222–233
    among assertive/sadistic personalities, 224–226
    among conscientious/compulsive personalities,
        229–231
    domain analysis, 225–226, 228, 230, 232–233
    general clinical picture, 222–223
    among nonconforming/antisocial personalities,
        224–226
    among shy/avoidant personalities, 231–233
    among skeptical/negativistic personalities,
        227–229
    treatment options, 224

Alexander, F., 38, 39

Alienated (self-image), 56, 91, 136, 199, 217, 232,
    243, 248

Amnesia, 170

Andrews, G., 124

Anguished (mood/affect), 58, 173

Antisocial personalities. *See* Nonconforming/
    antisocial personalities

Anxiety:
    pain polarity and, 25
    physical syndromes related to, 191–219
        conversion syndromes, 211–219
        somatoform syndromes, 192–211
    psychological syndromes related to, 153–189
        dissociative syndromes, 168–180
        obsessive-compulsive (Axis I) syndromes,
            180–189
        phobic syndromes, 156–158
    simple versus complex, 36

Anxiety management programs (AMP), 127

Anxiety syndromes, 115–152
    acute anxiety and panic reactions, 117–126
        general clinical picture, 121–122
        introduction, 115–117
        treatment options, 124–126
    generalized, 127–152
        among aggrieved/masochistic personalities, 149
        among capricious/borderline personalities,
            151–152
        among confident/narcissistic personalities, 142
        among conscientious/compulsive personalities,
            143
        domain analysis, 133, 136, 138–139, 141,
            144–145, 147–148, 150–151
        among dramatic/histrionic personalities,
            139–140

Anxiety syndromes (*Continued*)
    among eccentric/schizotypal personalities,
       131–132
    among forceful/sadistic personalities, 142–143
    gender, 130
    general clinical picture, 129–130
    Generalized Anxiety Disorder (GAD), 129
    introduction, 115–117, 127–129
    among needy/dependent personalities, 137
    among nonconforming/antisocial personalities,
       142–143
    among pessimistic/depressive personalities, 149
    among retiring/schizoid personalities, 131–132
    among shy/avoidant personalities, 134
    among skeptical/negativistic personalities, 146
    among suspicious/paranoid personalities, 152
    treatment options, 130–131
  posttraumatic stress syndromes, 126–127
Apathetic (mood/affect), 58, 243
Arkowitz, H., 12, 13
Arthur, A., 195
Asceticism (intrapsychic mechanisms), 61
Assertive/sadistic personalities:
    alcohol-related syndromes among, 224–226
    in circulargrams, 28, 29, 30
    domain analysis (code J in tables), 34, 51, 53, 55,
       57, 59, 61, 63, 65, 66
    generalized anxiety among, 142–143
    paranoid schizophrenic disorders among, 250
Attention-seeking (interpersonal conduct), 52, 88,
    95, 108, 141, 164, 179
Atwood, J. D., 97, 157
Auerbach, A. H., 5
Autistic (cognitive style/content), 54
Autonomous (self-image), 57, 225
Aversive (interpersonal conduct), 52, 161, 199, 217,
    233
Avoidant personalities. *See* Shy/avoidant personalities
Awakenings (Sacks), 70

Bacaltchuk, J., 99
Barlow, D. H., 125, 130, 158
Baron, D. A., 171
Barsky, A., 195
Bassoe, P., 5
Beard, G. M., 191
Beck, A. T., 25, 99, 125, 130, 136, 146, 151, 159,
    187, 226, 233
Behavioral learning theory, 44, 97, 99, 213

Bellack, A., 99
Benjamin, L. R., 171
Benjamin, L. S., 19, 25, 31, 109, 137, 139, 146, 167,
    174, 218, 226
Benjamin, R., 171
Berg, I. K., 173
Bergen, A. E., 5
Bergin, A. E., 76
Bernardini, R., 97
Beutler, L. E., 12
Binder, J. L., 139, 162
Bipolar syndromes, 105–113
  domain analysis, 108–109, 112
  euphoric mania:
    among confident/narcissistic personalities,
      109–110
    among needy/dependent personalities, 109
    among retiring/schizoid personalities, 110
    among shy/avoidant personalities, 110
    among sociable/histrionic personalities, 107
  general clinical picture, 106–107
  hostile mania:
    among capricious/borderline personalities,
      110
    among confident/narcissistic personalities, 113
    among conscientious/compulsive personalities,
      111
    among retiring/schizoid personalities, 110
    among shy/avoidant personalities, 110
    among skeptical/negativistic personalities, 113
    among suspicious/paranoid personalities,
      110–111
  introduction, 81–82, 105–106
  personalized psychotherapy, 107
  treatment options, 107
Blatt, Sidney J., 97
Bleiberg, K. L., 84
Bloom, C., 4, 29
Bockian, N., 82, 84
Bond, M., 99
Borderline personalities. *See* Capricious/borderline
    personalities
Borkovec, T. D., 131
Braun, B. G., 171
Braun, J. D., 125, 129, 213
Brief therapy, 7
Briquet, P., 191
Burton, Robert, 82
Butler, G., 131

Callous (mood/affect), 59

Cameron, N., 26

Capricious/borderline personalities:
  agitated depression among, 105
  in circulargrams, 28, 29, 30
  dissociation among, 180
  domain analysis (code N in tables), 34, 51, 53, 55, 57, 59, 61, 63, 65, 66
  dysthymia and brief manic episodes among, 92
  generalized anxiety among, 151–152
  hostile mania among, 110
  somatoform syndromes among, 210–211

Carroll, K., 224

Catalytic sequences, 68–72

Catatonia, rigid/withdrawn, 238–239, 242, 244, 246–247

Caul, D., 171

Cerny, J. A., 125

Chambless, D., 184

Chaotic (intrapsychic content), 62

Charcot, J. M., 168, 180, 211

Chester, R., 97, 157

Chevron, E. S., 96, 99

Christiensen, H., 124

Christos, P. J., 84

Cicchetti, D. V., 99

Clarkin, J., 11, 12

Clinical sciences, elements characterizing, 16

Cloninger, Robert, 19

Clum, G. A., 127

Cognitive dysfunction syndromes:
  endogenous (see Schizophrenic syndromes)
  exogenous (see Alcohol-related syndromes; Drug-related syndromes)

Cognitive style/content:
  in circulargram of functional domains, 29
  functional versus structural domains, 25
  trait descriptions checklist, 63–64
  trait descriptions framework explained, 48–49

Cognitive therapists, simple reactions versus complex syndromes, 44

Colby, C. A., 84

Collins, J. F., 89

Combative (self-image), 57

Compartmentalized (intrapsychic structure), 66

Complacent (self-image), 56

Complex syndromes (symptom clusters), 31–43
  personality domain traits underlying, 39–43
  versus simple reactions, 33–43

Compulsions, 183

Compulsive personalities. See Conscientious/compulsive personalities; Obsessive-compulsive (Axis I) syndromes

Concealed objects (intrapsychic content), 63, 176, 209

Conduct disorders, 41

Confident/narcissistic personalities:
  anxiety disorders among, 142
  in circulargrams, 28, 29, 30
  domain analysis (code G in tables), 34, 50, 52, 54, 56, 59, 60, 62, 65, 66
  dysthymia among, 96–97
  euphoric mania among, 109–110
  hostile mania among, 113
  paranoid schizophrenic disorders among, 250
  polarities and, 26
  somatoform syndromes among, 204

Conflict-resolution model, 213

Conscientious/compulsive personalities. See also Obsessive-compulsive (Axis I) syndromes
  agitated depression among, 105
  alcohol-related syndromes among, 229–231
  anxiety among, 25, 143–147, 156
  catatonic rigidity among, 244–247
  in circulargrams, 28, 29, 30
  complex syndromes and, 155, 156
  conversion syndromes among, 215–216
  as diagnostic example, 42
  disorganized schizophrenic disorders among, 249
  dissociation among, 174–177
  domain analysis (code O in tables), 34, 51, 53, 55, 57, 59, 61, 65, 66
  dysthymic syndromes among, 92–93
  hostile mania among, 111–113
  obsessive-compulsive syndromes among, 184–185
  phobias among, 165
  polarities, 25, 26–27
  somatoform syndromes among, 207–210
  subdued depression among, 101–102
  training to become compulsive, 40, 156

Conscientious self-image, 112, 176, 230, 246

Constricted (cognitive style/content), 55, 112, 145, 150, 197, 209, 230

Contrary (interpersonal conduct), 53, 104, 138–139, 148, 167, 206, 228, 230

Contrived (intrapsychic content), 62

Conversion syndromes, 193, 211–219
 among conscientious/compulsive personalities, 215–216
 general clinical picture, 212–213
 introduction, 191, 211–212
 among needy/dependent personalities, 215
 among shy/avoidant personalities, 216–218
 among skeptical/negativistic personalities, 218–219
 among sociable/histrionic personalities, 218
 treatment options, 214–215
Cooney, N. L., 224
Coons, P. M., 171
Cooper, N. A., 127
Coping styles, 34, 37
Costello, E., 131
Covi, L., 99
Cowley, D. S., 136
Craighead, L. W., 69
Craighead, W. E., 69
Cullington, A., 131
Culturally sensitive therapies, 7–10
Curtis, R. C., 91
Cyclothymia, 82
Cynical/skeptical (cognitive style/content), 64, 148, 200, 206, 228

Dadds, M. R., 125, 130
Dattilio, F., 184
Davidson, J., 127
Davis, D. D., 136
Davis, R. D., 20, 21, 22, 29, 40, 45, 131, 135, 147, 150, 156, 230
Dean, S. J., 5
Debased (intrapsychic content), 63
Defenseless (interpersonal conduct), 53
Defensive (expressive behavior), 51
Deferential (interpersonal conduct), 53
de Jesus, M. J., 99
DeJong, P., 173
Delaney, H., 224
de Mello, M. F., 99
Dependent personalities. See Needy/dependent personalities
Depleted (intrapsychic structure), 65
Depression. See also Bipolar syndromes; Dysthymic syndromes; Major depressive disorder:
 complex syndromes, 39
 developmental perspective, 97

Depressive personalities. See Pessimistic/melancholic (depressive) personalities
Deviant (cognitive style/content), 55
Diagnostic and Statistical Manual of Mental Disorders (DSM), 17, 22–24, 33, 43–44, 47, 76, 81, 97
Diffident (cognitive style/content), 55
Dion, G. L., 107
Disciplined (expressive behavior), 51
Disconsolate (expressive behavior), 51
Discontented (self-image), 57, 104, 206
Discredited representations (intrapsychic content), 63, 150
Disjointed (intrapsychic structure), 65
Disorganized type. See Schizophrenic syndromes
Displacement (intrapsychic mechanisms), 61, 181
Dissociation (intrapsychic mechanisms), 60, 179
Dissociative syndromes, 168–180
 among capricious/borderline personality disorders, 180
 among conscientious/compulsive personality disorders, 174–177
 general clinical picture, 169–171
 identity disorders, 170
 introduction, 153–156, 180–181
 among needy/dependent personality disorders, 174
 among shy/avoidant personalities, 171–174
 among skeptical/negativistic personality disorders, 179–180
 among sociable/histrionic personality disorders, 177–179
 treatment options, 171
Distracted (cognitive style/content), 54, 161, 232, 248
Distraught or Insentient (mood/affect), 58
Divergent (intrapsychic structure), 66
DNA, psychic, 4
Dogmatic (cognitive style/content), 55
Domains. See Personality-based evolutionary model
Drake, R. E., 5
Dramatic (expressive behavior), 50, 95, 109, 141
Dramatic personalities. See Sociable/histrionic personalities
Drive derivatives, 19
Drug-related syndromes, 234–236
Durham, R., 107
Durham, R. C., 130
Dysphoric (mood/affect), 59

Dysthymic syndromes, 41, 83–97
    among aggrieved/masochistic personality patterns, 41–42, 86–89
    among capricious/borderline personalities, 92
    among confident/narcissistic personalities, 96–97
    among conscientious/compulsive personalities, 92–93
    general clinical picture, 83–84
    introduction, 81–82, 83
    among needy/dependent personalities, 45, 86–89
    among negativistic personalities, 45
    among shy/avoidant personality patterns, 89–92
    among skeptical/negativistic personality patterns, 89
    among sociable/histrionic personalities, 93–94
    treatment options, 69, 84–85

Eccentric/schizotypal personalities:
    anxiety disorders among, 131–134
    in circulargrams, 28, 29, 30
    disorganized schizophrenic disorders among, 249–250
    domain analysis (code B in tables), 49, 50, 52, 54, 56, 58, 60, 62, 64
Eclecticism, 12–13
Edwards, C., 195
Eldridge, N., 74
Electroconvulsive therapy, 98–99
Ellis, A., 95, 146, 197, 249
Emery, G., 99, 125, 130, 151, 159
Emmelkamp, P. M. G., 224
Energetic (self-image), 56
Eruptive (intrapsychic structure), 65
Espie, C. A., 130
Estranged (self-image), 56, 133
Euphoric mania. *See* Bipolar syndromes
Evidence-based therapies, 7
Evolutionary model, 20–24, 27
Exaggeration (intrapsychic mechanisms), 70
Expansive (cognitive style/content), 54, 95, 167
Exploitive (interpersonal conduct), 52
Exposure procedures, 124–125, 158, 159, 184
Expressive behavior domain:
    in circulargram of functional domains, 29
    domain analysis in cases, 91, 95, 104, 109, 136, 141, 148, 202, 226, 248
    functional versus structural domains, 25
    trait descriptions checklist, 50–51
    trait descriptions framework explained, 48–49

Exuberant/hypomanic personalities:
    in circulargrams, 28, 29, 30
    domain analysis (code E in tables), 49, 50, 52, 54, 56, 58, 60, 62, 64

Family therapy, 171
Fantasy (intrapsychic mechanisms), 69, 173
Farber, B. A., 135
Fatalistic (cognitive style/content), 55
Fava, M., 107
Fawcett, J., 99
Feuchtersleben, E., 82
Fickle (mood/affect), 58, 164
Fiedler, S., 241
Fineberg, N., 184, 185
Fisher, J. E., 5
Fleeting (intrapsychic structure), 64
Flighty (cognitive style/content), 54
Fluctuating (intrapsychic content), 63
Foa, E. B., 127, 182
Fonagy, P., 84, 107, 125, 224
Forceful/sadistic personalities. *See* Assertive/sadistic personalities
Forsaken (intrapsychic content), 63
Fragile (intrapsychic structure), 64
Fragmented (intrapsychic structure), 64
Frances, A. J., 11, 12, 99
Frank, J. B., 5
Frank, J. D., 5
Frankl, V., 226
Freeman, A., 136
Frenzied states, 169
Fretful (expressive behavior), 50, 136
Freud, S., 153, 156, 170, 181, 192, 211, 212
Fugue (dissociative syndromes), 170
Fugue (musical metaphor), 23
Functional domains, 25, 29

Gabbard, G. O., 127
Gabhainn, S., 224
Gains, primary/secondary, 38–39, 154
Gale, T., 184, 185
Gansu, C. V., 130
Garfield, S. L., 5
Gays and lesbians, 9–10
Gelder, M., 131
Generalized Anxiety Disorder (GAD), 129. *See also* Anxiety; Anxiety syndromes
Genomic medicine, 4

Geringer, E., 195
Glasser, W., 197, 226
Goddard, A. W., 124
Goldfried, M. R., 5
Goldstein, A. P., 5
Goldstein, Kurt, 69
Goodheart, C. D., 5
Gorman, J. M., 5, 99, 107, 124, 125, 130, 131, 195
Götestam, K., 184
Gothard, K., 158
Gotlib, I. H., 84, 99
Gottschalk, L. A., 5
Gould, S., 74
Greenberg, R., 151
Gregarious (self-image), 56, 141
Greist, J. H., 184
Grossman, S., 4, 20, 21, 24, 29, 45, 86, 147
Grossman Facet Scales, 4, 87, 179
Grunbaum, A., 32
Guerney, B. G., 5
Guze, S., 191

Hadzi-Pavlovic, D., 124
Hakstian, A. R., 99
Haughty (expressive behavior), 50
Heindberg, R. G., 159
Hempel, C. G., 20
Heresco-Levy, U., 240
Hersen, M., 99
Hester, R., 224
Hettema, J., 136, 164
Hibbert, G., 131
High-Spirited (interpersonal conduct), 52
Himmelhoch, J. M., 99
Hirsch, I., 91
Histrionic personalities. See Sociable/histrionic
     personalities
Hoch, P. H., 5
Hofmann, S., 159
Hollon, S. D., 99, 125
Homeostasis, 73
Hood, E. M., 130
Hostile (mood/affect), 59
Hostile mania. See Bipolar syndromes
Humors, four, 81
Hypnosis, 214
Hypochondriacal syndromes, 39, 40, 193
Hypomanic personalities. See Exuberant/hypomanic
     personalities
Hysteria, 168, 211

Immature objects(intrapsychic content), 62, 202
Impassive (expressive behavior), 50
Impetuous (expressive behavior), 50
Impoverished (cognitive style/content), 54
Impulsive (expressive behavior), 51
Inchoate (intrapsychic structure), 64, 139
Incompatible (intrapsychic content), 63
Incompetent (expressive behavior), 50, 91, 202, 248
Inelastic (intrapsychic structure), 65
Inept (self-image), 56, 101, 138, 164, 187, 202
Insouciant (mood/affect), 59
Integrative therapies, 11–14
Intellectualization (intrapsychic mechanisms), 60,
     133
Interpersonal conduct domain:
   in circulargram of functional domains, 29
   domain analysis in cases:
      anxiety-related physical syndromes, 199, 206,
         209, 217
      anxiety-related psychological syndromes, 161,
         164, 167, 173, 179
      cognitive-dysfunction syndromes, 228, 230,
         233, 243
      generalized anxiety syndromes, 133, 138–139,
         141, 144–145, 148
      mood-related syndromes, 88, 95, 101, 104,
         108
   functional versus structural domains, 25
   trait descriptions checklist, 52–53
   trait descriptions framework explained, 48–49
Interpersonal tradition, 19, 25, 97, 98
Intrapsychic content domain:
   in circulargram of structural domains, 30
   domain analysis in cases, 62, 91, 150, 161, 176,
      202, 209, 217, 226, 228
   trait descriptions checklist, 62–63
   trait descriptions framework explained, 48–49
Intrapsychic mechanisms domain:
   in circulargram of functional domains, 29
   domain analysis in cases, 109, 112, 133, 173, 179,
      181, 187, 246
   trait descriptions checklist, 60–61
   trait descriptions framework explained, 48–49
Intrapsychic structure domain:
   domain analysis in cases, 139
   trait descriptions checklist, 64–66
   trait descriptions framework explained, 48–49
Intrapsychic therapists, 45, 98
Introjection (intrapsychic mechanisms), 60, 187
Inverted (intrapsychic structure), 65

Inviolable (self-image), 57
Irascible (mood/affect), 59
Irresponsible (interpersonal conduct), 53
Irritable (mood/affect), 59, 176, 245
Isolation (intrapsychic mechanisms), 61, 181

Jackson, D. N., 46
Janet, P., 168, 169, 170, 180, 181, 184, 211
Jefferson, J. W., 184
Jenike, M. A., 185
Joffe, R., 99
Judge, R., 150
Juster, H. R., 159

Kadden, R. M., 224
Kahler, J., 171
Kamp, M., 213
Kaplan, D. A., 158, 159
Kaskutas, L., 224
Kazdin, A. E., 5, 69
Kellner, R., 195
Kelly, K. R., 184
Kernberg, O. F., 22, 96, 137, 229
Kiesler, D. J., 25, 146, 218, 226
Kilpatrick, D. G., 127
Klerman, G. L., 96, 99
Klimes, I., 131
Klosko, J. S., 125
Kluft, R. P., 171
Kocsis, J. H., 84
Koenigsberg, H. W., 136
Kraepelin, Emil, 82, 97
Kubie, L. S., 171

Labile (mood/affect), 59
Lambert, M. J., 76
Landlaw, K., 195
Lane, J. S., 135
Lazarus, A. A., 5, 12
Lecrubier, Y., 150
Leigh, G., 234
Lemmens, G., 215
Lesbians/gays, 9–10
Levenson, H., 162
Levinson, M. H., 99
Lewin, Kurt, 1936, 20
Lewinsohn, P. M., 99
Lewis, A., 82
Lindsay, W. R., 130
Lipman, R. S., 99

Lithium, 107
Livesley, W. J., 46
Locke, John, 156
Luborsky, L., 5
Lupu, V., 214
Lynde, D., 5

MacVicar, B., 107
Magnavita, J. J., 91, 174
Magnification (intrapsychic mechanisms), 60
Mahoney, M. J., 69
Main, A., 124
Major depressive disorder, 97–105
   agitated depression, 97–98
      among capricious/borderline personalities, 105
      among conscientious/compulsive personalities, 105
      among shy/avoidant personalities, 102
      among skeptical/negativistic personalities, 103
   domain analysis, 100–101, 104
   general clinical picture, 97–98
   introduction, 81–82, 97
   subdued depression, 98
      among aggrieved/masochistic personalities, 102–103
      among conscientious/compulsive personalities, 101–102
      among needy/dependent personalities, 99–100
      among pessimistic/depressive personalities, 102
      among shy/avoidant personalities, 102
   treatment options, 98–99
Maldonado, J. R., 171
Mania. *See* Bipolar syndromes; Exuberant/hypomanic personalities
Manic episodes, brief, among capricious/borderline personalities, 92
Manning, D. W., 99
Markowitz, J. C., 84
Marks, I. M., 125
Marshall, R. D., 159
Marzuk, P. M., 107
Masochistic personalities. *See* Aggrieved/masochistic personalities
Matthews, K., 107
Mattick, R. P., 124, 159
Mavissakalian, M., 125
Maxmen, J. S., 158
McCracken, J., 214
McCrady, B. S., 224
McCullough, J. P., 84

McGlynn, F., 158
McKinney, R., 241
McLaughlin, E., 130
McLean, P. D., 99, 124, 125, 127, 130, 131
Meager (intrapsychic content), 62
Meagher, S., 147
Medications, 69, 98–99, 124–125, 127, 184
Melancholia, 81
Melancholic personalities. *See* Pessimistic/
    melancholic (depressive) personalities
Melancholic/woeful (mood/affect), 59, 197
Mercurial (mood/affect), 58
Merrens, M. R., 5
Messer, S. B., 5, 12, 13, 76
MG-PDC. *See* Millon-Grossman Personality Domain
    Checklist (MG-PDC)
Michels, R., 107
Michelson, M., 125
Miller, W., 136
Millon, C., 147
Millon, T., 3, 4, 7, 12, 14, 16, 17, 20, 21, 22, 23, 24,
    25, 29, 40, 45, 46, 70, 73, 81, 86, 116, 131,
    135, 143, 147, 150, 156, 174, 230
Millon Clinical Multiaxial Inventory (MCMI-III),
    Grossman Facet Scales, 4, 30, 87, 179
Millon-Grossman Personality Domain Checklist
    (MG-PDC), 4, 30, 45–68
Mistrustful (cognitive style/content), 55, 136
Modality-bound psychotherapy, 18–20
Monti, P. M., 224
Mood/affect domain:
    in circulargram of structural domains, 30
    domain analysis in cases, 101, 164, 173, 176, 197,
        243, 245
    trait descriptions checklist, 58–59
    trait descriptions framework explained, 48–49
Mood-related syndromes. *See* Bipolar syndromes;
    Dysthymic syndromes
Morrison, J., 171
Mueser, K. T., 240, 241
Murray, E. J., 14

Nagy, R., 171
Naive (cognitive style/content), 54
Narcissistic personalities. *See* Confident/narcissistic
    personalities
Narcosynthesis, 171
Nathan, P. E., 5, 99, 107, 124, 125, 130, 131,
    195

Needy/dependent personalities:
    anxiety disorders among, 137–139, 155
    catatonic withdrawal among, 244
    in circulargrams, 28, 29, 30
    conversion syndromes among, 215
    Dependent Personality Disorder, criterion, 43
    disorganized schizophrenic disorders among, 249
    dissociation among, 174
    domain analysis (code D in tables), 49, 50, 52, 54,
        56, 58, 60, 62, 64
    dysthymia syndromes among, 41–42, 86–89
    euphoric mania among, 109
    obsessive-compulsive syndromes among, 185–188
    phobias among, 159–160
    polarities, 26
    somatoform syndromes among, 200–203
    subdued depression among, 99–102
    tactical modality selection (example), 74
Negativistic personalities. *See* Skeptical/negativistic
    personalities
Neugebauer, R., 99
Neurasthenia, 191
Neuroses/neurotic symptoms, 128, 153, 180
Nierenberg, A., 107
Nietzel, M. T., 124
Nonconforming/antisocial personalities:
    alcohol-related syndromes among, 224–226
    anxiety among, 142–143
    in circulargrams, 28, 29, 30
    domain analysis (code I in tables), 49, 51, 53, 55,
        57, 59, 61, 63, 65
Norcross, J. C., 5

Oakley, D., 214
Object Representations, 25
Obsessive-compulsive (Axis I) syndromes, 180–189
    among conscientious/compulsive personalities,
        184–185
    general clinical picture, 182–183
    introduction, 153–156, 180–181
    among needy/dependent personalities, 185–188
    among retiring/schizoid personalities, 188–189
    among shy/avoidant personalities, 185
    among skeptical/negativistic personalities, 188
    among sociable/histrionic personalities, 188
    among suspicious/paranoid personalities, 189
    treatment options, 183–184
Obsessive-compulsive patterns. *See* Conscientious/
    compulsive personalities

Obsessive-compulsive personality disorder, criteria for, 43
Obsessive doubting, 182, 185
Obsessive thoughts, 182
O'Donohue, W. T., 5
Onken, L., 224
Osler, William, 82
Ost, L., 125

Pacific (mood/affect), 58, 101, 245
Pain disorders, 193, 214. *See also* Conversion syndromes; Somatoform syndromes
Pain/pleasure polarity, 21–22, 25–26, 71
Panic control treatment (PCT) program, 125
Panic reactions, 115, 117–126
Paradoxical (interpersonal conduct), 53
Paranoid personalities. *See* Suspicious/paranoid personalities
Paranoid schizophrenia. *See* Schizophrenic syndromes, paranoid type
Parloff, M. B., 5
Passive/active polarity, 22, 26, 72
Patient-based self-judgments, 46
Patrick, H. T., 5
PDM Task Force, 98
Peculiar (expressive behavior), 50
Penn, D. L., 240, 241
Pernicious (intrapsychic content), 63
Perry, J. C., 99
Perry, S., 11
Personality-based evolutionary model:
    circumplex representations:
        functional personologic domains, 29
        normal and abnormal personality patterns, 28
        structural personologic domains, 30
    domains checklist, descriptive trait choices, 48–49, 50–68
        cognitive style/content domain, 54–55
        expressive behavior, 50–51
        interpersonal conduct domain, 52–53
        intrapsychic content domain, 62–63
        intrapsychic mechanisms domain, 60–61
        intrapsychic structure domain, 64–66
        mood/affect domain, 58–59
        self-image domain, 56–57
    functional domains, 25, 29
    introduction/overview, 20–31
    psychic DNA, 4
    spectra and domains, 28–31, 67–68

Personalized psychotherapy:
    barriers to (two), 17
    versus eclecticism, 14
    emergence of, 14–15
    introduction, 3–4
    justification for name, 3, 11, 12
    methods/goals of, 68–72
    procedural caveats and considerations, 76–78
    tactics/strategies, 72–76
Personal styles (conflicted/deficient/imbalanced), 24
Pessimistic/melancholic (depressive) personalities:
    in circulargrams, 28, 29, 30
    domain analysis (code K in tables), 49, 51, 53, 55, 57, 59, 61, 63, 65
    generalized anxiety among, 149–151
    medications, 69
    phobias among, 159–160
    polarities (passivity), 26
    somatoform syndromes among, 196–198
    subdued depression among, 102
Peters, L., 159
Pharmacologic interventions, 69, 98–99, 124–125, 127, 184
Phobias/phobic syndromes, 156–158
    among aggrieved/masochistic personalities, 165
    complex/simple reactions, 36, 37, 39
    among conscientious/compulsive personalities, 165
    general clinical picture, 157–158
    introduction, 153–156
    among needy/dependent personalities, 159–160
    among pessimistic/depressive personalities, 159–160
    among shy/avoidant personalities, 160–163
    among skeptical/negativistic personalities, 165
    among sociable/histrionic personalities, 163
    trait domains and, 18
    treatment options, 158–159
Piecemeal (intrapsychic content), 62
Polarities of evolutionary model, 21–31, 71–72
Pollack, W. S., 107
Pollard, C., 184
Posttraumatic stress syndromes, 126–127
Potentiated pairings, 68–72
Power, K. G., 130
Precipitate (expressive behavior), 51, 148
Prince, Morton, 169
Projection (intrapsychic mechanisms), 61
Provocative (interpersonal conduct), 53

Psychic DNA, 4
Psychoanalytic model, 97, 156–157. *See also* Freud, S.
Psychopharmacology, 69, 98–99, 124–125, 127, 184
Psychotherapeutic practice today, reflections on, 4–15
    toward briefer and evidence-based therapies, 7
    diagnostic revolution, *DSM-III,* 6
    economic influences, 6–7
    historical perspective, 4–5
Punctuated equilibrium, 74

Quine, W. V. O., 20

Ramnath, R., 147
Rasmussen, P. R., 69
Rationalization (intrapsychic mechanisms), 60
Rauch, S. L., 185
Reaction formation (intrapsychic mechanisms), 61,
    112, 181, 246
Regression (intrapsychic mechanisms), 61
Regulatory mechanisms (functional domain), 25,
    47–48
Relaxation techniques, 158
Reliable (self-image), 57, 145
Renshaw, K., 184
Replication strategies, 22
Resentful (expressive behavior), 51, 104
Resick, P. A., 127
Resistances, 77
Respectful (interpersonal conduct), 53, 209
Retiring/schizoid personalities:
    anxiety disorders among, 131–134
    catatonic withdrawal among, 242–244
    in circulargrams, 28, 29, 30
    domain analysis (code A in tables), 49, 50, 52, 54,
        56, 58, 60, 62, 64
    obsessive-compulsive syndromes among, 188–189
    polarities, 26, 71–72
    somatoform syndromes among, 203–204
Riggs, D. S., 182
Rigid/withdrawn catatonia, 238–239, 242, 244,
    246–247
Risky behaviors, 76
Rosenbaum, J. F., 107
Roth, A., 84, 107, 125, 224
Rothbaum, B. O., 127
Rothberg, M., 5
Rounsaville, B. J., 96, 99
Roy-Byrne, P. P., 136
Rubinstein, E. A., 5
Rush, A. J., 99

Sachs, G., 107
Sacks, M., 84
Sacks, Oliver, 70
Sacks, R. G., 171
Sadistic personalities. *See* Assertive/sadistic
    personalities
Salvendy, J. T., 99
Scattered (cognitive style/content), 54
Schizoid personalities. *See* Retiring/schizoid
    personalities
Schizophrenic syndromes, 221, 236–251
    catatonic rigidity, 238–239
        among conscientious/compulsive personalities,
            244–247
        among shy/avoidant personalities, 246–247
    catatonic withdrawal, 238
        among needy/dependent personalities, 244
        among retiring/schizoid personalities,
            242–244
        among shy/avoidant personalities, 242–244
        among sociable/histrionic personalities, 244
    disorganized type, 239
        among conscientious/compulsive personalities,
            249
        among eccentric/schizotypal personalities,
            249–250
        among needy/dependent personalities, 249
        among shy/avoidant personalities, 247–249
    domain analysis in cases, 243, 245–246, 248
    general clinical picture, 236–240
    paranoid type, 239
        among assertive/sadistic personalities, 250
        among confident/narcissistic personalities, 250
        among suspicious/paranoid personalities,
            250–251
    subtypes, 238–240
    treatment options, 240–241
Schizotypal personalities. *See* Eccentric/schizotypal
    personalities
Schneier, F. R., 159
Schnicke, M. K., 127
Schroeder, M. L., 46
Secondary/primary gains, 39, 154
Secretive (interpersonal conduct), 52
Self-image domain:
    in circulargram of structural personologic
        domains, 30
    domain analysis in cases:
        anxiety-related physical syndromes, 197, 199,
            202, 206, 217

anxiety-related psychological syndromes, 164, 176, 187
  cognitive-dysfunction syndromes, 225, 230, 232, 243, 246, 248
  generalized anxiety syndromes, 133, 136, 138, 141, 145, 150–151
  mood-related syndromes, 88, 91, 101, 104, 112
trait descriptions checklist, 56–57
trait descriptions framework explained, 48–49
Self-judgments, patient, 46
Self-other polarity, 22, 72
Seligman, L., 85, 97
Sexual preference, 9–10
Shallow (intrapsychic content), 62
Shaw, B. F., 99
Shlien, J. M., 5
Shy/avoidant personalities:
  alcohol-related syndromes among, 231–233
  anxiety disorders among, 134–137
  Avoidant Personality Disorder, 158
  catatonic rigidity among, 246–247
  catatonic withdrawal among, 242–244
  in circulargrams, 28, 29, 30
  complex syndromes and, 155
  conversion syndromes among, 216–218
  disorganized schizophrenic disorders among, 247–249
  dissociation among, 171–174
  domain analysis (code C in tables), 49, 50, 52, 54, 56, 58, 60, 62, 64
  dysthymia among, 89–92
  euphoric and hostile mania among, 110
  obsessive-compulsive syndromes among, 185
  phobias among, 158, 160–163
  polarity framework, 23, 25, 26, 71
  somatoform syndromes among, 198–200
  subdued and agitated depression among, 102
  tactical modalities, 74
Siever, L. J., 136
Simple reactions (versus complex syndromes), 43–45, 129
Simpson, R. J., 130
Skeptical cognitive style. *See* Cynical/skeptical (cognitive style/content)
Skeptical/negativistic personalities:
  agitated depression among, 103–104
  alcohol-related syndromes among, 227–229
  anxiety among, 146–149
  in circulargrams, 28, 29, 30
  conversion syndromes among, 218–219

dissociation among, 179–180
  domain analysis (code M in tables), 49, 51, 53, 55, 57, 59, 61, 63, 66
  dysthymia in, 41, 89
  hostile mania among, 113
  obsessive-compulsive syndromes among, 188
  phobias among, 165–168
  somatoform syndromes among, 204–207
Slater, L., 69
Smitherman, T., 158
Sociable/histrionic personalities:
  anxiety disorders among, 139–142, 155, 156
  catatonic withdrawal among, 244
  in circulargrams, 28, 29, 30
  conversion syndromes among, 218
  dissociation among, 177–179
  domain analysis (code F in tables), 49, 50, 52, 54, 56, 58, 60, 62, 64
  dysthymic syndromes among, 93–96
  euphoric mania among, 107–109
  obsessive-compulsive syndromes among, 188
  phobias among, 163–165
  somatoform syndromes among, 203
Social phobias, 158, 162
Solemn (mood/affect), 68
Somatic discomfort, and acute anxiety and panic reactions, 123
Somatoform syndromes, 44, 192–211
  among aggrieved/masochistic personalities, 210
  among capricious/borderline personalities, 210–211
  among confident/narcissistic personalities, 204
  among conscientious/compulsive personalities, 207–210
  domain analysis, 197, 199–200, 202, 206, 209
  general clinical picture, 193–194
  hypochrondriasis, 193
  introduction, 191
  among needy/dependent personalities, 200–203
  pain disorders, 193
  personalized therapy, 195–211
  among pessimistic/depressive personalities, 196
  among retiring/schizoid personalities, 203–204
  among shy/avoidant personalities, 198–200
  among skeptical/negativistic personalities, 204–207
  among sociable/histrionic personalities, 203
  somatization, defined, 193
  treatment options, 194–195
Somnambulism, 169

Sorrell, E., 107
Spasmodic (expressive behavior), 51
Spence, S., 215
Sperry, L., 99
Spiegel, D., 171
Split (intrapsychic structure), 66
Spurious (intrapsychic structure), 65
Squires, D., 224
Steele, J., 136
Steketee, G., 184
Stephens, J. H., 213
Sternberg, R. J., 5
Steuer, J., 99
Stewart, M. O., 99
Stiles, T., 184
Stollak, G. E., 5
Strategic goals/tactical specificity, 72–76
Street, L., 159
Stress inoculation training (SIT), 127
Structural/functional attributes/domains, 25, 29, 47
Strunk, D., 99
Strupp, H. H., 5
Subdued depression. See Major depressive disorder, subdued depression
Submissive (interpersonal conduct), 52
Substance-related syndromes. See Alcohol-related syndromes; Drug-related syndromes
Suspicious/paranoid personalities:
    in circulargrams, 28, 29, 30
    diagnostic focus example, 42–43
    domain analysis (code H in tables), 49, 51, 53, 55, 57, 59, 61, 63, 65
    generalized anxiety among, 152
    hostile mania among, 110–111
    obsessive-compulsive syndromes among, 189
    pain polarities, 26
    paranoid schizophrenic disorders among, 250–251
Swan, J., 107
Swanson, V., 130
Swartz, M. S., 214
Systems perspective, 45, 73

Tactics/strategy, and tactical specificity, 72–76
Tafet, G. E., 97
Tassinari, R., 125
Tavris, C., 101, 246
Taylor, S., 125, 129, 213

Tazaki, M., 195
Temperamental characteristics. See Mood/affect domain
Theory, utility of, 20
Therapist competence, 77
Thought stopping, 184
Trance-like states, 169
Tringone, R., 46
Trull, T. J., 124
Turkus, J., 171
Turner, J., 195, 215–216

Unalterable (intrapsychic content), 63
Uncertain (self-image), 57
Undeserving (self-image), 57, 88, 150–151
Undifferentiated (intrapsychic structure), 64
Undoing (intrapsychic mechanisms), 60, 181
Unengaged (interpersonal conduct), 52, 133, 173, 243
Unruly (intrapsychic structure), 65

Vacillating (cognitive style/content), 55
Vacillating objects (intrapsychic content), 167, 178–179, 226, 228
Vassey, M. W., 125, 130
Verdeli, H., 99
Veronen, L. J., 127
Vexatious objects (intrapsychic content), 62, 91, 161, 217
Vogel, P., 184

Wallace, L. A., 130
Ward, N. G., 158
Wattar, U., 195
Weinberger, J., 2004, 46
Weissman, M. M., 96, 99
Westen, D., 46
Wexler, B. E., 99
Withdrawn/rigid catatonia, 238–239, 242, 244, 246–247
Woeful/melancholic (mood/affect), 59, 197
Wood, C. A., 195
Woody, S. R., 124, 125, 127, 130, 131
Woo-Ming, A. M., 136
Worthless (self-image), 57, 197

Zubin, J., 5